The Battleship Era

_The Battleship Era

Peter Padfield

David McKay Company, Inc.
New York

Contents

List of Illustrations

Plates

USS *Texas*
A German High Seas Fleet battleship at firing practice
HMS *Lion* leading the battle cruisers
The German battle cruiser *Seydlitz* after Jutland

Between pages 226 and 227

The German Dreadnought *Friedrich der Grosse* steaming to
  internment
The German battle cruiser *Derfflinger* scuttled at Scapa Flow
The German 'Badens', which closely resembled the 'Queen
  Elizabeths'
Aircraft carriers at Malta
USS *New Jersey* firing a broadside
A US triple 16-inch gun
The Japanese *Yamato* on trials
The *Yamato* wiped out by the US fleet air attack

Illustrations in the text

Acknowledgements

Much of my research was at the Naval Library, London, and I should like to thank Rear Admiral P. N. Buckley, CB, DSO, and the staff of the Library for their help and knowledge; I should like to express my gratitude as always to the Library Interlending Service, and the Staff of Sudbury County Library. I am also grateful to Mr Martin Holbrook for his splendid line diagrams. I should also like to thank Lord Fisher, DSO, for permission to quote from his grandfather's letters, Lord Beatty, DSC, for permission to quote from his father's letter, Admiral Sir Desmond Dreyer, GCB, DSC, for permission to quote from his father's autobiography, *The Sea Heritage*, and Lt Cdr W. B. Harvey and the Editor of *Navy* for permission to quote from his very evocative reminiscences, 'Broadside Mess', published in *Navy*. I should also like to thank the following publishers for permission to quote extracts from their books: HUTCHINSON for R. Bacon, *A Naval Scrapbook*, and *From 1900 Onwards*, A. B. Cunningham, *A Sailor's Odyssey*, K. C. Barnaby, *Some Ship Disasters and their Causes*, G. von Hase, *Kiel and Jutland*; GOLLANCZ for K. G. B. Dewar, *The Navy from Within*; JOHN MURRAY for C. V. Usborne, *Blast and Counterblast*; EDWARD ARNOLD for C. C. P. Fitzgerald, *Memories of the Sea*; METHUEN for C. Beresford, *Memoirs*; SEELEY SERVICE for O. Parkes, *British Battleships*; HER MAJESTY'S STATIONERY OFFICE for J. Corbett, *Naval Operations*.

'The British battlefleet is like the queen on the chessboard...Properly supported by other weapons it is the final arbiter at sea; to lose it is to lose the game...' *Admiral of the Fleet Lord Chatfield*

For England...the sea is not to be looked upon as a means of transport between the different Continents, but as a territory, a British territory of course. The English fleet which owns the empire of the seas, places its frontiers at the enemy's coasts, and will dispose of all commerce behind that frontier, just as an army disposes of the resources of a conquered province. *Paul Fontin*

Introduction

This is the story of the evolution, use and eclipse of the battleship, which succeeded the wooden sailing ship-of-the-line as the power behind command at sea. There are two ways of looking at the story: as a tale complete in its own right, starting with the industrial revolution and ended with aerial revolution, or simply as the last quarter of the story of the great gunned warship which took over from the galley in the sixteenth century, and was itself displaced by the aircraft carrier three and a half centuries later. This book takes the first approach, with a small concession to the second right at the beginning—where it might be expected.

It is essentially a story of change, and I have tried to trace the springs of change and follow wherever they lead rather than write an encyclopedia, a catalogue or a history of battles. At the centre is, of course, the evolving battleship, and the main theme is the battleship's struggle to maintain 'command' on its element; the villains of the piece are the torpedoes, torpedo craft, submarines and finally aeroplanes which disputed command. It is well known that these aspirant systems were regarded by the supreme battleship power, Great Britain, as beastly underhand weapons and damned un-English from the beginning; for the very good reason that British naval strategy, indeed world policy, was based on the battleship and Britain took great care to build more and on the whole better battleships than other powers. Inevitably, then, the main theme of the struggle between the battleship and its unfair enemies has a companion theme in the struggle between Great Britain and the lesser maritime powers, at first France and Russia, then Germany, and finally the United States and Japan. So while this is the story of the battleship it is also the story of British naval strategy, that is main fleet battle strategy, against all comers.

This strategy had powerful intellectual backing, epitomized by the American naval historian, A. T. Mahan, and its products, the great ships with long guns, made an equally powerful impression on men's imaginations. Although a number of independent naval thinkers rejected both, the combination was so successful that Britain was busy right up to the end keeping up with *other countries*' battleship building. In this light the age of battleships looks like an Anglo-Mahan confidence trick, which eventually rebounded on its own innocent perpetrators. But it was also an inevitable stage in an era of naval history dominated by the great gun, whose end had to await the perfection of more effective weapons. And if the end was delayed by established ideas, this is not unusual.

These are the main issues then, technology and strategy, or change and purpose, or even change *versus* purpose; in tracing them I have tried to convey the spirit of the times and the great ships themselves in the words of the men who sailed and designed them. What is a story without spirit—or a book that is not read?

The Sailing Navy

The sea is a wide road to all countries with coastline or navigable rivers; this is the great theme. From the earliest times it has been a road offering enormous economies to merchants who adventured upon it. Far less horsepower was needed to part water before a ship's prow than to turn wheels over rough country, and as there were few limits to sea tracks the free wind could be sought wherever it blew, and harnessed. Great argosies whose full bellies would have been immovable on land slid through the seas with marvellous economy of effort. Maritime cities and states grew wealthy, and as the source of their wealth came under attack at sea, they grew fighting navies to defend it. As with trade, so with the transport and supply of armies.

From pre-classical times up to the Middle Ages the fighting ship designed and organized to attack and defend trade, or military expeditions by sea, was the galley—a long, slim vessel, with a hardened spur projecting from her prow—whose main propulsion unit in action was massed oarsmen. Her tactics were to close with the enemy fast, attempt to ram or at least scatter the opposing oars, and to fight a soldier's battle on the water. Heavy missile weapons such as Roman *ballistae* and much later Venetian and Florentine heavy guns were carried aboard galleys, and no doubt increased the shock of impact, but they were slow in action, inaccurate and, due to the necessarily light design of the galley and the space taken up by the rowers, could not be massed aboard; so they did not affect the galley tactics of head-on attack in mutually supporting line *abreast*, indeed the guns were mounted in the bows to fire forward and made such tactics essential.

During the fifteenth century several factors combined to produce a new class of fighting ship, which was more than a match for the galley; this was the gunned sailing ship. She was essentially the trading argosy of full lines, now grown higher sides, defensive castles at bow and stern, and in these castles rows of light guns.

Many, notably the carracks and caravels of Portugal, had heavier pieces known as bombards on the main deck beneath the castles and as these were capable of wrecking the oars, oarsmen, masts, rigging and even the flimsy hulls of galleys, sailings ships kept away rather than closed, and attempted to reduce galleys with guns alone.

Proof of such early 'stand-off' tactics can be found by the turn of the fifteenth century in the instructions carried by Pedro Cabral, Portuguese-styled Admiral of the Indies, and in the tactics of Vicente Sodré, commanding the van division of caravels during Vasco da Gama's battle with a great Arab fleet of dhows off the Malabar coast of India in 1501. Sodré, according to a contemporary chronicler, ordered his caravels to haul up as close to the wind as possible and arranged them one astern of the other in a line'. The Portuguese destroyed the Arab fleet by gunfire without the loss of a single ship.[1]

This is the first record of a formation later raised to dogma as 'close-hauled line of battle', and the first great sea fight decided by stand-off tactics. It marks a fundamental reversal of traditional naval tactics, and it is instructive to see how it came about. Undoubtedly the main factor was technological, the superiority of the Portuguese guns to those carried by local Indian ocean craft. Next a chance factor based on advances in shipbuilding and navigation: their vessels were traders, sailing craft beamy and stout enough to mount guns along the sides of a hull free from oars and oarsmen. The Portuguese made a conscious policy decision to use these factors for a new form of naval warfare; Cabral's and da Gama's fighting instructions state 'you are not to come to close quarters with them if you can avoid it, but only with your artillery are you to compel them to strike sail...'.[2]

Having decided on the method, the actual formation to accomplish it was dictated by the unalterable shape of ships, rather longer than broad, and thus showing more guns on the side than ahead. To avoid masking or firing into or over consorts, ships had to form a single line, one astern of the other. It seems clear that 'line ahead' followed inevitably from the decision to make the gun the deciding weapon; we shall find this theme recurring.

The next 150 years or so was an age of transition in ship design and tactics. This was because the stout timbers of Atlantic sailing craft designed to withstand heavy seas could also withstand the low-powered pellets from the kind of bombards Vasco da Gama's ships mounted, and a stand-off battle between sailing ships would have been indecisive. From early in the sixteenth century however, a new type of cast gun, far more powerful than any bombard, began to appear in a few great ships and at about the same time gun ports were cut in the hulls of these ships below weather deck level, so that many more heavy guns could be carried. At first some of these reached monster proportions, but they proved too cumbersome and slow to load and fire, and were gradually replaced by lighter and generally longer pieces with a smaller ball but higher muzzle velocity. The lead in higher muzzle velocity, thus greater horizontal range, and the possibility of a slightly more distant stand-off fight appears to have been taken by Dutch, French, English corsairs and privateers against the established powers of Spain and Portugal; one of the reasons for this was no doubt that the centre of the most advanced gunfounding industry had moved to northern Europe.

By the middle of the age of transition, the 1580s, the galley, although still useful in certain conditions, had lost its place as the ultimate sanction of sea power. Its failure was partly due to lack of ocean-going sea-worthiness in a time of oceanic trade and colonizing, but mainly to its unsuitability for artillery battles. The new weapon, the developed great gun, had done for it; the galley could neither protect itself by stouter timbers, nor mass a battery equal to a sailing ship's broadside without sacrificing its own advantages of speed and mobility. More protection meant more weight and therefore less speed, more guns meant more weight and a smaller propulsion unit as well.

As for the great sailing ship which had taken over, she was in a halfway stage to final development. In general the established powers, Spain and Portugal, together with conservative elements among the aspirant powers, France, England and Holland, favoured 'high-charged' ships whose lofty castles to overtop the enemy were filled with quick-firing but light guns and hordes of soldiers for a traditional boarding and entering contest—the old type of soldiers' fight at sea – although as many heavy battering guns as could be found were carried in the hull to inspire terror before boarding. Meanwhile an influential school of adventurers and intruders, particularly among the English, favoured 'race-built' ships, longer for their beam, without towering castles or so many soldiers and light guns, but with a battery in the hull of long guns with high muzzle velocity, and the ability to sail fast and manoeuvre well. These vessels were designed for a stand-off fight; their tactics were group concentration on one of the weathermost enemy ships—passing her in line ahead and firing their broadsides in turn, then tacking and coming back in line to give the other broadside.[3]

As is well known, when the two opposed theories of naval warfare—soldiers' battle *versus* stand-off gun battle—were put to the test in the 1588 Spanish Armada campaign, the results were inconclusive. The English, firing from outside effective range because of the threat of Spanish heavy pieces, accomplished nothing by gunfire; there is plenty of evidence that their shot, even when it hit, did not penetrate Spanish timbers until the Spanish formation had been thrown into confusion by fire ships at Gravelines and Spanish shortage of powder and shot had allowed the English to close on individual galleons. As for the Spaniards, they could not board because the more manoeuvrable English ships kept safe distance.

So much for the transition; the great gun was not yet dominant in naval warfare, although the English had tried to make it so. What happened through the next 50 years was that gunpowder and gun-founding improved so that shorter but wider bored pieces, known as cannon, could throw their heavier balls with the same muzzle velocity as the long or culverin type of gun had previously. This increased the possibilities of real damage at effective range, which between rolling and pitching ships meant horizontal range; hitting outside the distance for a roughly horizontal trajectory of the ball was a matter of pure chance.

As this advance was taking place, the high-charged and the race-built types of ship merged into a fighting vessel which was fast, manoeuvrable and lofty throughout its length so that it could carry two or three tiers of heavy battery guns; this was in essentials the type of fighting ship that continued as the capital ship until the industrial revolution caught up with naval warfare in mid-nineteenth century.

There were, however, striking changes in tactics. The first change was that group or squadronal line tactics gave way to 'fleet line' tactics. This happened in a period of constant sea warfare between the Dutch and the Spanish and then the English. While the first example seems to be Dutch, in 1639, the first written instructions were English, in 1653 — the middle of the First Anglo-Dutch war. While no reasons were given, the instructions followed a battle in which two of the English generals-at-sea in their flagship *Triumph* had been isolated by massed Dutch, with the rest of the English ships unable to work up to windward to support them. It is reasonable to assume from this and from ample evidence of the defensive English attitude, that fleet line was an essentially defensive formation aimed at preventing groups from being overwhelmed by a massed enemy. It was also the formation best adapted for a stand-off artillery battle, which was what the English wanted as they had generally larger ships with more and heavier guns; this is made clear in an account from the Hague of the first battle fought under the English 'line' instructions.

And when the Dutch, finding the great disadvantage they were at endeavoured to get the wind that they might come nearer, the English by favour of the wind still prevented them ... always battering them with their great ordnance.[4]

Thirteen years later in the Second Anglo-Dutch war, the English were still dictating stand-off artillery battles. A French observer, de Guiche, wrote:

Nothing equals the beautiful order of the English at sea. Never was a line drawn straighter than that formed by their ships; thus they bring all their fire to bear upon those who draw near them... They fight like a line of cavalry which is handled according to rule, and applies itself solely to force back those who oppose; whereas the Dutch advance like cavalry whose squadrons leave their ranks and come separately to the charge.[5]

These early fleet line battles were not static, parallel exchanges, but affairs of manoeuvre, the lines cutting through and crossing each other in a follow-my-leader struggle for the windward position, known as the weather gage. The advantages of the weather gage were that the great clouds of smoke from the guns blew clear downwind instead of obscuring the decks, that the guns tended to depression rather than elevation and so were generally more effective against the enemy hulls, and—perhaps the main point—that the ship or fleet with the 'weather gage' controlled the *range* of the action, as the leeward vessels could not claw up to them against the wind.

The other main goal of fleet line manoeuvres at this time was to isolate a small portion of the enemy line and 'double' it with a superior concentration of ships. In practice these moves and counter moves, accompanied as they were by damage to masts and rigging and other chance factors which made precise manoeuvre impossible, led to separate mêlées in which both sides were liable to lose their isolated or weakest ships.

As a result, before the end of the seventeenth century fleet line had developed into a rigid and inflexible defensive posture: English fighting instructions directed that the fleet was to bear down upon the enemy van to van, centre to centre, rear to rear, taking care that no part of the enemy line was left unattended, and when within range to sail in the same direction as the enemy exchanging broadsides; if the enemy attempted any manoeuvre this was to be copied as quickly as possible so that no overlap might lead to 'doubling'. Offensive manoeuvres were out; no ships were permitted to leave the line, even to chase beaten opponents, until 'the main body [of the enemy] be disabled or run'.

The essence of fleet line was distilled by the French tactician Morogues in 1763:

in line of battle the inconsiderate or ill-judged bravery of a Captain might be attended with too fatal consequences, when his chief care and attention should be directed to the good of the whole, by keeping close in the line in a proper position, where all are mutually to support one another; and by their firm, impenetrable union, be the better able to resist the efforts of the enemy...[6]

In practice fleet line, which reigned supreme for the first three-quarters of the eighteenth century, proved an indecisive way of giving battle, and the English fighting instructions which enjoined it have received regular, undeviating disapproval from tacticians and naval historians ever since; its use marked a sterile period in which many commanders paid more attention to keeping the line than to beating the enemy. The only decisive tactical victories, in the sense of ships taken and destroyed, followed from a loophole in the Instructions which allowed an informal chase if the enemy was on the run.

One prime cause of inclusiveness was French defensive strategy, which sought to preserve ships and fleets for specific purposes which did not include getting knocked about or lost in action; to go with this strategy excellent line retiring tactics had been perfected. But this is not the whole story; there were 'offensive' French admirals, Suffren in particular, who hammered away within pistol shot in fleet line actions with 'offensive' British admirals, and still the results were draws. Dutch admirals were never loath to close, but again there were no real decisions in fleet line like those when Rodney, Jervis, Howe, Duncan, or Nelson 'broke the line'. So the line has been blamed for all this sterility.

But there is another way of looking at it. Fleet line had grown naturally out of a half century of some of the dourest naval battles ever fought; it was not the work of theorists. And the fighting sailors who had taken part in these slogging matches had been led to think that approximate equality in numbers and strength meant neither side could win. Victory then depended more on strategy than tactics, in massing more ships than the enemy at the point of action. This is how all the victories of the sterile period were gained; they were gained in general by the chase when formal line was thrown to the winds, not *because* formal line was thrown to the winds but because the victor had more ships; otherwise the chased would not have fled so precipately.

This view, that it was not 'the line' but approximate fighting equality that brought about the draws, could be supported by casualty figures. Anson is known to have smartened his squadron tactics and gun drill by constant practice, yet when in 1747 he chased and took a French squadron of less than a third his force under de la Jonquière, he suffered more than double the French casualties. Clearly the best French were equal to the best British at this date. But if we move on half a century to the 'triumphant' period of the British Navy, when Howe, Duncan, Nelson deliberately broke fleet line, the figures show what everyone knows in any case, that the French were not equal, nor anywhere near equal to the British in fighting efficiency. In all the major, minor and squadronal actions of the wars after 1793 the French casualties were some *four* times British; and in single-ship encounters British ships confidently took on odds of up to 3:2 against. All this was not because the line was broken; it was the other way about, the line was broken, the period of sterility turned into the period of triumph because the French were no longer equal enemies.

The great difference was in gunnery method: while the British husbanded their nervous energy and held their fire until well within decisive—that is horizontal—range, then unleashed the whole broadside in a shocking eruption directed at the enemy gun decks, the French in accordance with defensive strategy and retiring tactics fired at any distance at which they thought they might do some damage to masts and rigging—to immobilize their enemy. In practice, with the motion of ships and the uncertainties of cannon bores and balls, this threw a great deal of shot straight into the sea.

The first major demonstration of British gun superiority was given at the Battle of the Saintes in 1782. The British were quite confident of it by this time and during the peace after the Saintes and before the French Revolutionary wars British tacticians sought ways of quickly getting in and holding decisive gun range against their elusive opponents. The method adopted with such success after the outbreak of war was gaining the weather gage and steering straight down to cut through the enemy line, then engaging close from the lee side, holding their opponents from escaping downwind. There were great risks in this, risks of being raked by cool broadsides during the headlong approach, of firing into consorts, of separation and defeat in detail, but the British were prepared to accept them and forego the fighting advantages of the windward position to force a decision. As it happened the French service had been reduced to near chaos by the Revolution, and while the British, by unremitting attention to great gun drill, had brought their crew up to a rapidity and precision of fire surpassing their standards at the Saintes, the French had dropped below all previous standards. As a British gunnery officer noted, 'What state crews must be in when fully officered and superbly equipped they played batteries of 20 or more heavy guns for several rounds against large ships crowded with men, without any effect!'[7] By contrast we hear of the British *Culloden* at the Battle of St Vincent firing 'double-shotted broadsides as if by seconds' watch in the silence of a port admiral's inspection.' So it was that the British were able to gain decisive victories over numerically equal or superior fleets. Each 74-gun ship-of-the-line, by firing its broadside twice as rapidly and twice as effectively as each French ship, became equal to *four* of the French—or more properly, as this force was collected together, to one ship of 300 guns.

Now it is apparent why formal fleet line could be discarded by Howe and Nelson: every action became a chase with the actual odds overwhelmingly in favour of the British fleet whatever the numbers. This is the explanation of Trafalgar, where the British ships scrambled into action as best they could in two ragged columns, ship after separate ship wafted down on the light breeze to where, as a British officer put it, 'an enemy of equal spirit and equal ability in seamanship and gunnery would have annihilated the ships one after the other in detail...' Nelson knew his own strength.

The French naval historian, Admiral Jurien de la Gravière, summed up this extraordinary period: 'It's to this [British] superiority in gunnery that we must attribute most of our defeats since 1793: it's to this hail of cannonballs...that England owes her absolute mastery of the seas... They strew our decks with corpses.'[8]

So while tactics appeared to return full circle to the furious charges and mêlées of the early Dutch Wars, this is only true of British tactics, the tactics of superiority, even contempt, and it is probable that the true expression of tactics in the gunned sailing era remained the formal fleet line, to which even British fleets returned not long after Trafalgar.

However, in practice it was the 'offensive' dash of Hawke, Howe, Nelson which, through the long French wars, provided the golden pages of naval history; it was to these men that later naval officers turned for inspiration, and it was to their tactics, glowing with success beside the pale issues of the formal line, that naval historians naturally turned when they sought 'lessons'.

So far tactics have been considered mainly as a product of the dominant weapon, the great gun, and the vessel, the sailing ship, all seasoned by individual and collective genius. Of course other factors entered. Chief of these were geographical position, national policy and strategy. Britain, an island nation, sought to secure her coasts from invasion and her sea trade from interference by quantitatively outbuilding all her rivals and even combinations of rivals, all of whom had land frontiers to look after as well. British admirals then discovered that the best way to use their preponderance in fighting ships was to lock up the enemy fleets along their own coastline by blockade. This meant a close and so far as possible continuous watch on enemy fleets where they lay in harbour, with British fleets ready to bring them to action directly they sailed, and a flexible system of combination between British fleets in case the enemy should escape and manage to concentrate. With the enemy main fleets thus neutralized, the British could do almost as they wished on the broad oceans. Clearly in operation this was a highly offensive strategy and it is natural that offensive tactics sprang from it or became part of it. It was also demanding and arduous, calling for seamanship and moral and physical stamina of the highest order. In the French wars the British ships were always at sea, clinging to the Continental coastline like limpets against the buffetings of the weather, while the French lay snug in harbour. Small wonder that British sailors became arrogant in their superiority, while French fleets were further demoralized.

So Britain became mistress of the seas in a way never achieved before. And in so doing she became the final beneficiary of the gunned sailing ship with which western Europe had outflanked the East and established a dominant commercial and strategic position.

After Trafalgar, which set the seal on this extraordinary dominance, the French proposed to outflank the tight ring of British battleships by concentrating on constructing fast single-decked ships which could escape the blockade and prey on British commerce around the world; this policy proved a nuisance to the British as privateer and cruiser warfare always had, but it never began to look decisive and in all the years of the war only accounted for some 2½ per cent of British merchant ships. Meanwhile organized French shipping was swept from the ocean.

The lessons of these Anglo-French wars were burned into the consciousness of both rivals: for the British, seamanship, and cool courage for close action had been the decisive qualities, blockade and the capture of enemy battleships in fleet actions the decisive strategy. For practical and thoughtful officers victory had been the reward of attention to gun drill. The French drew the same conclusions on gunnery, denounced their policies of distant fire, and produced gunnery manuals advocating hulling fire on the best British model. As for fleet action and blockade they were as aware of their weakness as the British were sure of superiority, and this produced an ambivalent attitude, on the one hand respect for the battleship and attention to design and armament, on the other repeated attempts to devalue it by novel weapons and devices, or outflank it by ships designed for trade warfare.

The attitudes of both powers persisted throughout the nineteenth century.

French Challenge

March 4, 1858 marks the practical beginning of the revolution that displaced the wooden ship-of-the-line. On that day the French Navy laid down three frigates, that is single-main-gun-deck warships, designed to have shot- and shell-proof iron plates bolted over their timber sides; two days later another followed.

These were not the first armoured vessels by several hundred years, nor were they the first ironclads, but they ushered in the new era because they were ocean-going, and designed by the French both as a deliberate act of policy to outflank British superiority in conventional ships-of-the-line, and as the only logical way to build ships which would fight rifled shell guns. News of their construction reached England in May. In June the Surveyor of the Navy, Sir Baldwin Walker, expressed the British attitude to all such novelties:

> Although I have frequently stated it is not in the interest of Great Britain, possessing as she does so large a navy, to adopt any important change in the construction of ships of war which might have the effect of rendering necessary the introduction of a new class of very costly vessels until such a course is forced upon her by the adoption by Foreign powers of formidable ships of a novel character requiring similar ships to cope with them, yet it then becomes a matter not only of expediency but of absolute necessity.[1]

Such an attitude, which had distinguished British Boards of Admiralty throughout the period of known battle superiority, had great merits. It accorded with all natural instincts to preserve a familiar and if not physically comfortable at least comforting and highly successful way of life, and it kept costs down by preserving existing dockyards, ships and naval skills which were known to be superior. And, most important, it worked—because concealed beneath its bland surface was a riot of practical inventiveness which equalled the French or Americans, who were also prolific in ideas for devaluing British battle superiority; and because the country had engineering and industrial potential which exceeded anything elsewhere. This was perhaps the deciding factor throughout the century. It is difficult not to feel sympathy for the French as time after time they grasped new ideas or inventions to outflank British battlefleet strategy, only to be countered and outbuilt by British industrial supremacy. Of course the one rested on the other; British battlefleets had secured British sea trade, which had produced the conditions and wealth necessary for industry, at the same time denying such fruits to the French; industry then generated the conditions for securing battlefleet supremacy. The French, constantly pushing the British into fields where engineering skill and volume of production counted as much as seamanship and guts, in general devalued their own rather than their rival's fleet.

Such arguments, clear in hindsight, were not the main prop of the British policy to follow foreign novelties rather than lead the way; the concern seems to have been always to preserve *existing* superiority. Nevertheless the British lead in engineering, particularly marine engineering, must have influenced the deliberations of mid-century Boards of Admiralty, even if only unconsciously, like a comforting glow. And while there were many voices raised, many panics about the ridiculous simplicity of managing ships under steam power cancelling out the British monopoly of good seamanship and manoeuvre under sails (a nice conceit so sincerely held that all the world except the Americans believed it) there were practical Englishmen of the time who took another view; one was the naval gunnery expert, Sir Howard Douglas:

We have superior seamen and superior engines and engineers well known to have greater skill and more experience than men of the like class in other nations...Englishmen in fact are employed in foreign steamers...it may therefore be safely affirmed that the advantages which Great Britain has so long enjoyed in her maritime superiority will rather be increased than lessened under the new and as yet untried power of motion; and it may be reasonably supposed that other nations will continue to follow rather than lead us in the career of nautical warfare...[2]

So much for general attitudes; the particular novelty introduced by the French in 1858 was the thick iron side for seagoing warships, and the particular cause was a shell effective at ranges equal to solid shot effective range, an elongated shell thrown from a rifled gun.

Shells were nothing new in naval warfare; they had been used throughout the Anglo-French wars as 'bombs' thrown at high trajectory from mortars, but as a near-flat trajectory was necessary for effective hitting between moving and rolling ships, they had scarcely affected actions at sea, while the danger of their exploding while being loaded in a hot fight, and the slower rate of fire which proper precautions induced, made officers wary.

Then in the peace after the Napoleonic wars a French artillery officer, Colonel Paixhans, took up the question seriously. In 1822 he published *La Nouvelle Force Maritime et Artillerie*, the first of several books and pamphlets which hammered home the message that France could overcome Britain's superiority by building a fleet of small steam-powered, armour-plated vessels mounting shell guns; these would offer smaller targets than the high-sided wooden ships-of-the-line and each would hazard a far smaller proportion of total strength to the fearful results of successful shell fire, which he saw as complete destruction. Meanwhile they could deploy equal batteries if two or three concentrated on each ship-of-the-line.

This idea of small but highly mobile ships armed with devastating weaponry was one that recurred again and again under different guises in French thought and policy throughout the century. In one respect it accorded with the lessons of the previous century; it *was* far more difficult to hit a low target than a high one, and in heavy seas single-decked ships had often fired away for hours without hulling each other. In other respects the idea ran counter to past lessons, particularly to the principle of concentration of force, ably expounded by the French tactician Morogues in 1763, practised by most fighting admirals, and plainly discernible in the growth in size and power of individual ships-of-the-line throughout the life of the gunned sailing ship. There were other disadvantages connected with seaworthiness, endurance, steadiness as a gun platform, speed in a seaway, and difficulty of concentrating a large fleet, all of which appeared when similar ideas were tried later. But the great flaw which was never overcome was the assumption underlying each new plan that Britain would not or could not counter with similar ships or weapons directly her maritime predominance was threatened. This was a serious flaw because Britain's existence depended upon her command of the sea, or more to the point, whether it did or did not she knew very well that it did.

Paixhans could not foresee all this. In common with many other intelligent and progressive men on both sides of the Channel, he thought steam a revolutionary force which would make nonsense of all the rules of naval warfare and cancel Britain's advantage in seamen, just as shell guns would cancel her advantage in wooden ships-of-the-line—at that date 146:58.

While his ideas were premature—for the engine was still a wheezy infant and the concept of armour was generally discredited by experiment over the following years—his persistent efforts towards the naval adoption of shell guns, helped by the dramatic incendiary effects of shells fired into wooden hulks in several tests, had effect, and the Paixhans *canon-obusier* firing spherical shells fitted with time fuses to burst after penetration was adopted by the French Navy in 1824. The British immediately followed suit with a very similar shell gun. Few were allowed aboard however, as officers of both navies were concerned at the danger of carrying bombs; some five French ships-of-the-line and numerous smaller vessels were known to have been lost in this way during the previous wars. As for Paixhans' call for smaller ships, the final French Committee to report on the whole scheme recommended that comparatively small vessels should be introduced in place of large ones which, under the incendiary shell system, would be exposed to a *déflagration générale* or *explosion entière*.[3]

In theory Paixhans had won two out of his four points; in practice very little changed. French ships-of-the-line, like British, continued to increase in size and power despite the Report and they seldom mounted more than two *canons à bombe* among all the great pieces of the broadside. Nevertheless the movement away from conventional naval artillery, minute as it was, could be seen to favour the weaker power, the smaller ship, and it stimulated other European navies to follow suit, thus turning back on the French who, in 1837, adopted a more whole-hearted mix of shell and solid shot. The British followed immediately and in about the same proportion.

Serving officers regarded with horror this slide towards a 'merciless and barbarous system of warfare', perhaps wondering whether there might be truth in one admiral's forecast that future conflicts between ships would quickly be decided by one disappearing under the water, the other up in the air. Meanwhile it needed no genius to advocate armour for keeping shells out and iron rather than timber construction to prevent the sort of bonfires which Paixhans and his allies were arranging with mock-up wooden targets.

But the metal industry was not ready for armour; tests in nearly all countries with a navy produced uneven results, and it was always possible on the proving ground to bring up a heavier gun or insert a bigger charge and shatter the test-piece. Thus in French experiments at Metz in 1835 a 3.08 inch thick plate carefully rolled from forged iron failed to resist even a 24-pounder gun fired with a charge of only 6½ lbs of powder, while masses of cast iron 13 inches thick were shattered by quite moderate blows. In British tests in 1842 6 inch wrought iron armour laminated from thinner plates failed to survive a close-range pounding, and as late as 1854, when it had been found that solid masses were far stronger than an equal thickness made up from a number of plates, 4½ inches of wrought iron was penetrated by 68-pounder solid shot at 400 yards.[4]

As for iron construction, the deciding factor in the British decision against it was not, as one legend has it, that the Admiralty thought iron would sink, but the deadly shower of splinters which accompanied any penetration of iron plating; French conclusions appear to have been similar; they carried out the same sort of experiments and listed them with the British results when they declared themselves against iron construction in November 1847. However there is some evidence that the certainty of Britain following any change to an iron protection weighed with them; a general change would leave them where they started—with greater expenses.

Whatever the reasons, the logic of ironclad construction, although pressed by individuals in every maritime country, received no official approval by a major navy during the peace which followed the Napoleonic Wars. Only in the United States, which had actually built a steam-powered iron-sided floating battery in 1815 just too late to take part in the war against Britain, was such a project authorized, and that got little further than the planning stage. Protection against shell fire was held to lie in keeping outside shell range, for shells did not carry so far as solid shot. They were lighter and had to be fired with a smaller charge, and they were more liable to strange deviations in flight because their centres of gravity were seldom in the centre of the sphere. In action a ship firing solid shot and choosing her distance could be expected to batter an opponent mounting only shell guns, without being hit.

So much for peacetime experiment and theory. The first action test was provided by a Russian squadron headed by six ships-of-the-line, including three three-deckers, which in 1853 sailed into Sinope Bay on the Black Sea and, disregarding solid shot from shore batteries and the 10 Turkish frigates and corvettes which were its target, approached within 500 yards, flagship to flagship, and annihilated them. This result could have been predicted from the disparity in force; what caused interest was the way that the Turkish vessels caught fire and blew up. Paixhans—now a general—used this successful, and as always dramatic, demonstration to reiterate his views on replacing the wooden ship of the line with small, shell-firing craft:

> Guns which fire shells horizontally will destroy any vessel and will do this with greater certainty in proportion as the vessels are large, because the circulation of powder and projectiles during an action, being more multiplied for the service of a greater number of these guns, will multiply the chances of an entire explosion of the ship.[5]

This was not really tested in the Crimean War which followed Sinope as the Russian commander-in-chief, a soldier, overruled his admirals' plans to attack the Anglo-French expeditionary force by sea, but instead sank his own fleet to block the harbour of Sevastopol and provide more gunners for the shore forts, an interesting but premature idea for the employment of ships-of-the-line. The Anglo-French fleet subsequently bombarded the Russian forts from ranges of 1,000–2,000 yards with very little effect and the Russians returned red-hot shot and shells which were equally indecisive. Those shells which struck and exploded started fires but these were easily extinguished; ships dropped out to repair damages but there was no wholesale destruction.

The real naval lesson of the Crimean War followed one year later on 17 October 1855 with the bombardment of five Russian sand and stone works comprising Fort Kinburn. Since the affair at Sevastopol it had been appreciated that ships-of-the-line drew too much water to come within decisive range of the Russian forts, and the French had taken the lead in constructing shallow-draft floating batteries, whose timber hulls they covered with 4 inches of iron to keep out shot and shell. The first three of these 'formidable engines of war', *Devastation*, *Lave* and *Tonnant*, came into action against Fort Kinburn on the morning of the seventeenth at ranges between 900 and 1,200 yards and made good practice for three and a half hours, after which allied ships-of-the-line joined in the bombardment from about 1,600 yards. One and a half hours later the fort surrendered. The significance of the floating batteries' performance was that although hit over a hundred times by Russian shot and shell their armour casing had not been pierced and their total of 28 casualties had all been caused by shot or splinters entering through the gun ports or an imperfectly protected main hatch; for many French and British officers this battle proof of armour heralded the end of the wooden ship-of-the-line. The necessities of war swept away peace-time controversy.

There was, however, one other development largely unconnected with navies which confirmed the lesson: this was the elongated shell which spun in flight. It offered less resistance to air than spherical shells and so carried its velocity longer. It held a larger bursting charge than a spherical shell of the same diameter and its deviation from a straight course due to spin deliberately applied was a known factor instead of an eccentricity; in other words it had greater range, effect and accuracy than a spherical shell and the former theoretical protection for wooden ships of fighting with solid shot outside shell effective range had vanished.

Artillerists had been experimenting with these projectiles since the 1840s, a few even earlier, and during the fifties after the Crimean War varieties blossomed with wings, inclined flanges, fish-tails, belts, studs, ribs, propellers, even rocket assistance. Out of this playground of invention and industrial expertise several practical systems emerged; the two which had most immediate effect on warship construction were both rifled, the French *systeme la hitte*, whose shells had 12 protruding zinc studs which travelled in six shallow grooves cut slightly spirally into the gun bore, and a few years later the British Armstrong system, whose shells had a soft coating of lead which expanded into even shallower grooves.

The French 16-centimetre rifle, model 1855, whose studded shells were loaded through the muzzle in conventional style, was the first of the two to enter naval service. And it was this weapon which gave the *coup de grâce* to the wooden ship-of-the-line. Tests through 1856 against timber and armoured targets made it clear that no unprotected ship could sustain an action against it, and in January 1857 the *Conseil des Travaux* proposed that all wooden warship construction be stopped forthwith. This was particularly significant as it came within 18 months of a proposal for a programme of 40 *screw* ships-of-the-line.

The *directeur du matériel* responsible for the new policy was a brilliant naval architect named Dupuy de Lôme. Before the Crimean War he had submitted plans for a sea-going armourclad, but at this time the *Conseil* was turning away from iron and he had to wait some 12 years before his ideas were confirmed at Kinburn. In November 1856 he had been appointed with the then *directeur du matériel* and the naval historical analyst, Jurien de la Gravière, to report on future construction policy for the French Navy. Out of this collaboration had come the new sea-going ironclad policy which carried with it the rejection of the ship-of-the-line.

This collaboration was important for defining not only the broad principles of *la nouvelle force maritime*—that is complete shell gun armament in single-deck ships protected by armour impenetrable to shot and shell—but also the essential design requirements, many of which bear the marks of de la Gravière's conclusions from gunnery actions of the sailing era. Of prime importance was speed: the faster fleet had the steam equivalent of the weather gage and could dictate the range at which an action was fought. As the average modern screw ship-of-the-line could do perhaps 12 knots, but would probably be held to 11 or less by the slower ships of a fleet, 13 knots was chosen as a minumum. And for cruising the vessels were to be ship-rigged. The battery was to be at least 2 metres above the waterline so the guns could be fought in heavy weather, and the armour was to extend at least 1½ metres below the waterline to protect this most vulnerable section when the ship was heeled over. Finally the vessels were to be as small as was compatible with all this plus a powerful battery, as it was considered that other factors being equal the smallest ship, thus the smallest target, must win a sea action. These requirements, together with the results of the most recent armour tests which showed that the latest 4½-inch thick solid wrought iron was impenetrable by the heaviest solid shot and the largest of the new rifled shells, were translated by de Lôme into the frigate *Gloire* and two sister ships laid down at Toulon, L'Orient and Cherbourg, in March 1858. In addition to these three, which were of conventional timber construction with the wrought-iron plates bolted to the sides, an iron-built armourclad frigate, *Couronne*, was started at the same time. French naval officers in the know were convinced that these slight vessels were the capital ships of the future and that no more ships-of-the-line would be laid down. Dupuy de Lôme declared that one of them in the midst of a fleet of hostile wooden ships would be like a lion amongst a flock of sheep.[6,7]

3

Riposte

Meanwhile in Britain the same sort of armour and rifled shell gun tests, conducted with a greater wealth of engineering talent, were producing exactly the same results as in France, and those most concerned were drawing exactly the same conclusions—except the Lords of Admiralty, who were holding on tight to their *status quo*, They were not even compromising, as the French had at first, with a programme of two-deckers, unless six large timber frigates can be called such a compromise, but were building bigger and better three-deckers, the greatest of which mounted 131 guns almost equally divided between shot and spherical shell—monuments to British phlegm.

The naval estimates, which had dropped to around £6,000,000 in mid-century under the influence of government economy and real hopes for a stable European peace, had increased to nearly £9,000,000, but this was due to the adoption of steam power for ships-of-the-line and frigates following the French lead in 1850, also to pay rises and to troubles in India and China. It was reaction to events. It could almost be called a *policy* of reaction to events since it rested on not allowing France to gain the lead in steam ships-of-the-line, while patronizing experiments, which were never allowed to influence sound judgement. In the month before *La Gloire's* keel was laid at Toulon the Surveyor—or head of the *matériel* departments of the British Navy—produced rough plans for a steam corvette of almost the same tonnage as the French ship, rather longer and shallower, and carrying a rather small battery of 26 guns behind 4-inch armour. The flaw which betrayed her as a reflex action was her speed of 10 knots, 3 knots below the best 'line' ships and quite incapable of dictating events. She was shelved until it should be revealed how best to keep her proposed iron bottom clean.

That year a weakly Irish lad, Charles Beresford, who appears later in these pages as a far from weakly officer, went with his father to visit the flagship of the Channel Squadron after it came to anchor

B

in the Downs; he was rowed out behind the commander-in-chief in his six-oared galley.

> As we drew near the ships there arose a great tumult of shouting and I could see the men running to and fro and racing aloft, and presently they stood in rows along the yards, manning yards in honour of the arrival of the admiral. The neatness and order of the stately ships, the taut rigging, the snowy sails, the ropes coiled neatly down on deck; these things left an abiding impression upon my youthful mind.[1]

There was a grandeur and terror about the battleship, whether under sails or in the next century clad in grey steel, which touched the deepest chords in men; the sight of one was an argument in itself, and on a different level from the frenetic experimentation of theorists, it backed up all the profound feelings for security in familiar things and habits and rituals which moved British admirals as much as lesser men.

Even steam, with which admirals and Admiralty had apparently come to terms by having their great sailing ships built or converted so that they could screw through the water as fast as French ships, was not accepted in any positive sense. While French tacticians, American Admirals and even English artillerists like Howard Douglas, were devising manoeuvres for steam fleets designed to *use* the new powers of movement in any direction, and while the French Signal Book was changed in 1858 to bring in specific steam evolutions, the sole concession of the British Admiralty seems to have been a memo circulated for attachment to the 1853 Signal Book, directing that all sea going vessels under steam should exhibit a masthead white light and red and green sidelights between sunset and sunrise. The signals themselves remained Nelsonic with weather and lee divisions, cutting the enemy's line in the order of sailing, attacking from the lee position; Numerals 60: 'Keep the main topsail shivering.' However, no doubt a British admiral in command of a steam fleet would have extemporized efficiently; and the line tactics which occupied the greater part of the evolution signals were better adapted for naval warfare, even in the steam age, than the military ideas of advancing in echelon, turning the enemy's flank in oblique movement, or enfilading, which occupied the theorists. So the attitude of their Lordships, English, amusing and even elegant in the refusal to rush in too soon after brainy men, was nevertheless sound. How far this was a deliberate policy and how far mental torpor or obstinacy is more difficult to decide.

If any one person was responsible for getting the British Navy to grapple seriously with the problems created by the industrial revolution, it was Napoleon III. In the first place it was he who had initiated the ironclad floating batteries so successful at Kinburn, he who had been the main drive behind the French rifled field gun policy which had spread into the naval service, he who had chosen Dupuy de Lôme to reconstruct the French Navy, and in 1858 it was his martial ambition, or more properly British fear of his ambition, which created the conditions for a British reappraisal of defences—traditionally 'naval defences'.

One of the most obvious defects here was the number of ships, especially steam ships; an Admiralty minute of 27 March 1858 noted 'When determining upon the number of ships and upon the naval force generally which England should have, it should be borne in mind that the navies of France and Russia may very probably be combined against her.'[2] This minute, revealing the changed political situation so soon after the Crimean War, set the pattern for the rest of the century; so did the Admiralty response, an instinctive bid to outbuild these two great powers in capital ships, at this time steam ships-of-the-line.

In May, while this policy was being pressed forward, there came news of French construction of 'irresistable' iron-sided frigates, and the construction of vessels which could meet them became in the Surveyor's words 'a matter not only of expediency but of absolute necessity.' So it was treated. It became one of the Board's most urgent tasks to devise an answer to the French threat which 'would not only hold its own, but be superior.' In responding to the challenge, not simply by copying, but by moving deliberately into a superior class of vessel the British Admiralty of this date stands revealed as, after all, a creature of the industrial revolution. It is a significant moment of revelation.[3]

The Board did not go so far as the French in the logic of the change; the ironclad vessels they spent so many 'very anxious hours' debating were regarded rather as a match for the French experiment, and adjuncts to the battlefleet, than as the new type of capital ship. This was no doubt because, in the words of the Surveyor, 'no prudent man would at present consider it safe to risk, upon the performance of ships of this novel character, the naval superiority of Great Britain.'[4] In fact it is doubtful if Britain had much more than moral superiority: the Report of a Committee appointed that year to enquire into naval strength revealed that in screw line of battle ships completed the French had caught up—both nations had 29—while they had 11 others in progress in a more advanced state than the 21 building or converting in England. Although the English line ships carried more guns in total, this near-parity was dangerous by the standards of the great wars or even of the peace up to mid-century, when the capital ship ratio had been held at 2:1 in Britain's favour.

Such was the overall problem which faced the Board of Admiralty under Sir John Packington in 1858, the year of the ironclad. It responded with a traditional offensive programme, *quantities* of screw line of battle ships for blockade, and for the new ironclads *speed* to chase and bring to action any warship afloat, even against high seas and wind; thus 15 knots was stipulated as well as full ship rig for cruising anywhere in the world. Besides speed, the ironclad hulls were to provide steady platforms for a battery of 19 of the latest 68-pounders on each broadside; these were the most powerful guns available and more effective armour piercers than the French 50-pounders. Meanwhile armour tests at Portsmouth revealed that the latest rifled 68-pounder solid shot was capable of piercing 4 inches of solid wrought iron but not 4½ inches, which seemed impregnable to any existing guns.

This met the main requirements. Next, the bold decision was taken to build the ships of iron; this was contrary to previous Admiralty policy and opposed by service opinion generally, but the Surveyor pointed out that while a timber ship needed complete armour protection against shells, an iron vessel need only have an armoured box protecting the main portion of the battery from broadside and raking fire, leaving the forward and after ends of the ship unprotected. Penetration of these ends need not be fatal if they were divided into a number of watertight compartments to limit the water taken in. Thus the two opposed claims for speed, generally believed to require length and fine lines, and thick iron protection which if complete obviously added more weight the longer the ship, led directly to iron construction.

In addition, extreme length could not be achieved with a timber keel. The longest wooden warships ever built were the British frigates, *Mersey* and *Orlando*, designed the previous year for a speed of 13 knots, and it was said (as it turned out wrongly) that they lacked longitudinal strength. The new ironclad frigates were to be faster than these by two knots and if this meant even greater length at least the keel and associated structures had to be iron. Finally, it was well known that an all-iron hull weighed less than a timber hull of the same form, thus allowing a greater payload—in steam warship terms more guns, protection or horsepower.

Underpinning these technical considerations was the fact that Britain, unlike France, had a number of private yards experienced in building iron merchant steamers, and on 11 May 1859, roughly one year from the first news of the French programme, the Admiralty turned to these builders for tenders for their own ironclad frigate, whose details had been worked out by the Surveyor's department under the Chief Constructor, Isaac Watts. The Thames Iron Ship-building Company of Blackwall won the contract and laid the keel of the frigate, to be named *Warrior*, in June 1859. She was shortly followed by a sister, *Black Prince*.

So it was that the enthusiastic outsiders, Paixhans and Napoleon III, aided by the powerful minds of de la Gravière and de Lôme, at last moved the established naval power towards new fields of iron shipbuilding and engineering which, by one of the inscrutable accidents of history, were fields in which they could never hope to catch her, let alone overtake. Put another way, the logic of the industrial revolution was bound to change naval warfare sooner or later, and by the nature of things the logical men of the aspirant power had their message accepted before the logical men of the established power. But the tide of events was against them.

La Gloire was launched on 24 November 1859 and completed the following summer; on her trials she made just over 13 knots in a calm sea and 10 knots against heavy weather, fulfilling all de Lôme had hoped of her. On 22 September he submitted that in view of her success and her obvious superiority over the largest wooden warships, France should embark at once on transforming her fleet, beginning with 10 seagoing ironclads in addition to the four original frigates and two which had followed them on the stocks. This proposal was put into effect. The ironclad revolution was under way.

In October the same year the *Warrior* was launched; she was fitted out through 1861 and emerged in October, a 'stately and noble vessel, whose beauty was a delight to behold. The great spread of sail, long hull and yacht bows, the vast expanse of flush wooden deck, the solidity and grace, set her among the finest ships ever built.'[5] While the *Gloire*'s rather squat, bluff lines revealed her ancestry in the conventional timber ship-of-the-line, the *Warrior* evidently sprang from a different stable; the clipper bow decorated with gingerbread work, sharp entrance leading into a rounded mid-body, and the long sweet run up to the counter, were all from racing stock, the lovely little clipper ships, pioneered and brought to perfection in the United States and now making record ocean passages with tea, opium and emigrants under the Red Ensign as well. But she was twice as long as these, and between her fore and main masts, rigged on the scale of an 80-gun ship-of-the-line, were two telescopic funnels. On her trials she made nearly 14½ knots, faster than any warship afloat.

She was protected for some five-eighths of her length by 4½ inches of solid wrought-iron plates hammered from several thinner sheets, bolted through 18-inches of teak backing and extending from 5-feet below her waterline to the top of the battery deck. At the forward and after ends of this side armour similar bulkheads carried the 4½-inch iron across the ship to meet the other side, thus forming a central box imperforable even in test conditions by any existing gun. Forward and aft of the central armoured rectangle her un-armoured length was subdivided into a number of watertight flats. Her armament was a mixture of 68-pounders and a new Armstrong 110-pounder developed while she was building.

As she provided a much lower target than a ship-of-the-line and with superior speed and equal sea-keeping ability could choose her range outside the effective spherical shell and shot range of such a vessel, which in any case could do little damage to her battery, she was evidently the prototype of the new capital ship. This was recognized at the Admiralty that year; they stopped work on all timber line of battle ships, and commenced 11 new ironclads of various designs. But it was not apparent to the service at large, not even to her hand-picked crew; her gunnery lieutenant 'Jacky' Fisher wrote afterwards, 'it certainly was not then appreciated that this, our first armourclad ship of war, would cause a fundamental change in what had been in vogue for something like a thousand years...'[6]

By comparison with the really new concepts in this warship, the *Gloire* with her timber hull and conventional lines was almost a transitional type, and she was in most respects inferior: she was far smaller and carried her guns lower, so she would in theory have been no match for the *Warrior* in heavy weather. Her battery of 36 50-pounder rifles, although of a new breech-loading pattern which proved more satisfactory than Armstrong's original pattern, were not the equals of the British 68-pounders for armour-piercing, and they were mounted in wider embrasures behind slightly thinner armour. She was fully a knot slower than the British ship, had a restricted sail area and a smaller steaming radius. The one vital point in which her design was more effective was the complete protection for rudder and screw; the British ship with counter stern and no armour at all was dangerously exposed. *Warrior* also lacked handiness in manoeuvre because of her extreme length, and this was considered a disadvantage as the old galley tactic of ramming had come back into fashion now that warships had regained the power of free movement denied them in their sailing years. Indeed the *Warrior* had a strengthened stem for this purpose.

4

Battle Proof

While France and Britain laid down successors to the *Gloire* and *Warrior*, following their own different patterns, other European nations joined in. Two of the first were the rival powers of Austria and newly-united Italy. Indeed Italy ordered two small ironclads from France before the first Italian Parliament sat in March 1861, and that year she also ordered two larger vessels of the size and style of the *Gloire*-type from a New York shipyard. Similarly Austria started with two small ironclad corvettes, and in 1861 began three larger '*Gloire*' ironclads. Russia ordered a 3,300-ton ironclad, with a projecting ram bow, from the *Warrior*'s builders in 1861, and another the following year, meanwhile converting two timber frigates; Ottoman Turkey ordered three 6,400-ton ironclads also from England, and Spain started building against the US Navy with a home-grown 6,200-tonner, at the same time ordering a rather larger vessel from France; other minor naval powers followed suit.

Meanwhile across the Atlantic, two strange deviant types were being hammered together in the more urgent conditions of the American Civil War. The secessionist southern states, inferior to the northern states in ships, shipbuilding and engineering capacity, had started the competition. The secretary of their small navy claimed: 'Inequality of numbers may be compensated by invulnerability... a new and formidable type must be created.'[1] The screw frigate *Merrimack* had fallen into their hands at the occupation of Norfolk, Virginia, with lower hull timbers sound and engines capable of repair, so they cut her down to the waterline and built upon the lower body an armoured battery or casemate. This occupied some two-thirds of the wall length, and was built of 20-inch pine sloping inwards from the waterline at about 45 degrees; 4-inches of oak was laid over this and then two layers of railway irons rolled down to plates 8-inches wide by 2-inches thick. This casemate was pierced all round with 14 ports for 10 guns, four of which were 6-inch or 7-inch calibre rifles, six 9-inch smooth-bores; a single funnel projected through the top. There were no masts or sails.

This craft, which had a cast-iron ram attached to her bow, was only an extemporized floating battery which would have been overwhelmed by even moderate seas; nevertheless reports of her construction caused a little concern in the North, turning by degrees into a great scare which allowed a Swedish engineer inventor named John Ericsson to gain approval in September 1861 for a novel ironclad, the outlines of which had been maturing in his mind for some 20 years, despite repeated rebuffs. His idea was an 'impregnable fort' in the shape of a revolving armoured turret 'in the plain cylindrical form in order that attack from all quarters of the compass may be resisted with equal certainty'…mounted upon a wide armoured deck whose sides would be carried below the waterline and overhang a narrow raft hull, containing the machinery, by such a margin that any shot would have to 'pass through 20 feet of water' to strike the hull, while the propeller and rudder on the centreline would be 'absolutely protected'—this last feature Ericsson considered 'perhaps the most important'.[2]

As built the 'impregnable fort' of this craft, named *Monitor*, was a drum 20 feet in diameter by 9 feet high, formed of eight layers of 1-inch plating, inside which were mounted two 11-inch smooth bore guns each firing 166lb balls at a very slow rate, something like one aimed round every seven minutes. The 1-inch thick iron deck on which this turret turned floated some 2-feet above waterlevel with armoured sides extending down to 3-feet below the water. This was the weakest part of the design; as the volunteer crew found when they sailed her out of the sheltered waters of New York, open seas swept over the deck and leaked through between it and the turret and down the openings for two collapsible funnels and two ventilators abaft the turret, besides juddering up under the armoured overhang as if to tear it from the hull. She was not in any sense a sea-going ironclad; in this and in her laminated armour, inferior to the thinner but homogenous plates of the European ironclads, she resembled the *Merrimack*. Neither could have lived with the *Gloire* or the *Warrior*. They enter the story, not because they were an advance or a lesson, only because they were the first ironclads in action against ships.

By freak chance the two vessels were completed within days of one another, and when on the morning of Saturday, 8 March 1862, the *Merrimack*, renamed *Virginia*, steamed unsteadily out from Norfolk to give battle to a Federal blockading force in Hampton Roads, the *Monitor*, two days out from New York, was struggling down the East coast just 10 hours away. These 10 hours were

important though; they gave the *Virginia* time to prove in action
de Lôme's forecast about a lion amongst a flock of sheep, also Paixhans'
suggestion that the simple management of steam batteries would cancel
enemy advantages in seamanship. For while the Federal force was
composed of three fine frigates and a sloop manned by American
sailors renowned for skill and panache, the *Virginia*'s crew was
made up largely of Confederate soldiers with only a few days'
training aboard.

So the battery steamed slowly across bright water to where the
timber sloop *Cumberland* and the veteran frigate *Congress* lay at
anchor in a shoal channel near Newport News. Both thought so
little of the danger that they remained at anchor and simply waited
at their guns while 'the thing' they had been hearing so much about,
swung its ugly battery towards them. When the *Cumberland*
judged it within range, she fired her broadside of 9-inch smooth
bores; soon the *Congress* joined in with a few 8-inch and her
main battery of 32-pounders, and shore guns added to the flying
round shot, but any balls which hit simply bounced off the sloping
iron, neither making any impression nor diverting the battery's
progress towards the *Cumberland* which she eventually rammed
below the fore channels. The sloop listed as water rushed in, and
half an hour later she was gone, the first victim of ramming since
the days of the galley. The *Congress*, meanwhile, realizing how
irresistible was this opponent, set topsails and jib, slipped cable and
making towards Newport News ran aground; the *Virginia* followed,
took up a raking position off her stern and, silencing her, forced
her to strike and set her on fire.

That evening the *Monitor*—directed by the supreme dramatist—
arrived in the Roads; the *Virginia*'s crew made her out by the glow
of the burning frigate. News of impending conflict between the
two armoured craft spread quickly along both shores, and the next
morning, which again dawned bright, spectators were out in crowds
to watch the joust. The *Virginia* did not disappoint them. She
steamed out at 8 o'clock, making for one of the grounded wooden
frigates expecting the *Monitor* to interpose, as she did, and there
developed a ponderous, close duel which proved mightily indecisive.
Neither had the weapons to pierce the other's armour as the *Virginia*
was firing shell or grape, the *Monitor* cast iron balls which shattered
on impact. Besides this her turret, which was turned away from the
enemy during the seven minutes' loading interval to prevent any
accident to the gun port stoppers, developed the faults of all prototypes; the turning engine was hard to start and still harder to stop
and the crew took to firing on the swing as the target appeared
briefly through the ports. The *Virginia* directed volleys of musketry

towards the swinging ports with as little effect as her shells against the armour, then decided to make for her original prey, the grounded frigate *Minnesota*. The *Monitor* followed and a ramming duel developed. This too was indecisive as the *Monitor* failed in her clumsy passes while the *Virginia*, which succeeded once, had lost her ram in the affair of the previous day and so made no impression. As the vessels came together the *Monitor* fired one of her great pieces with the muzzle almost touching the *Virginia*'s casemate, but although a section was crushed in, it was not pierced. The southern commander, for his part, called away the boarders, but before they could scramble over the vessels had drifted apart. So it continued until the vessels finally parted after some four hours with some casualties and a little damage to both sides, but no lives lost. The result was a draw, although the *Monitor* could claim to have prevented further damage to the Federal timber ships.

The *Virginia* was repaired, given more armour below her vulnerable waterline, and sallied out again in April, capturing some merchant vessels; the *Monitor* failed to meet her, so this time the southern vessel could claim to have achieved her purpose. Then, before she could put into operation a plan to capture the *Monitor* by boarding and driving in wedges between her turret and deck, Federal troops forced the Confederates to evacuate Norfolk, and she was burned by her crew to keep her from enemy hands. As for the *Monitor* she foundered later on a voyage around the coast.

However both these famous prototypes were followed by descendants which took part in the naval struggle along the rivers and bays of the southern states, and provided material for later naval thinkers to ponder as they searched for lessons which might help to clarify the new naval warfare. For instance a Southern floating battery named the *Albemarle*, laid down in a cornfield up the Roanoke river and armoured on the style of the *Virginia* with iron worked into shape over an open forge, made another successful ramming attack under fire in 1864. And this same vessel was later the victim of a daring torpedo boat attack. The boat, commanded by a young lieutenant named Cushing, had to drive at and over a barrier of logs which surrounded the ironclad, so that the torpedo, a case of gunpowder held out on a spar over the bow, could be brought into contact with the target and then fired with a pull on a line attached to its detonator. Cushing accomplished this extraordinary feat in the dark and under fire with so much presence of mind that he was able to sink the *Albemarle* and afterwards escape by swimming down the river.

Later there was the famous episode at Mobile Bay when Admiral Faragut, crying 'Damn the torpedoes! Go ahead!' steamed the

Northern fleet under his command close under the guns of the Confederate Fort Mogan and through a double line of mines (then known as torpedoes) into the Bay, miraculously losing only one vessel and her crew as he did so. This unfortunate vessel was the *Tecumseh*, an enlarged 'monitor'. There were three other monitors with Farragut and one of these, the *Manhattan*, which carried two huge 15-inch smooth-bores in her 10-inch armoured turret, was responsible for putting paid to the most powerful Southern descendant of the *Virginia*, the *Tennessee* which came out to do battle with Farragut's entire fleet.

These and other events of the Civil War were analysed in works on naval warfare, naval gunnery and tactics for many years following, as there was little other modern action proof to go on. But really the armaments revolution was moving too fast for the 'lessons' to be of value, and the Southern ships and weapons were too extemporized to be considered as much more than the desperate essays of an agricultural community: the most effective of the 'torpedoes' which Farragut charged over were made of lager kegs waterproofed with pitch; the armour of the floating batteries, while ingenious, was too sectional; the guns were not designed for armour-piercing. The ironclad actions were fought in sheltered waters, and there were few conclusions to be drawn for open sea. Perhaps most instructive was the cruise of the Southern commerce raider, *Alabama*, which destroyed a number of northern merchant vessels and evaded capture for almost two years before USS *Kearsage* finally sank her. This lesson was not lost on the French, nor on the British whose merchant marine was particularly exposed to such a form of warfare.

The next ironclad battle occurred in 1866, when the fleets of Austria and Italy met off the island of Lissa in the Adriatic. This time there was real meat for analysis, or so it appeared, for the first-line vessels of both powers were sea-going warships in direct descent from the *Gloire*, some of the most recent construction. More important perhaps, it was the only fleet action which took place until the end of the century, so it had to be picked bare.

The conflict was an offshoot of Bismarck's grand policy for removing diverse north German states from Austria's orbit and uniting them under Prussian leadership. He arranged a war with Austria, first tempting Italy into an alliance with the prospect of Austrian Venetia and Lombardy, territories they needed to complete their unification. But, while Bismarck's army quickly defeated the Austrians at Sadowa, the Italians were beaten at Custozza; this was particularly embarrassing for the new nation, and weakened their position in any peace negotiations which Bismarck might achieve. They turned to their fleet. On paper it was superb. Since unification they had spent some £12 millions on it, millions they could ill afford, and materially it was far superior to the Austrian Navy which had been neglected since the initial burst into ironclad construction. However, the Italians' ships and armament had come from different countries and they had no pool of marine engineers or modern gunners; nor, it seems, a tradition of naval discipline. The new force was a young and artificial creation, and the Commander-in-Chief, Admiral Count Persano, seems to have been overwhelmed by the practical difficulties of the situation. He did little training and, when the war started, nothing offensive.

The Minister of Marine tried to sting him to action. 'Would you tell the people who in their mad vanity believe their sailors the best in the world, that in spite of the £12 millions we have added to their debt, the squadron we have collected is one incapable of facing the enemy?'[5] When Persano still showed reluctance, he was ordered to take the Austrian-held and fortified island of Lissa, across the Adriatic from Ancona. His attempts to do so were reported to the Austrian Commander-in-Chief, Rear Admiral Tegetthoff, who put to sea to fight him.

Tegetthoff flew his flag in the *Ferdinand Max*; she was a barque-rigged 5,140 ton vessel on the lines of the *Gloire* launched the previous year with complete armour plating reaching a maximum thickness of 5-inches on 26-inches of timber backing. However, while she had been designed for a powerful battery of Krupp rifles on each broadside, the Prussian firm had been backward in supply and instead she had been fitted with 16 obsolescent smooth-bores throwing 56 lb projectiles. She and a sister ship, *Habsburg*, which suffered the same disadvantage, were the spearhead of the fleet. In addition there were four smaller ironclad frigates of 3,000–3,600 tons which mounted in total 74 62-pounder rifles together with 66 smooth-bores. There were also numerous timber vessels including a ship-of-the-line, *Kaiser*.

The Italian fleet was more imposing. The flagship *Re d'Italia* and her sister *Re di Portogallo* were 5,700 tons, rather larger than the Austrian big ships and with rather thicker armour, although built to the same style. But their main theoretical advantage lay in their batteries; the flagship mounted 30 Armstrong 100-pounder rifles and two rifles throwing 150 lb shells, while her sister ship had 26 of the 100-pounders and two throwing 300 lb shells. In addition there were five ironclad frigates just over 4,000 tons mounting a total of 108 rifles and a few smooth bores, two smaller armoured vessels and a number of timber craft. Altogether the principal units in the Italian fleet were larger than their Austrian opposite numbers and mounted 200 modern rifled guns against only 74 smaller Austrian pieces.

The Italians also had a curious 4,000 ton vessel known as a turret ram, the *Affondatore*. Her design was probably due to the successful rammings of the American Civil War for she had a de Bergerac of a beak extending 26 feet; she also had a turret mounting two powerful Armstrong 300-pounder rifles, hence her designation, and she was armoured with 5-inch iron plate. The Italians expected great things from her.

So much for *matériel* comparisons: what was thought more important when the naval *post mortems* came to be written was the comparison between the querulous Count Persano and Tegetthoff, who ordered his mind and his fleet in a more positive way, exercised his ships and guns frequently, and was in all respects an inspiring leader.

He was certainly an agressive one. On the morning of 20 July, having sighted the Italian fleet, he formed his ships into three divisions behind one another each in double quarterline, like three arrowheads, with the ironclads leading, and charged at full fleet speed—something like 9 knots. His intention was to go through the Italian line and provoke a mêlée, partly because he knew the Italian rifles had the greater effective range and he needed to get in close, where the 'concentration' fire in which he had trained his gunners might tell, but primarily to ram, since his shells could not pierce the Italian armour. As the *Ferdinand Max* neared the grey-painted Italian vessels he signalled. 'Charge the enemy and sink him'.

Persano, who had collected his fleet together from various positions around the island, intended to fight a line battle and make use of his heavier guns; he was not averse to ramming but he meant to disable some enemy ships with broadsides first and ordered his captains to engage *unarmoured* ships at 1,000 metres, armoured ships *not* outside 500 metres. Then he formed up with his ironclads in three divisions in line ahead, steaming north-north-east to meet the Austrians coming down south-east, placing his flagship in the centre division and his turret ram just to starboard, thus on the disengaged side of the centre division. His unarmoured ships were ordered to the disengaged side, distant 3,000 metres. So far his tactics appear sound. But then he decided to shift his flag from the *Re d'Italia* to the turret ram *Affondatore*; this meant stopping the ships concerned and a gap opened up between the first division of three frigates, and the rest of the line. Meanwhile the first division, disregarding orders, opened fire at Tegetthoff's approaching ironclads, which were still about 1,000 metres off. The great clouds of smoke from their broadsides drifted astern, con-

32

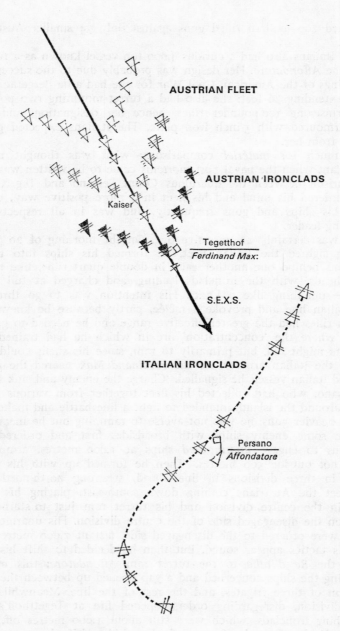

AUSTRIAN FLEET

AUSTRIAN IRONCLADS

Kaiser

Tegetthof
Ferdinand Max:

S.E.X.S.

ITALIAN IRONCLADS

Persano
Affondatore

Figure 1. Battle of Lissa

cealing the widening gap which Persano had created by his eccentric behaviour, and it was through this gap and smoke that Tegetthoff's whole ironclad division, holding its fire, soon passed.

Once they were through the line Tegetthoff's seven ironclads formed into two groups, one of which turned north to chase the Italian van (itself turning in to attack the Austrian unarmoured rear) while the main body of four frigates fell on the Italian centre. Meanwhile the second Austrian V formation of timber ships headed by the line-of-battle ship *Kaiser*, reached the Italian rear and, attempting to run down whatever they could see, provoked a mêlée which quickly became shrouded in dense gunsmoke. The situation was now exactly as Tegetthoff had hoped, a close, confused scramble, all central control lost and with it any possibility of cool, stand-off gunnery. Opportunism ruled the day.

It is impossible to follow all the contortions the ships were put through; the main object on both sides was to ram any enemy as they made him out, and while they held on with tight nerves for their target, often charging towards them for the same purpose, the guns' crews waited for the shock and the chance to get in a broadside as they came together or raced past. The collisions, near misses, touchings and scrapings, many between friends unable to get out of the way in time, were numerous, but at first none were fatal. Even the *Affondatore* failed to bring her prow into contact with such a ripe target as the *Kaiser* in two attempts, although she wrought fearful damage in the timber upperworks with 300-pounder shells at pistol-shot range. The *Kaiser* for her part, passed on from this desperate affair to try and ram the large frigate *Re di Portogallo*, which was steaming at her with the same intent, and spinning her wheel over at the last moment made contact abreast the Italian's engine room, but at far too fine an angle to enter. Instead she scraped down the iron side, losing her bowsprit and taking a broadside of shells which brought down her foremast, turned her gun decks into shambles and started numerous fires. The *Maria Pia*, astern of the *Portogallo*, put two more shells into her as she came past and she retired to put out fires and reorganize the fighting decks.

Meanwhile, around what had been the Italian centre, Tegetthoff, who had been no more successful in ramming than Persano, saw through the fog of battle the *Re d'Italia* apparently disabled; he made straight for her, his flag captain conning from the mizzen rigging. The Italian's rudder had been damaged by collision or a lucky shell and she couldn't turn her side as the *Ferdinand Max*'s steam approached at full speed, something over 10 knots, and drove straight in, tearing a gap of about 140 square feet, half below water. The Austrian flagship reversed engines and withdrew; the *Re d'Italia* listed slowly to starboard, suddenly lost stability, rolled to port and went down. Meanwhile a small Italian gunboat, *Palestro*, dashing in heroically to aid the ironclad, received a shell in her wardroom which set it alight and forced her to retire; later she blew up as the flames reached the magazine.

These were the only ship losses of the battle. For the rest, the astonishing series of abortive charges, scrapes and accidental collisions punctuated by broadsides at point-blank swinging targets continued until early afternoon. Then Persano led his scarred ships back to Ancona, while Teggethoff anchored his off Lissa, evidently the victor in possession of the field.

This battle again confirmed the value of armour as protection for ships and guns' crews. The Austrian ironclads fired 1,386 shot or shell, the three largest of their unarmoured ships fired another 1,400, and the rest of their fleet joined in as well, but the total Italian casualties, apart from those drowned in the *Re d'Italia* and blown up in the *Palestro*, were eight killed, 40 wounded. The Italian fleet fired at least 1,400 shells, probably many more, but the total Austrian casualties in their armoured division were three killed, 30 wounded; the unprotected *Kaiser* meanwhile lost 24 killed, 75 wounded. Armour was not the only reason for such comparatively low casualties: another was the small proportion of hits, and even smaller proportion of hulling hits. For instance the Austrian flagship received a total of 42 hits, but only eight were against her armour, the rest were above. This was not unusual in fights between rolling ships, particularly with indifferently trained gunners, but in this case it was exaggerated by the twisting, turning, listing, passing nature of the fight, which although close, forced gun captains to fire the instant they saw a target briefly through the ports. Effective hulling gunnery required steady ships and steady courses. However, hits on thick armour failed to pierce even from the closest range.

But the main lesson drawn from the battle was the power of the ram. The dramatic picture of the *Re d'Italia* disappearing at one blow, while so much gunnery had hardly accomplished anything, drove out all power rational analysis. The facts, clear enough in all reports, were that ramming, tried and accidentally achieved scores of times by dozens of ships in ideal conditions, had failed every time it had been attempted against a ship under command; the single success had been against a ship unable to steer. Individual reports showed how a ship about to be rammed could, by a sudden turn of the helm, herself become the rammer, though at too sharp an angle to be decisive.

However, it must be remembered that steam was still in its

Top The first ironclad, *La Gloire;* a French steam ship-of-the-line crossing her stern. (*National Maritime Museum*)

Bottom British riposte: H M S *Black Prince*, sister-ship of the *Warrior*

Top A 1st-class 'belt and battery' ironclad, H M S *Hercules*, launched 1867. (*Imperial War Museum*)

Bottom The British unarmoured frigate, *Shah* in action with a rebel Peruvian 'Coles'-turret' ironclad, *Huascar*, 1877. (*National Maritime Museum*)

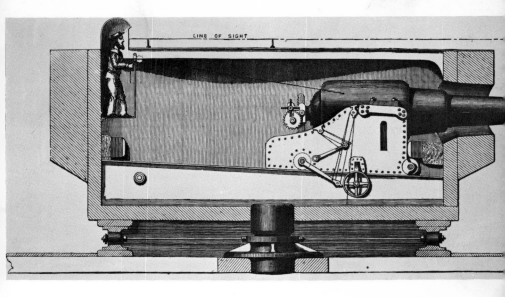

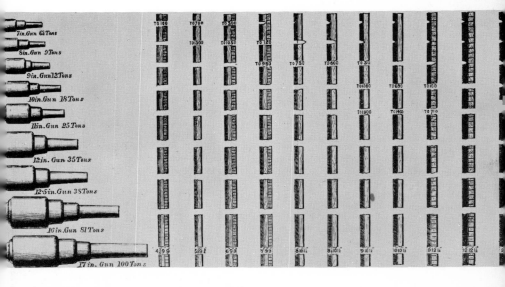

Top Section through a Coles'-type turret of the 1870's, showing a muzzle-loading gun on an iron carriage.

Bottom Competition between guns and armour: British Fraser-Woolwich naval muzzle-loaders of the 1870s and timber-backed, wrought-iron armour penetration.

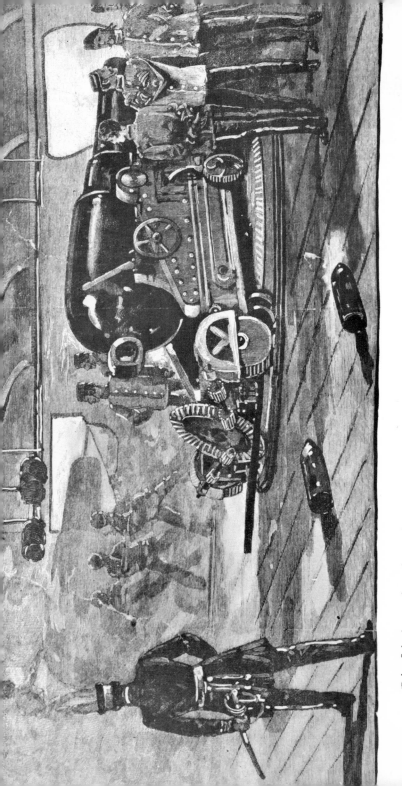

'Prize-firing'; a view from the battery deck of a British ironclad of the 1880s. (*Lt Col. C. E. J. Eagles, R.M.*)

infancy at sea, and naval officers, sail-trained and sail-thinking, while professing to despise engines, held them in some awe. Besides there was already a strong school, apparently logical and of French origin, in favour of ramming. The argument was: engines gave free movement, thus the ability to close and bring the whole gigantic momentum of the ship against the enemy at his most vulnerable point below the waterline, below armour. And compared with the energy of a ship in motion even the largest gun was little better than a pea-shooter. Such a logical approach took little account of an enemy's evasive tactics. Practical experiment with models or small steam boats might have put it into perspective and explained the extraordinary inefficiency of the ram in its own conditions at Lissa. This is clear from hindsight and in the light of modern theory; what was clear in 1866 was that the ram had proved itself in battle, and this led naval constructors and most naval tacticians up false trails for decades.

On the other hand armour was undoubtedly master over the gun at the time, and at first it was not evident that the situation was going to change; so while the ram was overestimated, it was a reasonable *addition* to the armament of a warship at the time. The mistake designers and tacticians made was to treat it as almost the prime feature of a ship, bending other features such as the arrangement of guns, or fleets, to suit.

The other two lessons extracted from the battle were that morale counted for more than material force, and that line ahead was a bad formation for steam warships. Like the conclusion on the ram, both these were already well established ideas among those who liked to theorize about naval warfare, and Teggetthoff's victory gave them practical respectability.

Probably the real conclusion to be drawn about the tactics of Lissa is that they were transitional. They belonged to a brief period during which the armourclad ship was impregnable to the great gun, and they appear to parallel the early days of the gunned sailing ship when the stout timbers of an Atlantic galleon could resist the heavy guns of the time and contests had to be decided by boarding and entering. All the principles of the massed charge and the attempts to clap vessels together distinguished that period too. And it was only as the great gun became sufficiently powerful to decide an action without recourse to boarding that tactics changed, and ships changed to take account of them.

As for Persano's line tactics, they were not pursued with determination, indeed they were thrown away. There can be few more extraordinary lapses in fleet command than his self-provoked break in formation in the face of an enemy under a mile away and bearing down upon him. As a result it is not possible to say whether a steady, compact line holding its fire until Teggetthoff had closed to 500 metres would have been successful in preventing a mêlée at the opening; the chances are that effective range was too low, ironclads too invulnerable and the guns too slow in loading and firing for such a cool order to have disorganized a resolute enemy like Teggetthoff.

5

The Iron Thickens

Technically the ironclad revolution had been a response to the challenge of the rifled shell gun. As it turned the tables on the gun so completely it became a challenge itself; because it was intolerable for the gunmakers of the engineering and metallurgical revolution to acknowledge defeat from a mere 4½-inches of wrought iron. The iron could be punctured, and would be; it simply needed more energy behind the blow.

This process began on armour-proving grounds before the first ironclad was launched, and was so successful that by 1861 the British Admiralty was stipulating 6-inch plates for their second generation of armoured ships, and the French 5.9-inch. This was more a response to the gunmakers' confidence than to actual holes in iron. 'The ship may be cased with armour which today is shot-proof; but tomorrow it may be pierced with ease by shot or shell thrown by some new iron monster.'[1] The confidence was not misplaced: in 1863 the British 'Somerset' 9.2-inch smooth-bore pierced 5½-inches of wrought iron at close range, in 1865 the Woolwich 7-inch, rifled on the French system, pierced 9½-inches. Ship designers responded by increasing the thickness of armour plating, whereupon the gunmakers produced larger pieces still, and so the leapfrog progressed until by the end of the sixties vessels were being designed with 12–14-inches of armour over their vitals to mount 12-inch calibre guns able to pierce 15-inches, at least in theory.[2]

The guns which generated and sustained this competition came in several varieties: the French, whose original *systeme la hitte* model had been little more than a traditional cast-iron muzzle-loader rifled for an elongated and studded shell, developed a breech loader which they put into service from 1864. This was still cast iron, but now strengthened with hoops of steel shrunk on over the main barrel. The breech end, through which the shell and charge were inserted, was sealed with a cylindrical breech block held in place by a screw thread; for speed in opening and closing, the thread was interrupted by wide channels, so that the block could be pushed straight in and given just one-sixth of a turn to screw it tight. This ingenious mechanism, the basis of most later breech-loading systems, were taken from a design patented by two Americans at the height of the 'rifling' revolution in the early fifties.

In Britain, meanwhile, was a ferment of innovation led, like iron ship building, by private firms and individuals. Most influential of these was William Armstrong, an engineer whose interest in ordnance had been aroused first by a despatch from the Crimean War describing the difficulties of dragging two ponderous cast-iron field guns over rough ground. Struck by the gap between these traditional pieces and the products of modern civil engineering, he had produced, by July 1855, a new type of gun, lighter and stronger. This consisted of a steel tube for the bore, over which ribbands of wrought iron had been wound and welded together at white heat, forming an outer tube of coils which cooled into a state of tension over the inner steel tube. This was closed at the breech end by a solid block, dropping through slots and held firm by a large-diameter screw which was hollow, so that the gun could be loaded through it once the breech block had been shifted. The steel bore was rifled and the shells were given a coat of lead to grip in the rifling.[3]

This novel piece proved so accurate in comparison with the products of the Royal Gun Foundry at Woolwich that its successors in the late fifties were adopted enthusiastically by the Ordnance Committee responsible for guns and ammunition for both Army and Navy. So the British Navy began to arm with breechloaders in 1861 before other navies and, as it turned out, before time; besides structural weaknesses they were no quicker to load and fire than muzzle-loaders and, designed for smaller charges of powder, they were less effective armour-piercing weapons. They also needed more attention from more skilled men. Their one advantage was great accuracy, but this was little use from rolling and pitching ships, and in 1864–5, just as the French service was going over to its more satisfactory breech-loading system, the British reverted to muzzle-loaders, rifled in the French style with studded projectiles. As manufactured at Woolwich these pieces were built-up of wrought-iron coils around a steel inner after the Armstrong style, but the coils, instead of being shrunk on separately, were made up first into a barrel and one or two massive hoops to contain it at the breech end, a method which proved as effective as Armstrong's early efforts and considerably cheaper and quicker.

Armstrong, meanwhile, continued to develop his own pieces as muzzle-loaders and was successful in selling them to foreign navies, notably Italy's. Other British private firms pioneered all-steel guns of various types. The only other important centre of innovation was Prussia, where Alfred Krupp, basking in the patronage of Wilhelm I and the army, was also developing all-steel breech-loaders. However his proved as deficient as the early Armstrong's until his sliding breech block mechanism was redesigned after the Austrian war of 1866. In armour-piercing power he could not equal Armstrong until 1869, when competitive tests showed him superior for the first time.

At this date the *system* of loading made little difference to efficiency; what counted was muzzle velocity. And as no method had been devised to control the burning rate of the gunpowder charges, muzzle velocity depended largely upon the strength of the metal around the breech end where the explosion took place; the more massive and weighty this was made the more power could be unleashed behind the shell. So the great pieces grew huge about the breech but comparatively short in the barrel, like dumpy soda-water bottles, and came to be described by weight rather than bore-diameter or projectile-size; weight for weight the British muzzle loaders had the advantage in velocity—1,300–1,400 feet per second at the muzzle against 1,100–1,200—and initial energy on target. They were also much simpler and just as quick to load.

As the guns grew in size and weight, ship designers struggled with the problem of carrying them, and the armour needed to resist their shells, in hulls which must form the smallest possible target area. The first solution was to concentrate armour and guns in a central battery like the *Warrior*'s leaving the ends unprotected save for a belt of armour just above and below the water-line, where penetration could endanger stability or disable the steering gear. Dupuy de Lôme adopted this style for the two-decked successors to the *Gloire* class in 1860, and it was repeated in subsequent French ships through the decade, the central armoured 'box' shortening as the armour itself had to be thickened.[4]

To give some of the heavy guns a higher platform so that they could be fought in a seaway or perhaps depressed to fire down through an enemy's decks, and to give them greater arcs of fire, two or four were carried above the armoured central battery on sponsons projecting some way beyond the sides of the upper deck which was brought in by giving the hull considerable 'tumble-home'. These upper guns were mounted each on its own turntable, which revolved inside an individual fixed armoured redoubt or barbette which was low enough to let the barrel swing above the top; the gun itself was unprotected, as were the crew—a disadvantage outweighed in French eyes by greater ease of sighting in open air instead of through gun-ports in the smoke of the battery, and by the greater arc of fire. Weight was also saved by the reduced armour. This was particularly important for the French, who lacked industrial resources to complete an all-iron fleet and consequently built their lower hulls of timber, which weighed more than iron for the same displacement, thus left less weight for fighting qualities. Of course the unarmoured ends of French ships above the waterline were built of iron against incendiary shell fire.

British ships meanwhile followed two distinct lines of development, 'belt-and-battery' vessels of this type (although worked out in very different ways) and 'turret' ships of various classes. But turrets proved difficult to combine with the masts and rigging still required on all ocean-going ships, and the belt-and-battery idea gained favour. The real prototype here was the *Bellerophon*, a remarkable warship, often held to be the first conceived as an ironclad rather than a steamer with iron bolted on. This does injustice to de Lôme, but it is certain that her design was rethought from the keel up both in terms of fighting requirements and engineering techniques, and this fresh approach led to a break with the earliest British ironclads developed from the *Warrior*.

Her designer, Edward Reed, came from outside the Admiralty and was an exile to practical shipbuilding, though he had served a conventional naval apprenticeship as a shipwright and studied the theory of naval architecture at the School of Mathematics and Naval Construction in Portsmouth. Afterwards he had moved into technical journalism and become Secretary of the Institution of Naval Architects, founded in 1860. So he was not unqualified, indeed he was more qualified than most practical shipbuilders. By happy chance his ideas on warship construction coincided with the tactical ideas of the Controller (late Surveyor) of the Navy, Vice Admiral Sir Spencer Robinson. We can see the trend of these in a confidential report submitted to the Board by Robinson in February 1863, some four months before Reed was called to the Admiralty as Head of the Constructors' Department. This Report compared the four French *Gloire* class ironclads in commission with the four British ironclads—two *Warrior* class and two *Warrior* diminutives —which would have to meet them. The one advantage Robinson could see for the British squadron was its rather higher batteries, but this he thought would only help in Atlantic conditions. In calm seas or the Mediterranean the French ships' completely protected steering gear and gun batteries, greater quickness in turning and 'average power of manoeuvring', and smaller 'exposed surfaces', would give them such an advantage that the British squadron would not be able to fight on equal terms.

The *Bellerophon* answered all these objections, plus another that exercised the Board—increasing expense. By building her very much shorter and broader than the *Warrior* with a bluff U bow to deaden pitching, instead of a fine clipper V, Reed produced a much handier, steadier and cheaper vessel.

Her battery was designed for a small number of the heaviest guns that could be mounted behind armour, rather than a complete deck of smaller pieces. Thus she carried five 12-ton Woolwich guns on each side of a central rectangular casemate of 6-inch iron on 16-inch teak, their muzzles 9½ feet above the waterline and their arcs of fire extending to 45 degrees from the fore-and-aft line. These were mounted on iron carriages and were trained and run in and out, although not loaded, by machinery. In addition there were 'chase' guns at the bow and stern. Beneath the battery deck the entire length, from 5 feet below to 6 feet above the waterline, was protected by armour 6-inches thick amidships, and 3¼-inches at the bow, where it sloped into a ram below water. Her engines drove her at 14.2 knots, virtually as fast as the *Warrior*.

Perhaps her most interesting feature was a cellular system of construction (apparently suggested by the Menai Bridge) adding strength and safety below water. By deepening the usual longitudinal girders that ran from end to end of iron ships, crossing them with deep bracket frames and adding a skin of iron plates to both outside and inside surfaces, Reed created a deep cellular double bottom extending along the underside of the vessel and up around the turn of the bilges. Together with watertight compartments inside the vessel these were conceived as protection against rocks, torpedoes or rams. Using steel in place of wrought iron wherever safe (steel came in variable and often brittle lots) lightened the ship by some 200–300 tons. The *Bellerophon* shows the Admiralty pulling ahead almost effortlessly in the ironclad revolution by harnessing British civil engineering; it says much for the Board and the Controller that they tapped this potential and could recognize genius—even outside their own service.

Here is Reed giving evidence on the genesis of the *Bellerophon* before the 1871 Committee on Designs.

I put the design in a finished form before their Lordships when Parliament had sanctioned the building of five armour-plated wooden frigates, and I requested their Lordships to build this iron frigate...instead of one of those wooden frigates...Of course in designing the *Bellerophon*, although I had acted under no orders as I had contemplated putting it forward myself to the Board, I may have been influenced by the known wishes of the Admiralty, but I think I may properly say that the *Bellerophon* represented at that time the kind of ship which I proposed.[5]

The *Bellerophon* was the only ship Reed was allowed to design in more or less complete freedom; afterwards he was restricted by the Board's instructions, usually on tonnage and nominal horse-power. Perhaps the main reason for this was economy, as the naval estimates, which had risen to £12¾ millions in the three decisive years 1859–1861, were thereafter pruned to below £11 millions. But larger ships made larger targets so economy went hand in hand with tactical requirements.

Another consideration: naval design was in a flux with few guide-lines of experience, but a bewildering number of contradictory theories superimposed on contradictory requirements: heavy guns and heavy armour *versus* small displacement, wide arcs of fire *versus* masts and rigging, steadiness as a gun platform *versus* stiffness as a sailing ship, speed as a screw steamer against weight of armament and efficiency as a sailer. And all these needed constant readjustment as the 'monster' gun revolution quickened. Ships were obsolescent before they were commissioned as guns were designed abroad which could penetrate their armour, ships laid down with armour impenetrable by their guns. In these conditions the Admiralty refused to hazard too much money or power in individual hulls which were in a sense experimental. Then there was the ram, which could send the largest, most heavily iron-clad ship to the bottom with one blow. So they built basic prototypes like the *Bellerophon* and then improved them in successive single-ship designs, meanwhile building classes of diminutives to balance French classes.

The improvement on the *Bellerophon* was the *Hercules*, launched in 1867 with 18-ton as well as 12-ton guns and a waterline belt of 9-inch armour. Her sides were recessed immediately before and abaft the central armoured battery to permit bow and stern fire from the battery itself within 15 degrees of the fore and aft line. This drive towards greater end-on fire continued in the diminutives, the *Audacious* class, and the attempted improvement, *Sultan*, because the ram was considered the primary weapon and it was thought that future naval battles would start with both sides steering straight for each other in a series of line abreast charges, followed by mêlée. It was also thought that steam might give an opponent the chance to place herself easily in the favourite sailing ship position across the bow or stern to rake.

It is plain there was a confusion of tactical thought here, and it was drawing design away from the natural lines of development based on the shape of ships. Powerful fore and aft fire was difficult to achieve (since vessels steam in the direction of their longer axis) especially if masts and rigging were needed. It could be obtained in part by sacrificing other qualities, particularly stability, spread of shrouds, and working space in the battery, but was impossible to maximise.

'Many officers think the gun a comparatively subordinate form of offence as compared with the ram?'
Edward Reed: 'I am quite of that opinion.'[6]

6

Turrets

While the belt-and-battery type evolved through the 1860s as the new capital ship, turret vessels formed a secondary line of development. So far as ocean-going ships were concerned, this was the result of the enthusiasm of two men, John Ericsson in America, and in Britain Captain Cowper Coles, RN, a talented, restless officer in the British tradition of practical innovators. The seed of his idea was sown in action during the Crimean War: frustrated by the shallows which protected Russian forts and depots from effective naval bombardment, he had a raft constructed to mount a long 32-pounder gun together with its ammunition, towed it inshore and destroyed a quantity of enemy stores, thereby gaining his commander-in-chief's esteem, and some fame as a public hero. Fired by this success, Coles developed the idea into a ship-shaped raft mounting a heavier gun protected by a hemispherical shield; he was sent to England to show his plans to the Admiralty, and suggest that a fleet of these be built to attack the Kronstadt forts. The Admiralty showed interest, but the war came to an end, and Coles's plan with it.

However, he had tasted success as a designer, and while on half pay the idea of the raft as a stable gun platform offering hardly any target to enemy fire continued to exercise his mind, soon growing into a more ambitious project altogether: the raft became a low profile sea-going ship, the single gun a number of guns, each mounted upon its own turntable to command wide arcs of fire, and each with its own convex shield which revolved with it —the whole the very shape of the future capital ship, Marc Brunel, father of the famous engineer and iron shipbuilder, has been credited with the idea of mounting gun and shield together on a turntable; but it was certainly Coles who patented the idea in March 1859 and who thereafter promoted his 'cupola' ship with fanatic persistence.

The trouble with Coles's 'invention' was that the glittering theoretical advantages of turrets on the centre line of the ship, commanding wide arcs on *both* broadsides—thus halving the number of guns needed—and the stability and low target area of a low freeboard vessel with guns raised in individual armoured positions (as compared with a conventional broadside ship which had to be tall to carry its guns sufficiently high) blinded its creator to its impracticality for a ship which had to sail as well as steam. Coles refused to see his own limitations as a ship designer. When he offered the Admiralty his plan for a 10-cupola ship mounting 20 heavy guns, the drawing was, as K. C. Barnaby put it, 'amateurish in the extreme, even childish. Only token masts were shown with no rigging and there was just room for a slender funnel. The only clear areas were short spaces at bow and stern.'[1]

The Surveyor pointed out that masts needed shrouds, and the Chief Constructor, Isaac Watts, who unlike Coles had received a proper training in subjects like ship stability, reported that the proposed ship laboured under 'every disadvantage in point of efficiency as a sea-going man of war'.[2]

Coles's enthusiasm remained unquenched by such 'theories' and he started a campaign to reverse the Admiralty decision, gaining the powerful support of Prince Albert, who was struck by the sheer logic of the thing. So in 1861 the Admiralty, who had never been averse to the turret so long as it was not to be mounted in a sea-going ship, built an experimental turret to Coles's design, fitted it to a floating battery at Shoeburyness and pounded it with their heaviest guns, the 68-pounder and the new 100-pounder. Thirty-three hits failed to damage its turning gear and Coles, waiting only long enough to see to the construction of another mock-up turret housing *two* 100-pounders, wrote to the Admiralty:

> I will undertake to prove that on my principle a vessel shall be built nearly 100 feet shorter than the *Warrior* and in all respects equal to her with one exception—that I will guarantee to disable and capture her in an hour; she shall draw four feet less water, require only half the crew, and cost the Country for building at least £10,000 less.[3]

This celebrated challenge was written in October 1861; it was backed up by a letter from the Prince Consort and in the following January the Board agreed to build a coast defence vessel with six, later four, turrets on the centre line. She was designed by the Constructor's Department and laid down on 29 April 1862, to be named, appropriately, *Prince Albert*.

This, of course, was more than a month after the *Monitor* had gone into action at Hampton Road, six months after Ericsson had started building her. But for any dispute about who 'invented' the turret the facts are that Coles's first patent had been filed in March 1859, that the US Navy Department had decided on a number of Coles's double-turreted craft when they ordered the *Monitor* in the autumn of 1861 (although these were never built) and going further back, that Ericsson had sent plans of a turreted iron-clad battery to Napoleon III in 1854; obviously both these men and probably Marc Brunel as well, were the 'inventors'. Ericsson himself gave the credit to the ancient Greeks.

Of the two types of turret Coles's was probably the more practical and less easily damaged. As originally conceived it was in the shape of a cone with the top half removed, but this was altered during the construction of the *Prince Albert* to a plain cylinder. It was turned by hand-power upon a circumferential roller path set in the lower deck, and its upper 4½ feet of armour reared up through the main or upper deck which formed an armoured glacis to protect the lower part. The guns within were mounted on iron carriages which recoiled along slides whose ends could be raised or lowered by screw gear to elevate or depress the muzzles; the crew and ammunition entered through a hollow central cylinder from below. Ericsson's turret, on the other hand, was all above the upper deck on which it rested. Before turning, it had to be lifted by rack and pinion from contact with the deck, and trained by a central spindle driven through gearing by a steam engine. This was a more vulnerable system, but of course was designed for a raft-like vessel with scarcely any freeboard; Coles's was for a conventional hull. Both were extremely clumsy in operation.

Towards the end of 1862, the French began studies on the use of turrets aboard ship, and de Lôme came up with a new type altogether, whose turntable was protected by a circular armoured barbette rising from the deck around it; this was adopted for coast defence vessels and the new class of 'rams', but for ocean-going ships with masts and rigging the turret itself was omitted and the upper deck guns were mounted on separate turntables without any protection save for the low barbette. This system seemed to lack all the turret's advantages : neither gun nor gunners were in an 'impregnable fort', and there was no saving in weight of armament nor gain in power; the main feature of the design was the saving in weight of armour that allowed the guns to be carried higher above water. As for its apparently wider arcs of fire, these were more theoretical than real; here is a French critic writing of de Lôme's Ocean class of 1868–70:

The fore and aft fire of the guns placed in the turrets, in fact barbettes, to which so much has been sacrificed both in the spread of the shrouds, the position of the boats...and the light armament of the upper deck, appears to me a perfect chimera. The Commission appointed to carry out experiments were so struck with the injury occasioned by the concussion from a 24-cm 15½-ton gun that they determined that the guns should not be trained within 15½ degrees of the line of the keel.[4]

When firing at less than 45 degrees to the fore and aft line, the crew had to be withdrawn from the extremities on that side of the ship.

In fact neither turrets nor barbettes could be employed to full advantage in ships which, because contemporary steam engines were uneconomical and worldwide coaling stations scarce, had to be masted if they were to cruise the oceans. This was appreciated by the professional designers: de Lôme compromised with wing barbettes, Ericsson built ocean-going monitors without sails but carrying enough coal to cross the Atlantic under steam alone— although the crews were dreadfully weakened in the process—and Reed, when he was persuaded to build a rigged turret ship, sacrificed fore and aft fire to seaworthiness. Only Coles persisted in seeking *all* advantages in one hull, at least he was the only man with the obstinacy, successful design record, backing and flair for press support, to succeed against all professional advice in having such a ship built.

To understand how he succeeded one must realize that shipbuilding was still a craft largely undisturbed by scientific calculation. The form of ships and their sail plans had developed by trial and error and observation—and lately by competition—and the naval officers who sailed them, who shifted a weight here, tautened a stay there, adjusted the tight spread of canvas to each trick of the wind, regarded themselves as quite competent, if not to draw detailed designs of ships, at least to argue the merits of any vessel with anyone. They, after all, knew the wind and sea as no shore-bound architect could, fought them and mastered them every day of their professional lives; they knew ships, handled them, even loved them. Against such practical knowledge theoretic calculations were little more than dalliance for mathematicians; they could help in defining the weights and centres of gravity of all the new metal pieces that went into an ironclad, but when it came to the general shape and form of a ship a sailor was as good a judge as a mathematical designer, while for sail plans, trim, and all the problems of fighting a ship he was far better. This view was not restricted to the shellbacks who despised 'book learning' for its own sake, but found expression among those many lively and enquiring naval officers who had become Associates of the newly formed Institution of Naval Architects, and amongst informed lay opinion, notably Prince Albert, various First Lords of the Admiralty, *The Times* and most other leading newspapers; these supported Coles in his campaign for low freeboard thus low target, fully-rigged, thus ocean-going, heavily-gunned turret ships for Britain's first line of defence.

As for Coles, he was carried along by the momentum of success and the enthusiasm of his supporters. After the *Prince Albert* had been laid down, he had persuaded the Admiralty to cut down a new timber ship of the line, *Royal Sovereign*, and convert her to an armoured turret ship; Denmark, Peru and the Southern states of America had ordered other turret vessels from British builders. And along with all these independent testimonies to his genius, the *Royal Sovereign*, which was the first to be completed for the British Navy, came through her trials successfully in 1864, with her turrets reported on favourably. Coles issued another ebullient challenge to the Admiralty. This time it was the *Bellerophon* which he compared unfavourably with a turret ship of the same dimensions; however he tempered his former presumptuous tone and asked for the services of a competent naval architect from the Constructors' Department to help him design one. The resulting draft was examined by a Committee appointed for the purpose, which recommended that a sea-going ship of this type *should* be tried out. However, as they suggested two turrets in place of the single one on the new Coles/-Admiralty draughtsman design, Reed set about planning a larger vessel altogether.

She was laid down in June 1866, in essentials a large version of his *Bellerophon* with a foc's'le added housing two bow chase guns, and with two turrets rising on the centre line at either end of the central armoured box. Each turret, which could be turned by steam or hand gear, eventually mounted two 12-inch 25-ton guns 3 feet above upper deck level, 17 feet above the waterline; these pieces, the first of their great size mounted in the British service, threw a 609 lb shell capable in theory of piercing 12-inches of iron at 1,000 yards. Over the turrets a flying deck extended between the fore and main masts to take the rigging. She was named *Monarch*.

Alas, the design did not meet with Coles's approval; all he could see was a normal belt-and-battery vessel with central turrets substituted for broadside gun ports, turrets whose fore and aft fire was blocked by the foc'sle and the supports for the flying deck. Gone was the low silhouette and the full armour protection for the whole ship. He 'most respectfully but earnestly' recorded his opinion 'that it is disadvantageous and unnecessary to add to her tonnage by giving her guns the unprecedented height of 17 feet out of the water, tending to make her top-heavy and to labour heavily in a seaway. A good sea boat does not altogether depend on height out of water.'[5]

Here was the naval officer confident in his practical judgement, quite unclouded by scientific theory. Unfortunately he was wrong. Height out of the water, which was built in to all sailing men-of-war not on theoretical principle but to carry the guns high, *was* needed for a ship under press of sail; it increased the range of stability — the angle a ship could heel before the righting moment began to decline and then vanish.

Reed knew this and refused to alter his designs. The Controller, Sir Spencer Robinson, backed him. But the First Lord was a Coles supporter, and when all the other Coles supporters in press and parliament rose and declared the *Monarch* no fair test of their paragon's views, the Board agreed to finance a second sea-going turret ship to be built to Coles's specification — in other words with a freeboard of only 8 feet for a length of at least 300, and a full sail plan. But 'entire responsibility' was to rest with him and the builders. Coles chose Lairds of Birkenhead and the vessel they designed to his specifications was laid down on 30 January 1867; she was named *Captain*. Reed wrote:

> The very cause of the *Captain*'s being designed and of her being built was the assumption that the opinions of Sir Spencer Robinson and myself were not to be trusted and that we were showing some prejudiced opposition to the views of Captain Coles. So strongly did I feel that we were clear of responsibility for this ship, and that the time would come when it would be necessary for us to prove our exemption from that responsibility, that I forbade my assistants ever to employ the phrase 'approved' even for the most minor details, and I directed them never to employ a stronger phrase than 'no objection would be offered.'[6]

The *Captain*, as built, was nearly as long as the *Monarch*, but less beamy and at 7,767 tons displacement over 500 tons smaller. Her main hull rose little higher than a conventional ship's 'belt' and was consequently fully armoured up to the weather deck, but an unprotected foc's'le and poop rose from it to add ocean-worthiness and support a narrow flying deck for the rigging above two double 12-inch gun turrets on the centreline; there was also a small deck-house between the turrets which supported the flying deck at mid-length. The need for all these structures above the weather deck must have irked Coles as they limited the fore and aft fire quite as much as the *Monarch's* 'obstructions'. Nevertheless he had specified the fullest possible rig and there was no other solution.

The ship was completed in January 1870, seven months after the *Monarch*, but unfortunately not to specification; due to insufficient control over her weights while building, or incorrect initial estimates, she floated 1½ feet lower than her designed freeboard of 8 feet, an alarming exaggeration of Coles' ideas on raft-like hulls; when Lairds calculated her stability they found that she would have a maximum righting moment at only 21 degrees—compared with 40 degrees for the *Monarch*—after which it would decline and vanish at 54½ degrees; if the foc's'le and poop were damaged, it would vanish at only 40 degrees. Despite this she came through her trials well, appeared to stand up stiffly under her canvas, and also steamed well at 14¼ knots, no doubt due to the slimness of her lines. When, in addition, she weathered a May gale off Finisterre without any signs of distress, all doubts vanished and she came to be considered one of the finest ships in the service. Even the Constructors' Department were lulled by the good reports of the officers who had sailed her. They made their own stability calculations which confirmed Lairds', but had no means of knowing whether such a low freeboard vessel would in fact heel beyond the danger point; all experience with monitors and rafts suggested that their hulls did not roll as much as conventional vessels'.

Meanwhile the *Captain* had already sailed with her creator on what was to be her last voyage. She continued to prove a good sailer, and on the afternoon of 6 September, during a trial with all ships of the Channel Squadron off Finisterre, she made 9½ knots in a force 6 wind under plain sail including royals, gradually increasing to an average between 11 and 13 knots as the wind freshened. Both her Captain, Hugh Talbot Burgoyne, VC, and Cowper Coles were well pleased with the performance, although the commander-in-chief of the squadron who was aboard at the time and not so used to seeing a lee gunwale driven down to the very level of the sea, was uneasy as a swell from the lee bow continually washed aboard over the weather deck. Burgoyne and Coles assured him that they knew exactly how far they could go, but he returned to his flagship not entirely convinced.

That evening the wind freshened with rain, the barometer dropped and by midnight a gale lashed the squadron; the *Captain* was reduced to fore topmast staysail and fore and main topsails double reefed, their yards braced sharply to the wind from the port bow so that she had little way. As a new watch came on deck at midnight she lurched to starboard, but righted herself, then a short time later fell over again. The Captain, on deck, called out 'How much is she heeling now?' 'Eighteen degrees,' came the answer.

'Let go the foretopsail halyards! Let go fore and maintopsail sheets!'

But as the men worked their way along the narrow flying deck and started casting the ropes off the pins the ship continued to fall over on her side in a smooth roll that took her masts down into the sea and brought her keel uppermost; then she sank stern first. Captain Burgoyne, Cowper Coles and all but 18 of her crew of over 500 went down with her.

The court martial found that the *Captain* was lost 'on the morning of 7th September 1870 by pressure of sail assisted by the heave of the sea, and that the sail carried at the time of her loss...was insufficient to have endangered a ship endued with the proper amount of stability'. And they found that she had been built in deference to public opinion expressed in parliament, 'in opposition to the views of the Controller and his department'.

The terrible vindication of Reed's views did, perhaps, serve one purpose: it had been a very practical lesson, and it carved the curve of stability into naval design as no theoretical exposition could have done. It also stimulated further investigation into the problems of stability and the interaction of sea, wind and hull form, prompting one authority to call it 'one of the landmarks in the history of warship design'.

As for the specific failure to comprehend the danger the *Captain* was running, this was due not simply to the supposed 'theoretical' nature of the stability curves which had been worked out by one of Reed's mathematically inclined assistants, F. K. Barnes, only two years before the disaster, but to a 'static' concept of stability which assumed a fixed wind pressure on the sails being met by a known righting moment. In fact, as K. C. Barnaby puts it:

The effect of a sudden squall is very different...instead of a fixed 'dead' load, a 'live' load is suddenly imposed and an angle of heel is approximately doubled. If any reader doubts the vast difference between a 'dead' and a 'live' load he has only to suddenly impose a weight on his bathroom scales, and he will at once find a momentary indication of twice the actual weight.[7]

As the *Captain* went down, another vessel embodying all Coles's ideas except the fatal sail plan, was completing in England to Reed's design. This was the *Cerberus*, a 3,340 ton coast defence

c

vessel for the State of Victoria in Australia. She was the first of a type—designated 'breastwork monitor'—which was to provide the true line of development for the ironclad battleship. Reed had taken the raft-like hull of the monitor and built centrally upon it an armoured citadel or breastwork about half as long and three-quarters as wide as the hull; from each end of this rose a Coles turret mounting two guns with uninterrupted axial fire, and between the turrets was a small midships structure supporting a flying deck for the boats, conning position and rigging for the short pole mast. Her advantages over the plain monitor type, for which Reed had little use, were of course increased height of the guns above water, protection for the turret bases, and the greater stability afforded by the additional freeboard of the breastwork, small as it was.

In 1869 Reed developed her into the first British sea-going mastless warships, *Devastation* and *Thunderer*. These two might be called the first real battleships; in any case they were direct prototypes for the species of first class fighting ship which eventually won the evolutionary struggle—not that this could be foreseen at the time. Indeed, they were designed, not as rivals for the *Captain*, *Monarch* or *Hercules*, as sails were still essential for Britain's world-wide needs, but rather as capital ships for European waters where the main strength of the enemy was likely to be found. In a sense they were an expression of the confusion in traditional strategy and tactics since steam had upset all certainties, particularly the ideas on the defence of Britain and her Empire by locally stationed forces centred on impregnable floating fortresses, rather than by a battle fleet holding the general 'maritime superiority' and able to move anywhere. They were also in a sense experimental, the result of an awareness that all ironclads could not be all things and fulfil all roles, but that different types would be necessary and each type would have to sacrifice some qualities. This awareness, so soon after the plunge for an ironclad type which combined invincibility, power, good steaming and cruising qualities all in one hull, was a result of the problem created by the increasing weight of guns and their ascendancy over all but the thickest armour, combined with the principal of making each ship the smallest possible target to enemy guns. This impossible conflict could only be resolved by different types with different qualities, so it fed back and encouraged ideas of piecemeal defence and group attack—each group including ships with different advantages so that together they combined them all. Thus technical and tactical confusion interacted with each other.

In another sense the 'Devastations' were an expression of genius and sheer clear-headness; here is Reed in March 1869, some months before their keels were laid:

> My clear and strong conviction at the moment of writing these lines is that no satisfactory designed turret ship with rigging has yet been built or even laid down...The middle of the upper deck of a full-rigged ship is not a very eligible position for fighting large guns. Anyone who has stood upon the deck of a frigate, amid the maze of ropes of all kinds and sizes that surrounds him, must feel that to bring guns of a moderate size away from the port holes to place them in the midst of these ropes and discharge them there is utterly out of the question...[8]

By doing away with all the ropes, Reed could bring the great guns away from the portholes, and build a virtually impregnable fort to float them: his design for the *Devastation* showed a main hull 285 feet long by 58 feet beam with only 4½ feet freeboard; bolted around this was a band of armour 9¼ feet deep which was composed, from the side out, of two layers of ¾-inch iron plates, 18 inches of teak backing then 12 inches of solid wrought iron plate which tapered to 8 inches at the ends. The whole was decked over with 3-inch wrought iron covered by two layers of teak planks. Upon the mid-156 foot length of this hull and leaving a 6 foot gangway down each side, was a 7 foot high 'breastwork' similarly armoured and decked with a turret rising from either end. The turret armour was made up in a deep sandwich of two inner iron plates, 6 inches of teak laid horizontally, 6 inches of solid wrought iron, another 6 inches of teak set vertically and finally an outside surface of 8 inches of wrought iron. The total weight of armour in the ship was 2,540 tons, 27 per cent of the total displacement. Hitherto the standard proportion had been about 15 per cent.

The turrets, cylindrical with an inside diameter of 24¼ feet, each mounted two 35-ton guns with a theoretical penetration of 15 inches of iron at 1,000 yards. Their ports were 13½ feet above sea level, quite as high as those of a conventional broadside battery ship. Between the turrets was a small superstructure supporting a flying deck to which the main hatches and openings were led, and from which the funnels and a single pole mast projected. Her speed of nearly 14 knots under twin screws was to be only marginally less than other first class warships, and with a length-breadth ratio of only 1: 4.57, as against 1: 5.38 for even such a handy vessel as the *Bellerophon*, she would have great powers of manoeuvre for a ramming contest.

The advantages derived by freeing this class from masts and rigging led to the birth of a ship virtually indestructible by contemporary gunfire, but whose own guns could pierce anything afloat; as she was seagoing, with a wide radius of action allowed by 1,400–1,800 tons of coal, she was evidently the new capital ship—especially if compared with the French class laid down the same year. These were the 'Colberts', a standard de Lôme belt, battery and upper deck barbette, timber-hulled and fully-masted type with 15½-ton guns—theoretical penetration 11 inches of wrought iron—protected by only 6¼-inch battery armour with an 8½-inch waterline belt.

However, all this is plainer now than it was in 1869, much plainer than in 1870 after the loss of the *Captain*. For the *Devastation* had an even lower main hull freeboard and her curves of stability were very similar, showing a maximum righting movement at 19 degrees, vanishing altogether at only 43 degrees. And the public, who had clamoured for Coles and the *Captain*, now distrusted low freeboard to such an extent that they were blind to the essential difference in masting between the two types; the *Devastation* plans were criticised freely—by naval officers as well.

Before she was completed Reed left the Admiralty, whether due to pique, disagreement with the First Lord, or the financial advantages of commercial ship-designing is not clear. What is clear now is that in the *Hercules*, *Devastation* and *Monarch* he had designed the finest warships of the decade in these three distinct first class types, and set high standards of engineering excellence which no other country could match at the time. He had taken the steamer plated with iron into the ironclad proper, and finally shown the way towards the mastless battleship.

Torpedoes

While most energies in the world's navies were directed towards heavy armour and guns to smash through it, there were more subtle schemes afoot which aimed at getting in underneath and attacking the vulnerable lower hull. These ideas can be traced back to the beginning of the century, long before the *Gloire* and the *Warrior*, when charges of gunpowder were towed behind small rowing boats in attempts to open underwater breaches in the timbers of blockading warships. But it was the steam/ironclad revolution which gave the ideas real stimulus. It seemed at first as though the ironclad was going to be invulnerable to gunfire; this naturally encouraged underwater attack both by explosive charges known as 'torpedoes', and by ramming—and ramming led directly back again to the torpedo, both as a protection against being rammed and as an apparently ideal weapon for the close quarters mêlée which a ramming attack involved. The theory meanwhile gained practical merit and ingenuity with the progress in engineering and metallurgical skills.

So Torpedoes were adopted by all navies, both as static, moored charges to defend harbours and river mouths (in which role they came to be known by the military term 'mines') and as weapons which could be moved into action. The simplest of the moving torpedoes were the 'spar' type carried like a dipping bowsprit before a small steam boat and exploded by electricity on contact—after the style so skillfully and daringly exploited by Lieutenant Cushing in the American Civil War—and the 'outrigger', which was the same device extended from the *side* of its steam launch. By the late sixties probably all ironclads carried steam boats equipped with these devices.

Another early type was a modern version of the towing torpedo. In its new form it stemmed from a proposal by Captain John Harvey of the British service in 1862; a buoy attached to the charge by line kept it up to a set depth, and it was designed to explode on contact with any object it struck. In 1867 a Commander F. Harvey improved the idea by shaping the metal container for the charge so that it diverged out from the wake of the towing ship some 30 degrees, and in this or similar form the 'Harvey' was adopted by all navies; the Germans carried one whose divergence could be changed from side to side at will.

These weapons were regarded with scepticism by most naval officers; 'We had some curious toys in the shape of torpedoes,' wrote Admiral Penrose Fitzgerald of his days in the Channel Squadron of 1870. 'There was for instance the spar or pole torpedo...you were supposed to steam quietly up to your enemy while he was at anchor, poke the charge under his bottom and explode it by electricity, then return to your ship and report, "Enemy sunk, sir; found him fast asleep."' From the US service we have the reminiscences of Robley D. Evans about the early seventies: 'We tried all the kinds of torpedoes then known to us and decided that they were good only for newspaper stories or to scare timid people with. The much-talked-of Harvey towing torpedo was towed about for days in an effort to make it strike a ship, but it would not do it.' In any case the danger of blowing up friend instead of foe in the confusion of a mêlée was clear, and efforts were made to give it a more selective firing mechanism than the simple percussion head.

Before these could come to anything the self-propelled or auto-mobile torpedo had proved its superior potential. The earliest and most successful of these was pioneered by an Austrian naval officer, Commander Lupis, from 1860. In 1864, he called in an English engineer, Robert Whitehead, manager of an engineering works at Fiume, to help him with the technical problems, and by January 1867 the Lupis-Whitehead fish torpedo had become a practical weapon. It was then a slim wrought-iron cylinder 13 feet long by 14 inches in diameter, tapered and pointed at both ends with a keel along upper and lower sides, two horizontal fins, and at its rear a horizontal balanced rudder behind a single screw propeller which was driven by compressed air contained in the after part of the body. The forward part contained 16–18 lbs of dynamite with a percussion igniter, and in the centre was the mechanism which kept the torpedo to the set depth; this was the most ingenious part of the machine and it came to be known as the Whitehead 'secret' as it was never patented; governments who bought manufactur-ing rights were sworn not to divulge its processes.

Later it became quite an open secret, described in various articles as a chamber exposed to the sea by small holes in the outside casing of the torpedo, and containing a spring which could be set to resist the water pressure at the desired depth; if the torpedo sank below this depth, the pressure on the chamber acted on the spring, thereby operating a rod connected to the horizontal rudder at the rear. In addition there was a pendulum arrangement which also acted upon the rudder as the nose dipped or rose; thus the torpedoes' horizontal course was not a straight line but a constantly corrected series of undulations.

It was fired from below water, issuing from a pipe in the ship's side with valves at either end, and travelling beneath the surface at 6 knots; after trials it was said to 'hit a target with certainty at a cable's length (200 yards), and that its propelling power; would carry it three cable's length with fair precision...' The Austrian and French governments immediately negotiated for rights.

In August 1868 the machine was brought to the attention of the British service by the commander-in-chief on the Mediterranean station; his report was filed. In October Whitehead himself arrived in England to sell his 'secret' to the greatest maritime power, the Director General of Naval Ordnance reported, 'the invention is one of the *very highest importance*', an opinion corroborated the following year by a committee of officers sent out to Fiume for demonstrations. Finally, after further tests in 1870 the British government purchased manufacturing rights, and experts at Woolwich set about improving the weapon; by 1875 the wrought iron body had become steel, a second contra-rotating propeller had been fitted, also a vertical rudder at a fixed angle, and both speed and maximum range had been increased—300 yards at 12 knots or 1,200 yards at 9 knots. Tests suggested that the new model could be launched from a moving vessel 'with sufficient accuracy to hit a broadside ship at 400 yards and from a stationary ship with sufficient accuracy up to extreme range.'

By this time many officers were convinced that the torpedo was about to revolutionize naval warfare; perhaps the most convinced, certainly the most enthusiastic, were a group of French officers, later to become known as the *jeune école*, who were attracted by the prospect of countering British battlefleet superiority—now measured in numbers of ironclads—with small, fast torpedo-carrying boats which could be built at a fraction of the cost of an ironclad, but which would be able to sink the largest, most heavily protected and expensive ship with one blow. The British Admiralty was alive to the danger, equally alive to the possibilities; here is Sir Spencer Robinson giving evidence before the Committee on Designs in 1871, just after leaving his post as Controller of the Navy:

We are on the eve in my opinion of a total change in naval warfare. We are on the eve of discovering the best way of using that formidable weapon, the torpedo, if we have not already got to that point...we should do well to turn our attention to the best form of torpedo ship which would be the master of the *Devastation* and *Thunderer*...I should like to have them with great speed and with immensely thick armour plating. I know the ship would turn out an ugly, horrid, uncomfortable looking vessel, but still she would be the master of an enemy in battle.

Before Reed left the Admiralty he was discussing filling watertight compartments with cork to provide flotation after torpedo hits, his successor Barnaby set up experiments against a hulk, and numerous devices were tried out for catching torpedoes before they ever reached the side of a ship. The most successful of these was galvanized wire net with an 8-inch mesh weighted at the foot and hung out around the ship from 40-foot booms; in 1874 tests these nets arrested all torpedoes fired, and an Admiralty committee set up to inquire into all aspects of torpedo warfare recommended their adoption by ironclads, together with light rapid-firing machine guns, such as the American Gatling, to repel torpedo boats. All these, together with electric searchlights and a system of patrolling by the ironclads' own boats would, the committee thought, ensure safety while at anchor. For the open sea they were not so happy, indeed they were quite as gloomy as the *jeune école* would have wished.

Offensive torpedoes will also play a most important part in future *ocean* warfare. The Committee recognizes the introduction of the latter as specially inimical to the manoeuvrings of large squadrons and as having a tendency to reduce to one common level the Naval Power of the greatest and the least significant nations...the Committee desire to lay special stress upon the imperative necessity for providing some description of defence, for without it the most powerful ship is liable to be destroyed by a torpedo projected from a vessel of the utmost comparative insignificance...

As for Britain's traditional strategy of blockade, the committee had 'no hesitation in expressing their opinion that none of our large vessels could remain for any length of time during war off an enemy's port without imminent risk of destruction by offensive torpedoes; experiments in this and other countries have furnished data which leave no room for doubt on this head.'

As it turned out these alarmist views were premature: the great gun was fast gaining over armour; penetration of the thickest wrought iron was becoming possible at 1,000 yards, way outside effective torpedo range, and as for accuracy against moving targets, the relative times of flight—over three minutes for a torpedo travelling 1,000 yards as against three seconds for a shell—tell their own story. In addition there was, as yet, little realization of the difficulties of combining oceanworthiness, habitability and range with the small, narrow hulls of fast torpedo craft, such as the British firm of Thorneycroft were pioneering from 1873.

But once again, this was not clear in the 1870s; the potential of this devastating weapon seemed more important than its limitations, which were considered only temporary. So 'Whiteheads' joined the other industrial novelties projecting naval design and tactics into a wilderness of conjecture. There was no certainty, very little agreement. Gunnery and torpedo specialists went their separate ways, improving the efficiency of their own weapons; commanders-in-chief went a different way, exercising their squadrons in steam manoeuvres which aped military precision and with formations like the 'naval square' which had little to do with gunnery or torpedoes. Meanwhile the majority of officers contented themselves with, indeed carried out enthusiastically, the directions in Admiralty Circular 177 which enjoined them to work their ships without the aid of steam 'not only on the score of economy, but for the important purpose of ensuring the efficiency of screw ships as sailing ships'.

Naval Supremacy in the 1870s

As the first decade of ironclad building came to a close it was evident that Britain had shrugged off the French challenge. The tension that had marked the first desperate years, when the Admiralty tried to make up lost ground, had faded mainly because France's attention had been diverted to far more pressing affairs: Bismarck was shaking out the map of Central Europe and the resulting tremors throughout the Continent forced her to concentrate on European diplomacy and her land frontiers. The British Admiralty, for its part, had been unable to continue its traditional provocative stance of two ships for each one of the French in every class because Gladstone's crusade against public expenditure had by 1870 cut the estimates down to little over £9 millions, and the cost of ironclads was high. Thus, while the three-decker steam line-of-battle ship of 1858 had cost £170,000, the *Warrior* had cost £370,000, the super-*Warrior* £480,000, and the latest Reed types, the *Sultan* and *Devastation*, some £360,000. However, the Admiralty had been able to maintain a real advantage by building individually larger, more powerful ships; there is little doubt, for instance, that there were only four vessels afloat in 1871 which could have been termed first class warships by the standards of that time, and while none of these were French, three were British; the *Sultan*, 9,290 tons with a 9-inch belt and 18-ton guns, the similar *Hercules*, 8,680 tons, and the *Monarch*, 8,320 tons, with 25-ton turret guns. The *Devastation* and *Thunderer*, which were building, were in a new class altogether. Even the much smaller British belt-and-battery *Audacious* class of little over 6,000 tons with 8-inch belts and 12½-ton guns were believed to be a match for the three largest French ships, *Ocean*, *Marengo* and *Suffren*. For although the French ships displaced some 1,600 tons more, a proportion of this was wasted by their timber hulls, and their armour, marginally thicker in places, was spread further and was thinner on average; in addition their 14-ton guns were less powerful armour-piercing weapons and the four upper ones, mounted *en barbette* were less protected.

Apart from France there were no naval powers of any consequence to trouble the Admiralty. Russia, which had been considered France's most likely ally in any maritime war against Britain, had scarcely entered the ironclad age; apart from two timber ships which had been cut down and armoured with $4\frac{1}{2}$-inch iron in 1861 she had three frigates with full-length batteries covered with $4\frac{1}{2}$-6-inch iron and one central battery frigate with $4\frac{1}{2}$-inch iron. The US fleet consisted of monitors, and although six were designated ocean-going, and had a wide steaming radius, their laminated armour, ponderous smooth bore guns, and largely submarine progress made their offensive value doubtful. After one of these, the *Miantonomoh*, had successfully crossed the Atlantic, a British officer who went aboard reported that the crew 'seemed to have no go in them and crawled about the decks in a state of debility one and all. I was shocked and immensely struck by their inactive appearance. The vessel was compared to a dungeon under water filled with a stifling atmosphere by a steam engine...'

Of the other minor powers, Austria and Italy had done little, since the battle of Lissa, and Turkey was probably the most powerful minor naval power in the Mediterranean—at least on paper. The only other countries with any sea-going force were Spain, and Bismarck's North German confederation which had a 9,600-ton all-iron ship, *König Wilhelm*, on paper the only non-British first class warship. She had been built in England, originally for Turkey, and launched in 1868 as one of the most powerful vessels in the world, with 8-inch armour, a long battery mounting $15\frac{1}{2}$-ton guns, and a designed speed of $14\frac{1}{2}$ knots. But Germany lacked marine engineering experience or even a dock large enough to take her, and by 1870 her hull was so covered with barnacles that she could manage no more than ten knots.

Outside Europe and North America there was virtually nothing; Japan had not been aroused from her isolation long enough to have gained industrial or naval experience and her fleet 'were curious craft...built and rigged up on Dutch models of the sixteenth century, and anyone who knows Van der Velde's sea pieces will be able to picture to himself exactly what they were like, with their high sterns, round tops and other characteristics of that date.'[1]

Plainly the fleets of Britain and France had no serious rivals anywhere. And while the British fleet was not so overwhelmingly powerful in numbers as her traditional strategy demanded (indeed both countries had approximately the same number of ironclads built and building—40:35 in Britain's favour) they were by all rational calculation more than a match for any French force in action; in addition the Constructors' Department had drawn up detailed plans for cutting down and armour-plating existing timber ships to swell the number of ironclads quickly in the event of any serious threat.

The main British strength, however, still lay in her maritime and engineering potential, which had increased both actually and comparatively since 1859. In that year only one-third of the merchant tonnage leaving her shipbuilding yards had been iron; by 1870 the proportion was five-sixths, while the French Navy still built with timber. In steam ships her lead was equally impressive; due in the main to a government policy of postal subventions, which had both encouraged pioneer steamship lines as early as 1840 and enabled them to survive while the steam engine was still clumsy and uneconomic. Her mail companies, Cunard, P & O, Royal Mail, Castle Line were not only vigorous themselves but supported a vigorous marine engineering industry whose products had become a byeword for efficiency and sound craftsmanship. Most major foreign steamship Lines, Hamburg-Amerika, North German Lloyd, the Netherland Steamship Company, the Guion Line of America, had their ships built and engined in Britain.

The total British steam fleet amounted to 1.1 million tons, her only rivals, the US had 0.2 million, and France 0.15 million; indeed Britain's steam fleet was larger than the total steam and sailing fleet of any country save the United States, which still had a vast, technically efficient and savagely driven fleet of sailing ships. But using the usual 4:1 conversion ratio for steam/sailing tonnage Britain's 5.6 million tons of merchant shipping amounted to some 56 per cent of the world total. With such a lead in technical expertise, such a reserve of strength in nautical and engineering manpower and material, Britain enjoyed a maritime supremacy in the new conditions of peaceful competition which was quite equal to her earlier fighting supremacy. And despite the economy campaign which had reduced the first line fighting strength to a level which earlier would have been regarded as dangerously low, and despite the prevailing confusion about the influence of all the new elements in naval warfare, it is difficult to see how she could have been seriously challenged in a fighting war. This supremacy was as clear at the time as it is in the light of the cold statistics; it was evident in the assured style of British naval officers, in the pride and smartness of the main squadrons—'the immaculate decks, the glittering perfection, the spirit and fire and pride of the *Marlborough*, the flagship of the world';[2] as Captain D. Evans, USN, wrote, 'it was not well to monkey with such a buzz saw as the sea power of England'.[3]

But it is interesting that this naval supremacy, to use the popular expression of the time, was largely a matter of habit; it rested on no scientific principles nor any deep-thought strategy. There was some strategic controversy in the country and in Parliament which obviously affected the Admiralty but the actual decisions on ship construction were taken solely in the light of such practical considerations as the amount of money granted in the estimates, the number and type of ships building abroad and the size of guns which could be produced by the Royal Foundries. The Admiralty reacted to events foreign, internal and technological; it did not dictate them nor even conduct studies into the size and composition of the fleet necessary to protect Britain, her overseas possessions and vast trade. Thought and scientific measurement was confined to technical considerations like shipbuilding and ordnance performance, leaving superiority in design—helped by 'British guts' —to give general 'maritime superiority'. If 'maritime superiority' were analysed it turned out to be battlefleet superiority. Here is Vice Admiral Sir Spencer Robinson again, the man who as Controller through the greater part of the sixties had the judgement to pick Reed and guide material policy commonsensically through a gale of technical change. Having given his opinion to the 1871 Committee on Designs that Britain should build two distinct classes of warship, 'special ships' generally unmasted for European waters— preferably the 'Devastation' type—and cruising ships moderately masted for service anywhere in the world, he was asked how these types might be employed.

The only description I could give is that, wherever it is known that the enemy is, these ships would go and endeavour to destroy him. Supposing you knew—I am putting a supposition which I know to be very unlikely—that in latitude 40 degrees North and longitude 35 degrees West, by some unaccountable and inscrutable cause, there was a fleet of 10 hostile ironclads which would remain there for a considerable time you would at once send 10 ironclads there, either to destroy or capture them. If you saw a fleet assembling at a stated port you would send your fleet to that port to attack it. That is my view of the way in which war would be carried on.[4]

The same year, the First Lord of the Admiralty, Viscount Goschen, countered claims that the Navy was inadequate to protect the Australian colonies and trade by stating that its role was not defensive, but was to destroy enemy fleets early in a war, to ensure the safety of all colonies and trades. This was to be accomplished by immediate blockade. Such an offensive policy was of course ingrained in British naval thinking and was triumphantly supported by history and common sense alike; the easiest way to find the enemy was to appear before his ports before he left them, the easiest way to assure general maritime supremacy was to contain his main fleets or to defeat them if they put to sea. The policy, the habit, was sound but it was hedged about by all the coast-defensive ideas which had led to laying down unseaworthy floating fortresses. The vital questions 'how many ships are necessary?' and 'of what types?' were not asked until 1873, and the answers not translated into action until the following decade. As Reed complained, 'I think that in this country if a first class war vessel is wanted the essential elements should first be determined, and that size is not one of them.' But the Boards of Admiralty might justly have replied that they could not be expected to determine 'essential elements' amidst constantly changing technical factors and tactical theories; further, it was no use building to great size or in great numbers until it was clear what type of ship would emerge from all the conflicting theories, in their words until there was some 'finality in naval design'.

In the event this commonsense policy proved safe, even correct, because the French were thoroughly occupied on land in Europe and because Britain had the industrial potential and talent to make good the serious deficiencies in numbers and design, both for blockading and wider trade protection, which would have been revealed by war. Naval supremacy in the sixties and seventies was in this sense quite unplanned, the result of historic and geographical factors, specifically the scattered oceanic empire and chain of defensive bases, mostly acquired during the great French wars, the coal and iron deposits together near rivers in the homeland, and of course the surrounding sea, which both allowed these deposits to be developed in safety into a commanding industry and forced attention on maritime affairs. While we can applaud the practical men in successive Boards of Admiralty who refused to be diverted by too much speculation or scientific investigation, to have swum against the tide of events and actually allowed Britain's maritime supremacy to lapse they would have needed a good deal more solid Devon oak in their heads than even their sternest critics have alleged. Admiral of the Fleet Lord Fisher noted:

> Time and the Ocean and some guiding star,
> In High cabal have made us what we are.

By contrast the French were most unfortunately placed. They had a long coastline to defend and several colonies, notably across the Mediterranean in North Africa, and at the same time a long land frontier abutting a Continental empire which had developed recently from a loose collection of North German agricultural states into an industrial power with a greater population than France, bent on asserting itself commercially and militarily, in Bismarck's design, 'mit Eisen und Blut'. He might more accurately have said 'mit Stahl' for as in the United States it was steel for railroads and railroad tyres that provided the necessary communications and much of the impetus for industrial expansion, and it was steel, Kruppstahl, that provided the decisive military weapons, high muzzle-velocity rifled cannon.

When France was drawn into war with Germany in 1870 it was these which outranged the French bronze field pieces and cut down their spirited soldiery like flax at Worth and Sedan, destroying Napoleon III, heralding the new giant of Central Europe.

In this conflict the overwhelming French naval superiority played only a minor part. Although their plans were to use battlefleet strength to cover an expeditionary force to attack North Germany, the essential Danish co-operation was withheld; without it there was nowhere they could use as a base, and so their Channel squadron was confined to blockading the German warships in Wilhelmshaven and stopping German sea trade, both of which they accomplished successfully; at the same time French trade and troop transport from North Africa proceeded without check. In this sense their maritime superiority was useful; also as the threat of a landing in the north caused the Germans to hold back four Prussian corps in defence. But it only acted on the periphery of the main land conflict. Some people afterwards saw this failure of a great navy as an indication that warships were of little account outside coast defence. More informed opinion on both sides of the Channel noted the complete success of the French maritime blockade—noted that Britain's vulnerability to such a form of attack increased every year as her factories processed more imported raw materials, her population ate more imported grain, her prosperity fed on exports and the ships which carried them.

This realization was not new: in 1851 a French naval commission had recommended that if a war should break out 'we must at its very commencement strike at the trade of the enemy simultaneously at every point. To strike at the trade of England is to strike her at the heart...',[5] in 1863 the US Navy anticipating a British alliance with the Southern states had laid down commerce raiders 'for business and not for glory...solely to attack the enemy's purse, and to bring him to tears of repentance in that most tender point';[6]

and in 1867 a former Royal Marine officer, Sir John Colomb, who had retired early and spent his leisure analysing British naval history, had published a pamphlet identifying trade protection, not coastal or local colonial defence, as the vital task of the British Navy.

Colomb had seen the empire as a whole for the first time, bound together by sea routes and the merchant ships upon them; he realized that if these routes were severed, Britain would be ruined, her empire toppled before any conventional battles need be fought; invasion, which had been the bogey distorting traditional strategic concepts ever since steam power had threatened surprise landings, would in his view be a mere postscript after the homeland had been starved to defeat. To prevent this he saw the Navy's main fleets blockading enemy main fleets in their home ports while cruisers acted from various points of concentration in the further oceans to keep open the trade routes. This of course was traditional British strategy, but it was the first time it had been presented with a reasoned theoretical as opposed to a commonsense basis, and the first time that the confusion caused by steam power and the other technical changes of mid-century had been cut through and exposed; it was clear and brilliant. Moreover it provided a solid framework outside technical and financial considerations for calculation of the British Navy's real needs in numbers and types of vessels.

The message had taken time to gain acceptance, but by the early seventies it had caught hold of a number of thinking officers, the noisiest of whom was Lord Charles Beresford, now a lieutenant and a Member of Parliament, where he proclaimed it forcefully. In 1873 the new First Naval Lord, Admiral Sir Alexander Milne, called for a report on trade protection; the resulting paper revealed that British merchant ships were wide open to attack throughout the world, their natural sanctuaries such as the Cape of Good Hope, undefended, and the Navy hopelessly short of modern cruisers to protect them. Milne wrote a strong plea for a vast cruiser-building programme and his arguments and suggested programme, determined by the enormous trade that needed protection, were repeated by subsequent Naval Lords through the decade—but with little success. In 1879 the whole matter became the subject of a commission of inquiry under Lord Carnarvon, whose detailed reports through 1881 and 1882 confirmed that British shipping and thus Britain herself would face a disastrous situation in the event of a determined trade attack.

Meanwhile precisely the same point was being argued from the opposite standpoint across the Channel. Admiral Aube, whose first article on the subject was published in *Revue des deux mondes* on 1 July 1874, was the leader of this school. He started from the premise that an organized attack on any part of British territory was impossible because of Britain's marked superiority in ironclads, which would undoubtedly be used to confine French ironclad fleets to their own harbours: 'Supremacy at sea, the empire of the sea (which was disputed no more with England after the Nile and Trafalgar) belongs to her for ever...'[7] But while France's main fleets would be locked up, Britain would be incapable of blockading her entire coastline and preventing fast steamers from going out one by one as 'pirates' to bombard coast towns, hold them to ransom, destroy any merchant ships they saw—yet by their speed remain unapproachable. He saw commerce and riches as the sinews of war, and their attack as legitimate and indeed obligatory for the weaker naval power.

His argument had the same fatal weakness as Paixhans' and de Lôme's before it; there was nothing to prevent Britain, the superior industrial power, countering with even faster vessels to catch the 'pirates'. However, this weakness was endemic to any French *matériel* programme and Aube's idea, if carried out systematically, had more chance of success than any direct assault on Britain's battle fleets or territory.

But neither the logic from across the Channel, nor the Colomb or 'blue water' school of thought in England (and especially within the Admiralty) could persuade British politicians of either party to spend much more on naval defence.[8]

Tactics and Design: the 1870s

While the strategy of maritime supremacy had received its first scripture as early as 1867, growing into dogma during the following decade, tactics when considered at all, remained speculative, so speculative that many thoughtful officers in all navies came to dismiss the study as one that could have no theoretical or practical basis. The cause of the disillusion was the ram—or more properly, regard for the ram as the supreme naval weapon. This unscientific obsession led straight to the ramming mêlée, and naval officers came to believe that 'mêlée' and 'tactics' were contradictions in terms. As Admiral Aube put it: 'all vestige of formation disappears after a ramming attack...a happy chance becomes the decisive event of the day.'[1]

The French school, such a sensible analyst as de la Gravière among them, compared modern naval actions with medieval tourneys, the ram as the knight's lance, the torpedo his dagger: 'each combatant will be valued for what she is by her speed, her turning powers, her armour, her guns, by the coolness and grasp of her captain, but in which the unknown effects of shock, of gunfire and of torpedoes, in one word the material element, may neutralize the wisest plans, even the genius of the admiral...' From this individualist view of naval action it was but a step to the proposition that numbers alone could triumph; as the ships disappeared beneath the water 'by happy chance' and in roughly equal numbers, side for side, the fleet with the overlap must be in possession at the end of the day.

It is pleasant to record that there were dissentient voices; here is Admiral Warden, commanding the British Channel Fleet in 1868:

It is as clear as anything can be that, so long as a ship has good way on her, and a good command of steam to increase her steam at pleasure, that ship cannot be what is called 'rammed'; she cannot even be struck to any purpose so long as she has room and is properly handled. The use of ships as rams, it appears to me, will only be called into play after an action has commenced, when ships of necessity are reduced to a low rate of speed.[2]

Admiral Warden stands out as a practical genius among his more famous contemporaries. Majority opinion was against him; here is a passage from the Recommendations of the Committee on Designs 1871:

> The importance of ramming in future naval warfare is likely to be so great that in designing armour-clad ships particular attention should...be paid to the best methods of resisting it...[3]

Commander G. H. Noel, author of the 1874 prize essay of the Royal United Service Institution, later printed as *The Gun, Ram and Torpedo*—the only textbook of naval tactics written by an English officer in the nineteenth century—believed it generally held by officers who studied fleet manoeuvring 'that the *ram* is fast supplanting the gun in import...'; 'There can be little doubt', he went on, 'of the prominent part that rams will play in the next naval battle.'[4] Other essayists that year stressed the advantages of small, highly manoeuvrable ships for ramming. The current signal book, which dated from 1868, also showed signs of the fetish. '20: Break through the enemy's line in all its parts...Captains of ships fitted as rams must use their discretion as to striking their opponents instead of passing them...28: Attack the enemy by endeavouring to run them down...80: Close doors of watertight bulkheads...'[5]
The main reason for the ramming doctrine, apart from the theoretical attractions and the few misread demonstrations from actual warfare, was not so much the impregnability of the ironclad to gunfire—as it had been earlier—rather the clumsiness of the great pieces which were needed to rupture armour, which made the rate of fire slow and the likelihood of hitting a moving target remote—disadvantages which increased with the size of gun. Thus in 1870, on Mediterranean firing tests with the *Hercules*, *Monarch* and *Captain*—just before her fatal cruise home—the four 10-inch guns of the *Hercules*' main broadside fired 17 rounds in five minutes, starting loaded; the four 12-inch guns in each of the two turret ships fired only 12 and 11 rounds respectively. While the slower fire resulted in part from the disadvantages of loading and aiming in turrets, this was still only one round every 2½ minutes against one

every 1¼ minutes for the smaller pieces. As for accuracy, the *Hercules* made 10 hits on the target, a rock 200 yards long and 60 feet high in the centre, about 1,000 yards from the ships, the *Monarch* made five hits and the *Captain* four, three of them from the first broadside.[6]

These results seem startlingly poor: the day was clear, the sea quite smooth, the ships steady—until they fired—the guns all rifles, the target twice the length of a contemporary hull and more important twice as high. The problem lay in the method of laying the pieces. The routine was thus: after firing, the wrought iron carriage carrying the gun ran back along its slides, which were inclined slightly upwards, against friction imposed by a braking arrangement of longitudinally arranged plates known as 'compressors'. These held it at the limit of recoil while the bore was sponged to extinguish any smouldering remnants of the cartridge. The charge of gunpowder made up in a silk bag was placed in the barrel and rammed home; the studded shell was hoisted by purchase then swung in after it, so that the studs engaged in the rifled grooves. This was similarly rammed home with a staff with rope tails. Then the compressors were eased and the weight of the gun and carriage took it down the inclined slides till the muzzle protruded through the gun port—as this was a hazardous business in rolling weather. The gun captain then ordered the gun laid to the required elevation for the range; this was done with hand levers operating gears on the carriage which engaged in teeth on the breech. The silk of the cartridge inside the gun was pierced by a long gimlet thrust down the vent, and afterwards the firing tube was placed in the vent, the firing lanyard was hooked to the top of the tube and the gun captain, taking the other end in his hand, retreated beyond the recoil distance of the gun and looked through the V of the backsight (now some seven feet from him) past the raised bead of the foresight (four feet beyond that) to the target, and gave orders for training the piece. With the larger guns this was done by steam winches. Now all was ready—provided that the ship had not yawed off course—and as the roll brought the target, the foresight and the backsight into horizontal line the Gun Captain pulled his lanyard sharply, friction fired the tube, the tube fired the charge and the expanding gasses moved the shell smartly up the barrel.

The system did not make for speed for speed or accuracy; in the words of one great gunner. Admiral Sir Percy Scott: 'It called upon the eye to do more than any camera will do unless it is very much stopped down.'[7] As for speed, this was a question of working the guns' crews up to a high standard of teamwork; it is said that the repetitive drills necessary to accomplish this were a significant factor tending to change the individualistic spirit of sailing ship sailors, who knew no discipline in the military sense but had to be capable of instant, independent action without orders, into a more orderly 'service' manner. Lord Charles Beresford who served through the change believed this, and, significantly, *The Times* military correspondent compared British naval gun drill of the seventies to that of Prussian field artillery. One British officer wrote, 'the battery deck of a smart ship during General Quarters in those days did present a remarkable display of high pressure muscular activity organized on an impressive scale.'[8]

However good the drill, the large pieces could only be fired every two minutes or so, and as only a few could be carried, because of their size and weight, and as the accuracy achievable was not great, naval officers doubted if many shells would hit their target in action, especially as fleets would charge and attempt to ram, presenting the most difficult aiming problem. In these circumstances 'concentration fire' was the favourite method of controlling batteries of broadside ships; all the guns were trained to converge their fire at one point, then fired simultaneously either from a director sight on the upper deck, or from one of their own sights as the target ship moved on to the point of aim. The training racers of the guns were fitted with stops which enabled the pieces to be pointed for 'concentration' in the minimum time.

Even when 'concentration fire' was not possible, as from turret or barbette positions, it was accepted that fire should never be opened outside 'decisive range', probably not more than 1,000 yards. In the British service this was habitual, it had been embodied in every set of fighting instructions from the sixteenth century onwards, and it was well known that Howe and Nelson pressed in so close that the shot could not miss. Throughout the second half of the nineteenth century this tradition was expressed in the signal books:

> Great care is at all times to be taken not to fire at the Enemy over any ships of the fleet; nor, though the signal for action should be flying, is any ship to fire until she is placed in a proper position, and sufficiently close to the enemy.[9]

The French, who had suffered most during the seventeenth and eighteenth centuries from a policy of firing 'at random', had been taught the error of their ways by Jurien de la Gravière, and it was established in their mid-century Gunnery Manuals:

> . The Captain of the gun ought never to fire if his object is not on...to fire at random is to waste stores, heat the gun, fatigue

the crew, make smoke and lose time uselessly. He ought never to fire if not sure of his aim.[10]

The need to wait until close had increased as guns grew, loading and aiming became slower, and ships' speed increased; if two fleets were approaching head on at full speed, and this expectation conditioned all thinking, a broadside released outside effective range would mean that the guns would not be ready at the decisive moment, and gun-smoke might hamper the officers conning the ship or gun captains themselves. This was no doubt why the sights and laying methods remained primitive in all navies, and such subtleties as range-finding and calculation of 'aim-off' or 'deflection' for the relative movement of the target were only hobbies for a very few enthusiasts.[11]

All the practical limitations of naval gunnery, well known to serving officers, caused friction between them and experts and manufacturers ashore, who were more concerned with the pieces' potential under test conditions. Naval officers, anticipating a very low proportion of hits to shots fired ($2\frac{1}{2}$ per cent according to Captain Philip Colomb who had taken over his brother's mantle as leading historical analyst to the British service) deplored the increasing size and consequent decreasing number of guns on modern ships; besides lacking speed of fire they reduced the number of chances of hitting. Commander Noel worked out that 30 12-ton guns could fire 50 tons of shells in 10 minutes whereas 20 18-tonners—the same total weight—could only get off 30. Shore experts on the other hand, enthralled by the enormous thickness of solid iron which could be punctured by the latest pieces, and aware of their ballistic accuracy, advocated 'monster' guns both for long range fire and as irresistable hammers of the enemy. Most extreme was Sir William Armstrong; he was so impressed with the power of his own pieces that he advocated removing all armour from ships, arguing that if the thickest iron could be so easily penetrated, it was ridiculous to burden ships with it. Sir Spencer Robinsons's commonsense rebuttal was that the most heavily armoured ship was, or could become, vulnerable to *something*, but great guns 'by their cost and difficulty of manufacture must always be uncommon'.[12] In any case naval officers knew that long-range fire was a sure way of wasting ammunition and giving the enemy an initial advantage.

In view of these doubts and conflicts, it is not surprising that the ram was admired for its simplicity and 'irresistable effect', nor that French tacticians, basing their thought on the ram, became sceptical of pre-thought manoeuvres or fleet cohesion in a mêlée, and advocated *plotons de combats*,[13] small groups of ships acting together, keeping their relative bearing from their leader. British tactical thought, where it existed, appeared to follow the French, no doubt because it fitted in well with 'offensive' traditions and conveniently disposed of theory. A few hard-headed officers like Colomb deplored 'groups' as a negation of basic 'concentration' principles in offence and defence, inviting defeat in detail. Nevertheless they were popular through the 1870s, and the favourite was the 'scalene' triangle—three ships ahead of one another, with the second ship on one quarter of the leader and the third on the opposite quarter of the second. The theory of 'groups', as expounded by Noel in his prizewinning essay was that each ship, by constantly holding the same place, would get to know its position and its companions' movements, thus comparatively few manoeuvres would be required. Noel saw each group working together under its leader, keeping well clear of other groups while retaining 'distance and bearing from the commander-in-chief'.[14] This dual system of relative bearings and distances, ships within the group, and groups from the Commander in Chief, eventually proved unnecessarily complicated and inflexible. In this sense the French *laisser aller* school was sounder.

Meanwhile the fighting instructions in the Admiralty signal book expressed an opposite philosophy, which had come down almost unchanged from the eighteenth century: 'No ship is to quit her station in the fleet' and 'No ships are to separate from the body of the fleet in time of action to pursue any small number of the enemy's ships which may be endeavouring to escape. Such ships as have disabled or beaten their opponents are to assist any ships of the fleet which appear to be much pressed, and to continue their attack until the main body of the enemy be broken or disabled.'[15] This insistence on the whole fleet working together, Captains mutually supporting one another, was a message literally from history; whether it remained in the instructions by intention or default is not clear—majority opinion was that sailing methods had no relevance whatever to the steam age. Here is Vice Admiral Sir Spencer Robinson:

I think it is a false analogy to compare the way in which naval warfare will be carried on by ironclads with the way it was carried on in Lord Howe's time. It is misleading and using terms which have no relation to each other to compare the old line of battle ships and their manoeuvres with the iron clad ships of the present time...[16]

Probably the clearest contribution to the theory of tactics came from Philip Colomb; he recognized the value of historic principles, particularly concentration of force, and analysed the various formations a steam fleet might adopt, arriving at four basic types: the extended front with small depth, the narrow front with great depth, the mass or square of equal front and depth, and the 'group' system. These formed the basis for the steam tactics exercised by fleet commanders through the seventies. However the experimental stage, when battle contingencies were debated, soon moved into a formal stage, more concerned with the techniques of putting a fleet through elaborate convolutions and training captains in ship-handling than with the possibilities of real warfare; admirals gained their reputations for precision of steam choreography, so it is difficult to say what British fleet commanders might have done in battle. If they had arranged their own ships to conform to the enemy's it is probable that fleet battles which were not chases would have been started by both forces charging directly at each other in 'extended front with small depth', the favourite form of which was indented line abreast—two lines abreast, the ships in the rear line or rank steaming on the quarters of the ships in the leading line, to allow all bow guns clear arcs of fire on approach. However, as 'groups' were briefly popular it is possible that a disciple of Colomb might have kept his fleet concentrated in close order to meet a French attack begun with groups in line abreast. There are many possibilities because there was no doctrine; tactics were still in the transitional stage. The only agreed principal was that the bow attack would probably be adopted.

As in tactics, so in naval architecture, the seventies saw a flowering of transitional types. The first landmark was the British Committee on Designs set up in January 1871 in the shadow of the *Captain*'s loss, because of disquiet about low freeboard ships, specifically the 'Devastation' class. It became a wide-ranging enquiry into all types of warship, but its report, while establishing the pattern of building for the rest of the decade, was really just a restatement of the attitudes and policies of Robinson and Reed.

A simple and perhaps under ordinary circumstances a safe method by which the requirements of the British navy may from time to time be administered is to watch carefully the progress of other nations in designing and constructing ships of war, and to take care that our own fleet shall be more than equal both in number and power of its ships...[17]

The *Devastation* herself was found to have sufficient stability, though it was recommended that her breastwork be extended out to the sides of the hull with an unarmoured watertight structure, to give additional buoyancy. More important, this class was considered 'in its broad features the first class fighting ship of the immediate future.' The reason was:

> ...the inevitable failure of the attempt to unite in one ship a very high degree of offensive and defensive power with real efficiency under sail...we find ourselves compelled to regard the attainment of this very desirable object as an insoluble problem; and we believe that our transmarine possessions, and other important interests in distant parts of the world, will be more efficiently protected by the establishment, where requisite, of centres of naval power, from which vessels of the 'Devastation' class may operate, than by relying on cruising ships of such limited fighting power as the *Monarch*...[18]

And, for coast defence vessels:

> As a powerful armament, thick armour, speed and light draught cannot be combined in one ship, although all are needed for the defence of the country, there is no alternative but to give preponderance to each in turn amongst different classes of ships which shall mutually supplement one another.[19]

Obviously John Colomb's message had not been hoisted aboard. In hindsight the prime failure of the Committee and of the Boards of Admiralty through the seventies was the assumption that the size of warships had to be kept as small as possible. Both Reed and his successor, Barnaby, complained about this, but there is no evidence that either put forward positive proposals while in office to show how most of the apparently irreconcilable elements in warship design could be combined quite easily on larger displacements—no doubt because they, too, accepted the arguments for small size: economy, handiness, not hazarding too much to 'one fatal blow', and small target area. All were false; the ram was the major wrong turning of the century, and as for economy, it would have been cheaper to have built an ocean-going fleet of large ships with great power able to move *anywhere* in European waters than lots of small craft tucked away all over the world *and* a sea-going fleet as well. This was the lesson of history—the concentration of greater force in fewer hulls—and it would have been practical realization of Colomb's 'historical' strategy.

But neither the Committee nor any of the naval and technical witnesses even hinted at such an idea. All were lost in a quicksand of conflicting technical requirements and current prejudice.

'Do you think you could turn the vessel in a single-reef topsail breeze at sea if the rudder were injured?' 'Have you found any difficulty in working the ship from that box amidships?' 'Yes rather so. It is a cramped space...' 'Further experiments against inclined targets are about to be made with improved chilled projectiles and until they have taken place, this question cannot, I think, be answered.' 'Ironclads will not rise to the sea, the sea comes right over them, they have not the life the wooden ships have...' 'Are you in favour of the broadside or the turret principle?' 'For a general action I am for having both classes. I am not a party man at all...'[20]

Here is a picture of men imprisoned by experiences and concepts, from which in all probability it was impossible to break free without some outside agency. As it turned out several agencies co-operated: one was the scientific study of naval history (although this later degenerated into exactly the same sort of prison of fixed ideas), another the increasing pace of material change forced by technical developments and international competition, and sheer practical experience with ironclads was another.

One of the most interesting constructional suggestions to the Committee came from Reed; this was to do away with the waterline belt at both ends of ironclads and use the weight saved both to increase the thickness over the vital central portion and to build a full length horizontal armoured deck below the water-line, so that the hull beneath would form a raft impenetrable by shot or shell. This raft, combined with the central armoured 'citadel', would float the vessel however much damage the unarmoured ends might suffer. Reed originally thought the ends of such ships about the waterline should be divided into empty tanks; on going into action these tanks would be filled with seawater to decrease the freeboard and make sure that both the central side armour and the horizontal armoured deck were low enought to prevent any chance of a shot reaching the raft under-body. As amended by the Committee the empty tanks became a cellular system, perhaps filled with cork or other buoyant substance.

Ships of the 1870s

With the wealth of classes and methods of protection recommended by the Committee on Designs, it is not surprising that the seventies saw the most prolific variation of warship types ever to amaze naval men. The first in commission was Reed's *Devastation*. Despite her clean bill of stability, her low freeboard was still suspect and, according to Nathaniel Barnaby 'the entire Navy outside the Admiralty and highly placed persons at Court held that to send such a ship to sea would be criminal';[1] a notice appeared on her gangway, 'Letters for the *Captain* may be posted here'. The science of naval architecture meant nothing to naval officers; one remarked, 'We had probably heard that there was such a thing as a metacentre—at any rate in modern ships—but whether it was in the maintop or the forepeak we did not much care.'[2] In the event the ugly-looking craft passed her trials well, proving steadier than a conventional broadside ironclad when beam on to the sea, because of the weight of water flowing over her decks and acting as a stabilizer, and performing adequately against head seas, although she had to reduce speed drastically for even moderate conditions. Here she is at seven knots, dipping into 20–26 foot waves twice her own length from crest to crest:

> The scene from the fore end of the flying deck...was very imposing. There was repeatedly a rush of water over the fo'c'sle, the various fittings, riding bitts, capstans, anchors etc. churning it up into a beautiful cataract of foam; while occasionally a wall of water would appear to rise up in front of the vessel, and, dashing on board in the most threatening style as though it would carry all before it, rush aft against the fore turret with great violence, and after throwing a cloud of heavy spray off the turret into the air, dividing into two, pass overboard on either side.[3]

But her defect was lack of habitability; it is doubtful if her crew could have stood Atlantic blockade work for long. She was never-theless the strongest vessel in the world. And the same year, 1872, a scaled-up, rather higher freeboard version was laid down—the *Dreadnought*—to be 10,866 tons, some 2,000 tons more than the French first class vessels laid down that year. The main improvement on the *Devastation* and *Thunderer* (still building) was that the armoured breastwork was carried right out to the sides of the hull to protect a greater stability. As the thickest portions of this and also the hull armour were increased to 14 inches of iron, the total weight of armour was brought up to 3,690 tons, no less than 35 per cent of displacement. By contrast only 520 tons, or just under 5 per cent, was devoted to the armament of four 38-ton guns, which each fired 810 lb shells capable of penetrating some 18 inches of iron at 1,000 yards. The question was, of course, whether they would actually hit in action; despite hydraulic loading and steam training gear, they could not fire more than once every two minutes.

The *Dreadnought*, not completed until 1879, was the ultimate product of Ericsson's 'impregnable fort' concept; no other breast-work monitors were laid down after her. Yet in the positioning of her turrets and the distribution and relative weight of her armour she was closer to the evolved battleship than any other vessel of the decade; what she lacked was sufficient displacement to allow the weight of the turrets to be carried higher and thus permit greater freeboard throughout. But higher freeboard for all-weather effective-ness was not yet a requirement for her type.

The French, meanwhile, fresh from humiliation in Europe and constricted as never before by a united German Empire whose army had become the new model for military efficiency, directed atten-tion towards replacing their obsolescent timber-hulled fleet. Prob-ably the expanding Italian Navy provided as much incentive as the British which they could never hope to outmatch. However, while they decided to construct with *steel* frames, beams, deck plates, bulkheads and inner bottoms, leaving only outer hull plates and rivets of wrought iron (thus taking a small jump ahead of British practice, which still required iron frames) they would not dispense with full-masted rig for first class warships. Consequently the big ship designs by the new *directeur du matériel*, de Bussy, were restricted and fell way off the true line of evolution. The first one was the *Redoubtable*, laid down at L'Orient in 1872; she was 8,800 tons and had a 14-inch belt, above which the hull sloped inwards very sharply to leave a short mid-length 9½-inch armoured battery projecting; at each corner of this battery a 38½-ton gun was mounted to fire through ports angled to permit fire on the broadside or in line with the keel; on the deck above were two smaller pieces firing on the broadside. These guns were a new French pattern with a steel lining tube inside the cast iron body strengthened by steel rings outside, and their muzzle velocities were now equal to the British Woolwich pieces in the 1,400 feet per second range. The 38½-tonner could penetrate 14½-inches of iron. The *Redoubtable* was followed by two scaled-up versions laid down in 1876, the *Devastation* and *Foudroyant*, which had a rather greater average thickness of iron on the belt so that altogether their armour accounted for nearly 30 per cent of displacement.

Then, perhaps depressed by the uniformity of the belt, battery and barbette type which had served them since almost the beginning of the ironclad revolution, the French Navy acquired another new *directeur du matériel*, Sabattier, who gave them a new design altogether, the 'barbette ship'. The first of these was the *Admiral Duperre*, of 11,000 tons, laid down at the end of 1876. Here the armoured battery was omitted and the entire hull was left unprotected above a 21⅝-inch thick belt. The main armament was carried on the upper deck where there were four 12-inch circular barbettes, each mounting one new pattern all-steel 46-ton gun which could penetrate some 19 inches of iron at 1,000 yards. Two of these were arranged on sponsons projecting from either side just abaft the foremast shrouds—for the ship was fully rigged—with arcs of fire extending from ahead to some 25 degrees from astern, and two were placed on the centreline abaft the main and mizzen masts respectively. The great advantage of this design was that the big guns were carried high, some 27½ feet above the water, and would thus be effective in the roughest weather, provide their gunlayers with a good, clear aim and, the French claimed, fire down through the *decks* of an opponent in close action. Whether any opponent, however lightly armed, would have allowed such a ship as this to get so close without wreaking havoc through her completely unprotected sides and perhaps bringing down masts, yards or rigging upon her open barbette positions, must be doubted. In addition, her belt, owing to its great thickness, only extended 2 feet 6 inches above the waterline. The type must have proved extremely vulnerable in action, and it would have been a brave captain who brought her close to a *Devastation* or a *Dreadnought*.

In Britain the first class rigged ship took slightly different directions. The first was the *Alexandra* of 9,490 tons, laid down in 1872, the same year as the *Dreadnought*. She was designed by Barnaby, but was really the final expression of Reed's belt-and-battery type with even stronger emphasis placed on ahead fire; thus the armoured battery was in two tiers, and the hull before it was recessed to allow the two forward guns on each level to fire out in line with the keel.

There was a similar, though higher-cut-away, aft to allow two guns to fire directly astern. In all she mounted ten 18-ton and two 25-ton guns, and while these were individually smaller than those in the contemporary French class, the total broadside weight was rather greater and the chances of hitting six to three in favour.

The following year she was followed on the stocks by *Temeraire*, 8,540 tons, which had a similar although lower battery, but no upper level; instead there were on the upper deck two lozenge-shaped barbettes, one before the foremast, one abaft the mizzen, each of which housed a remarkable disappearing gun mounted on a turntable. These 25-ton pieces recoiled back and down after firing, thus hiding themselves below the barbette armour on a principle first devised by Captain Eades USN for coastal monitors, and since refined with hydraulic power. They were never repeated however, as the mounting absorbed far too much weight and space; the *Temeraire* joined the growing list of unique vessels.

Perhaps the main glory of all the large belt-and-battery ships, especially in that age of maritime peace, was the splendid accommodation, which resulted from the great size of the guns they carried between decks.

The mind of an officer who has passed his sea life on board wooden ships of the old type and become accustomed to their low, dark 'between decks' will be struck by the great additional capacity of our modern men of war when he enters the batteries of the *Alexandra* and sees the great rifled guns mounted on Scott's system of wrought iron carriages, and the unusual height between decks of 10 feet 4 inches in the upper battery and 9 feet 6 inches in the main. But lofty and spacious as these are, his surprise would be still greater upon seeing the mess or living deck, which has the extraordinary height of 11 feet 6 inches from deck to underside of beam...He would also be impressed with the large air ports, the pleasant, light and commodious cabins for officers...[4]

Men from the modern breastwork monitors would have been struck even more forcibly by the contrast.

Before either of these (as it proved) final versions of the British belt-and-battery type were in commission, Nathaniel Barnaby had been diverted up another false and more freakish trail. This time it was Italy that provoked the change, specifically the Chief Constructor, Benedetto Brin. The Italian service had roughly the same relation to France as France to Britain; to make up for comparative lack of finance and industry, they determined to build first class ships individually far more powerful than the rather small French vessels, with guns which could penetrate their armour, armour impenetrable to their guns, and at the same time with the speed, radius and sea-keeping ability to meet a challenge anywhere in the Mediterranean—precisely the class of capital ship which Britain would have seen the need for had she been able to break out of her 'local defence' strategy.

Such ships might, perhaps, have been built as improved 'Devastations' had it not been that the latest 38-ton guns could penetrate nearly 20 inches of iron, and there was too great an area of iron over the breastwork monitors to spread it that thick. Brin therefore followed Reed's suggestion and concentrated all his armour in a short box extending across the vessel at mid-length—$21\frac{5}{8}$-inches thick about the waterline, $17\frac{3}{4}$-inches thick above and around two turrets which protruded from the top. From this central citadel he extended a 2-inch armoured deck 4 feet 9 inches below the waterline to both ends to protect the lower hull—the 'raft'—from any shells which might penetrate the unprotected sides above. The space between this deck and the first deck above waterlevel he subdivided into small compartments, many of which were to be filled with coal to restrict the entry of water in the event of damage. Originally this class, the *Duilio* and *Dandalo*, laid down in 1872 and 1873, were to have two 38-ton guns in each of their turrets, but when Armstrong announced 60-ton pieces Brin amended his design to incorporate two of these in each turret.

Britain of course had to respond; no longer just a matter of instinct, it was actually written in to the 1871 Committee Report: 'Watch carefully the progress of other nations...take care that our own fleet shall be more than equal...' As Barnaby was confronted with the same heavy armour problem as Brin and was not allowed by his Board to exceed the cost or dimensions of previous first class ships, and in view of continuing criticism of the *Devastation*'s low freeboard, he came up with a very similar answer to Brin's. He was able to make her rather larger than the Italian's though, 11,900 tons displacement against 10,400, with thicker although shorter armour against the 60-tonners, and mounting two 81-ton guns in each of two turrets; these pieces had a theoretical penetration of 22 inches of wrought iron.

The vessel was laid down in 1874, and launched two years later as HMS *Inflexible*. Barnaby wrote:

This is the ship which the progress of invention in artillery has finally driven us to resort to...There could be no question that we could not allow foreign seamen to have guns afloat more powerful than any of our own, however ready we might have been to allow them to defend themselves with thicker armour... The first of the ruling conditions [in her design] was that she should be able to mount the heaviest guns which could possibly be made now...[5]

In the event Brin won the ordnance competition as before the *Duilio* was finished Armstrongs produced a 100-ton monster gun of 45 centimetre bore throwing a 2,000 lb shell which could penetrate *three feet* of solid wrought iron, and he mounted two of these in each of her turrets. The turrets themselves were centred slightly off the keel line on opposite sides of the citadel so that, theoretically, the outside gun of the after turret could join the two guns of the forward turret in direct ahead fire. In practice it proved hazardous to fire more than one piece at a time as the portentous recoil from the 550 lb gunpowder charges strained the whole structure of the ship; so it is probable that in action the enthusiastic punch of these vessels would have proved considerably less effective than the *Devastation*'s. The ships themselves were certainly more vulnerable to gunfire.

It was this point which exercised Edward Reed and prompted his return to the front line of public naval controversy. After visiting the Italian yards in 1875 while they were rivetting together the parts of the ships, which were arriving from all over the world (constructional iron and steel from France, armour from Sheffield and the French Creusot works, guns from Newcastle, engines from Maudsleys of London) he thought the completed vessels would be exposed 'beyond all doubt or question to speedy destruction', for their citadels were far too small in relation to the unprotected ends. And stirred by such misuse of his original ideas, he visited HMS *Inflexible* at Portsmouth and found the same fault in her. Although Barnaby had subdivided the ends about the waterline into small compartments to be packed with coal and stores, and had constructed elaborate ship's side cells filled with cork and bounded inboard by cofferdams filled with canvas and oakum and extending 37 feet aft and 30 feet forward of the central citadel, Reed considered that in action it could all be blown away. 'Observing this...I designed an *Inflexible* in my own office and had the whole of the calculations made, the result showing that when these cork chambers were destroyed the vessel would have no stability whatsoever, and would be in a condition of capsize.'[6] His conclusions were printed in a letter in *The Times*.

Barnaby replied that the possibility of the ship being reduced to such a state was 'infinitely remote, although not absolutely impossible...If the water be kept out of the coal spaces by the cofferdams, as I believe it will be, the ship will retain an amount of stability far in excess of the *Devastation*...'[7] The Director of Naval Ordnance agreed that the conditions Reed suggested 'cannot be brought about in a naval engagement. These conditions are, practically that the fore and aft ends of the ship are to be utterly demolished. Should the *Inflexible* be made the target for continued practice... it is possible that the unarmoured parts above water might be destroyed', but 'the difficulty is great of striking a ship at or below the waterline...', and 'considering the few guns that are likely to be carried by any ship engaging the *Inflexible*, and the ever varying distances and bearings that must exist in any future naval action, it is next to impossible that any number of shells could be planted in a ship in such an exact position... as to blow out the cork from the chambers in which it will be fixed...'[8]

Nevertheless the public debate was not stilled and an *Inflexible* Committee was set up in 1877 to adjudicate between Reed and the Board of Admiralty. Their report in December came down squarely on the side of the Admiralty: it was highly improbable the stores and cork would be blown out in action unless she was attacked by 'enemies of such preponderating force as to render her entering into any engagement in the highest degree imprudent'. The inaccuracy of naval gunnery, the rude means of ascertaining range, the high speed of ships were among the considerations they noted, as well as the fact that the most effective armament to bring against the ends would be numerous shell guns, and these could not be combined with armour 'of a thickness to be of the least avail against the *Inflexible*'s guns.'[9] The Committee concluded that a 'just balance has been maintained in the design'. Exit Reed, muttering 'these are not armoured ships; they are armoured in places'. But the test of battle on other central-citadel ships later supports the Committee beyond reasonable doubt.

The *Inflexible*—together with the four diminutives which followed her before the end of the decade—was the crowning example of the instability of naval design brought about by the great gunmakers. She reflected in her ungainly, piecemeal structure, stubby guns, eccentric turret positioning, curious systems of protection and compromise sail plan on two masts, all the contradictions of a building policy governed by reaction to outside events and lacking any theory save naval supremacy and technological superiority. She was a folly which would have brought smiles of astonishment from eighteenth-and twentieth-century sailors alike. She was splendid.

It is worth examining her in some detail to see how far the art of warship building had progressed by the beginning of the eighties

D

when she was completed, and to note with the eccentricities, touches of the future. First of all, her lines had been fixed after experiments with models in the testing tank established by the Admiralty in 1870 after pioneer work by William Froude on the correlation of models to full-scale ships. Barnaby wanted a ship both beamy to give maximum transverse stability and short to leave as little unprotected side as possible beyond the mid-length citadel. Froude went to work with his models and showed these requirements were not incompatible, that a vessel with a length/breadth ratio smaller even than Reed's extreme designs would make the required speed without greatly increased horsepower. Barnaby accepted his findings—with some incredulity—and fixed the *Inflexible*'s length at 320 feet, the same as the *Dreadnought*, 21 feet less than the *Duilio*, and her breadth at 75 feet, 11 feet more than the *Dreadnought*, 10 feet more than the *Duilio*. This gave her a length/breadth ratio of 1:4.27 which was the smallest ever reached in any first class warship apart from the timber ship-of-the-line.

The mid-length 110 feet from 6½ feet below the waterline to 9½ feet above was a rectangular citadel cased with 41 inches of protection—on the outside 12 inches of wrought iron, then 11 inches of teak reinforced with 11-inch deep vertical angle irons three feet apart, then another 12 inches of wrought iron on 6-inch teak reinforced by horizontal angle irons fastened to two layers of skin plating over the transverse frames of the ship, the whole bound together by 4-inch diameter bolts with large conical heads flush with the outer surface of the armour and spring washers and nuts inboard. This was the maximum ironwork about the waterline; above and below the iron was slightly reduced in thickness and the teak backing increased to keep a uniform 41-inch layer. Rising above the citadel through a 3-inch armour deck were the armoured top halves of the two turrets arranged in echelon, more exaggerated than the Italian formation, to permit ahead and astern fire either side of long, narrow accommodation superstructures forward and aft of them; each was 28 feet in diameter internally and nearly 34 feet externally. Their armour was a similar sandwich, although the outside layer was itself compound—a steel face for hardness welded to wrought iron for toughness, 16 inches in all. The total weight of each turret including its two 81-ton guns and their iron slides was 750 tons; hydraulic power could rotate them 360 degrees in 1 minute 16 seconds.

The guns themselves, which cost £10,000 each as against £2,150 for a 35-ton piece, had been built up in the usual Fraser-Woolwich style but with a 'chamber' for the powder charge which was of larger diameter than the bore, and were designed for an Armstrong rifling system whereby a copper disc or 'gas check' at the base of the shell expanded into the rifling grooves—no longer the old zinc studs. In tests the prototype gun of 16-inch calibre, penetrated three 8-inch plates and 2 inches into a fourth at 120 yards.

The pieces were loaded through the muzzle by an Armstrong hydraulic system tried out first in the *Thunderer*; this was arranged at two fixed loading positions situated beneath a glacis formed by an upward incline of the armoured deck, and consisted mainly of twin loading tubes or ports, a loading trolley behind each which could be raised or lowered hydraulically, and behind these telescopic rammers, also hydraulically operated, which had sponges around the rammer heads and valves which opened to admit water into the bores when the sponges were thrust up to their fullest extent. The drill after firing was to swing the turret round and depress the gun muzzles until they formed a continuation of the loading tubes. Then the turret was locked in position and a signal given to 'sponge and load'. The hands in the glacis pushed their ramming levers forward to extend the sponges up the bores, then reversed them; after this the loading numbers placed cartridges in the loading tubes by hand, motioned to their trolley operators, who raised the loading trolleys containing the shells until they formed continuations of the loading tubes. Papier maché discs were placed over the rammer heads to hold the shells once loaded, and the rammer levers were pushed forward to thrust the charges, shells and wads to the breech end. Then the levers were reversed again and the signal 'gun loaded' passed into the turret by electric tell-tale. The turret was unlocked, the captain of the turret started the training engine, 'number one' hands worked the hydraulic gear to elevate the gun muzzles, 'number two' hands stood by the levers which would run the guns out by hydraulic pressure, and others placed a firing tube in each vent and hooked on the firing lanyards; the guns could be fired electrically from the conning tower or by percussion or electric tube from within the turret. They were aimed from 'sighting hoods' projecting above the armoured top of the turret in rear of the breeches, and could manage one aimed round per gun every two minutes.

The ship was also equipped with the most advanced submerged torpedo tubes, one on each bow. These were massive cast-iron cylinders swivelling at their outboard end on cup and socket joints, their inboard ends travelling on graduated training racers. To be fired each 14-inch torpedo had to be placed in a brass cylinder which was then rammed into the iron torpedo tube; the inboard end valve was closed, the outboard valve opened to admit the sea, and an open guide was run out from the tube extending 10 feet beyond the side to protect the torpedo from the eddies caused by the ship's progress. When all was ready and the tube had been trained to the orders of the officer in the conning tower, he could trigger a piston in the brass cylinder to force the torpedo out at speed, at the same time activating the torpedo's own motor.

The other weapon was of course the ram. This was a solid iron forging bolted to the stem so that it could be unshipped if it endangered friend more than foe; there is no evidence that it ever was removed although other ships of the time carried their rams on board, only to be shipped in time of war—for good reasons. The 3-inch armoured deck which protected the lower 'raft' hull was inclined downwards to join the stem behind the ram to give it support.

The propelling machinery which gave this vessel, bluff-bowed and beamy as she was, a speed of 14¾ knots on trials, consisted of two compound engines by John Elder & Co., the pioneers of this type for merchant steamers. Each had one high pressure cylinder and two low pressure cylinders with 9-inch diameter connecting rods working on crankshaft bearings 17½ inches in diameter, driving hollow steel propeller shafts to the two screws. At full speed they made 75 revolutions a minute. At either end of the engine room which was situated at mid-length under the citadel were two boiler rooms, each of which housed two 17 foot and two 9 foot cylindrical boilers. All were clothed with four layers of felt and galvanized sheet iron, were internally stayed for a working pressure of 61 lbs per square inch, and externally stayed to prevent them shifting under the concussion of a ramming encounter. They were fed by gangs of stokers shovelling and wheeling coal from bunkers all along the unarmoured ship's side. The first big ships in the British service to be fitted with this type of cylindrical boiler working at what was then a high pressure, and the compound engines which rendered such pressures economical, had been the *Alexandra* and the *Temeraire*; before them even such recent types as the 'Devastations' had rectangular boilers only working up to 30 lbs per square inch and feeding single-cylinder engines.

Besides the main propelling machinery there were no less than 39 auxiliary engines, all the most important of which were duplicated or quadruplicated; thus there were four steam and two bilge pumps capable of discharging 300 tons of water per hour from the 135 watertight compartments into which the hull was divided, there were four engines working the fans which drew air into the ship and blew it around the hull through a system of main and branch pipes, there were of course steering engines, engines for all the hydraulic operations of the guns, for the torpedo air compressors, for the capstans, engines to turn the main engines when idle, to hoist coal, ash or provisions, to force water through the condensers, and to generate electricity for the Brush electric lighting system. The shattering din of their clattering pistons, the heat and the mazy atmosphere may be gathered from Admiral Bacon's description of the engine-room of a later steam battleship:

It was impossible to make a remark plainly audible and telephones were useless. The deck plates were greasy with oil and water so that it was difficult to walk about without slipping. Some gland was certain to be blowing a little, which made the atmosphere murky with steam. One or more hoses played on a bearing which threatened trouble. Men constantly working round the engines would be feeling the bearings to see if they were running cool or showed signs of heating; and the officers could be seen with their coats buttoned up to their throats and perhaps in oilskins, black in the face and with their clothes wet with oil and water.[10]

There were other ways in which the naval engineer of these days was not to be envied: although first rate ships by now depended on his class for almost every power of movement and offence they possessed, as the catalogue of the *Inflexible*'s auxiliary machinery makes clear, the engineer officer himself was still regarded as literally a usurper. He was a 'grease' or a 'fat', obliged to mess separately from the fighting officers and, according to Reed who steamed into action on this question in 1877, was a 'snubbed, subdued, subordinated man, with a dozen officers put above him to look down upon him...' Part of this must have been natural hostility which any new class of men would arouse in a service with such long and splendid traditions, especially if their beastly accoutrements were changing the old customs and methods out of all recognition, but it was largely a matter of social class: the engineers, who arrived on board by way of a workshop bench, were 'emphatically cads...neither fitted by manners, education or *savoir faire* to be given commissions as officers in HM Navy'.[11] Similarly in France, America, Germany the average run of engineer was not regarded as a social asset.

Of course there were exceptions; there were gentlemen who became engineers, there were aristocratic naval officers like Lord Charles Beresford who learnt to operate a lathe, but in general in all the navies of the world the engineers got on with their practical business down below and the military officers got on with theirs above—in every sense. So we may sympathize with the engineer officer who, Admiral Bacon recounts, believed himself to be a glass boiler and lay on his back all day puffing hard, convinced that if he stopped he would burst; also with Captain Sir Algernon Heneage, a sailing man with his whole way of life under threat, who refused to learn the names of any of his chief engineers, simply calling them all by the name of the first one he had known as a youth.

To return to the *Inflexible*: all her engines and boilers were contained within the armoured citadel; Barnaby wrote: 'the defence against... the ram and the torpedo, must rest with the officer in command. But to resist them he must retain command of speed and steering gear. He therefore requires that these and the floating power should be equally defended against the gun, which he cannot avoid...'[12]

The design was considered a success, indeed the first rate type of the future long before the great ship herself was completed, and in 1876 two 8,400-ton 'Inflexible' types were laid down, and then in 1879 two 9,150-ton rather finer-lined versions without sails. One of these, *Colossus*, was the first large ship in the British service to follow the French lead in all-steel construction; only the great forgings for stem and stern, and the rivets, were of wrought iron. This followed a dialogue between Barnaby and Dr Siemens, whose steel-making process, employed at the French Creusot and Terre Noire Works, had made possible the revolution in their naval yards. Dr Siemens insisted that steel, unlike wrought iron, *could* be made to give precise sets of qualities depending upon the elements added after the carbon had been driven out of the raw iron. Even so the tradition of brittleness and irregularity in British Bessemer steel, which had kept it out of private yards and prevented its whole-hearted use in warships, made Barnaby wary:

Mr Barnaby has insisted upon very stringent precautions being observed in dealing with a material apparently so erratic in its behaviour as steel. All plates or bars which can be bent cold are so treated, and if the whole length cannot be, heating over as small an area as possible.[13]

The use of steel for all structural purposes, by bringing the hull weight down to some 36 per cent of total displacement, allowed more weight to be put into the fighting qualities of warships—the all-iron hull of the *Warrior* for instance had absorbed 52 per cent. Of even greater significance was the steelmakers' bid to produce armour as well. Because of its harder surface steel had been the subject of armour experiments from the earliest days of shell guns but it had always shivered and cracked under impact from even wrought iron projectiles, and had been rejected; in 1876, however, the Creusot Company produced a 22-inch thick mild steel plate, forged under a 100-ton steam hammer, which resisted all guns of that date. When this was tested at Spezia by the new 100-ton Armstrong gun produced for the *Duilio* is was broken up, but nevertheless stopped the shell; wrought-iron plates of the same thickness which were tried at the same time were pierced right through; Italy consequently adopted the 22-inch Creusot plates for the citadels of their great ships, the first country to use all-steel armour.

Meanwhile in Sheffield, the ancient home of steel-making, two companies, Cammell's and Brown's, were experimenting with 'compound' armour—a steel face for hardness upon a wrought iron back for flexibility and toughness; Cammell's produced it by casting open-hearth steel on a hot wrought-iron plate, Brown's by pouring molten steel between an iron and a steel plate, cementing them together. Although these plates failed to withstand the 100-ton guns as well as Creusot all-steel armour they were preferred for a short while by most navies as they were not so liable to crack. They had a resisting power 25 per cent greater than simple wrought iron. However, it was not to be expected that ordnance men would let the matter rest there, and the new hard face stimulated the use of steel, instead of chilled wrought iron for armour-piercing projectiles.

While Barnaby laid down his last two 'Inflexible' diminutives in 1879 with steel construction and compound armour for their virtually impregnable citadels, Benedetto Brin was flying off to the opposite extreme with the successors to the *Duilio*, named *Italia* and *Lepanto*, by dropping side armour altogether and relying entirely on waterline cellular construction and an end-to-end armoured deck below. This, of course, was Armstrong's preference; Barnaby himself was adopting a similar approach with cruising vessels to protect trade and distant possessions, and the French had gone some way towards it with the narrow waterline belts and otherwise unprotected sides of the *Admiral Duperre* and her successors. 'The gun is certain to be victorious over armour; hence safety must be sought as much as possible without armour...'[14] Brin joined to this belief enthusiasms for the very heaviest guns that could be produced, the highest speeds and the greatest cruising radius, all quite logical in view of the more numerous French ships and the very long Italian coastline. His two ships were in fact giant cruisers and with enormous offensive power designed to crack the armour of first rates, they may be called the first 'battle-cruisers': the similarity between Brin's ideas and the aphorisms of Fisher, who inspired what came to be known as the battle-cruiser some 25 years later, is remarkable. The *Italia* and *Lepanto* were laid down at Castellammare and Leghorn in 1877 and 1878 to be assembled in the Italian fashion with parts from all over western Europe. To achieve 16 knots and to carry four 103-ton guns 33 feet above the water, Brin fixed the dimensions at 400½ by 72¾ feet, and the displacement at 13,480 tons, considerably more than any warship hitherto. The fine-lined hulls were divided internally into 53 compartments, each horizontally divided into four watertight decks. The lowest of these, 5½ feet below the waterline, was of 3-inch steel, and between this and the first deck above the waterline the side was lined with cork-filled cells like the *Inflexible's*. Four compound engines, two to each of the propeller shafts, and 26 boilers, were all carried below the submerged armoured deck, as were the magazines; the ammunition was hoisted through armoured cylinders to the upper deck, where the four big guns were mounted in two pairs, each pair on turntables arranged in echelon either side; all were protected by one 17-inch steel barbette which extended diagonally across the deck, and all had direct ahead, astern and broadside fire.

Edward Reed expected these extraordinary ships to succumb rapidly in an artillery duel; Barnaby was 'not at all confident that the Italians are not in the right'.[15] The argument became academic as before they were completed the 'quick-firing' gun of medium calibre had appeared on the naval scene, and by threatening their unprotected sides with a 'hail of fire' before the great guns could get off more than a few rounds, rendered them obsolete. While they were probably as good an answer as the *Inflexible*, possibly better than the *Duperre* at the time of their conception, they are an interesting example of how abstract theory could be overtaken by the rapid technological advances of the time. Nevertheless, as Oscar Parkes noted, they 'will always rank among the masterpieces of naval architecture.'[16]

Despite Italy's inspired bid to put her navy into the first rank with the principle of concentration of force, there were still only two major navies by the early eighties, and of these the British still had the commanding lead. While the variety of experiments during the decade makes it impossible to arrive at any definition of a first class ship which would be universally agreed, if recent construction, displacement, thickness of belt armour, and weight (thus penetrative power) of guns are taken as the criteria, Britain had nine first class warships in the early eighties and five building, France had four and six building, Italy two and two building, Russia one, Turkey one and one building—although the state of the Turkish fleet, rusting hulks rottings at moorings from which they never moved, eliminates it. The British line-up of the *Inflexible*, *Dreadnought*, *Thunderer*, *Devastation*, probably the four most powerful ships in the world, the *Monarch* and a similar turret ship *Neptune*, together with the *Alexandra*, *Temeraire* and *Superb*, all powerful belt-and-battery types, represented over 50 per cent of the world total of first class ships, and would have been impossible odds for the French *Admiral Duperre* and the three 'belt, battery and barbette' types, *Devastation*, *Foudroyant*, *Redoubtable*. In ships of the second rank Britain was not so far ahead on paper, but the French vessels were smaller and timber-hulled; in any case there was little conceivable danger as France's natural allies, Russia and the United States, hadn't a second class sea-going ship between them —unless the old monitors were so classed—and the only first-rate ship, the Russian *Devastation* type, *Peter the Great*, sheered rivet heads and cracked cylinders when she fired her 12-inch guns in practice, 'leaked like a sieve and could only be steered in the calmest weather'![17]

By contrast France's natural rivals, the central European powers, had concentrated on fleets appropriate to their position: Germany had built up a powerful short-sea or coastal fleet of shallow draft vessels protected by 9–10 inches of armour and mounting Krupp guns with a theoretical penetration of 13 inches of iron, which must have been more than a match for the older French vessels of the second class.

Only a diplomatic blunder which set the whole western world about her ears could conceivably have placed Britain in any danger so far as her battle fleet was concerned; commerce was a different story.

Actions, Accidents and Other Alarms

During these experimental years while capital ship design was being blown from one extreme to another on the winds of theory, there was little action experience to go on, and that little was not helpful in solving the major problems concerning first rate ships.

First, there were a few more practical demonstrations of the power of the ram: in 1872 HMS *Northumberland*, at anchor off Madeira, parted her cable and blew down upon the *Hercules*, impaling her side upon that vessel's specially pointed beak which tore a hole 'a horse and cart could have driven through'.[1] However, she was saved by her compartmentation and did not sink. Three years later there was another collision between British ironclads and this time it was far more serious: both vessels, of Reed's 'Audacious' class, were steaming off the Irish coast one behind the other and about four cables on the port beam of two other ships of the squadron, but rather astern of station so that they had increased to eight knots to catch up. On the port bow was a Norwegian barque. They all ran into dense fog and visibility dropped to less than 100 yards. The Captain of the leading port column ship, *Vanguard*, was called to the bridge and, anxious about the speed they were making in such conditions, started easing the engine revolutions down and blowing the steam whistle to let the *Iron Duke*, astern, know where he was. The watch officer of the *Iron Duke* meanwhile sheered his charge out of line and followed on what he supposed to be the *Vanguard*'s port quarter as he felt he would be safer; he also increased engine revolutions as, just before the fog clamped down, he had been dropping further astern of the *Vanguard*. Then his captain arrived on deck, and told of the alteration out of line, remarked 'That won't do—get into line again!' and ordered the helm over.

About the same time in the *Vanguard* the Norwegian barque was spotted dangerously close and standing across the bow from port to starboard. The ironclad's engines were immediately stopped and the wheel put over to pass astern of her, thus to port, a manoeuvre which caused her to drop back upon the *Iron Duke* and across her course. The sailing vessel had hardly disappeared before this new threat was seen less than a ship's length away. Seconds later the *Iron Duke*'s ram penetrated the *Vanguard*'s hull just abaft the watertight bulkhead separating the engine and boiler rooms, a most fatal point as, although the ram stopped some inches short of the inner plating of the double bottom and did not directly breach any main compartment it drove in the armour plates and structure of the ship above, causing numerous relatively small leaks which flooded both vital compartments at some 800 tons an hour, extinguishing the boiler fires in minutes and leaving the ship without any power for the pumps. As the two main compartments filled and others flooded through imperfectly fastened watertight doors it was only a matter of time before the ship went down. The captain set about saving the crew, and seventy minutes after the collision the *Vanguard* rolled over and sank.

The court martial into her loss considered that the captain should have concentrated his efforts on saving the ship by stuffing sails into the breach, manning the hand pumps and towing her towards shoal water instead of employing the crew hoisting out the boats, and judged that he should be severely reprimanded and dismissed from his command. The captain of the *Iron Duke*, which had done all the damage despite the steam whistling from the *Vanguard*, was exonerated from all blame on the grounds that he was justified in regaining station as quickly as possible! These findings come down the years as unjust, unscientific, essentially transitional; the court was composed of nine captains and admirals, only three from ironclads, and all naturally bred in timber seamanship, who apparently ignored evidence that water was entering at the rate of 800 tons an hour and that the hand pumps which they advocated were only capable of discharging 30 tons an hour! Perhaps it was felt necessary to preserve the credibility of British ironclads with a scapegoat; it is not the only example.

Three years later there was an even worse disaster, this time in a German squadron in clear weather. The squadron was steaming westerly in two columns close off the south Kent coast, the *König Wilhelm* as flagship followed by the *Preussen*, forming the port column and one cable to starboard and slightly ahead the *Grosser Kurfurst*, a rigged turret ship like the *Monarch*. Two small sailing vessels were beating off the coast to cross ahead of them from starboard to port, and the *König Wilhelm* altered to starboard to pass under their sterns; as she came to turn back on course, the men at the wheel became flustered, and putting it the wrong way, pointed her straight at the unfortunate *Grosser Kurfurst*, which was far too close to get out of the way. The ram struck, pierced and tore off the side armour as the *Kurfurst* steamed ahead, opening her stern sections to a torrent of seawater which took her down in only seven minutes and—because of the shortage of time—284 of the crew with her.

So much for the ram; as Barnaby inferred, the main defence was to keep out of the way—although smaller subdivisions, main watertight bulkheads unpierced for access, and more efficient, quicker-acting, watertight doors were also called for.

As for the gun, the British service had its first and only action experience against an armoured ship before the 1914 War when in 1877 the large unarmoured iron frigate, HMS *Shah* accompanied by an unarmoured corvette, *Amethyst*, fought a Peruvian turret ironclad called the *Huascar*, whose crew had mutinied in support of a bid to overthrow their president, and afterwards interfered with British merchant shipping. The *Huascar* was a monitor designed by Cowper Coles in 1864, with a single turret rising behind a short forecastle which sloped into a ram below water; her hull was protected by 4-inch armour tapering at the ends and her turret, which contained two 12½-ton Armstrong guns, by 5½-inch armour. Against this, the *Shah* brought two 12-ton pieces with a theoretical penetration of 10 inches at 1,000 yards and, on each side of her battery deck, eight 6½-ton guns with a theoretical penetration of 7 inches; she also carried a few of the smaller 64 pounders, which formed the sole armament of the *Amethyst*. However, the British ships, being totally unarmoured and not even protected on the cellular system, had to keep moving and keep the range long, generally between 2,000 and 1,500 yards, to try and avoid being hit, while the low freeboard and frequently end-on position of the turret vessel which steamed about at 11 knots made her an extremely difficult target. In the event the fight, described as partly a following and partly a revolving one, lasted two hours and 40 minutes, during which time the *Shah* fired 241 rounds and made about 30 hits, mainly on the gear above deck; she did however succeed in hulling the Peruvian vessel with four 9-inch and two 7-inch—2½ per cent of the shots fired; the *Amethyst* hit her another 30–40 times from 190 rounds. Altogether this was a creditable performance at such a target at such ranges and speeds with such muzzle loading guns and probably justified Colomb's claim that British naval gunnery was the best in the world. What was disappointing was the low penetration achieved; the only shell to get through the armour was not an armour-piercing shell at all, but a common 9-inch, which pierced a 3½-inch plate and exploded in the timber backing, causing the only four casualties of the action. These results, which compared so unfavourably with theoretical penetrations, continued to be a feature of naval warfare between armourclads, not simply because of inefficient projectiles or charges, mainly because in the words of a French analyst: 'It is extremely rare, in practice, for a projectile to hit a ship's armour at exactly a right angle.'[2]

The *Huascar*, for her part, only fired some eight times and failed to do more than part some rigging on the *Shah*; she also failed in a ramming attempt as the British ships kept their distance. The lowest range reached was some 400 yards for a brief time, at which point the *Shah* got off a Whitehead torpedo, the first ever used in action, but at that distance there was little chance of hitting especially as the *Huascar* outsteamed it! Finally the *Huascar* retired into shoal water off the town of Ilo where the British ships could neither close because of their deeper draft, nor fire without the chance of putting some shots into the town. The following day she surrendered to her own authorities.

Two years later the *Huascar* was in action again, this time as a regular member of the Peruvian navy in a war against Chile. She had been engaged on tip and run raids along the Chilean coast when she was caught between two divisions of Chilean ships and forced to fight, which she did most bravely although thoroughly outclassed. The most powerful of the Chilean ships were two Reed-designed belt-and-battery vessels, the *Blanco Encelada* and the *Almirante Cochrane*, of 3,500 tons mounting three 12-ton Armstrong guns each side of their armoured batteries. The first to attack held her fire until within 700 yards of the monitor, then unleashed a broadside, one of whose shells pierced the *Huascar*'s side armour below the turret and, exploding inside, jammed it temporarily and put paid to a number of men working the training gear. Shortly afterwards she hit the conning tower, blowing the captain to pieces, and then came in to ram, failing twice, but pouring in fire at point blank range which pierced the turret and the side armour again. Then she was joined by her sister ship and the *Huascar*, turning as if to ram and missing by only a few yards received another fearful broadside which completed the shambles within her turret and between decks. With dead and mutilated bodies lying everywhere and both guns' crews destroyed some of the crew ran on deck waving white towels. In all the *Huascar* had been hit by 27 heavy shells out of 76 fired; two had penetrated the 5½-inch turret armour from point blank range, and five others had passed through the thinner hull armour and exploded within, an exhibition of decisive gunnery creditable both to the Armstrong guns and the Chilean crews, although these had been under no pressure after the first accurate broadside, and had done their most fatal work at extremely close range. Perhaps most significant (but apparently unnoticed) were the ramming failures.

Meanwhile during 1877–8 the Russians had been providing some torpedo action data during their struggle with the Turks around the Black Sea. The Turkish fleet dominated that sea simply by lying at anchor, as the Russians had no sea-going ironclads and no chance of getting any in while Turkish forts and ships' guns dominated the narrows to Constantinople; so the Russians had no alternative to using torpedo boats for offensive operations, and they carried out a number of raids by night with specially constructed 15-knot boats some 50 or 60 feet long, carried by mother ships, usually fast merchantmen. However the earlier attacks were made with spar and towing torpedoes, and to get close enough without alerting the enemy with sparks from the funnels and considerable engine noise, they had to drop their speed to walking pace and creep in. Even so they did not escape detection, and were only successful on one occasion when they found the coastal monitor *Siefé* unprotected by the usual torpedo boat obstructions placed around the Turkish ships. Despite detection by the sentry, they pressed in under her turret guns as they misfired three times and touched a spar torpedo off close by the sternpost; the *Siefé* sank in a short time. As for the 'Whitehead', this was also tried and on one occasion on the night of 25–6 January 1878, the Russians claimed to have sunk a Turkish guard-ship anchored at the entrance to Batum harbour from 80 yards range; although the Turks denied any loss it is possible that this was the first Whitehead success in action. Despite the poor condition of the Turkish fleet and the great resolution of the Russian officers, these were the only effective torpedo attacks of the war. They were modest successes, and it was evident that torpedoes would be little use against an efficient fleet at anchor and guarded as recommended by the British 1875 Torpedo Committee, by nets, lights, Gatling guns and guard boats.

More important than any *matériel* lessons from the Russo-Turkish war were the strategic issues. Historically Britain's policy in the eastern Mediterranean had been to support Turkey as a barrier against Russian expansion towards Britain's Indian Empire and the overland links with that Empire through Mesopotamia or across the sands of Egypt. This policy had been stiffened since 1869 by the opening of the Suez Canal, which seemed to offer French and Russian ships, acting on interior lines from Toulon and the Black Sea, the chance to enter the Indian Ocean and play havoc with all British routes to the East, besides blocking Britain's own short cut. This was the view of the military departments.

Parallel with this was the strong commercial view: the canal had cut several thousand miles off the routes around the Cape to India and the Far East, and had naturally gathered to itself an increasing volume of steam shipping; by 1875, when Disraeli made his celebrated purchase of Suez Canal shares, over two million tons of British ships were using the waterway every year, 75 per cent of the total traffic. Then, as a symptom of both commercial and military views—or simply as an expression of British expansionist vitality—there was the maritime chauvinist view which by its very nature exaggerated the position; thus *The Times* could write: 'The Canal is in fact the sea'; everyone knew who was mistress of the sea! And the *Bristol Times and Daily News* could go so far as to say, 'holding that [canal] we hold Turkey and Egypt in the hollow of our hands, and the Mediterranean is an English lake, and the Suez Canal is only another name for the Thames and Mersey.'[3] In fact the Canal was a part of the Turkish Empire!

When Russia declared war on that Empire in April 1877, Britain was immediately involved, both because there was strong support in the country for the Turks and against the traditional threat to their eastern Empire, and because the Canal, which by now carried three million tons of British shipping a year, might become the scene of warlike operations which would stop commercial traffic. Britain sent a note to Russia, asking her not to 'blockade or otherwise interfere with the Canal or its approaches', and moved her Mediterranean ironclad squadron to Port Said.

We don't want to fight, but by Jingo if we do,
We've got the ships, we've got the men, we've got the money too.

Russia, with her armies fully occupied in a movement around the Black Sea, shortly renounced her belligerent rights against the Canal as an 'international work', and agreed to exclude Egypt from her sphere of operations; the following day, as if by reflex, the British squadron weighed and steamed out of Port Said.

The next year, with victorious Russian armies approaching Constantinople Disraeli's cabinet ordered an even more explicit demonstration: the British ironclad squadron was to steam up the Dardanelles and anchor off the city itself. This was called off temporarily at the request of the Turks who sought an armistice, but was carried out three weeks later while peace terms were being negotiated. It had no effect: Turkey was forced to give up her Balkan Empire to Russian influence, and allow Russia access to the Mediterranean, a defeat for British policy and prestige which threatened war, and a conference was called at Berlin to try and avert it.

While preliminary discussions were being held, Disraeli couldn't resist another naval show: he summoned 8,000 troops from India through the Suez Canal, covered by three ironclads at Port Said, to concentrate at Malta. This was the first time the Indian Army had been used for grand Imperial designs, and while the numbers were not impressive, the manner of their smooth and rapid transfer by water, and the potential of the vast continent they represented, were significant. *The Times* noted: 'they revealed England's capacity for the first time in her history to fight a great Continental war without an ally.'[4]

The actual effect of Disraeli's demonstration cannot be determined—all parties at Berlin wanted peace—but the upshot was a compromise: Russia gave back to Turkey a great slice of Bulgaria she had acquired at the peace conference, and Disraeli, in a separate convention, took Cyprus from Turkey; he returned to London satisfied that he had brought 'peace with honour'. Historians have seen in this peace the beginning of an end to the British policy of maintaining the Turkish Empire against Russia at all costs, and— more important for the history of the battleship—the beginning of a new Russian interest in sea power. Four years later they brought out their first systematic naval plan, for 15 battleships, 10 cruisers, later raised to 20 battleships, 24 cruisers, and various smaller craft. The threat of these squadrons in alliance with France provided the main stimulus to British building for the rest of the century.

The same year, 1882, also saw the logical result of Britain's strategic and commercial interest in the Suez Canal combined with her new-found 'by jingo' expansionism; she established military and political control over Egypt. That this happened under a Liberal prime minister, Gladstone, anti-imperial, anti-military, champion of self-determination for all peoples, violent opponent of all that Disraeli had so extravagantly stood for, is an indication of just how inevitable this move was.

It was provoked by a nationalist revolt, itself largely a response to the increasing Europeanization of Egypt since the Canal. When Britain and France sent warships to Alexandria and the Canal to protect their nationals and property and overthrow the nationalist leader, Colonel Arabi, the Egyptian army started throwing up fortifications and mounting guns opposite the ships as they lay at anchor. At which point the French government fell and the new administration, alarmed that the Egyptian crisis might be a sinister German plot to lure French troops from their own borders, recalled their squadrons. Britain was left on her own. Now, while Gladstone was opposed to unilateral action, and tried to seek a solution imposed by the European 'concert of nations', he was defeated by

Top A magnificent freak:
H M S *Inflexible* in 1881. (*National Maritime Museum*)

Bottom The first 'mastless'
battleship: H M S *Devastation*,
1871.

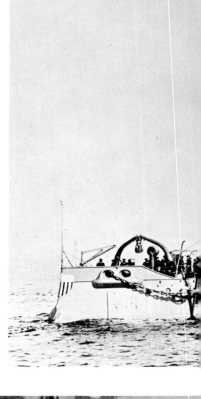

Opposite bottom The true line of evolution of the modern battleship, H M S *Royal Sovereign*, 1892.

Opposite top The United States becomes a battleship power; U S S *Oregon* in 1898. (*U. S. Navy*)

Above The accuracy revolution starts in the Royal Navy: Captain Percy Scott timing 'dotter' practice.

Below Artist's impression of the Russian battle line at Tsushima. (*Radio Times Hulton Picture Library*)

Top Grand Admiral von Tirpitz, creator of a German battle-fleet to challenge British sea supremacy at the turn of the century. (*Radio Times Hulton Picture Library*)

Bottom 'Jacky' Fisher, the Royal Navy's great administrator at the height of the battleship era; this was Fisher's favourite photograph of himself. (*National Maritime Museum*)

his service departments, who took a more practical view after anti-Christian riots and a massacre of 50 foreigners at Alexandria. It became imperative to restore European prestige, and Gladstone sanctioned a naval bombardment of the forts at Alexandria as the quickest and most economical way.

So it was that the first British armoured ships ever to fire their guns in earnest cleared for action on the morning of 11 July 1882, and steamed in to position opposite the forts. They were a diverse collection. Largest and most modern was the *Inflexible*, commanded by Captain 'Jackie' Fisher, a dynamic man already marked for the highest positions; next came the flagship of the Mediterranean station, the *Alexandra*, the ultimate in British belt-and-battery ships, then the similar *Sultan* and *Superb*, and one of the scaled-down versions, the *Invincible*, to which the commander-in-chief had transferred his flag because of her shallower draft; then there was the *Temeraire* with her unique arrangement of central battery and disappearing guns at either end above, and finally of the big ships, Reed's double-turret, fully-rigged, *Monarch*. There were in addition one smaller ironclad and a number of gunboats. In all, the fleet mounted 43 heavy rifled muzzle-loaders on any one broadside, ranging from the *Inflexible*'s four 80-ton pieces down to 9-tonners.

Against them the forts mounted only 41 rifled muzzle-loaders, besides 211 obsolete smooth-bores which were little use against armoured ships. Nevertheless, if these batteries had been manned by skilled guns' crews they would have had all the theoretical advantages: they had steady platforms not deranged by other guns firing alongside, their guns could be set accurately for distance, their shot could be 'spotted' on to target by the high splashes it made in the water, and they had the whole of a ship to aim at and damage while a ship had to make a direct hit on a gun or its embrasure to put it out of action.

The theoretical odds didn't worry the British; it was a bright, clear morning, the sea barely rippled by an offshore breeze, and the guns' crews, stripped to the waist as in the old days, were eager to give what they considered an Arab rabble a taste of British powder. As the *Invincible* made the signal for general action a rumble like thunder spread through the separate detachments opposite the forts, and great clouds of thick, white smoke burst from the black hulls of the ships, rising and hanging about the taut rigging, only dispersing slowly. Below, the loading numbers went through their heavy precision drill, now spiced with the urgency of real action.

Again and again, from the smaller calibres first, came 'the full-toned bellow of an old-fashioned muzzle-loader', then more dense smoke as the pieces slid back. In the tops officers peered through it to watch the shells rising and growing smaller towards the dun shore some 1,500 yards away, then reported where they landed to the officers of the quarters. Punctuating the continuous thud and chatter came the great concussion of the *Inflexible*'s turret guns followed by a rumbling sound as the great shells 'wobbled in the air with a noise like that of a distant train'.

So it went through the glistening day in almost target practice conditions; at one stage when the splashes from the Egyptian shells moved too close it became necessary for some ships to shift themselves with springs from the anchor cables, and for others to weigh and steam to and fro, but the Egyptian reply was not enough to divert the guns' crews. And gradually the sheer volume of ships' fire, the exploding shells, the noise and the occasional direct hit which wiped out a gun and its crew, wore the defenders down. Having suffered some 550 killed and wounded, against only 53 British casualties, they evacuated the forts after dark and the sailors and marines walked in on the thirteenth.

They found only 15 of the rifles and nine of the smooth bores disabled by hits from the 1,750 heavy shells, 1,730 lighter shells and 16,000 Nordenfelt bullets fired, and only about 5 per cent of the fire had actually hit the target area, the parapets of the forts. The best shooting appeared to have been made by the two ships with hydraulic laying and training gear, the *Inflexible* and *Temeraire*; however, most of the guns of the fleet had mechanical elevating gear and this had proved too slow and clumsy for the smooth water conditions at Alexandria. Had there been any swell the gunlayers could have set the elevation and waited until the ship rolled the sights on target; lacking such customary help one ship at least had bodies of men moving from one side of the deck to the other to produce an artificial roll. The report from the captain of the *Monarch* illustrates some of the difficulties:

> After the captain of the turret had ascertained and communicated the heel to the numbers laying the gun, the time necessarily taken to work the elevating gear, lay the guns by means of the crude wooden scales and make ready is so great that probably another gun or turret will have fired in the interim, and consequently the heel of the ship will be so affected that a relay of the gun is necessary unless a bad or chance shot is purposely delivered.[5]

In addition, there were no more aids to fire control than there had been at the beginning of the century, when effective range had been 300 yards or less; there were no rangefinders, no telegraphs to pass orders or range corrections from the officers stationed aloft to watch the fall of shot, and messages passed by voicepipe were frequently inaudible in the din of battle. The giant products of the ordnance revolution had outgrown the methods of controlling them; had the bombardment of Alexandria failed it is just possible that this lesson might have been heeded, but as the firing had been infinitely better than the Egyptians', and the victory had been clear-cut and most economical, the reports were filed and there is no evidence that any improvements followed.

The evacuation of the forts took the fighting and destruction into Alexandria itself, hardened the Egyptians behind Arabi and boosted the military and colonial departments in England, whose Cabinet representatives virtually took over from Gladstone and forced him to alter the emphasis of the campaign from a limited punitive demonstration by the Navy to a full-scale invasion by the Army. When the French again refused to co-operate unless the security of the Canal were threatened the British cabinet called in Indian troops; meantime a British admiral who had won a VC in the Crimean War for refusing orders to retreat, ignored instructions to wait for the troops, seized and held Suez with his own squadron, and unilaterally closed the canal. Next month the British army annihilated Arabi's forces at Tel-el-Kebir, and Britain became sole master of Egypt. The Canal had become at last (almost) as British as the Thames and the Mersey.

These events in the eastern Mediterranean from 1877–82 illustrate the importance Britain attached to command in that sea and over Egypt, a vital link of Empire. This feeling, practical or paranoic depending upon viewpoint, was a major factor behind ironclad, or as they came to be known battleship, building programmes to the end of the century. The scale of these programmes was determined by Russian and French building which, at least in the former case, stemmed directly from the arrogant displays of British naval supremacy. It was well enough for British first lords and naval historians after this to complain that Russia was a 'land power' with scarcely any sea trade and therefore no need for a navy, but it was a remarkably one-sided view which expected any great power to take humiliations lying down. On the other hand British interests in the area seemed to practical men in England to demand protection: besides the four million tons of merchant shipping passing through Suez annually by 1882—over 80 per cent of total traffic—and the British investment in the area, there was the awful possibility of such a vital hinge of maritime strategy falling to France or Russia. In this sense the acquisition of real power in Egypt was a natural development of the policy or instinct which had given Britain chains of island and mainland bases from which to protect her shipping throughout the world. The flag had to follow trade.

Whether the Egyptian move was an essential consequence of maritime strategy, or a high-handed demonstration of naval power, or both of these and a bit of the bond-holder's dilemma, whether it was part reaction to France's pretensions to a North African empire or was itself powerful stimulus to European powers to carve up bits of the undeveloped world for themselves—as they did with increased frenzy during the following decades—for the purposes of this story it was provocation for a naval race. It not only upset the balance at the meeting point of East and West and extended Britain's naval commitments, it provided France and Russia with sufficient envy and resentment to begin building programmes which might—at least in alliance—prevent future unilateral action by the 'mistress of the seas'.

The Development of the Battleship

The decade of the 1880s began with 'ironclads'—*cuirassés d'escadre, gardes-côtes cuirassés*—and ended with 'battleships', a change of term which corresponds with a significant crystallization in design and function. Other changes and constant improvements were to come but the eighties saw the last violent swings between heavy guns and heavy armour, the last eccentric distribution of main armament, the end of sails for heavy ships, the end of experimental designs, the last serious doubts occasioned by torpedo boats, and in Britain the scientific establishment of naval strength based on homogenous battle squadrons designed to maintain command in all weathers by virtue of artillery. Hence the first programme for a class of sea-keeping—as opposed to sea-going—first rates; these were in essentials evolved battleships.

They marked the triumph of the gun. Just as, after a much longer transitional period in the sixteenth century the great gun had developed till it dictated battle terms outside the range of those who sought to board, so the ordnance of the eighties gained such an ascendancy that ramming and torpedoing, the new forms of close combat, became unfeasible. Philip Colomb noted in 1887: 'English officers are getting out of the habit of mixing up the gun, the ram and the torpedo as though they were weapons on the same level, and they have a more present reflection that the ram does not influence an action fought at a minimum distance of 600 yards; and that the torpedo does not influence one fought at a minimum distance of 1,000 yards.'[1]

The first phase of this ordnance development was an increase in muzzle velocity; it was brought about by the development of slow-burning powders, pioneered by the American artillerist, General Rodman, who thought that if holes were bored into solid blocks of gunpowder the surface area of powder exposed would actually increase during combustion—as the holes became larger—and the production of gas would consequently develop during the whole of the projectile's travel up the bore; thus the shell would receive a steadily-increasing thrust instead of an initial sharp jab. As a bonus it was found that the cubes, prisms or whatever shape the powder was moulded into, broke up in the final stages of combustion, presenting a suddenly increased surface area and giving a final boost; the trick for manufacturers was to make this boost coincide with the end of the shell's flight up the bore. By 1880 all leading gunmakers were capable of achieving this and several transitional guns, notably the Armstrong 100-tonners for the *Duilio* and the Woolwich 81-ton replies, were ready for mounting aboard. These had larger powder chambers than former guns as slowing the explosion allowed larger charges to be fired without bursting the breech end.

This quiet revolution in ballistics, demanding longer barrels for the powder to complete its work, saw the British muzzle-loaders out. The War Office had called for an experimental breech-loader as early as 1878, and in 1880 the director of naval ordnance had asked Armstrongs for an experimental 43-ton breech-loader as long guns were particularly difficult to load through the muzzle on board ship: the longer the barrel, the longer the rammer which meant fixed loading positions at some distance from the turret with all the design problems and slowness this entailed. Breech-loaders required only a very short rammer which could follow the breech of the gun around. The Ordnance Department of the Admiralty had such an experimental all-round loading gear under construction before the change to breech-loading was announced in 1880.

Both Armstrongs and Woolwich adapted the French interrupted screw mechanism for their breech-loaders, as did the American service later, leaving only Krupp and the Russian Obukoff copies employing a laterally sliding wedge to close the breech. At the same time the British service followed the Continental gunmakers into all-steel construction. The first big ships to mount these new weapons were the final 'Inflexible' diminutives, *Colossus* and *Majestic* (later *Edinburgh*), laid down in 1879, which each mounted four 45-ton 12-inch pieces with a muzzle velocity of 2,000 feet per second and a theoretical penetration of 19 inches of iron at 2,000 yards. All-round loading gear was not out of the development stage when they were completed in 1886, and they had the same fixed station hydraulic gear as the *Inflexible* but adapted for ramming through the breech.

The British and Italian Navies were the last to adopt—or in the former case re-adopt—breech-loading, apart from the United States and Turkish services, both of which were in a very low *matériel* state. However, it was not until the eighties that the *system* of loading made any difference to speed of fire or penetration: George

Rendel of Armstrongs thought it 'a very difficult matter to establish a really exact comparison. In small guns you may say that you will gain in rapidity by loading at the breech; in large guns you will, I think, lose rapidity';[2] this was in 1880. It was only the potential for all-round loading noted above which seemed about to give large breech-loaders a real advantage. As for penetrating power, the British guns only began to fall seriously behind in the final years of the 1870s, about the time that new style muzzle-loaders like those for the *Inflexible* and an altogether new breech-loading system were being developed for the new powders. For their part muzzle-loaders were simpler to handle and maintain—an important consideration during the transition period from the old navy of marline spikes to the new technical service—and were half the price of steel breech-loaders.

Slow-burning powders and the longer guns that came into service with them raised muzzle velocities to over 2,000 feet per second. Besides increasing penetration this allowed a far flatter trajectory for any given range: a standard British 35-ton gun needed nearly nine degrees of elevation to reach 4,000 yards, the new Armstrong 35-ton piece for slow-burning powders only four. In the absence of range finders this greatly extended the range of likely hitting. But this was a side effect; the whole drive towards higher velocities, and the British change to breech loading, were aimed at armour-piercing power.

The other major development in ordnance was medium calibre quick-firing (QF) guns. This stemmed from the threat posed by fast 'Whitehead' torpedo boats which were constructed with increasing enthusiasm, especially by France and Russia, from 1877 onwards. At first the various multi-barrel machine guns by Gatling, Nordenfelt and Hotchkiss, which could repel 'spar' torpedo boats, were considered adequate, but as torpedo boats grew larger and faster heavier weapons were needed, and as larger-calibre guns with five to ten barrels would have been excessively heavy and clumsy the British Admiralty in 1881 invited designs for a single-barrel gun firing a 6 lb projectile at a rate of 12 aimed rounds per minute. Both Hotchkiss and Nordenfelt produced successful guns which entered the British service within two years; the basis of their rapid fire was a cartridge case containing both powder and projectile whose base provided a perfect check against gases escaping through the interrupted screw mechanism of the breech, and made it unnecessary to clean or sponge the bore between rounds. Encouraged by success both companies soon increased the calibre to 4 inches, and other firms joined in, notably Armstrong and Krupp who produced 4.7-inch or 120 millimetre pieces. Armstrongs gave a great boost to accuracy against fast moving targets by mounting theirs on a central pivot with hand-wheels geared for rapid training and elevating. In trials in 1887 one of these 4.7s fired 15 rounds in one minute; this was exactly 10 times the rate achieved by the new service 5-inch breech-loader, and although such a speed was seldom achieved in service, 12 rounds was quite normal. Armstrongs went on to produce 6-inch QF guns on low slide mountings with similar handwheels; these could fire six aimed rounds a minute.

In this field Britain led the way—once again Admiralty reaction to a threat against the battlefleet, followed by mobilization of private industry. The side effect of the rapid development which follow-ed through the eighties was that battleships acquired a secondary armament of these medium-calibre QFs for use not so much against torpedo boats as against the unprotected parts of other battleships. They answered increasingly vocal criticism about the small volume of fire from modern first rates, promising to bring back the Nelsonic battle-winner, a 'hail of fire' to overwhelm enemy *men*; as they came into service they rendered unarmoured ships like the *Italia*, and ships showing a large proportion of unarmoured side like the *Admiral Duperre* and her successors, obsolete for the first line. They also restored the broadside to its former predominance.

However, all this was not apparent until midway through the eighties; at first the drive was all towards monster guns to pierce armour, and France entered the decade with two first rates under construction similar to the *Admiral Duperre* in appearance and armour distribution, but mounting three 75-ton guns in three separate centre-line barbettes; although this reduced direct ahead fire to one heavy piece there was a gain in real arcs of fire as France had at last followed Reed in abandoning sails for first line ships.

To compete with this class Barnaby produced designs for the first British barbette ship—apart from the *Temeraire*—and she was laid down in July 1880, a year after the last two *Inflexible* types; she was named *Collingwood*. The prime advantage of the barbette system was that it saved weight of armour and of engines turning heavy turrets, and so enabled the guns to be carried higher—an advantage in a seaway and, it was claimed, for plunging fire through the enemy's decks in close action (although it is difficult to visualize such warm work between ships fitted with Whitehead torpedoes and machine guns on their upperworks and fighting tops). Open barbette guns were also said to have an advantage in sighting, but this simply reflects the crudity of all sighting systems of the time. For her general features Barnaby returned to the *Dreadnought* idea, four big guns in pairs on turntables at either end of an unprotected mid-length super-structure. However the guns were much higher, 20 feet above the water, and consequently the armour could not be distributed on the same pattern; instead it formed a central box belt rising 2½ feet out of the water. This was covered by a 3-inch armoured deck, and the protection for the ammunition hoists rose from either end to open barbettes. The maximum thickness of the midlength belt was 18 inches of compound armour, equivalent to some 23 inches of iron. Beyond the citadel the sides were quite unarmoured and the *Italia/Inflexible* system of underwater armoured deck and cellular subdivision and coal bunkers was used to protect stability—although the cork cells and canvas-filled cofferdams of the *Inflexible* were omitted. To attack the enemy's unarmoured sides a secondary battery of six 6-inch breech-loaders were mounted in the unprotected superstructure between the barbettes.

The *Collingwood* marked a return to practical balanced design, particularly for artillery, and was the final step towards the evolved battleship, which must have been appreciated as she was followed by five other 'Admirals', the first 'class' of British first rates since the coming of the ironclad. Her successors of 10,600 tons, laid down between 1882 and 1883, each mounted four 13.5-inch guns, theoretical penetration 26-inch compound armour at 2,000 yards, thus enough in theory to smash the low French belts, but the final one, the *Benbow*, mounted just two monster pieces, 16.25-inch calibre and weighing 110 tons each, an actual reduction in power as they could only fire once every four minutes or so.

Sound as the 'Admirals' were in conception, Barnaby was working on far too small a displacement. The most obvious symptom was the low freeboard; steaming head to even a moderate sea a great deal of water was shipped over the bows and as the barbettes had only light canvas covers, which could be ripped away fairly easily, much of it found its way down the hoists. Admiral Bacon recalled one occasion when he was paddling about the ammunition passages above his knees in water.[3] Another defect was the extent of the unarmoured waterline at both ends; Admiral Fitzgerald recalled that serving officers were at loggerheads with the naval architects over this point, thinking they 'miscalculated the chances of battle'. And as all the contemporary French first rates had complete water-line belts, Fitzgerald, in command of the *Collingwood*, 'felt somewhat anxious as to what would happen if we had to fight our hereditary enemy while I was in command of a 'soft-ender'.[4] Reed was publicly with the officers on this point, as he had been ever since seeing the *Duilio*, and although the Admiralty fought back well: 'it is quite certain that the admission of only moderate quantities of water will not prejudice the stability of the vessels to an important extent'[5]—the coming of the QF forced a reaction towards defence.

This first appeared in the *Victoria* and *Sans Pareil*, laid down in 1885, which had the same style of hull protection as the 'Admirals', increased in thickness to a maximum of 18 inches, but in place of high and open barbettes at either end one massive and necessarily low 18-inch armoured turret at the fore end mounting two of the 110-ton monster guns that had gone into the *Benbow*. Aft of it the unarmoured superstructure housing the secondary 6-inch battery extended right to the stern. This design sacrificed rate of fire and efficiency in a seaway to the unlikely chance of piercing an enemy's belt and finishing him with one great blow, and it still left a great deal of the hull and all the secondary battery at the mercy of any shells that might strike.

Following them on the stocks the next year came two more first rates, the *Nile* and *Trafalgar*, which marked a complete return to Reed's ideas; indeed they were virtually up-to-date breastwork monitors with short unarmoured ends to increase length and thus speed. Each mounted four 13.5-inch guns in two turrets, and between them six 4.7-inch QF guns, the first of these weapons to be mounted in heavy ships. The 'Trafalgars' marked a return to sanity so far as the size and distribution of the main guns were concerned, but the accent on protection, which brought the proportion of armour to over 35 per cent of displacement, and sacrificed freeboard and gun height, was too much for Barnaby; he resigned. In fact he had set himself an impossible task; certain to the end that the size of armoured ships should be kept down, he was unable to produce a satisfactory sea-keeping armoured battleship. Nevertheless, the 'Admirals' in their general features and the relative weights of armour, guns and displacement, came close to the ideal; if subsequent development is anything to go by they came closer than contemporary French ships.

For the French in 1880 laid down a class of four ships, *Magenta*, *Marceau*, *Neptune* and *Hoche*, similar to the *Admiral Duperre*'s two successors, but rather shorter, 1,000 tons less displacement and with even more unprotected side and higher unprotected superstructure. They had the complete waterline belt of all French armoured ships (similarly narrow and topped by a 3½-inch armoured deck) and although it was 17¾-inch maximum steel of a remarkably uniform thickness, it rose little more than two feet above the water at full load, and this left little margin for misadventure; in a seaway or with the ship under helm a few holes in the completely unprotected sides above might have brought the belt down to sea level and, as there was no cellular subdivision, produced a free surface of water above the armoured deck which would have seriously affected stability. The danger was accentuated by the sides' sloping steeply inwards, reducing the righting moment at angles of heel. The *Hoche*, for instance, which was being built with turrets instead of barbettes, was said to heel no less than 15 degrees under moderate helm with her guns trained abeam. The British Admiralty certainly thought that Barnaby's compromise solution for the 'Admiral' class was better, and pointed out that a short, high belt amidship where the vessel was broad cost no more per foot than where the ship was narrow, but had much greater value in maintaining buoyancy and stability than the same armoured area spread lower over the whole ship's length. The heeling and sinking of the *Osliaba* after gun wounds at the battle of Tsushima in the following century has been held to confirm the theoretical danger of the French system, for she had a complete low belt and great tumble-home; but in her case the danger was exaggerated by overloading which had practically submerged the belt before the battle began.

The reason for the French tumble-home seems to have been, as before, end-on fire. The main armament of four 13.4-inch guns was arranged in four separate barbettes, one forward, one aft, one on each beam at mid-length, and these two were on sponsons projecting out beyond the tumble-home to command direct ahead and astern as well as broadside fire. This 'lozenge' arrangement allowed three heavy guns to bear on most arcs and also reduced the number of guns hazarded to a direct hit in or about a barbette. However, if anything like ahead or astern fire were attempted, the secondary armament became untenable and a bugle blew to call all hands away from the sides. For broadside work they opposed only three pieces to the 'Admirals' ' four. Probably their strongest point was the secondary armament of nine 5½-inch pieces on each broadside— though carried lower than the main armament and unprotected. The vast unprotected area of these French ships and their predecessors is odd since 22 per cent of their displacement was devoted to armour.

While these vessels were still under construction Admiral Aube and his disciples in *la jeune école* produced a sustained theoretical attack on armoured warships that persuaded many people on both sides of the Channel that they would soon be obsolete. The Admiral was still convinced that only ruthless cruiser warfare against trade and coastal towns could be effective against England, but now believed that her battlefleet also could be attacked successfully by small, fast, specialized craft, the majority armed with Whitehead torpedoes, some with just one great gun, some with only a ram. All should be faster than heavy ships, thus able to press their attack to decisive range, escaping annihilation by speed and dispersion.

As expounded in 1886 by Gabriel Charmes in *La Reforme de la Marine* such small craft 'group' attack would not only be irresistable, especially at night or in fog, but also considerably cheaper. The three torpedo boats necessary to sink each armourclad would only cost 600,000 francs and need 39 men, against 20 million francs and 700 men hazarded in the big ship.

Similar views influenced policy in all European navies. Russia built up a large torpedo boat fleet, and Germany also; no doubt remembering her impotence against the French Navy in 1870, she saw these craft chiefly in terms of coast defence, rendering blockade 'almost impossible'.

> Every night the blockading ships would be compelled to withdraw to a distance under steam. Their coal consumption would thereby be much increased, the tension of the crews...would become intolerable, and at night the blockaded harbours would become accessible. Even when in motion the blockading ships would not be safe at night...[6]

To many people in England these predictions seemed only too reasonable; in 1885 the financial secretary to the Admiralty described the *Nile* and *Trafalgar* as 'probably the last ironclads of this type that will ever be built in this or any other country'.[7] This may have been an extreme view, though, as the First Lord in private correspondence confessed, 'we are in a period of transition, even as regards guns and shipbuilding. No two naval officers will agree as to what in a few years will be the fighting ships of that time...'[8]

This uncertainty, which actually put a stop to big-ship programmes in England for three years after 1886, was even more evident in France, no doubt because there they faced a tougher problem: they were in financial crisis, felt compelled to keep a large army on the German border, and a naval force in the Mediterranean to contain the Italians, and in addition they had to contend with England, now once again the colonial rival as the scramble for Africa and eastern influence gathered way. Caught in these impossible circumstances their policy veered more than most. At first it was pragmatic; the report that accompanied the Estimates for 1885 could almost have been drawn up by a British Board of Admiralty:

> The torpedo boats are the last arrivals in the successive phases which our naval policy has undergone. It does not follow that they should take the place of everything else, inaugurate a new era, still less form the definitive termination to an edifice to which so much intelligence and devotion have already as-

sisted. It is a step, nothing more: and they would be very simple who would not understand that these dangerous machines have need of support and that these supports will present themselves according to the circumstances under the form of forts, coast defence ships or sea-going ironclads...[9]

Then in January 1886, Aube was entrusted with the service, and such exasperatingly English policy went overboard, to be replaced by a ruthlessly intellectual conception worked through from British battlefleet predominance now, and as Aube saw it, for ever. Like Paixhans and de Lôme he saw that France must choose her own weapons; like them he saw his chance in the frailty of the existing capital ship, burdened with such a weight of armour and all the instruments of offence in one hull; like them he determined to upset it. Two heavy ships, *Brennus* and *Charles Martel*, which had been occupying much intelligence and devotion in the *Department du Matériel*, were erased from the Navy List, and programmes were set in hand for sea-going torpedo boats and very light draft, high-speed vessels each carrying one great gun capable of puncturing an ironclad. He also aimed to add a new element, invisibility, to 'combine offence and defence in the highest degree', and ordered experimental submersible boats both as torpedo carriers, troop transports and as portable craft to be carried by privateers.

While Aube's policies were sound in not breaking the French economy between the army and a costly armourclad fleet, meanwhile concentrating on the rival's weak point (in this case trade), he was in most respects a victim of his own 'thoroughly French conception'. He was trying to advance the art of naval warfare by sudden theoretical leaps instead of moving gradually after testing the ground. Leaving aside the submersible boats, which were so far-sighted as to be visionary, the cornerstone of his battle policy was the sea-going torpedo boat, which he expected to do more than current development allowed; he also 'mixed up the gun and the torpedo as though they were weapons on the same level'. They were not. The torpedo lacked range and gyroscopic control and was not effective between moving ships outside 400 yards; on the other hand the gun was effective at 1,500 yards, was developing rapid fire, had passed the point of minimum numbers aboard ship, was spreading along the broadside again, and was unavoidable if truly aimed. In this respect Aube's policy was already out of date. And the few boats he was building for great guns were too small to be suitable aiming platforms in anything but the calmest water. As for substituting numbers for armour protection, Philip Colomb, trying to imagine concentrating and manoeuvring 24 gunboats, 48 offensive and 48 defensive torpedo boats which Aube's policy would oppose to 12 armourclads, 'was struck by the thought of the practical difficulties of the undertaking'.[10] He was not the only one.

Other practical limitations were apparent even before Aube came to power: in the British manoeuvres of 1885 designed to test defences against torpedo-boats, flotillas attacking at night never succeeded in getting closer than 800 yards to the ironclad squadron at anchor before they were discovered, and the only two torpedoes to travel straight at their target were caught in the wire net around it; at sea the armoured squadron did get into theoretical trouble when it pressed on towards a flotilla attack, but such rashness was not expected in action and the principle was established that 'attacked ships will always endeavour to turn 16 points',[11] in other words directly away to oppose their stern fire to the attackers and reduce the relative speed of approach of any torpedoes. As for the sea-keeping qualities of contemporary boats, Admiral Phipps Hornby reported, 'six of them have done what they were never intended to do, viz accompany a squadron at sea. They have accomplished the voyage only through the pluck of the men that were in them and at the cost of great fatigue and considerable suffering.' And he recommended a programme of *sea-going* torpedo boats '*to supplement our ironclads*', suggesting that at least two should be attached to every ironclad 'and that they should be provided with an alternative gun armament so as to serve as torpedo boat destroyers when so required...Probably the best distribution will be to have half the boats arranged as torpedo boat destroyers and placed ahead of the squadron on going into action, and the remainder armed as torpedo boats close astern of their respective ironclads ready to act in the smoke and confusion...'[12] In short, the British answer to torpedo boat attack was spelled out in some detail before Aube gained power. And as always France could not hope to outbuild Britain either in numbers or in the speed of individual craft.

Many French officers were left with similar doubts about the effectiveness of extreme torpedo boat policy after fleet manoeuvres in 1886, but Aube and his disciples remained convinced, and it was not until the following year, when manoeuvres were held in appalling weather, that the limitations were really driven home; one torpedo boat was lost, two so badly damaged that they had to be paid off, and others so injured that the flotilla was reduced to 50 per cent strength; the admiral commanding was so occupied in preserving these that he failed to attack the ironclad squadron which came through it all 'perfectly ready to put to sea at once'.

This demonstration coincided with Aube's replacement by a new minister of marine, who reverted to a more immediately practical policy—particularly in view of France's relation to lesser European navies—and restored the *cuirasse d'escadre* as backbone of the fleet. Of all the French attempts to revolutionize naval warfare and dictate the strategy Aube's was the most dramatic failure.

Meanwhile British historical thought and practical experience fused into a battlefleet doctrine that for the first time had a real intellectual basis. For the lessons that the brothers Colomb had extracted from naval history had been absorbed in the places where it mattered. The change is illustrated in the 1887 report of the newly established Naval Intelligence Division (one of the first—if not the first—to use the term 'battleship' instead of 'ironclad' in comparisons of British and French fleet strengths):

> France and Russia have been selected as the countries most likely to combine against England...Our policy in the past always was to endeavour to prevent the enemy vessels putting to sea or to follow and attack them if they succeeded in escaping, and for the purposes of this comparison it is assumed that our policy will be the same in the future...our blockading vessels, which must be 'sea-keeping' vessels, have opposed to them not only the 'sea-keeping' vessels of the enemy in port, but his coast defence vessels and torpedo-boats, which though not capable of keeping the sea for any time are quite competent to proceed out of harbour and attack the blockading vessels, and are also able to cross the English Channel. Moreover, to allow for the temporary absence of some of our vessels coaling, refitting etc. our squadrons must be decidely superior to those of the enemy...[18]

While this sounds very like the views which had guided British naval policy right through the century, there is a difference in the more precise definition of strategic *requirements*. Formerly battlefleet equality with France and Russia had served as a rough yardstick for maritime supremacy, and all thought and effort had gone into creating technically superior ships on as small a displacement as possible. Now thought was going into the work, specifically blockade work, which the battlefleet would have to perform in war, a development which had to lead to technical considerations being ruled by strategic requirements. This was not because the technical problems were solved, for they were in 1887 quite as baffling as ever, it was because there was at last an agreed *theoretical* base to work from. This base, this solid doctrine which stood like a rock among the constantly shifting sands of the technical revolution, was largely the triumph of the Colomb brothers, although it was helped by various political crises with France and Russia which had served to impress commanders-in-chief, Mediterranean, with the practical difficulties of blockade in the new conditions of the steam navy, the considerable superiority in numbers which they would need, and the shortage of cruisers for lookout and commerce protection.

These points were tested in the annual manoeuvres of 1888 and 1889 and it was found that for a battlefleet 'to mask the fleet of an enemy from a suitable strategic base or bases' it would need a superiority of at least 5:3 in battleships and 2:1 in fast cruisers. This was because ships had to be relieved at intervals for coaling and repairs. The famous Report of the Three Admirals after the 1888 Manoeuvres drew the wider lesson that the country did not have this kind of superiority; the Navy was 'altogether inadequate ...to take the offensive in a war with only one great power, and supposing a combination of even two powers to be allied against her, the balance of maritime strength would be seriously against England.'[14]

Meanwhile there was a war scare. France massed most of her battlefleet in the Mediterranean at Toulon; combined with Russian battleship building for the Black Sea, and evidence of increasing Franco-Russian cordiality this served to create a climate of anxiety about 'the first line of defence' in the country as a whole. Actually this had been building up since 1884 when W. T. Stead had written a series of articles, 'The Truth about the Navy', using inside information supplied by Captain Fisher among others. Since then a group of 'panic mongers and chronic alarmists' among serving officers, ably assisted by the press, had kept the public informed about the deficiencies of the Navy, particularly the lack of cruisers for trade protection. All this resulted in the appointment of a Select Committee on Naval Estimates which reported in 1889 that the amount spent on the Navy was quite inadequate considering—this is pure Colomb—'Britain's unique dependence on sea supplies...The command of the sea once being lost it would not require the landing of a single soldier upon her shores to bring her to an ignominious capitulation.'[15]

The use of the phrase 'command of the sea' instead of 'maritime supremacy' was as significant as the change from 'ironclad' to 'battleship'. It was a Colomb term, shortly to be immortalized and stamped indelibly on naval thought by the American naval captain, Alfred Thayer Mahan; it specified the strategic use to which 'supremacy' was to be put—had been put in Britain's naval past—and it clearly expressed the change that had come over British naval thinking. That there was a significant change is clear from a comparison of the Select Committee's comments with the actual position of the national fleets. The first line battleships were:

Completed Great Britain	France	Russia
4 'Admiral' class	1 *Adml. Duperre*	3 'Trafalgar' type
1 *Dreadnought*	2 „ „	
1 *Inflexible*	enlargements	
1 *Alexandra*	2 'Devastation'	
2 'Devastation'	class	
class	4 Caiman (coast	
1 *Neptune*	service barbette	
1 *Superb*	vessels)	
4 'Inflexible'		
diminutives		
15	9	3

Building		
2 'Admiral' class	4 'Magenta' class	3 of 9–10,000 tons
2 'Trafalgar 'class	1 *Brennus*	
2 'Victoria' class		
6	5	3

This showed a clear superiority for Britain quantitavely and qualitatively; the Naval Intelligence Department projection forward to the end of 1890 gave an even greater overall superiority:

	England	France	Russia
First class	22	14	6
Second class	15	7	nil
Third class	3	3	1
Total	40	24	7

This justified the First Lord's assertion to the Select Committee that the strength of the Navy was relatively greater than it had been for years. It was; by the standards which had guided British naval policy since mid-century there had been no failure at the

Admiralty. 'Maritime supremacy' was assured, probably more than at any previous stage of the ironclad revolution, and the criticisms in the reports of the Three Admirals and the Select Committee were plainly exaggerated, if not mischievous. This was the opinion across the Channel.

It is only by substituting the phrase 'command of the sea' for 'maritime supremacy' and realizing this meant that the British fleet —to paraphrase Paul Fontin—placed its frontiers at the enemy's coasts and disposed of all commerce behind that frontier, just as an army disposes of the resources of a conquered province, that the 'chronic alarmists' can be understood. For this sort of command the Navy was patently inadequate. The most glaring shortage was in cruisers needed for the current doctrine of 'concentrating at the focal points of trade' and 'patrolling the sea routes'—analogies from the Roman Empire are clear.[16]

As for the battle fleet which had to ensure the cruisers a free hand, it was a motley collection, and the new, 'scientific' idea of relating design to war strategy found it wanting: even the newest class, the 'Admirals', had a lukewarm report after their mock blockade work:

> These vessels are good sea boats, and their speed is not affected when steaming against a moderate wind and sea; but we are of opinion that their low freeboard renders them unsuitable as sea-going armourclads for general service with the fleet, as their speed must be rapidly reduced when it is necessary to force them against a head sea or swell...[17]

In 1889 the evolved naval doctrine, together with political fears about the designs of France and Russia, naval fears for the Mediterranean junction of their fleets, commercial fears about the apparent vulnerability of Britain's vast seaborne trade, now £700 million a year, chauvinism and the sheer triumphantly expansionist mood of the country represented by the influential group of 'navalists', 'imperialists', journalists and even poets—'You-you—*if* you have failed to understand, the fleet of England is her all in all...'— brought about the Naval Defence Act which provided the unprecedented sum of £21½ millions to add 70 vessels to the fleet over the next five years—18 torpedo gunboats, 42 cruisers and 10 battleships, 8 of the first class; these were the ships which were to give meaning to the doctrine of 'command'—'On you will come the curse of all the land if that old England fall, which Nelson left so great—.' Appropriately enough they were evolved battleships.

The general features of the battleships were conceived at a special meeting of the Board of Admiralty in August 1888, at which the questions of speed, coal endurance, freeboard, principal and secondary armament, and armour protection were debated separately; the Board's conclusions were then endorsed at a wider meeting in November chaired by the First Lord, Lord George Hamilton, and including among other officers the directors of naval construction and naval ordnance. In both these discussions the ruling considerations were guns and protection against gunfire in a high-speed, sea-keeping vessel; the former confusion of torpedo and ramming theory had been dropped and these ships were gun platforms to dictate a stand-off fight and keep station in all weathers. The 13.5-inch breech-loaders which had already proved themselves were chosen for the main armament; four were to be mounted *en barbette* to allow a high freeboard—18 feet as against 11¼ feet for a turret ship of the same form and dimensions—'in two protected stations situated at a considerable distance apart, each pair of guns having an arc of training of about 260 degrees...all four of these guns to be available on each broadside'. The secondary armament of ten 6-inch QF guns was to be placed 'in a long central battery situated between the two heavy gun stations, and so disposed that there should be practically no interference with the fire of any one gun by that of any other'.[18] This was the disposition of armament in the 'Admirals' and 'Trafalgars'; it was preferred to the French system of dispersing the main guns in four separate barbettes, as the greater weight of armour required to protect the separated positions and the interference to the secondary armament of their fire, might outweigh any advantages. As for the 'central citadel' principle of concentrating the heavy guns at mid-length and thickening the armour by diminishing its area, this was ruled out 'in view of the risk of simultaneous disablement of the heavy guns, and the interference of those guns with the effective fighting of the auxiliary armament'.[19]

For protection, there was substantial support for a complete waterline belt, but this was rejected in favour of a shorter but thicker belt about two-thirds of the total length of the ship—like the 'Trafalgars'—with an underwater armoured deck extending to the ends. Above the belt, which was closed at both ends by transverse armoured bulkheads, 4-inch side armour was to be laid outside coal bunkers subdivided into compartments. This was due to the 'development of high explosive [shells] and QF guns of large calibre', and because French experiments had shown that 4-inch steel armour, while quite insufficient to resist penetration, did burst shells outside and so minimise destruction. In the event more weight became available during the detailed design work and this secondary armour was increased to 5-inch. Above it the 6-inch QF guns were carried on two decks, again 'in view of the development of high explosives ...to secure the widest possible distribution of the guns'. The speed was to be 15 knots for continuous steaming, with 17 available for spurts.

The specifications were left with the new Director of Naval Construction, William White:

> In the preliminary stages the processes [of design] are necessarily tentative and subject to correction. The various features of design are to a large extent, interdependent. At the outset the dimensions, form and displacement are undetermined. Yet upon them depends the power which the engines must develop to give the desired speed, the weight of the hull and the weight of certain parts of the equipment. In the finished ship the sum of the weights of the hull structure, propelling apparatus, equipment, coals and load must equal the displacement to the specified load line. Apart from experience a problem involving so many unknown factors could scarcely be solved. On the basis of experience, recorded data and model experiments it is dealt with readily. Approximate dimensions and form are first assumed. The weight of the hull is then approximated to for the system of construction adopted and the type of ship. An estimate of the probable engine power is made...[20]

White fixed the dimensions of the new class, the 'Royal Sovereigns', at 380 feet by 75, giving a length/breadth ratio of 1:5.07—against 1:4.82 for the 'Admirals' and 1:5.5 or more for the French ships—and the displacement at 14,360 tons. The belt was 18-inch compound armour which stood three feet above the waterline, 5½ feet below, and was topped by a 3-inch steel deck; at either end pear-shaped barbettes 17 inches thick rose through two decks to protect the ammunition supply, the fixed loading positions and turntables for the great guns which were carried 23 feet above the water. Between the barbettes, the lower tier of two 6-inch QF guns on each broadside were housed in 6-inch steel casemates in the ship's side, the three above on the open deck were unprotected save for thin steel shields which revolved with them. This lack of protection for the guns' crews of main and secondary batteries was the main fault of the class, particularly as no less than 32 per cent of displacement was devoted to armour. However, it was a choice deliberately made, and never regretted. The last of the class, *Hood*, was built with turrets instead of barbettes (thus with one deck less freeboard due to additional topweight) and proved inferior as a sea-keeper and at firing practice.

Curiously, the French had by now abandoned open barbettes and adopted cylindrical turrets both for main and secondary armament for their one contemporary big ship, the *Brennus*, of 11,200 ships. This ship, designed before the 'Royal Sovereigns', had the same disposition of main armament at both ends and secondary armament grouped on two levels between although she was otherwise in the typical French style with complete waterline belt, pronounced tumble-home and piled-up superstructure. The Russian ships under construction had a similar gun arrangement, so did the latest Brin designs for the Italian Navy, also designed before the 'Royal Sovereigns'. As planned, these large Italian ships of 13,500 tons were to be protected on the lines of the *Italia*, that is with a submerged armoured deck, cellular subdivision about the waterline, armoured ammunition tubes to upper deck barbettes and *no side armour at all*. But by the time that the first one, *Re Umberto*, was launched in October 1888 it was obvious that the QF had made such schemes as absurd as Reed had always maintained. Something had to be done, and it was decided to spread 3.9-inch steel over the whole of the side between the barbettes, an additional weight of 900 tons paid for by reducing the thickness of barbette and deck armour.

Of all the battleships of the late eighties, roughly similar as they were in armament distribution, there is no doubt that the final class, the 'Royal Sovereigns', were outstanding for balance between offence, protection, speed and sea-keeping, and when all were complete in the remarkably short space of five years they 'provided the British Navy with the finest group of fighting ships afloat', according to the First Sea Lord. They were the model of the battleship which served as the basis for all subsequent designs. Meanwhile they served as the symbol for Britain's 'empire of the seas':

> They sat in the water with majesty and distinction. For the first time since the *Devastation* set a new standard for unsightliness, a British battleship presented a proud, pleasing and symmetrical profile which was unmatched by any other warship afloat, initiating a new era of vulcanic beauty after two decades of sullen and mishapen misfits.[21]

As if to mark this consummation, a book appeared which opened the eyes of the world to battlefleet doctrine—*The Influence of Sea Power on History*, by Alfred Thayer Mahan. The impact was astonishing; it was as if this was the tablet the European nations had been awaiting. Even British officers, whose chief defect according to Mahan was that they were not *instruit* nor ever disposed to become so, that they preferred to deal with problems as they arose rather than analyse them beforehand, began to find an interest in 'theory'.

> It was not until Captain Mahan wrote *The Influence of Sea Power on History* that the curtain was raised and the study of naval strategy became universal. I can remember no event in my time in the Navy so epoch-making as the publication of Mahan's first works...[22]

Just how epoch-making it was in practice is debatable. Kaiser Wilhelm II, recently ascended, made *Sea Power* and its weighty successors his bedside reading—but then he was already a convinced and enthusiastic big-ship man, having acquired his passion as a boy, watching and going aboard the ships of the British fleet from his grandmother, Queen Victoria's palace in the Isle of Wight. Then again the British Admiralty had always worked on a battlefleet policy, first instinctively and later guided by the Colomb school —to which Mahan acknowledged his debt. The French and Russians continued, despite Mahan, to strive to get around Britain's battlefleet policy with cruiser warfare. America and Japan appeared to heed the doctrine, but both were in an expansive mood at the time, and probably the 'Royal Sovereigns' provided just as good a lesson in practical sea power as Mahan in theory; the leader in any field will be made the model for aspirants, as the French army was before Sedan. So it is doubtful if Mahan had anything more than marginal influence on the battleship story, perhaps stiffening those who were already predisposed towards great ships, weakening the arguments of the weaker *guerre de course* men.

If the influence of Mahan on Sea Power was more apparent than real, it is also true that there has never been a more influential exposition of the battlefleet doctrine, which ruled naval thought for the rest of the battleship era. Here are its two most important faces. From Napoleon's wars:

> The English fleets girdled the shores of France and Spain...step by step and point by point the rugged but disciplined seamen, the rusty and battered, but well-handled ships blocked each move of their unpractised opponents. Disposed in force before each arsenal of the enemy, and linked together by chains of smaller vessels, they might fail now and again to check a raid,

but they effectually stopped all grand combinations of the enemy's squadrons.[23]

And of the war against trade:

This *guerre de course* as the French call it...must if successful, greatly embarrass the foreign government and distress its people. Such a war however cannot stand alone; it must be *supported*...unsubstantial and evanescent in itself it cannot reach far from its base. That base must be either home ports or some solid outpost of national power...a distant dependency or a powerful fleet...It was not the policy of 1667 (when Charles II of England maintained a maritime war with cruisers and privateers only), but Cromwell's powerful fleets of ships-of-the-line in 1652 that shut the Dutch merchantmen in their ports and caused the grass to grow in the streets of Amsterdam.[24]

Usage and Abusage: 1880s and 1890s

By the end of the eighties the strategic use of the battleship had been clearly defined and was clearly understood: as a result and because of rapid ordnance developments, the mature battleship had emerged, at least in design. What had not yet emerged was a clear tactical doctrine; this was not surprising because those tactical exercises which were held had to be conducted with all the curious ships and weaponry created during the experimental years, many with an accent on ahead fire and ramming. Besides this, emphasis had moved from steam evolutions which might be performed against a hostile fleet towards manoeuvres either to avoid or press home a torpedo boat attack. Nonetheless, there was some advance. So far as the British service was concerned, the evidence comes from the manual of naval manoeuvres, 1889:

> The term 'group' as a formation does not appear in the revised General Signal Book. In the opinion of a large number of officers the arrangement of ships in the scalene triangle...was undesirable, being awkward for manoeuvring and difficult to maintain; whilst in action the fire of one ship in the group necessarily enveloped her consorts in smoke...[1]

This cut out one transitional tactic already condemned by Philip Colomb as against all principles of concentration and mutual support. There are other signs in the book that a good deal of thought and practical experience had gone into providing signals which would enable commanders-in-chief to form close-order lines ahead and abreast and lines of bearing from the usual cruising formations of divisions in line ahead disposed abeam; these were the essential bricks on which the tacticians of the nineties built. And there is evidence from the 1891 annual manoeuvres, the first since 1885 to investigate tactical rather than strategic questions, that the majority of senior officers taking part favoured line ahead for battle formation, or indented line ahead—in effect two parallel lines ahead with the second line ships covering the spaces between the first line ships instead of lying abreast of them. These manoeuvres, copying the French exercises of the previous year, attempted to obtain scientific results. The two opposing squadrons passed each other in different formations, and fired blank as rapidly as they could, tabulating the results as if all shots inside 2,000 yards had hit, and thus finding out which formation was the best for gunfire. Those shots which would have struck their target within 15 degrees of a right angle were classified as 'beam', and all others as 'wide'. Significantly the old favourite 'line abreast'—for ramming—was only tried once, and divisions in quarter line astern once; all the other passes were made in line ahead, four times, and indented line ahead, twice.

The actual results were difficult to analyse; all that could be said with certainty was that the lighter the gun the more shots it could get off in a given time, and if it was a QF the barrel fairly sizzled—which was disappointing after such a serious attempt to copy *la méthode scientifique*. In the one pass which might have been illuminating, that between line ahead, the obvious formation for broadside gunned ships, and line abreast, the line abreast squadron, having the only ship with a battery of QF guns, won by 46–35 'beam' hits, 535–164 'wide' hits.[2] So much for the artificial conditions of peace exercises. In fact Philip Colomb had already come to the conclusion that line ahead was the only formation that made sense, and that line abreast had neither strength nor flexibility; he was the hardest-headed naval thinker of the time.

Meanwhile the French were undecided between line ahead, double indented line ahead (more or less a rectangle or 'wedge' of ships) and 'groups'. Those who favoured 'groups' differed on whether they should be homogenous or composed of different types with different strong points; probably the weight of opinion in their 1890 naval manoeuvres favoured groups of three with one strong bow-fire ship and two strong broadside vessels—so much had ship design in the ramming era left its mark on tactics. This concern with a faulty and essentially transitional formation suggests that the French were some way behind the British at this time. Line ahead did, however, have strong support from some officers because of its flexibility 'and the possibility of the admiral leading in battle without signals',[3] but whether this survived theoretical failures during the manoeuvres is not clear; for as in the British mock battles line ahead lost to line abreast, and it was concluded afterwards that the leading ship in line ahead would be crushed by concentrated fire from the enemy's heavy guns. The image of opposing fleets charging directly at each other and passing on opposite courses was still fixed in tactical theory.

Of the authorities who went into print at this time, only two, Colomb, and the Frenchman Larminat, came out in favour of line ahead: Larminat's exposition was reminiscent of the classic French tacticians, particularly Morogues, in its stress on mutual support between ships-of-the-line, and the ability to concentrate easily on any part of the enemy. Both pointed out that line ahead was easily formed, easily maintained, left captains free to fight their ships without watching signals or bearings, and was the most flexible formation possible. By contrast other Frenchmen, particularly those associated with the *jeune école*, advocated complicated group, line abreast, or quarter line charges, as did an astonishing number of Italian authorities still transfixed by the brilliance of Tegetthoff's attack at Lissa, and favouring group attack in double quarter line — charging arrowheads of ships. As most of the Italian big ships were either unprotected by side armour or dangerously 'soft-ended', thus only suitable for long range stand-off duels when their great guns might have had some advantage, they had less excuse than most other tacticians.

The inference from all this is that Britain was as far ahead in tactics as she was in ship design. When ship design finally moved back to broadside emphasis as it did with the appearance of the 'Royal Sovereigns' in the early nineties, 'line ahead' was ready. In the British tactical exercises of 1895, the first held since 1891, Admiral Seymour's general orders stated:

If possible I shall form single line ahead with the battle squadron, and place the cruisers in cruising formation No. 1... This formation is intended to resemble what might be done in actual war when closing with an enemy's fleet. The admiral would thus have ahead of him only three scouts well within signal call, which could soon get out of the way, and no friendly ships would intervene between the line of battle and the enemy. Furthermore the battle column would have the mobility of a single line, as the cruisers could easily get out of its way...and in the event of the enemy charging through the battle line, powerful cruisers thus stationed would be well placed to ram the enemy's battle ships the moment they emerged on that side.[4]

Seymour's reiteration of the phrase 'line of battle' which had been discredited since the beginning of the ironclad revolution, is in its way historic; it marks clearly the end of the period of transitional tactics. There are other indications from other navies: the Japanese had fought in line ahead at the Battle of the Yalu—about which more below—and the German service, according to Tirpitz, had 'discovered line tactics' during tactical exercises 1892–4; 'the main feature of these was to keep the enemy in the centre of our line no matter how he manoeuvred'. On the basis of these results Tirpitz reintroduced the term *Linienschiff*.

This evidence of mental activity among naval officers of the eighties and nineties does not accord with the many memoirs which have come down from the period; this is because it was confined to relatively few exceptional figures and was manifest mainly in reports which made no great stir as they circulated; by contrast the old navy of sail-trained officers and men made a loud and immediate impact, especially on the younger officers.

> The eighties and early nineties were years in which the old officers were still embedded in sails and all the thought that pertained to them. They hated engines and modern guns; the mine and torpedo were anathema to them...nor had they the technical education that was now being given to young officers to enable them to make use of...modern material.[5]

This sort of criticism by the young men was in part due to rapid change and the natural resistance to it by successive generations, in part to the rigid authoritarianism of the age and the service, which made any 'dialogue' between senior and junior difficult. 'He was considered a smart officer who could put the fear of God into everyone, including his own second in command...no one for example thought any the worse of a certain captain who during General Drill shouted at the quartermaster to bring him a bucket because the commander made him sick.'[6] At the top of the apex of 'respect for rank and passive obedience in thought and action'[7] were the admirals, who kept their own counsel with God. As tactics and fleet handling were the prerogative of these men it is not surprising that lieutenants were left with the impression that no progress was being made. There was another reason, at least in the British service: the school of naval historians and historically-minded naval officers had long since established the doctrine that the indecisive naval encounters of the first three-quarters of the eighteenth century had been the result of the rigid code of fighting instructions then in force, consequently any tactical dogma had become suspect. At the same time the historical school saw with

Napoleon and de la Gravière that the real battle winner was the spirit that animated officers and men, not the *matériel* with which they fought—a truly remarkable doctrine after Sedan and in the midst of a *matériel* revolution. In naval terms this meant the spirit of individual captains in keeping their ships within the modern equivalent of Nelson's close range, and of 'the men behind the guns' in keeping up such a hail of fire that they demoralized enemy guns' crews. Such a doctrine easily became a formula for rapid rather than especially accurate fire, and mêlée. And while a few leading spirits had re-established 'line of battle' by the nineties to their own satisfaction, the accepted tactical feeling until the end of the century was undoubtedly for mêlée, a ramming, boarding mêlée at that; this explains how other junior officers later 'discovered' line of battle for themselves.

However, such theoretical arguments give an unbalanced picture; theorising was not endemic. More obvious in all navies was the stress on competitive but often redundant drills, rush, show, ceremonial, excessive 'housemaiding'—in short all the natural results of a long maritime peace. This was especially marked in the British service whose total ascendancy was held responsible for the peace, and it was nowhere more evident than in the Mediterranean squadron, where the pick of the battlefleet was to be found. Here is a view from the lower deck in 1886; the scene is Malta Harbour:

Monday morning was devoted to general sail drill, when ship competed with ship for first place, and a sacrifice of life and limb was thought a cheap price if the object could be attained. Not that commanding officers were careless of their men, it was the men who were careless of themselves, for a spirit of wild rivalry animated the fleet when evolutions were under way, and if accidents happened, why, it was part of the game; certainly any commanding officer who had insisted on the precautions laid down by the regulations would have found his ship eternally last, and would have earned the contempt of his men for being a milksop...Every evening the upper yards were sent down, some times the topgallant masts as well, and every morning at 8 o'clock they were crossed. This evolution only took a very few minutes but it was more keenly contested than any other. The upper yard men were specially picked men, being chosen on account of their smartness aloft, and to be referred to as the smartest royal yard man in the fleet was to reach a pinnacle of fame...the eyes of the whole fleet were on these men, who were the star actors of the piece. It may not have been much use from the point of view of war efficiency, but it was just glorious while it lasted![8]

Sails had already been dropped from first class battleships but they were still useful for all other classes in case of engine break-down and as a steadying influence in a gale; then as these arguments grew more far-fetched towards the end of the eighties with the introduction of twin screws and other technical developments, the debate turned increasingly on the qualities of nerve, hardihood, physical fitness which sailors acquired in the gymnasium of the rigging. From there in the British service it went spiralling up in flights of fancy which would have delighted Edward Lear. As British seamen had laid the foundations of her empire, so any decline in British seamanship—that was understood as sailing sea-manship—would see 'the decline of the British Empire'. There were serious aspects to all this, or would have been if other navies had not been equally wedded to sail; they were put cogently and wittily by Captain C. C. Penrose Fitzgerald, himself a superb sailing ship-handler, in a lecture to the Royal United Service Institution in 1887:

> The retention of masts and sails in men of war diverts so much attention and energy and resources of both officers and men from the real work of their profession, and from the study of modern naval warfare...Evolutions aloft are so attractive and so showy, and there is so much swagger about them, our admirals have always so highly commended and attached so much value to the smart shifting of topsails or topgallant-sails and so many first lieutenants have worked their promotions out of the successful cultivation of this sort of seamanship in their ship's companies, that we seem to have lost sight of the fact that it has nothing to do with the fighting efficiency of a ship in the present day. I know it is said that a ship's company which is smart at drill aloft is smart at everything else. This I beg leave to doubt...we don't teach men to make hats if we want them to make boots...[9]

Fitzgerald suggested that if it were necessary to attune the men to danger 'they could be given so many hours a day to fiddle with the live heads of Whitehead torpedoes...or set to work to hammer sensitive fuzes into filled shells'; he ended on a note which has been echoed in most memoirs from this period: 'We are not ready for war, and thus we invite attack.'

Alongside the sailing cult went an enthusiasm for brightwork and polish, some of whose manifestations were, again, more appropriate to Lear or Lewis Carroll than a fighting service. While British naval constructors were evolving the modern battleship, Admiralty strategists pondering over the implications of a Franco-Russian battlefleet junction in the Mediterranean, their battleship commanders were devoting enormous energy and time to having the great guns burnished until they blazed under the Mediterranean sun, the massive armoured battery doors taken off their hinges and similarly rubbed up, the watertight doors below decks filed to take a shine until they were no longer watertight, even the ring bolts on deck polished and lovingly fitted with little flannel nightcaps to protect them between inspections. A sailor looking back from 20 years on saw it all as 'excruciatingly funny'.

> No one realized it at the time, and I am sure that we all had a dim idea that the efficiency of the ship rested in the proper polish of a battery door. After all man is the outcome of his environment, and had anyone on that ship been so far ahead of his time as to suggest that fighting efficiency lay in knowing how to shoot with the guns, and not polishing them, he would have been looked on as a lunatic and treated accordingly.[10]

As the last sailing ironclads were progressively replaced by modern mastless battleships in the early nineties the paint and brightwork cult reached a peak. The yellow funnels, white upperworks, black hulls, timber and brasswork allowed a commander plenty of scope for his decorative talents and 'money spent on gold leaf, cleaning material etc. was recognized as a good investment for promotion.' Meanwhile the panache of the sailing evolutions had been replaced by a more mechanical, but none the less impressive and intricate formation steaming.

> Tactics took the form of quadrille-like movements carried out at equal speed in accordance with geometrical diagrams in the signal book. These corybantic exercises, which entirely ignored all questions of gun and torpedo fire, laid tremendous stress on accuracy and precision of movement. Exactitude of station-keeping and rigidity of formation were everything...[11]

Such was the background to the final, disastrous demonstration of the power of the ram in the British Navy. It occurred on 22 June 1893, off Tripoli, French North Africa. The Mediterranean squadron —eight battleships and five cruisers under the command of Vice Admiral Sir George Tryon flying his flag in the *Victoria*—was performing a showy manoeuvre to get the ships into station for anchoring. This involved the fleet steaming in two parallel columns *past* the anchorage, then reversing its course by each column turning inwards, ships in succession as they reached the leaders' turning point, thus preserving the order of the fleet for anchoring. It was not a particularly dangerous manoeuvre provided that the two columns were a sufficient distance apart to start with; the ships had turning circles of three and a half cables without juggling with the engines (of which Sir George disapproved) and a distance of eight or nine cables between the columns would have been ample for safety. The odd thing is that Sir George, who was an acknowledged master-mind at steam manoeuvres, had a curious blind spot about this one. He had ordered it at least once before in the 1890 Annual Manoeuvres when his two columns were only four cables apart; on that occasion the danger had been brought to his attention in time. Now, three years later, Tryon ordered it performed from a starting distance of six cables. Again he was warned, this time by his own staff commander before the signal for forming the fleet in columns was made, and again Tryon apparently saw the danger and agreed, 'Yes, it shall be eight cables.'

However, the staff commander had no sooner left the great man's presence than Tryon sent for his flag lieutenant and ordered him to make the signal for the fleet, which was steaming in line abreast, to form columns of divisions in line ahead, columns to be *six* cables apart; at the same time he handed him a slip of paper with the figure '6' written on it, and nothing else. When this signal was hoisted, but before it was hauled down and made executive, the staff commander saw it flying and told the flag lieutenant to go below and make sure that the admiral meant six cables. The lieutenant did so but Tryon replied shortly, 'Leave it at six cables.'

There are several clues to the disaster that resulted; the first is that men did not argue with Sir George Tryon. He was an iron disciplinarian. The next is that he was famous for the novelty and precision of his fleet manoeuvres; he was not typical of what some of the younger officers liked to believe was the old school of mindless martinets who ordained 'corybantic exercises' because they had nothing better to do; he was well aware of the legacy of a long peace and Britain's undisputed superiority and was constantly trying to shake his captains out of complacent formalism by thrusting unexpected situations upon them and devising novel manoeuvres which would make them think. He was acknowledged a mastermind at it, and recognized as one of the brightest stars in the service.

The signal was hoisted, and at 2.20 p.m. made executive; the battleships began to fall back on the leaders of their divisions,

HMS *Victoria*, and six cables on her port beam, HMS *Camperdown*, one of the 'Admiral' class flying the flag of Rear Admiral A. H. Markham. Shortly afterwards the two columns, one of six ships, the other of five, rounded the light tower at the south-western side of the roughly semi-circular bay of Tripoli and set course east by north directly for the eastern shore. Three-quarters of an hour later while the officers of the fleet were wondering what surprise Tryon had in store to deflect them from the shoals that spread out from the land ahead, the fatal flags broke out from the *Victoria*'s yard-arm; as there was no single signal for the manoeuvre there were two hoists: 'SECOND DIVISION ALTER COURSE IN SUCCESSION 16 POINTS TO STARBOARD' and inferior to this, FIRST DIVISION ALTER COURSE IN SUCCESSION 16 POINTS TO PORT. There was bewilderment in the ships astern as they looked at their opposite numbers in the column only 1,200 yards distant; in the *Camperdown* there was incredulity. Markham said, 'It's impossible. It's an impossible manoeuvre,' and he ordered his own flags to be kept at the dip to indicate that he did not understand, at the same time ordering his flag lieutenant to semaphore the *Victoria* and ask the commander-in-chief if he wished the evolution performed as indicated. Before this could be accomplished, Tryon, impatient at the *Camperdown*'s delay, directed his own flag lieutenant to signal her and while the message was being spelled out, 'WHAT ARE YOU WAITING FOR?' the *Camperdown*'s pendants were hoisted at the *Victoria*'s yardarm as a very public rebuke for her tardiness; she was now the only ship which had not hoisted her flags close up.

Markham looked at the land and the shoal water towards which the fleet was steaming at 8¾ knots, then back to the *Victoria*'s flags.

> It then flashed across my mind that there was only one inter-
> pretation of the signal and that was that I was to put my helm
> down and turn 16 points to starboard and the *Victoria* would
> ease her helm and circle round outside my division. I was all
> the more led to believe this as the signal to the second division
> was hoisted superior to that of the first division. I conferred
> hurriedly with the flag captain and Captain Johnstone. They were
> both of my way of thinking, and seeing that was the only
> safe way of performing the evolution I hoisted the signal...
> THE COURT: With the columns at six cables apart, supposing the
> ships to turn towards each other with their full helm, did the
> absolute certainty of a collision occur to you?
> MARKHAM: Most certainly.[12]

Moments afterwards, the *Victoria*'s two hoists were hauled down not one after the other as Markham had supposed they would be, but simultaneously; the *Victoria*'s wheel was put hard over for a port turn, and Markham ordered the *Camperdown*'s wheel hard over for a starboard turn. Meanwhile all eyes were on the green and red balls at the *Victoria*'s yardarm, which indicated how her helm was placed; Markham ordered his flag lieutenant to let him know when she eased her helm. He also took the precaution of having the men sent to collision stations!

At the same time on the *Victoria*'s fore bridge Captain the Hon. Maurice Bourke had been trying to indicate his own apprehensions to Tryon. He had first very audibly directed a midshipman to take the distance to the *Camperdown*, then remarked to Tryon that they would come very close to her and then, as the two ships' bows swung closer still, asked for permission to put the port engine astern. Tryon made no reply; he was watching the ships following astern. Bourke asked again, 'May I go astern full speed with the port screw?' Tryon turned and seeing the *Camperdown* approaching head on and only 450 yards away, replied 'Yes.'

Markham, meanwhile, had been deterred from easing his own helm to circle outside the *Victoria*, mainly because he was still convinced that Tryon was going to circle outside him, but when at last he realized that Tryon was not intending any such course he ordered his starboard engine reversed, then 'Full astern both!', meanwhile ordering all watertight doors closed.

The last-minute engine orders were too late to save the situation; the momentum of the ships carried them inexorably together, and the *Camperdown*, which had turned on a slightly wider circle, struck the flagship on the starboard bow with her ram at something greater than a right angle, and unfortunately in the way of a transverse watertight bulkhead; as the ships continued to swing the ram tore a hole in the side over 100 square feet before they disengaged. Up above Tryon murmured as if to himself, 'It was all my fault.'

At first, as the *Victoria* listed eight degrees to starboard with the inrush of water and dippered her foredeck, which was low enough at the best of times, no immediate danger was apprehended; the order to close watertight doors had been given a minute before the collision, and the cellular compartmentation in the region of the blow was expected to keep her afloat. However, at least three minutes was normally required to close all watertight doors, and on this occasion as it was a hot Mediterranean afternoon every door, port and vent which could be open was. So the list increased, the fore deck became awash and the sea started pouring below through the mooring bitts which also served as vents; very soon the massive fore turret with its 110-ton guns was left as an island in the sea. Just abaft it was the battery deck and as the starboard door and several ports had been left open when the foredeck party retired the water began to pour in, destroying the remaining stability of the ship. She gave a lurch, and twelve minutes after the collision turned over until her keel was uppermost, then sank bows first, taking Tryon and nearly all her engine and stokehold complement with her; of her total crew of nearly 700, 358 were lost.

The most serious question for the Admiralty, indeed the real shock after the first incredulity at Tryon's order had worn off, was how a first class battleship struck in a well-subdivided position well forward of the vitals had sunk so quickly—why she had sunk at all. This was answered in the official report: 'had the doors and ports been closed and the entry of water into the upper deck battery thus prevented, then calculation shows that sorely wounded as she was, the *Victoria* would not have capsized.'[13] Apart from this, the great number of watertight doors which needed closing was obviously a great source of danger in any emergency and a potentially fatal defect in the principle of watertight compartmentation. But nothing was done to reduce the number in future designs as it was felt that access and habitability would be too severely restricted if all bulkheads were solid and the compartments could only be approached from above.

The question that has puzzled the scores of commentators on the disaster ever since is how Tryon came to make his fatal miscalculation and how he, apparently alone of all the senior officers in the fleet, failed to see that his own manoeuvre was impossible despite several warnings from his own staff. The best solution to the problem, from Admiral Mark Kerr, is that he confused a half circle turn with a quarter circle turn. 'Half circle turns are very seldom executed, while quarter circle turns in manoeuvres are constantly made. When manoeuvring the fleet one gets accustomed to allowing two cables of sea room for a quarter circle turn.' Allowing two cables for each column and two cables between the columns for anchoring, the result would have been six cables as ordered. Afterwards Mark Kerr spoke of his theory to a lieutenant who had been officer of the watch in the *Victoria* at the time of the disaster; he replied 'that was exactly the reason'.

Markham was the Admiralty's chosen scapegoat. Despite the court martial findings that 'it would be fatal to the best interests of the service to say that he was to blame for carrying out the orders of the commander-in-chief present in person', the Admiralty issued and published a minute regretting that he had not carried out his first intention of semaphoring his doubts about the signal.

For the most interesting practical lesson in tactics and the naval *matériel* of the early 1890s it is necessary to look east to Japan, another island nation with an industrious population in a mood of expansion. Although she lay in much the same position off Asia as Great Britain off the coast of Europe, she had until recently used the sea as a barrier instead of a highway; this had started in the seventeenth century when realization of the greater power of European guns and fighting ships had forced her into self-imposed total isolation. When in mid-nineteenth century she had been forcibly opened to western trade, the same realization of western fighting superiority had been the main spur behind a complete reversal of her former policy; she had plunged into forced industrial revolution and westernization, centred on ships, guns and heavy engineering. And as the European nations through the following decades penetrated into the neighbouring mainland of China and Manchuria, opening up spheres of influence for trade and annexing territories from that once great empire, Japan also developed an export trade, first in hand-made silks and cottons, then in machined products which undercut western goods in price and began to penetrate the rest of the Pacific to the west coast of America.

Meanwhile her shipping was able to prosper, as British lines had rather neglected the area, and from 1888 a system of shipbuilding and navigating subsidies provided further stimulation. At the same time she was acquiring a modern navy. She could not afford battleships, so she adopted a policy very similar to Italy's, centred on fast but not-so-large cruisers with complete armoured decks below water, coal and cellulose or cork in cellular compartments about the waterline, and a heavy armament. The first of these were built by Armstrongs and launched in 1885. They were followed by six more powerful vessels, two built in France to French design, two in Britain, and two at her own yards at Yokosuka, as copies of each type. All these mounted broadsides of 6-inch or 4.7-inch QF guns; in addition the three to French design each carried one great 66-ton 12.6-inch gun in a 12-inch stel barbette on the upper deck. By 1894, with these advanced vessels as the spearhead of her fleet and with an equally well-equipped army, she felt able to take her new-found Western spirit of technology and commercial expansion a stage further, and like the westerners themselves lop off pieces of continental Asia for herself.

The first piece she chose was the peninsula of Korea, barely 100 miles from her southern islands and of great strategic value, flanking the southern entrance to the Sea of Japan, commanding the Yellow Sea and the northern Chinese commercial ports. She established disputes with China over this nominally independent territory, declared war with her guns in a manner to become familiar in the next century, and started landing troops in the north west of the peninsula. When the Chinese, finding they could not concentrate their own troops fast enough by land, also started moving them by sea, using their warships to cover the transports, they came in sight of the Japanese fleet off the mouth of the River Yalu, and battle ensued.

The main Chinese strength lay in two battleships, *Chen Yuen* and *Ting Yuen*, about 7,500 tons each, which had been built in 1881–2 as smaller versions of the *Inflexible*, but with their main armament mounted *en barbette* instead of in turrets. Their central citadels were protected by 14-inch compound armour and each mounted four 12-inch, 35-ton Krupp guns in two pairs arranged in echelon, so that they all had direct ahead and astern fire; their broadside arcs were, however, restricted by the opposite guns and the funnels and other obstructions. They also mounted a 6-inch breech loader at either end, some light guns and two torpedo tubes. Their unarmoured ends were closely subdivided, packed with cork around the sides, and protected below the water by a 3-inch armoured deck. They had been the Barnaby ideal of well-balanced second class battleships when originally commissioned. Now, their absence of QF guns and their speed, which had sunk to 10 knots at most, rendered them obsolescent. By contrast the latest Japanese cruiser *Yoshino*, built by Armstrongs, could make 23 knots.

Apart from the two big ships, the Chinese had another pair of smaller barbette ships each mounting two 8¼-inch Krupp breech-loaders and protected by cork cellular subdivision and a short armoured belt whose top was flush with the waterline, therefore little use; and also six smaller cruisers. The fatal defects of all these ships were low speed and a complete lack of medium or large calibre QF guns; it was calculated after the battle that all together could only fire 33 rounds in 10 minutes, against the Japanese 185. Besides this the service was poorly maintained and corruption was rife in the administration; while the accommodation of the ships was exquisitely carved, lacquered and gilded, some of the shells for the heavy guns had been filled with sand instead of bursting charges, or left empty.

The Japanese fleet on the other hand was efficient to the point of fanaticism. Its officers had been brought up in the warrior code of the *Bushi*, which imposed knightly ideals of courage, simplicity, self-sacrifice and absolute loyalty to the Emperor above all personal interests. They despised luxury, even pleasure, as corrupting influences, and lived only for their profession, working longer hours than their men, exposing themselves to more danger, eating the same simple food, sleeping like them on a straw mat—all the time training and preparing for war. The naval service, like the army, was a simple extension of the intense nationalism of this emergent nation.

At the Yalu it proved its worth. The Chinese, led by Admiral Ting in the *Ting Yuen*, advanced to action at 6 knots in line abreast; no doubt because all the ships had been built in the 'strong ahead-fire' period. Ting had previously given three principal orders: that all ships should fight in pairs, fight bows-on if possible, and follow his movements if they could; thus he adopted the tactics of the French school, long since discarded in the British, German and even sections of the French service. He placed his two strong ships in the centre of the line, flanked by three smaller ironclads, flanked by the cruisers; the smallest, oldest and weakest were on the right wing.

The Japanese approached this formation in two divisions formed in one long line ahead. Leading was the fast *Yoshino*, with the Japanese-built cruiser of the same class and the two older Armstrong cruisers; these formed the flying squadron. After them came the main body containing the French-designed cruisers with 66-ton guns, led by the *Matsushima* flying the flag of Admiral Ito, and following them were four older and smaller ships which would have been better left out of the battle. Ito headed for the Chinese centre at first, but seeing the weak ships on their right, he altered course across their front and signalled his intentions to attack the right and fight at 2,000 to 3,000 yards; the fleets were then perhaps six miles apart, the sea between them smooth as glass. As the range came down to 5,000 or 6,000 yards the Chinese big ships opened fire, but the shots plunged harmlessly into the water and the Japanese did not reply until some 15 minutes later when the leaders came abreast of the Chinese right wing at something outside 3,000 yards. At the same time they altered to starboard. As they did so Admiral Ting led his two battleships out from the Chinese centre in an attempt to close and perhaps ram the main body of the Japanese.

Almost at once the Chinese force lost cohesion; trying to wheel their front round to face the Japanese attack on the right, they lacked the speed and simply turned in pairs to face the right, becoming hopelessly scrambled as rising waterspouts from the Japanese QF guns, at first several hundred yards short, moved up to them. The Japanese ships, mostly hidden in funnel and gun smoke, meanwhile kept perfect line ahead formation as they passed down the right wing. Then the flying squadron, running out of ships to fight, led around to port 180 degrees and opened their other broadsides as they came back to the weaker Chinese ships, many of which were already ablaze. In the meantime the main Japanese squadron turned to starboard and completed a full turn right around the Chinese, eventually returning to Ting's pair of battleships, which they started to circle like hungry wolves at about 2,000 yards range, firing everything they had, and soon reducing the upperworks to shambles of torn, twisted metal and starting fires whose smoke made it difficult for the gunners to see. The *Chen Yuen* did, however, succeed in putting one 12-inch shell into the *Matsushima's* battery, which burst with devastating effect, firing the ammunition, decimating the guns' crews and forcing her to retire to put out the fires.

The flagship was the third Japanese to be so seriously damaged as to be out of the fight; previously two of the old vessels at the end of the line had come too close to the Chinese heavy guns. Meanwhile four of the Chinese had been destroyed by gunfire and one sunk in collision, and after over four hours of firing the Chinese admiral retired. Sunset was approaching and Ito decided not to pursue, possibly for fear of torpedo attack after dark. Nevertheless it was an undoubted Japanese victory, and while all except the three severely damaged Japanese ships kept the sea, the Chinese put into Port Arthur to effect repairs, only coming out again to retire across the Straits to the harbour of Wei-hai-wai.

As the first fleet engagement since Lissa, the battle attracted a great deal of professional comment and analysis, much of it restatement of previously held convictions. Probably the main verification was the great value of side armour; this was particularly noticeable in the engagement between the two Chinese battleships and the main body of the Japanese, for while these powerful cruisers had been circling and firing continuously, achieving some 200 hits with their QF guns on each of the big ships from short range, they had not destroyed the battleships' flotation or stability, nor had they pierced the central citadel once—the deepest impression they made in the armour was about 3 inches, which makes it improbable that they hit at all with their 66-tonners—and although they had reduced the unarmoured portions to tangled, charred wreckage the total casualties from both battleships had only been 17 killed, 35 wounded. Against this the *Matsushima* had lost 57 killed and 54 wounded; she was however the heaviest sufferer. Among the *jeune école*, of course, the battle was held to prove that unarmoured ships could stand up to and even beat armoured ships. But this was an extreme and unscientific view as the Japanese had only been hit by 10 12-inch and some 60 smaller projectiles and many of these had failed to explode. For the British historical school the Japanese 'hail of fire' from 'decisive range' had been the battle winner—together with the spirit of their officers and men.

As for tactics, line ahead appeared to have proved indisputably the better formation; only a very few diehard theoreticians, noting the faulty disposition of the Chinese line abreast with the heaviest ships in the centre instead of at the wings, doubted it. Fewer still adhered to the 'group' ideas which had been tried by the Chinese, and had led to utter confusion, one fatal ramming and complete lack of cohesion. All in all, and despite the inequality in moral and *matériel* factors, the action suggested that in tactics, design and ordnance the battleship was developing along the right lines. It was noticeable, for instance, that neither ramming nor torpedoes had influenced the fighting at all; the Chinese had fired theirs at about 2,000 yards range, way outside any possibility of hitting and the Japanese had never approached closer than about 1,500 yards, three times Whitehead effective range.

After this action the naval war was confined to troop transporting, Japanese naval bombardments in support of their troops ashore, and torpedo boat attacks on the thoroughly demoralized remnants of Ting's ships in Wei-hai-wei; here the Chinese boom and mine defences proved ineffective and as there were no anti-torpedo boat patrols nor net defences, nor medium calibre QF guns, the Japanese boats were able to get right into the harbour and sink the flagship, *Ting Yuen*, and one other ship for the loss of only two boats and twelve men.

The complete ascendancy that the Japanese Navy attained at the Yalu and subsequently allowed them practically undisputed movement by sea, and they used this to encircle and take Port Arthur and then Wei-hai-wei, where the only remaining Chinese ship of force, the *Chen Yuen*, fell into their hands. Then, holding all the keys to the Yellow Sea Japan imposed a treaty on China which gave her not only Korea and the island of Formosa way to the south, but also the spur of Manchuria just to the west of Korea known as the Liao-Tung peninsula which terminated at Dairen and Port Arthur; she also extracted a cash indemnity perhaps 50 per cent more than the cost of the war.

This sudden triumph of a colonial intruder came as an unpleasant shock to the European powers already in China, particularly Russia: Vladivostock, her principle maritime outlet in the East and the terminal to which the trans-Siberian railway engineers were slowly progressing, was now completely surrounded by Japanese territory and at the mercy of a Japanese naval blockade, moreover Japan had established a commanding foothold in Manchuria, which Russia had long disputed with China, and which she had expected to acquire for herself now that China had become, in the words of one of her contemporary statesmen, an 'outlived Oriental State'.

So when the established colonial powers protested at the Japanese treaty it was Russia, together with her friend and financial partner France, and also Germany in a violently expansionist and opportunist mood, who forced Japan to give up some of her gains, particularly the Liao-Tung peninsula. Russia and France then joined to pay China's war indemnity, as a reward for which the Chinese allowed the trans-Siberian railway to be built straight across Manchuria to Vladivostok. This was a major triumph for Russian diplomacy; when complete the railway and its hinterland became an extension of Russian power in the heart of the disputed province, and gave her a new mobility of force and influence in the area. Not content with this, a Russian fleet two years later took over Port Arthur, the key base which their diplomats had denied the Japanese, and following this Moscow forced a railway concession up the length of the peninsula to become eventually the southern extension of the trans-Siberian.

These cynical and dangerous Russian gains not only increased tensions around the carcass of China, but thrust Japan firmly into what the French and Germans regarded as an Anglo-Saxon orbit: Great Britain and America wanted to preserve China so that she would be open to the trade of all nations, and as Russia became the most immediate threat to this policy, so their interests coincided with Japan's, still smarting with resentment at being denied some of the chief fruits of victory.

Meanwhile Japan was on the way to becoming a first class naval power: in 1895 she had ordered from Britain two 12,300-ton battleships, virtually reduced 'Royal Sovereigns' with 12-inch main armament and 6-inch QF as a secondary battery, and two years later three 15,000-ton ships similar to the British class which followed the 'Royal Sovereigns'. The Russians could scarcely allow such a strong force to go unchallenged if they wished to retain Port Arthur so they introduced a new naval programme in 1898, headed by eight battleships. In keeping with their French *entente* these were in the French style with long or complete waterline belts, great tumble-home, high and mostly unprotected sides, and towering superstructures. Like the French ships their stability was suspect: they were narrow and their main belts rose less than a foot above the waterline. Both main and secondary batteries were, however, protected in turrets.

From the British point of view the emergence of two battleship powers outside Europe, where they could not be blockaded or brought to battle by the Mediterranean or Home squadrons, threatened to compromise the policy of command given expression in the 1889 Naval Defence Act. Although the immediate response was to strengthen the China squadron with second class battleships and to build a class of smaller, lighter draft battleships which could traverse the Suez canal and quickly reinforce the eastern ships, realization was coming that complete sovereignty over the oceans of the world could not be maintained for ever. It was not expressed thus, indeed 'navalists' and 'jingos' were having a high time urging the British public to reckon up their battleships ('Ten, twenty, thirty, there they go...') but in the background there were voices in favour of a formal alliance with Japan to safeguard British trade and interests in the East.

Equally significant, there were stirrings within the Admiralty, again not expressed in policy, for an unofficial alliance with the United States Navy, or at least a pooling of information so that both services could act in concert in support of free trade and the *status quo* in the Pacific. No doubt behind this was a feeling that America and England should spread Anglo-Saxon 'civilised' values throughout the world, but it was also a practical response to the emergence of yet another ocean-going battlefleet outside Europe.

It would have been unthinkable the previous decade. Then the American service had been in a state of absolute and relative decline with its main offensive weapons smooth-bore guns scarcely changed from the Civil War, mounted in turrets of monitors whose design had drawn inspiration from its lessons. Here is Lieutenant William Sims USN on the monitor *Monterey*:

> She is a double-elliptical, high-uffen-buffen, double-turreted, back-acting submarine war junk. She carries two twelve- and two ten-inch guns in round boxes on each end. You put the shell in, close the plugs, get outside, batten down, send the mail and list of probable changes ashore, and touch her off. The following day, when she cooled off, they try it again if enough of the men have come to. She is about the shape of a sweet potato that has bust in the boiling. She draws fourteen feet of mud forward and 16 feet 6 inches of slime aft, and has three feet of discoloured water over the main deck in fair weather...[14]

Even allowing for Sims' sharp critical faculties, this was a re-markably obsolete class of vessel which mirrored the isolationist and essentially coast-defensive views of the United States; the oceans were regarded as a barrier against the iniquities of Europe. The real barrier of course had been the British Navy, behind whose un-conscious shelter industrial eastern America had spread across the entire continent. However that may be, by 1890 the mood had changed. As the American historian, Frederick J. Turner noted, the westward drive had ended at the Pacific shore; the frontier was closed, and expansion, which had been the main fact of American life since the Europeans first landed, would need outlets overseas if it were to be sustained. Simultaneously came Mahan, the epoch-maker or sublime interpreter, showing that Britain's wealth and influence had come from the 'three interlocking rings' of sea power —colonies, trade, battlefleet command of the seas. It is interesting that this message came just as railways, thus inland transport and communication, were set fair to tilt the balance of wealth away from maritime trading nations towards the great continental states. This was nowhere more evident than in the United States itself, which was knit together by a network of steel ways whose manufacture had set new standards of sheer scale and finance. Hand in hand with Mahan and Carnegie were the influential Americans, sounding like British empire-builders who saw that the world would be a much better and safer place if the Anglo-Saxons, with their genius for colonizing and bringing order to barbaric peoples, could between them police a universal order.

Out of it all came a revitalized ocean-going navy, the first three battleships for which, still described as coast-line battleships, were authorized in 1890. These were the 'Indiana' class of 10,300 tons, following the lines of the 'Royal Sovereigns' in shape and hull protection, but with turrets protecting both main and secondary armament, consequently a lower freeboard. True to the late-eighteenth-century policy of the US service of building ships individually more powerful than their European equivalents, these were the most heavily-armed battleships of their time, with a pair of 13-inch breech-loaders at each end, four pairs of 8-inch breech-loaders in turrets at the four corners of the midships superstructure, and four 6-inch and 24 small-calibre QF pieces. This apparently great offensive power was obtained at some cost in speed, only 16 knots, sea-keeping ability, and interference between guns when they were firing. There were other problems too, which were natural to such a new development in the service. Robley Evans as captain of the *Indiana* in 1895 described how in an Atlantic gale both the 8-inch and 13-inch turrets broke loose, destroyed their controlling devices and thrashed from side to side as the ship rolled and pitched; to bring them under control the gun muzzles had to be lashed with hawsers to the towing bitts on the quarterdeck—a desperate task in the storm.

These ships were followed by the *Iowa*, a larger, higher freeboard version launched in 1896, and by two 'Kearsage' and three 'Alabama' class, all launched in 1898. The 'Kearsages' of 11,500 tons were remarkable for having their 8-inch turrets fixed atop the 13-inch turrets and moving with them, a novel idea abandoned because it presented a large target, and risked disablement with one blow, a risk increased, in Sims's opinion, by enormous gunports in the turrets and an uninterrupted ammunition hoist to the magazines directly below. Sims, soon to become one of the most influential officers in the US service, regarded them not as battleships but as 'a crime against the white race', and after serving in the USS *Kentucky* wrote a famous report to the President of the United States, '...the protection and armament of even our most modern battleships are so glaringly inferior in principle as well as in details to those of our possible enemies including the Japanese, and our marksmanship is so crushingly inferior to theirs that one or more of our ships would, in their present condition, inevitably suffer humiliating defeat at the hands of an equal number of enemy's vessels of the same class and displacement.'[15] Of course it is possible to find such criticisms of any country's ships from the officers who served in them, indeed this is a theme of the battleship's evolution; nevertheless the 'Kearsages' were generally poor and unbalanced ships which repeated mistakes long since discovered in the British service. On the other hand the contemporary 'Alabamas', of approximately the same tonnage, were much better balanced, with a longer foredeck, raised forecastle for speed and sea-keeping and a long secondary battery of fourteen 6-inch QF guns on two levels in place of the intermediate 8-inch pieces. These were very similar to reduced British battleships.

Before any of the later classes had been completed, the United States, as if determined to bear out F. J. Turner's expansionist thesis, was engaged in an overseas war. This started with a Cuban rebellion against their Spanish imperial masters and somehow led, through an apparent threat to American lives in the island and a mysterious explosion which destroyed the US cruiser *Maine*, to war between the United States and Spain. During the tense and, on the American part, bellicose period before the actual declaration, the US Navy had been preparing itself with tremendous enthusiasm. Robley Evans, now in command of the latest battleship, *Iowa*, remembered:

> We had constant torpedo drill until each torpedo on board could be made to run with all the accuracy it was capable of. The firing was systematic and continued until the gun captains could hit the target with reasonable certainty...I am sure no such persistent work was ever done before by any fleet.[16]

Before the war was declared on 25 April 1898, the battleship squadron was on its way to Cuba, and shortly afterwards the US China squadron of cruisers and gunboats in the Pacific steamed for Manila, the capital of the Spanish Philipines, where a force of generally older and smaller, certainly less well-trained Spanish cruisers lay behind the protection of shore batteries. The American ships under Commodore Dewey passed the batteries in the early hours of 1 May without being hit, proceeded in line ahead to where the Spanish ships lay at anchor and opened fire while passing at ranges of about 5,000–2,000 yards in a succession of counter-marches; the superior American equipment, drill, and marksman-ship through telescopic sights soon told. The last Spanish gun was silenced shortly after noon.

Meanwhile, in the Caribbean, the main US squadron under Com-modore Schley which contained the *Iowa*, two 'Indiana' class battle-ships, one smaller battleship and two armoured cruisers, was block-ading another Spanish cruiser force which lay behind mines and, as it turned out, obsolete shore batteries in the harbour of Santiago de Cuba; the Spanish admiral, Cervera, knew that his ships could not hope to escape the great guns of the battlefleet waiting outside, but in July he received orders to break out, and he made the attempt with great dash and courage, leading with his flagship, *Maria Teresa*.

She presented a magnificent appearance with her splendid new battle flags and her polished brasswork. Her bright coat of paint was in marked contrast to the lead-coloured, iron-rusted ships that were rushing full speed at her. As she passed the Diamond shoal she swung off to the westward and opened fire smartly with her port broadside and turret guns...[17]

After her three other armoured cruisers charged out 'like mad bulls' making an equally splendid appearance against the calm sea and the clear day. The American force closed and, keeping the Spaniards on their starboard bow in an attempt to get in to torpedo or even ramming range, opened with their starboard forward guns. Then seeing that they did not have the superiority of speed necessary for such tactics they swung around on to a parallel course and chased, firing all the miscellaneous guns on their starboard sides at ranges which soon came down to between 1,600 and 1,200 yards. The leading Spanish ships, caught by the concentrated fire of several battleships, 'rolled and staggered' under the barrage and finally, with flames bursting from shell holes and gun ports in their sides and reaching up to the military tops in the masts, they made for the shore and ran aground. Evans, watching from the *Iowa*'s conning tower found it a 'magnificent sad sight to see these beautiful ships in their death agonies'; the men yelled and cheered until their throats were sore.

In this annihilation the Americans lost one man killed, one wounded, from 33 hits. They themselves had fired some 8,000 rounds and had made 121 countable hits on the cruisers, only two of which had been from large-calibre guns. Most of the damage had been done by the intermediate 8-inch pieces, as a result of which they came back into favour for subsequent US battleships—as it turned out another false trail from action experience. However, the great fires which had consumed all the Spanish craft demonstrated the danger of timber deck fittings, and the danger of ammunition about the decks in action, particularly live torpedoes; these lessons, and of course the value of rapid fire and the difficulty of torpedo and ramming attack, had already been drawn from the battle of the Yalu, but Santiago provided a powerful reinforcement. Subsequent battleships carried all their torpedoes for submerged firing, had their decks beneath the weather decks covered with linoleum instead of timber and had furniture and fittings made from steel.

Manila Bay and Santiago were remarkable demonstrations of the fighting efficiency that the US Navy had acquired in a comparatively short period, or perhaps, like the Yalu, demonstrations of what industrial power harnessed to the sea service could do against a brave but technically backward navy. In any case they were perfect illustrations of the Colomb/Mahan theory of command at sea. Neither the Chinese after the Yalu nor the Spanish after the blockade of Santiago could reinforce or supply their land forces, and both conflicts turned on maritime command.

In the month following the Battle of Santiago, Spain sought an armistice and the United States, after hesitating to lay bare its conscience by the light of the Declaration of Independence, took up the Anglo-Saxon burden, buying from her the Philippines, taking over Puerto Rico and the Pacific island of Guam, and establishing a naval base in Cuba. And in response to her now defined status as a world power with oceanic bases from which to operate, she embarked on programmes for a series of large, fast, very heavily-gunned battleships. These programmes were carried through with such drive and efficiency, not to mention swollen naval budgets under the 'Anglo-Saxon navalist' President Roosevelt, that by 1907 she had risen to second place among the world's navies. Had Mahan sown the seed—or simply caught and expressed the mood of the times?

14

The Age of Battleships

To pick up the main threads of battleship development it is necessary to return to the early 1890s—from as yet peripheral questions in the Pacific to the centre of naval power in London. Here the concern for naval parity with France and Russia combined, and the threat that these two held out to British shipping, grew as the two Continental powers drew closer and more ostentatiously together and increased their naval budgets—apparently in response to the British Naval Defence Act of 1889, though in fact mainly in response to the triple alliance of Germany, Austria and Italy. Germany, the most dynamic industrial and commercial power in Europe whose great conscript army was ever-present along the borders of French thought, had been expanding into Africa, Italy into the Mediterreanean, both under the shield of British naval power which sought as ever to preserve a European 'balance' while remaining aloof from any formal or informal alliance. And it was suspicion of Italian and German building as much as hostility to Britain which provided the stimulus to French naval policy: Bardoux's report to the Senate on the Navy Estimates for 1890, for instance, justified the construction of 40 sea-going or coast defence torpedo boats by comparing the French strength of 146 vessels of this class with 170 German and 145 Italian boats. In the matter of battleships, Bardoux compared 21 French ships, six of which were built of timber and were about to be struck off the Navy list, with 55 British, 16 German and 13 Italian assorted types.[1] The same year an article in the influential Le Yacht, after drawing attention to increased naval estimates in Germany and Italy, concluded, 'As England wishes to be in a position to resist a coalition of any two powers, ought we not in the same way to make it our aim to be on a level with the two Continental powers whose maritime ambition is now so plainly brought to light?'[2] The pressure for increased construction was coming from below as a result of the suspicions and ambitions of the two groupings of major powers in Europe.

Meanwhile both French and Russian building, in despite of Mahan, continued to reflect some of the views of the *Jeune École*—not perhaps so *jeune* since the setbacks to Aube's torpedo boat battle policy but quite as desperately vocal for the war against trade. Whether or not this was directed specifically against Great Britain, hers was the wealthiest maritime empire and the policy held the very greatest dangers for her. Aube made this clear:

> ...a torpedo boat has sighted one of these ocean steamers freighted with a cargo of greater value than that of the richest galleons of Spain; the torpedo boat will follow at a distance, keeping out of sight, and when night comes on will, unobserved, close with the steamer and send to the bottom cargo, crew and passengers, not only without remorse but proud of their achievement. In every part of the ocean similar atrocities would be seen...[3]

While majority French opinion was against such a logical expression of the current ideas about war as a struggle between *peoples*— it was felt that barbarities of this sort would lead to an alliance of all civilized nations against France—there was no doubt that the basic idea could be given more chivalrous and probably more effective expression with fast, ocean-going cruisers. Thus France's 1891 'Gervais' programme, which followed the Naval Defence Act in setting out a fixed sum for naval building over a fixed number of years, in this case £37 millions over 10 years, was for 10 battleships, one coast defence vessel and no less than 45 cruisers, as well as torpedo boats.

This large programme, together with French plans for fortified nests of torpedo boats around the Channel and Atlantic coasts, and a first class naval base at Bizerta on the North African coast, plus Russian battleship building in the Black Sea, from where they could swoop down and join the French Mediterranean squadron, and rumours of a great Russian commerce-raiding cruiser, all combined to produce another series of panics in Britain. This was not confined to the professional alarmists like Lord Charles Beresford, although they had a hand in educating the public, but extended throughout the Board of Admiralty, the government and the shipping and commercial classes. The London Chamber of Commerce, for instance, published a pamphlet in 1893 pointing out that Britain had 12½ million tons of merchant shipping afloat against only 1½ million tons for France and Russia combined, and had sea-borne trade to the value of £970 millions against only £331 millions for France and Russia, yet she had fewer armoured ships in the Mediterranean than the

French and her total tonnage of armoured ships built and building was rather less than France and Russia combined. In these alarms the naval comparisons, so different from the comparisons made by the French, credited the potential enemies with every obsolete coast defence vessel still on the active list and every armoured vessel authorized in their future programmes; in fact neither the French nor the Russians ever succeeded in completing a programme and were never able to build as quickly or for that matter as cheaply as the British. This could not be foreseen, nor counted upon. The country recognized danger, so did the Admiralty, and the first response was to look to the battlefleet, so much were all officers now imbued with the doctrine of Philip Colomb 'that the blockade of the enemy's ports is the main protection, both of the [shipping] routes and of the coaling stations bordering them...'[4]

The Admiralty's own analysis of the situation was:

First Class battleships—December 1893

	England	France	Russia	France + Russia
Built	16	10	4	14
Building	6	5	5	10
Projected	–	3	2	5
	22	18	11	29 by 1898[5]

On the strength of this the new First Sea Lord, Sir Frederick Richards, who had been one of the 'Three Admirals' responsible for the 1888 report which had contributed so much to the Naval Defence Act, recommended a minimum programme of seven first class battleships to give parity with the two powers five years hence, at the same time stressing that 10 ships would be 'desirable' because of Britain's offensive policy.

> They have powerful fleets which can remain sheltered within their harbours until the opportune moment for breaking out presents itself, while the role of our fleets must be one of constant wearying vigilance without any possibility of relaxing from the very outset of war.[6]

Lord Spencer, First Lord of the Admiralty, accepted the minimum proposal for seven battleships at a cost of £7.24 millions and discussed it with the Prime Minister, Gladstone now back in power for the last time. Gladstone, who had lost none of his mid-century Liberal idealism, and particularly detested public expenditure on arms, was shocked; he considered Spencer a traitor to the Liberal cause who had succumbed to a conspiracy of sea lords, and the proposed increase in naval estimates as an act of defiance which 'would end in a race towards bankruptcy by all the powers of Europe'.[7] The entire Cabinet was against him; in the strained international atmosphere of the time—with France and Russia, confident in a recently-published military alliance, pursuing adventurous expansionist policies in Africa and Asia, with the evident danger to British trade in the Mediterranean and the Far East, the ministers reacted according to sound historical precedent, or reflex, when they sided with the sea lords. Here is Admiral Sir Frederick Richards:

There can be no greater danger to the maintenance of the peace of Europe than a relatively weak British Navy. It is abundantly clear that the aim for which France...makes such sacrifices to compete with England on the sea is directed by hostility towards England—the same may be said of Russia in her efforts to become a first class naval power. And there can be little doubt that the navies of these two countries...must be regarded as one in the determination of the naval policy of England...[8]

'Mad! Mad! Mad!' Gladstone fumed, and left public life for ever, a pathetic figure, left behind by the tide of European militarism; he had scarcely gone, in March 1894, before the Cabinet approved the minimum programme for seven battleships, six cruisers, 36 destroyers. This continuation of the naval expansion which had started in 1889 on the urgent grounds of trade protection was now more clearly a policy of deterrence—anything you can build, we can build more of—and better, and quicker. This was literally true. And it did give brief meaning to the phrase Pax Britannica.

The seven battleships were the 'Majestics'. They were of 14,900 tons, virtually enlarged 'Royal Sovereigns' but with a number of improvements and technical refinements. The most obvious of these was the protection afforded the big guns, not turrets in the Coles sense, but enclosing shields with light, sloping tops and 10 inch thick sloping fronts which revolved with the guns above the barbette. Inside the housing at the rear were two hydraulic rammers which moved around with the guns on their turntable and allowed eight rounds to be loaded at any angle of training; after these had been fired the guns had to return to a keel-line position for replenishment. This system allowed a rate of fire of a round every 45 seconds, but was improved to nearly two rounds a minute in the last two of the class, which were fitted with chain instead of telescopic rammers and

F

continuous all-round loading. This form of barbette turret, developed by Armstrong's engineers, was adopted by all major navies except France and Russia, who retained an earlier French adaptation of the Coles conception of cylindrical turret.

The great guns of the 'Majestics' were also of a new type, constructed by winding ¼ inch wide steel ribband at tension around the inner steel tube which formed the bore of the piece—a system not copied by any other power. These pieces in the 'Majestics' were 12 inch calibre, 46 tons; they made up for their comparatively small size by an increase from 30 to 35 calibres in length which gave them a muzzle velocity of 2,350 feet per second and a theoretical penetration of some 18 inches of steel at 1,500 yards.

By the time they came into service gunpowder was being replaced by 'smokeless' powders in all navies; this resulted from decades of experimental work in which scientists had tried to produce a slow-burning and stable compound out of the very unstable and rapid burning 'high' explosives nitrocellulose or nitro-glycerine. In the British service the result was 'cordite', a blend of both high explosives gelatinized with 5 per cent vaseline to lubricate the gun bore, and manufactured in long cords, hence the name. Other services produced different variations of the same basic compounds, although the Americans adopted a single-base 'explosive D' of nitro-cellulose and preservatives only. All had far greater strength than gunpowder and hence reduced the weight of the charges necessary. But their chief advantage was the elimination of the clouds of dense smoke which had been an obstacle to accurate gunfire from the beginning of the gunnery era. This was particularly important for the QF guns, and further increased their advantage over torpedoes from torpedo-boats.

Meanwhile armour had also advanced. The French Schneider works had taken the first step at the end of the 80's by adding some 3–4 per cent of nickel to their steel armour plates, reducing their tendency to crack. In 1890 an American, H. A. Harvey, improved on this 'nickel' steel armour by raising the carbon content of the outer inch or so from 0.2 per cent to over 1 per cent; this was accomplished by covering a plate with bone charcoal—usually making a sandwich of charcoal between two plates—and keeping it at a high temperature in a gas oven for up to three weeks, after which it was removed and 'quenched' with oil and then water to harden it. 'Harvey' plates had roughly twice the resisting power of wrought iron against about one and a half times for the best compound armour. Some four years later the indefatigable Krupp engineers took all the improvements to their final stage by adding chromium and manganese to 'nickel' steel, thus hardening as well as toughening it, and performing the carburizing process by heating the carbon-packed face only while the mass of the plate was buried in clay. The Krupp process, which involved elaborate drills over several months, both increased the hardness of the face and the toughness and elasticity of the back; it was adopted by all major navies as Krupp cemented (KC) armour, more than two and a half times better than iron.

At the same time chrome steel came into use for shells designed to pierce steel armour, and the Russian service, quickly followed by the French and then all others, adopted the practice of covering the hardened point with soft 'cap' which took the force of impact and pre-stressed the armour before it broke aside and allowed the main shell to do its work in the most favourable conditions; 'capped' shell proved some 15 per cent more effective than uncapped provided they struck within 15 degrees of a right angle.

To return to the 'Majestics'; they were constructed in the brief period of 'Harvey' armour and at the height of the ascendancy of medium-calibre QF guns; as a result their armour belt was both thinned to 9 inch and extended up to main deck level so that it was no less than 16 feet deep while still covering two-thirds of the length of the ships. While this was theoretically penetrable by heavy guns there was also a 3 inch armoured deck at what had been normal belt-top level, some three feet above the waterline, which sloped down at each side to meet the *bottom* of the armour, five feet below the waterline. This meant that any shells or fragments of shells penetrating the side armour would be stopped by the armoured 'splinter deck' for it was impossible that they could strike both vertical and horizontal armour at a right angle. The vitals below the splinter deck were thus protected from heavy shells, while the whole citadel was safe from penetration by the heaviest 8 inch calibre QF shells. Outside this citadel the ends were unarmoured, with flotation and stability protected by the usual underwater deck and cellular subdivision. This system was copied in essentials by all other navies except the French and Russian, who continued to build complete, very thick waterline belts usually rising less than two feet above the water with armoured decks meeting their top and bottom and the space between closely subdivided.

Besides well-protected main armament, the 'Majestics' had twelve 6-inch QF guns protected in 6 inch armoured casemates on two decks. These were for anti-ship work; there were also 3 inch QF and other light guns for anti-torpedo-boat work. The speed of the ships was 17½ knots and they could carry 2,200 tons of coal, enough to steam 7,600 miles at ten knots. All in all their prodigious endurance, high top speed, good freeboard, well-protected vitals, great offensive powers fully protected and widely-separated, made these ships perfect expressions of British offensive strategy, and there is little doubt that they and their very numerous successors in the same mould were the best balanced and most effective capital ships of the decade.

They did, however, bring to a head one of those bitter arguments which seemed inseparable from any new design era. This one, which had started with the 'Royal Sovereigns', was about their great size; actually they were nothing out of the ordinary, as a comparison with the contemporary Atlantic liner, *Georgic* of 1895 makes clear:

		HMS *Majestic*		White Star Line *Georgic*	
length breadth } length/breadth ratio		390 feet 75 „ }	5.2	559 feet 60 „ }	9.3
displacement		14,900 tons		c.14,000 tons	

However the professional critics like Nathaniel Barnaby were concerned about their vulnerability. The great gun was clearly mastering even the thickest steel armour, medium calibre QFs could wreak havoc through the sides necessarily left unprotected above the thickest armour, high-explosive shells would prove irresistibly devastating—not to mention blows below the belt from torpedoes—and it seemed madness to lock up a million pounds and enormous force in one large hull when two or three smaller hulls could carry equal offensive power for the same money but *distribute* the risk. This was precisely the attitude of the *jeune école*: 'Let us be sure that the three main elements of success in the naval battle of the future will be speed, the distribution of attack and superiority of the number of ships which can be brought into action.'[9]

There was also concern that increased size would encourage other nations to build bigger, thus stimulating a 'naval race', waste of resources as older, smaller ships quickly became obsolete—and ultimately financial ruin. Yet another criticism of the new British battleships was that despite their vastly increased size they lacked the weight of guns and armour of some foreign classes.

Such arguments got short shrift from Richards:

> The role of the British fleet in war must always be the offensive …the main object from the moment hostilities commence must be to keep the enemy's home squadrons 'sealed up' in port…and to clear the ocean highways of his cruisers. …All this means staying power and staying power means coal.[10]

He went on to point out that French battleships with only 580–

680 tons of coal were clearly designed to fight in home waters making short forays from the shelter of their own bases, and that most of the difference in size was due to this difference in coal capacity, for every extra ton of coal needed two extra tons of displacement if the ship were to float at the required draft and steam at the required speed.

Admiralty policy was to design a fleet, 'the ships in the line of battle in which shall be of equal size, equal power, equal speed and equal freeboard...'. When the 'Majestics' were complete, they and the 'Royal Sovereigns' would form 'a fleet of 16 ships which for mobility and power of acting together is altogether unique and unrivalled. The perfection with which a fleet such as this can be handled is obvious and we have no need to work backwards for inferior vessels.'[11] As for two small ships being equal to one large one, Richards thought this 'all right in theory', but it presupposed the smaller ships could always be together and meet their antagonist on favourable terms; separated they were 'liable to destruction in detail by more powerful ships choosing their own distance.' Sir William White's own defence of the battleships he had created expanded this: 'Many experienced naval tacticians regard concentrated attack by many small vessels as impossible in practice. Experience is against it.' On the other hand a large ship could be given 'an enormous increase in the power of *concentrated attack* since she carried her armament in a single bottom and under one direction.'[12]

This accorded with the history of the gunned warship in the sailing era, first the increasing power of artillery leading to the stand-off battle, then the ships themselves growing larger and larger for greater concentration of force in one hull. In the sailing era this growth had reached a point where it ran against speed and manoeuvrability, but in the steam age all factors were working together, the larger the ship the easier it was to give it high speed, good steaming radius and sea-keeping ability. So the various classes laid down after the 'Majestics', while preserving the basic formula, gradually increased in size, gunpower and speed, also in protection, as strong service reaction against 'soft-enders' led to complete waterline belts with submerged protective decks at either end.

In marked contrast to the confidence, style and uniformity of design which distinguished these classes and reflected the nature strategic and tactical doctrines from which they sprung, French battleships continued to show extraordinary variation on a much smaller displacement. After the *Brennus* of 11,200 tons with its armament distribution similar to the 'Royal Sovereigns' came three 12,000-ton 'Charles Martel' class in 1893–4 which reverted to the French 'lozenge' arrangement of single great-gun turrets. Each of these main turrets had two secondary gun turrets close by so that there were, in effect, four mixed batteries as widely separated as the length and the breadth of the ships allowed—an extraordinarily retrograde design, as apart from reducing the main armament broadside to only three guns for the very doubtful prospect in practice of obtaining three-gun direct ahead or astern fire it produced all the old interference between main and secondary guns on wide arcs of fire. It also needed the old exaggerated slope to the sides to allow theoretical ahead fire from the beam turrets. Above the turrets, which were placed deliberately high over the high, narrowing hulls, there arose a confusion of superstructure, flying decks, funnels, stout military masts with circular platforms like inverted pagodas, all according to the whim or design of principal constructors at different dockyards, and resulting in generally high centres of gravity. This, combined with the great tumble-home and consequently lowered righting moment at angles of heel, the very low armour belts and otherwise unprotected sides made the ships potentially unstable directly the sides were penetrated to admit water. It is difficult to believe that these ships could have lived long with the 'Majestics'.

Following them in 1895-6 came two similar and equally grotesque-looking modifications of the class, together with a new, rather smaller class, the 'Charlemagnes'; these reverted to the *Brennus* main armament arrangement with a long, lightly protected secondary battery between the two end turrets. However, they still had great tumble-home, high sides completely unprotected below the battery deck, and belts rising barely 18 inches above the waterline, and it was not until nearly the end of the century that the improvements on the class, the *Jena*, 11,900 tons and *Suffren*, 12,500 tons, had belts taken up to a reasonably safe height, 3 feet and 3 feet 6 inches respectively. After them in the new century came the 'Republique' class of 14,600 tons: extreme tumble-home was abandoned and the armament distribution, stability and protection began to look like something by White—except that a complete thick belt, thus largely unprotected side above, was still preferred to thinner armour spread higher against QF guns.

This succession of design changes reflected continuing uncertainty in French naval policy; should the Navy be designed to challenge British battlefleet doctrine with an ocean-going battlefleet—or with torpedo boats—or should it be designed to attack trade with cruisers and torpedo boats, keeping small, low-radius battleships and torpedo boats for coast defence? Should it be designed primarily against the Triple Alliance powers, Italy in the Mediterranean, Germany in the North Sea? Different administrations sought different emphases and there were 31 different ministers of marine in the 30 years after

1870. Besides this, French dockyards were still unable to match the British in speed or cheapness. A first class British battleship cost some £750,000 for hull and engines, perhaps £75,000 for gun mountings, £200,000 for armament and £20,000 for fitting out after delivery, but a French battleship some 3,000 tons smaller cost almost as much, £980,000 for hull and engines alone. Above all, of course, there was the French Army, which had to match the German. It was an imposs- ible situation. From it issued the ungainly, monstrously piecemeal oddities that made up the French battlefleet of the nineties.

The *dénouement* came in 1898 when parties of Empire builders from France and Great Britain converged on the Sudan and met at Fashoda. Their physical confrontation seemed to threaten war; the Toulon fleet was mobilized. The British Admiralty carefully avoided any similar overt action which might precipitate matters but the Mediterranean squadron received its war orders, the Channel squadron prepared to concentrate with it, and at Portland the Reserve Squad- ron of older ships completed with coal and stores. But as it turned out the French were unprepared for a great war; the fleet was going through one of its *guerre de course* phases induced by the knowledge that Britain was outbuilding it decisively and meant to continue— and there was nothing they could do about it. Their mobilization had been defensive, inspired by fear that Britain might be tempted to provoke a conflict and settle the colonial rivalry by severing France from her overseas empire. And when the Russians refused to become involved they had no option but to back down and order the evacua- tion of the Sudan. On 11 December the Union Jack was hoisted at Fashoda beside the Egyptian flag, and in January the following year the Anglo-Egyptian condominium of Sudan was established.

> We are getting it by degrees, we are getting it by degrees,
> We get a bit here, we get a bit there,
> The Union Jack is everywhere,
> And now and then we give it a gentle squeeze.
> We haven't got quite the whole world yet—but we're getting it
>   by degrees.

So the Gunner of HMS *Caesar* sang to Joseph Chamberlain, the 'high priest of British imperialism' when he visited the Mediterranean fleet that year.[13] It was an appropriate setting for the popular song. No one doubted that the 'Majestics' and 'Royal Sovereigns' of the Mediterranean fleet had been the instruments of the bloodless triumph which had finally secured the north-east corner of Africa for Britain, thus safe-guarding her Red Sea–Suez route from flank attack. This was accepted throughout Europe. At the Admiralty it was taken as the classic example of how a strong British fleet was the surest guarantee of world peace, and frequently quoted against the 'little Englanders' and 'little navyites' who bobbed to the surface struggling against the current from time to time—right down to 1914. Meanwhile in 1899 the naval estimates moved up to £26½ millions, of which £15½ millions was for new construction, repairs and armament; the comparable figure for France was nearly £6 millions, and for Russia the same. As Richards had said in 1895 before the last great increase, 'What this country wants is clear and undisputed superiority...'.

The country got this, and value for money. While White turned out class after class of improved 'Majestics'—Formidables', 'Londons', 'Duncans', 'King Edward VIIs'—private firms like Thorneycroft, Yarrow and Lairds put the Royal Navy well ahead both in design and then in numbers of smaller craft to destroy the battleships' most dangerous enemies. These boats which started life as 'torpedo boat catchers' soon became 'torpedo boat destroyers'. By 1899 they were some 300 tons displacement, could make 30 knots and were well able to accompany the fleet at sea, although it was not until a few years later that they became a regular advance guard of the fleet.

For the French, the bitter lesson of Fashoda, the subsequent increase in British naval estimates under a first sea lord singlemindedly devoted to outbuilding their Russian alliance, and a knowledge from history of the frailty of all fleet alliances, were sufficient to set them off on another bid to change naval warfare with the submarine. This time the signs were more auspicious. Since Aube's brave attempt in 1886 a great deal of work had been done on the problem, particularly in France and the United States. France already had two practical craft: one, named after the pioneer Gustave Zédé, had succeeded in torpedoing the anchored battleship *Magenta* in exercises in January 1898. The same year in Trieste an Austrian engineer, Obry, succeeded in controlling a torpedo's vertical rudders with a gyroscope, thereby removing one of the chief uncertainties in the performance of the submarine's irresistible weapon. The next year France launched the *Narval*, of 200 tons submerged displacement, which had four 18 inch torpedoes, could make 8 knots under water and had a radius of 70 miles at 5 knots. Two years later the *Gustave Zédé* became the first submarine to torpedo a moving battleship in exercises. By this date even Britain had embarked on a submarine building policy—chiefly to gain experience in how to deal with the beastly, underhand things. The

French were not worried. For the first time in their successive bids to outflank British battle superiority it didn't seem to matter that Britain could outbuild them. For submarines could not fight submarines, at least not under water.[14] Britain could build as many as she liked and still France would be able to send out her own invisible, invulnerable flotillas to prey on battlefleet or trade. This seemed to the descendants of the *jeune école* to strike at the heart of British supremacy, which lay not so much in her battlefleet as in the battlefleet doctrine with which she had mesmerized the world—with the help of Mahan—and prevented naval thought from advancing beyond the Battles of the Nile and Trafalgar. Here is Paul Fontin, Head of Department at the French Admiralty, writing in 1902:

It is the part of all the rival powers with France at their head to applaud, to precipitate themselves on the great English doctrine like a moth rushing to the light which dazzles it. There is not a naval programme which is not established upon this [British] model. Never has England gained a more complete and decisive victory. In this she triumphs over the whole world, for her security and her power at the present time depend less upon her formidable squadrons than upon this universal spirit which she has created, and which is indeed the masterpiece of her policy. Let us sum up this policy: (1) Naval strategy is unchangeable in its rules, independent of the engines of war. (2) The fighting unit is the battleship, the direct descendant of the ship-of-the-line of former times. (3) The fortunes of war depend exclusively upon the squadrons which together constitute the fleet. (4) The empire of the seas can only be obtained in two ways which are derived from the same principle: first by annihilation in pitched battle of the enemy's navy, second by the powerlessness to which this navy is reduced when, not daring to face its adversaries, it takes refuge in its ports, which are then closed upon it in an impassable blockade...This policy of England at the threshold of the twentieth century was the policy which secured her all her successes in the eighteenth and nineteenth centuries. England cannot change it. But France? Will she always leave to her great historic adversary the choice of arms?[15]

No, said Fontin, France should build at once a fleet of submersibles as an offensive arm so that British battleships would be unable to show their bottoms off her coasts, or for that matter off her own coasts.

Before such a policy could become effective, the great historic rivals came together in an *entente* directed against Germany, the new Titan of Europe.

While Britain and France had been sparring throughout the eighties and nineties, German industry had been expanding at a prodigious rate. By the turn of the century she was second only to the United States—the other boom economy—in iron and steel production, was producing twice as much iron annually as Great Britain, rather more steel, and was actually entering the British market with specialist forgings and castings, particularly for shipbuilding. With this spectacular advance—Britain's expansion had flattened out—came increasing population, increasing overseas trade and merchant shipping integrated in giant cartels and colonial possessions, particularly in Africa where her diplomacy had exploited the Franco-Russian *entente* against Britain skillfully and ruthlessly. Ruthlessness was the hallmark of her expansionist policy—or so the British believed. They saw her moving into their established world-wide markets and shipping routes, and despite (or because of) having 50 per cent of world shipping tonnage, British businessmen began to feel that they were engaged in a life-or-death struggle with German industry. A similar attitude was evident in Germany. And in both countries the friendly feelings which had existed from the Battle of Waterloo right through to the eighties were giving way to enmity, in extreme cases hatred: nationalist Germans saw Britain's world empire as an Anglo-Saxon conspiracy strangling the growth of Germanism, the British began to see Prussian militarism advancing in the wake of her industry towards world domination.

Up to 1898 such views were probably confined to extremists. But that year the Reichstag passed a naval law authorizing construction of a sea-going battlefleet, thereby touching Britain's tenderest nerve, and significantly hardening attitudes in both countries. At the time the German battlefleet was a minor force in world terms. It neither reflected her industrial strength nor her growing merchant marine, and was little more than a balance for France's northern squadron or the Russian Baltic fleet, indeed its strategic aims were limited to supporting the army's flanks in a two-front war against France and Russia. Regarded as an extension of the German army, it had actually been run by a general officer of the army until Wilhelm II's accession in 1888.

Wilhelm II, from the beginning of his reign, had tried to extend this land-locked view. His imagination was inflamed with boyhood images of the British fleet and the power that flowed from it, and he tried to awaken his people to the vision. He made speeches dwelling on the glories of the old Germanic Hansa League which had raised fleets 'such as the broad back of the sea had probably never borne up to that time', he made sure that copies of Mahan's works were aboard each of his ships, and telegraphed friends that he didn't read 'but devoured' them himself, trying to learn them by heart.[16] And he constantly harangued the Reichstag on the need for Germany to acquire sea power commensurate with her status in the world. For the first ten years it all fell on stony ground. The Reichstag, and the people themselves, felt it sufficient to bear the burden of the greatest army in Europe without building a great navy as well, and liberal elements disliked the power policies implied. Besides Germany had acquired extensive colonies, overseas markets and political influence without a great fleet, and creating one would only antagonize England and thus hamper foreign policy.

Then in 1897 Wilhelm appointed Admiral Tirpitz his Minister of Marine and there was a remarkable change. Where his own extravagant lectures had antagonized the Reichstag, and his former minister had failed to convince, Tirpitz reasoned patiently, explaining his proposals in moderate terms with inexhaustible good humour, urbanity and guile, carefully inserting the thin end of the wedge of an ocean-going fleet and explaining it in terms less of *Weltpolitik* than of defence of essential interests. Beneath it all he was quite as much a naval evangelist as his Kaiser.

> Germans did not realize that our development on the broad back of British free trade and the British world empire would continue only *until it was stopped.* The *'open door'*, which could so easily be closed combined with our hemmed in and dangerous continental position, strengthened me in my conviction that no time was to be lost in beginning the attempt to constitute ourselves a sea power. For only a fleet which represented alliance value to other great powers, in other words a competent battle fleet, could put into the hands of our diplomats the tool, which if used to good purpose, could supplement our power on land...[17]

In adition to its primary purpose as a great weight to be thrust into whichever side of the international power balance seemed appropriate at the time, Tirpitz saw his navy as the bearer of 'Germanism' throughout a world embraced by the 'polypus of Anglo-Saxonism'.

Tirpitz worked at his twin goal with a single-mindedness and devotion equal to his great opposite number at the British Admiralty, Sir Frederick Richards, and with the same battlefleet doctrine to guide him. The first evidence of this is found in the debates on the 1898 naval vote; hitherto money had been voted annually, but Tirpitz was determined that the size and composition of the fleet and the age of individual ships should be fixed by law. His argument was that while designs might change, the *units* of the fleet, based around its battle-ships, remained the same, and it was only by fixing a steady growth and maintenance that the infant German shipbuilding industry, which relied almost exclusively on government orders, could be ex-panded in a planned and rational manner. He achieved his aim despite intense opposition, and a Naval Law was passed which fixed the size of the fleet to be attained over six years as 19 battleships, 8 armoured coast defence vessels and 22 cruisers of various sizes, together with various cruisers for overseas service—in itself a very modest force compared with Germany's size and strength. In fact Tirpitz had trimmed his proposals to what he thought the Reichstag would accept; he had no intention of making this his final position: 'we should have to bring forward supplementary demands after the con-clusion of the six years' limit.'[18]

In the event the chance came much sooner than expected. British expansion in southern Africa had already provoked a wave of Anglo-phobia in Germany at the time of the notorious Jameson Raid, and when in 1899 another Boer War broke out, all the old feelings were revived, then fanned into a blaze by the British seizure of German steamers suspected of aiding the Boers. Tirpitz had already enrolled press support in his campaign for a big navy and had founded a Navy League on the British model to publicise the benefits of sea power. No doubt all this groundwork helped. But it was the immed-iate wounding lesson of complete German impotence in the face of the seizure of their own vessels on the high seas that gave Tirpitz his opportunity. In 1900 he introduced a supplementary Navy Bill as Wilhelm had been 'persistently and impetuously urging' him, which increased the battle fleet to 38 battleships and 32 cruisers, with four battleships and seven cruisers in reserve; this was passed into law. One of the most remarkable and frequently quoted parts of this Bill was the explanatory memorandum or preamble which was published with it.

When working out the second Navy Bill, we hesitated a long time whether or not to bring the idea of the English menace into the preamble...But such an unusual demand as was presented here, namely the doubling of our small naval force, made it scarcely possible to avoid hinting at the real reason for it...[19]

The preamble started with the proposition that the security of the German empire, its economic development and world trade was a 'life question' for which Germany needed peace, 'not however peace at any price, but peace with honour'. It went on to say that Germany's small 'sortie navy' could easily be shut up in its harbours and Germany's sea trade thereafter destroyed with consequent disaster to her economic and social life but at little cost to the enemy; then the conclusion:

> To protect Germany's sea trade and colonies in the existing circumstances there is only one means—Germany must have a battle fleet so strong that even for the adversary with the greatest sea power a war against it would involve such dangers as to imperil his position in the world.
>
> For this purpose it is not absolutely necessary that the German battlefleet should be as strong as that of the greatest naval power, for a great naval power will not, as a rule, be in a position to concentrate all its striking forces against us. But even if it should succeed in meeting us with considerable superiority of strength, the defeat of a strong German fleet would so substantially weaken the enemy, that in spite of victory he might have obtained, his own position in the world would no longer be secured by an adequate fleet...[20]

This was Tirpitz's 'risk fleet' theory. Quite obviously it was aimed at England. Whether it was intended by Tirpitz simply to give 'alliance value' to the German empire as he always claimed, or as a step towards seizing the trident from Britannia, as Wilhelm's more extravagant oratory suggested, made little difference to the British Admiralty; their recognition of danger increased year by year, not simply on account of the numbers involved and the consequent escalation of French and Russian growth to match, but because in marked contrast to the gross venality and bureaucratic inefficiency prevailing in the Russian service, the gadfly policies of the French and the chronic inefficiency of the Italian navy, the German service was notoriously hard-working, was backed by great industrial strength and was administered with single-minded determination. The danger of this combination under such an inflammatory pan-Germanist as Wilhelm II was considered so real that at the end of 1904 the new first lord, Admiral Sir John Fisher, suggested to his King that the German service be nipped in the bud by a preventive assault. Such schemes had been aired against the French Navy at the height of the Fashoda crisis, but they had never been considered seriously, and while this may be more of a comment on Fisher's character than the German threat, it is a revealing indiscretion. Early the following year when a crisis in Morocco threatened war between Germany and

France/England, Fisher was again 'longing to have a go', and wrote to the Foreign Secretary, 'We could have the German fleet, the Kiel Canal and Schleswig-Holstein within a fortnight.'[21]

The German battleships which provoked Fisher were not so formidable as his violent attitude might suggest, for Tirpitz had many difficulties to surmount. Among these were a comparative lack of finance—despite the grandiose objectives of the Naval Law the German estimates stood fifth in the naval league—the shallowness of the Kiel canal, which had to be traversed by the fleet if it was to command both the Baltic and the North Sea, the narrowness of the locks at Wilhelmshaven, and the shifting sandbanks outside. All this limited the size of the ships just as it had limited the Dutch in their seventeenth-century struggles against England. As then, the size of the great guns was seriously affected. The first two classes of the Tirpitz administration carried only 9.4-inch guns, scarcely larger than the secondary guns of the later classes of improved 'Majesticos'. This was partly due to Tirpitz's addiction to the 'hail of fire' as battle-winner, to which end the German ships carried powerful batteries of no less than 18 6-inch QF guns. After the 1900 expansion of the Naval Law the size of the ships was increased to 13,000 tons and their main batteries were increased to four 11-inch pieces; however these were still smaller than the guns favoured by all other major navies.

While these later classes, the 'Braunschweigs' and 'Deutschlands', were being laid down, Tirpitz conducted a number of experiments with full-scale models of a ship's section to determine the best protection against torpedo attack. This was not a novel idea; similar experiments had been carried out by the British Admiralty as an obvious response to the torpedo threat in the 1870s, and by Benedetto Brin at Spezia in the late eighties. As then, it was found that coal absorbed the first force of an explosion and that a steel 'torpedo bulkhead' in association with side bunkers could protect the vitals of a ship from damage. It was also found, as it had been in British experiments and disasters, that solid watertight bulkheads were better than bulkheads pierced with sliding doors; this was taken to its logical conclusion in later classes and, combined with detailed attention to stability control by counter-flooding, helped to give German ships their deserved reputation for unsinkability. Very solid compartmentation also helped to localize flooding from shell damage.

The detailed attention to defence begun here was natural for a navy with so little money, whose object was to challenge the naval power well known for outbuilding competition. A ship which could be got back to base, could be repaired much more quickly and cheaply than a replacement could be built.

Perhaps the most interesting feature of Tirpitz's long administration was his complete rejection of the ideas of the *jeune école*. Although a torpedo specialist, he was also a tactician of note, and the fact that he chose to build his fleet around battleships is impartial evidence that this battle doctrine was correct for the beginning of the twentieth century; gunned battleships supported by cruisers *were* more than a match for far more numerous torpedo craft. But the *jeune école* cannot be dismissed; their realization that submarines would fundamentally alter naval strategy and tactics and bite deep into Mahan's strictures on the *guerre de course*, if not render his whole thesis obsolete, was more prescient than Tirpitz's view. It could be argued that Tirpitz's impressive strength of mind in holding to a battlefleet policy while Britain predictably outbuilt him, thus 'precipitating himself on the great English doctrine like a moth rushing to the light that dazzles it',[22] was a blunder of the first magnitude. But that is looking ahead.

15

Gunnery Renaissance, in Practice and Anger

As Tirpitz was beginning his task an extraordinary gunnery renaissance began to tip the scales even more heavily towards the battleship. This had to happen at some time in the early twentieth century because ordnance technology had run way beyond aiming and sighting methods. Although the great guns were capable of hitting the service target every time at 6,000 yards, they seldom hit one in practice at 1,500. Of course every sailor knew the reason: accurate fire was impossible from a moving and rolling ship. And they knew the Nelsonic answer: close to decisive range and pour in smothering fire. This was dogma. The long peace had exaggerated the resultant emphasis on drill for rapid rather than accurate fire. Smart drill made more impression on inspecting admirals than splashes around a target, which in any case took time to lay out and recover; clean guns were easier to commend than marksmanship.

There were other reasons. The paintwork fetish had by the nineties taken over from mast and sail drill as the criterion of efficiency, and commanders' promotions had become entangled with the prettiness of the ships they ran. As gunnery lieutenants were junior and had to ask for men and time to exercise the guns, and as their powder charges had 'a most deleterious effect on the paintwork', they worked under some difficulties. One commander, who had his whole ship enamelled at his own expense complained that it cost him £100 to repaint her after target practice!

Another factor tending to discourage accuracy, or at least to promote complacency, was the system of scoring in the annual prizefiring; it was not necessary to actually hit the target to score, only to put the shots close enough for the umpires to judge that they would have hit a theoretical ship whose hull extended each side of the target.

I well remember that on one of our annual prizefirings the Captain of the foremost port 11-inch gun sent two shots in

Entente Cordiale; the French
flagship, *Massena* (*top*) coming
up Portsmouth harbour, 1905.
(H M S *Excellent*) Her obsolete
design and armament arrangement was emphasised by H M S
Dreadnought (*bottom*) then taking shape at Portsmouth.
(*Richard Perkins/National Maritime Museum*)

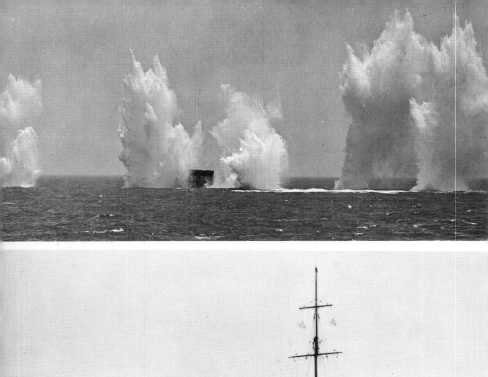

Top Battlepractice target straddled. (*Cdr J. Hale, D.S.O.*)

Bottom H M S *Thunderer*,
whose shooting by director (on
tripod foremast) established
director-firing in the Royal Navy
in 1913. (*Imperial War Museum*)

Top The foundation of battle-ship supremacy, the great gun: this is a 12-inch Armstrong. (*Vickers Ltd*)

Middle U S S *Texas*, the first American Dreadnought to be fitted with director-firing, 1916. (*U S Navy*)

Bottom German High Seas Fleet battleship at firing practice. (*Collection Unimare/E Groner*)

H M S *Lion* leading the battle-cruisers at Jutland. *Top (National Maritime Museum)*

Bottom German battlecruiser, *Seydlitz,* after the battle. *(Imperial War Museum)*

succession through the canvas of the target, and all hands were watching what seemed to us phenomenal shooting. With another round he knocked away one of the poles from which the canvas was suspended, when I heard a querulous voice mutter, 'What is the damn fool doing? Does he want to keep us out here all day?' It was one of our lieutenants.[1]

The whole system was out of balance so far as war preparation was concerned; while there was fierce competition between ships for drills like boat-pulling, sailing, rifle-shooting, all of which offered a cup or shield to the top ship, the annual prizefiring was a solitary unrewarded event in which the guns' crews of each ship competed against *themselves*. Training was carried out in similar isolation. There was a quarterly allowance of ammunition for the purpose, and it was usual, when ships were cruising, for the commander-in-chief to order them to 'spread for target practice' and rejoin the flag at a certain time. It was up to each captain how he spent his time; some enthusiastic officers made great efforts, others got rid of the ammunition as smartly as possible and quickly got things ship-shape again.

Besides being uncompetitive, the annual prizefiring was thoroughly unrealistic. Each ship made a number of passes at eight knots up a straight, buoyed course at a known distance from the target varying from 1,600 yards to 1,400 yards when abeam, and each gun in turn was allowed six minutes to get off as many rounds as possible. This gave no impression of the confusion of a multitude of shells dropping around the target and mixing up the gunlayers, who would be trying to 'spot' their own shells, no impression of the speeds and varying courses likely in action and no impression of the actual range at which firing was likely. Consequently there was little realization of the need for fire control, and as the average 'estimated' hits for the whole fleet was 30 per cent—some well-drilled ships scored as high as 43 per cent—there was a natural complacency.

As for the sights and other aids, there was only one real improvement on the cannon era at the beginning of the century; this was the Barr & Stroud 4-feet 6-inch base-length rangefinder, introduced in 1892. Some individuals, notably Bradley Fiske of the US service, had poineered electric range telegraphs and other aids to control of fire, but for the most part there were only bugle calls and voicepipes, while the sighting system itself was in essence that developed by British officers shortly after Trafalgar. Each gun had a raised foresight and a V backsight which could be moved up or down a graduated shank so that the gun had to be given the required elevation to bring it in a horizontal line with the foresight. The most recent ones had an H instead of a V for the backsight so they could be lined up for training even if they were not spot-on for elevation; these Hs could also be moved horizontally along a deflection 'leaf' so that the guns could be given deflection or 'aim-off' for the relative speed of target or wind. Deflection tables were worked out for an enemy right abeam and steaming a parallel course at 1,500 yards range; no doubt keen gunnery lieutenants could add to these official tables for various angles of approach and different ranges, but the method would still have been slow and inflexible against high-speed battleships.

As an illustration of the most advanced ideas of gunnery control in the British service of the last years of the nineteenth century, here is the 1898 'Plan for Battle' for the 'Majestic' class *Magnificent*. It is not typical; it shows more thought than most.

> Direction of approach of the enemy will be passed to the different quarters from the conning tower, as well as the speed of ship, deflection for this speed as well as for an estimated enemy speed of ten knots to be used. A gun in fore lower top will be used as a rangefinder and range thus obtained will be passed to 6-inch and 12 pounder quarters. After 'Commence fire' sounds (by bugle) officers of the quarters must estimate the distance. Captains of all guns are to aim halfway between the waterline and the upper deck except when close to.
>
> If enemy passes in line ahead as soon as leader is abeam, bow group of guns shift their aim to her next astern, after group keeping on leader until second ship comes abeam when they shift their aim to her (second ship), bow group at same time shifting to third ship and so on to last ship on which all guns are kept concentrated until 'Cease fire' sounds (by bugle).[2]

To a gunnery officer only 10 years later this was 'stone age gunnery'. However, there is no evidence that other navies were very much better. The French certainly tried harder and they credited themselves with 100 per cent more hits per minute in their annual firings than the British achieved. If this was right the British Naval Intelligence Department was unaware of the potentially disastrous gap between them. As for the Americans, who were extraordinarily pleased with their shooting against the Spanish, gunnery reports from shortly after the turn of the century showed that their squadrons exercised against British targets in British practice conditions made one-fifth the hits that British ships made; the same year their battleships fired 200 rounds at a stationary condemned lightship at 2,800 yards, scoring just two hits!

Such conditions obviously called for a revolution. As it turned out the revolutionary was a British officer, Captain Percy Scott, a small, brisk, forceful man of independent, indeed insubordinate, mind with a genius for invention already manifested in several devices for range telegraphs and signalling systems. His most obvious characteristic was dissatisfaction with existing practice and as he was a gunnery specialist he was particularly dissatisfied with gunnery methods. But his early attempts at reform while a commander were resisted by the sheer inertia of the system.

> In the end we had to do as the others were doing. We gave up instruction in gunnery, spent money on enamel paint, burnished up every bit of steel on board, and soon get the reputation of being a very smart ship.[3]

He had to await promotion to captain before he could do things his own way. Then his first command, a small cruiser, *Scylla*, startled the service with 80 per cent hits in the 1898 prizefiring. This incredible rate was disbelieved, but when he repeated it with his next command in the China Squadron and explained his methods to gunnery officers invited as witnesses, they returned to their ships converted and burning to spread the flame of the 'new gunnery'.[4]

Scott's methods were very simple. First and probably foremost he had taken an interest in target practice. By posting results on the ships' notice board after each practice and giving privileges to the most successful gun captains he had encouraged a competitive instead of a 'let's get it over with' attitude. Next, he had replaced the service sights with telescopes, the cross hairs of which he made with the fine hairs of a midshipman aboard. Then he had watched what happened. In the watching he had the good fortune to see a natural gunlaying genius at work one wild day when few other ships would have bothered to practice at all. This man, instead of waiting for the ship to roll his sights on target as the system had been from the very earliest days of shipborne gunnery, operated his elevating wheel with such dexterity that he kept his telescope on target through all the movements of the ship, scoring faster and more surely, and using—for the first time in such conditions—the speed of fire of which QF guns were capable. Instead of dismissing this performance as a freak Scott had his carpenters construct a machine so that all gun captains could be exercised at what this one man had done naturally. The machine was a framework carrying a target which could be moved up and down by one man turning a handle geared to a bicycle chain. The gun captain at practice had to follow through his sight as the target was swung up and down to simulate rolling and press his trigger each time he had a good aim. As he pressed the trigger a pencil arranged with a solenoid on the muzzle of the gun extended forward and made a mark—a dot—on a card which moved beside the target and had two horizontal lines extending tangentially from the top and bottom of the bull. All dots between these lines scored as hits. At first the gun captains at practice on the diabolical device, christened the 'dotter', found it almost impossible to work their wheels fast enough, but weeks of practice made them proficient.

Following this, Scott had devised a 'deflection teacher' to do the same job for a target moving horizontally, and then a 'loader' to speed the work of the loading numbers; this was simply a mock-up of the breech of a gun with a tray beyond it down which the shells and charges slid after being loaded. These three extemporized machines, telescopic sights, unremitting hard work, his own drive and enthusiasm, and his men's love of competition, were the only tools Scott used to revolutionize gunnery, but they were so effective that by 1903 'continuous aim firing' had spread throughout the British fleet and the Admiralty were having 'dotters', 'loaders' and 'deflection teachers' manufactured and supplied to all ships. Scott was fortunate in one way: the time was ripe for change; the younger, more scientifically-educated men were reaching ranks where they could alter traditional methods which had lost their usefulness, and there was a new spirit in the air which was soon to manifest itself in response to the German challenge. Scott's contribution was to give this spirit a practical application and a twist of his own genius which soon put Britain well ahead of all other European navies. In 1903 the French noted with astonishment that where they had been ahead in target practice they were now trailing 1:2 hits per minute.

Meanwhile the flame had spread to the United States. The carrier was another forceful and dissatisfied officer—in the best sense— Lieutenant William Sims. He chanced to be in the Pacific in 1901 while Scott's enthusiasm was transforming the gunnery of the British squadron and he made it his business to meet Scott. He was rewarded by full details of all Scott's methods, and fired by the little man's personality and his remarkable results, set about trying them out in the American squadron, while writing long reports to his service bureaux in Washington; he described the new British methods, the remarkable results they produced, and detailed deficiencies in American gear which prevented their full application in the US service. The reports were filed. Sims, infuriated, wrote a letter to President Roosevelt, then a devastating paper 'The crushing superiority of British naval marksmanship over ours...', then a second letter to the President. The Bureau of Ordnance now had to respond, and it did so by proving that 'continuous aim' was impossible—surely the most interesting testimony to Scott's genius. However Sims had the President of the United States on his side and it was not long before he was called back to take up a newly-created post, Inspector of Target Practice, in which he was able to introduce all the 'dotters', 'loaders' and competitive practices that he had advocated. This was in 1903, two years before a similar post was created in the British service for Scott himself, and the result was that American gunnery soon equalled, if it did not excel, that of the Royal Navy.

Scott's complete openness with Sims in 1901 and the continuing interchange of ideas and experience between the two men throughout the exciting gunnery advances of the next decade were, on the face of it, remarkable. They illustrate the new cordiality between the two 'Anglo-Saxon nations' and also a feeling among British officers that the growing pace of naval expansion outside Europe must lead to some sharing of the Royal Navy's self-imposed burden by alliance or co-operation.

In fact it led to both; there was continuing informal co-operation between the British and US Navies, particularly about the Pacific, and in 1902 Britain signed a formal alliance with Japan. Whether this last was to prevent a Russo-Japanese reconcilation—if such were possible for long—or whether it formalized the common interests of the two island nations in preventing further Russian expansion in Manchuria and Korea, it was, so far as the Admiralty were concerned, a simple recognition of the fact that they could no longer 'command' both Europe and Far Eastern waters by themselves; they called in the Japanese navy, now headed by five battleships, to help secure British trade and the principle of free trade in Chinese waters. The terms of this historic agreement were that if either party to the alliance were at war with a third party, the other would remain neutral unless the third party were joined by an ally, in which case it would come in with its partner. For Japan it meant that the British Navy would hold the ring if she should come to blows with Russia, whose Port Arthur fleet was now headed by five battleships, whose trans-Siberian railway was approaching completion, and whose plain ambitions extended to the annexation of Manchuria and Korea—and then?

What seems an inevitable collision occurred two years later in February 1904. The Japanese declared war with a torpedo boat night attack on the Russian fleet at anchor in Port Arthur. On paper this fleet, now headed by seven battleships—four of the most recent construction—was more than a match for Japan's entire navy, and it had to be whittled down if the sea was to be used for troop transport and supply. The Russians, for their part, had ample warning of the attack. Their naval attaché in Tokyo had been reporting Japanese preparations for some months; nevertheless Moscow had ordered the Port

Arthur fleet not to make any moves which could be interpreted as provocative, and so the ships had stayed in port unexercised and largely unprepared for war. They had, however, taken certain precautions against surprise attack and inefficiently as these were carried out they were sufficient to confuse the Japanese. Only the first division of four destroyers made hits with torpedoes; all these passed the extremities of ships' nets at bow or stern, damaging the two latest battleships and one cruiser, though not vitally. Disappointing as this result was, it temporarily reduced the Russian battlefleet to numerical equality with the Japanese, who were allowed to land troops in Korea unopposed; these pressed across the Yalu towards Port Arthur.

Meanwhile the Russians, in an effort to inspire their fleet with more 'military spirit', appointed admiral Makarov as commander-in-chief; he was by all accounts an exceptional man, technically and as a leader. But most unfortunately for the Russian Port Arthur Squadron he was cut short while engaged in one of the daily sea-going exercises with which he soon began to transform the fleet: his flagship *Petro Pavlovsk* struck a mine laid by Japanese torpedo-boats, and the explosion triggered off her magazines and blew the ship apart. There were fewer than 30 survivors. 'The Admiral was not among them, and all our hopes were lost as nobody could substitute Makaroff.'[5] In the Tsarist Navy this was literally true: most of the senior officers were stout-hearted, full-bearded martinets bred in the sailing navy and quite unable to fathom the technicalities of the modern ships and guns which had been thrust upon them in the recent sudden expansion; admirals and captains all relied heavily on their subordinate technicians, making up for lack of comprehension with arbitrary decisiveness and great rages. The state of their fleets reflected this, a fact very well known both inside and outside Russia; the French, for instance, were apprehensive of combining their own naval forces with any Russian fleet: 'They are so poorly handled that their cumbersome mass could do nothing but weigh down and paralyze our own.'[6]

Makarov was succeeded by Admiral Vitgeft, a man who lacked martial ardour. When the Japanese, who were blockading him from a nearby island anchorage, lost two battleships in one day to mines outside Port Arthur, thus leaving themselves in a 4:6 minority in heavy ships, he failed to take advantage, but continued meekly inside.

Meanwhile the Japanese army was fighting its way overland towards Port Arthur and by early August had reached the outskirts and were able to fire over the surrounding hills into the Russian fleet at their moorings. Realizing that it was only a matter of time before the field guns would be able to fire directly into his ships,

Vitgeft decided to break out and run the gauntlet of the Japan Sea to Vladivostok; on 10 August he led out in his flagship *Tsarevitch*. Seeing him coming, the Japanese Commander-in-Chief, Admiral Togo, steamed seawards to entice him further, then turned in line of battle to parallel him at about seven miles distance, leading in his flagship *Mikasa*. As he approached, the two new Russian ships at the head of the line, *Tsarevitch* and *Retvisan*, opened a deliberate but ineffective fire with their heavy guns. Togo waited until he had closed to some 14,000 yards before he replied, but as this was still some 9,000 yards outside the practice range for any navy in the world, and the British Barr & Stroud 4 feet 6 inch rangefinders—on which both fleets relied—could not cope with these sort of distances, his fire was equally ineffective.

Operating the *Tsarevitch*'s Barr & Stroud in an exposed position above the conning tower was Lieutenant Daragan:

> I had a splendid view over the whole situation. The first projectiles from *Mikasa* came very short, ricocheted, flew over us and fell somewhere behind our ships. These richochet-flying projectiles flew very slowly, turned in the air and made such a noise which reminded [one of] the flight of big birds. For at least five minutes I was sure that these were birds frightened by the Japanese firing...[7]

The two fleets were very evenly matched in gunpower; there were six Russian battleships mounting between them 16 12-inch and eight 10-inch primary guns, and on the Japanese side four battleships mounting 16 12-inch pieces, an inferiority in main armament balanced by far stronger secondary batteries, and particularly by powerful batteries of 8-inch and 6-inch QFs in four modern Japanese armoured cruisers opposing three less well-armed Russian cruisers. This Japanese preponderance in secondary and QF guns made Togo's position particularly difficult. On the one hand their effective range was far less than that of the heavy guns and he needed to close well inside heavy gun effective range to use them to advantage, on the other hand the battlefleet with him was Japan's first and *last* line. Whereas the Russians had their Baltic fleet battleships as a powerful reserve, he had only cruisers and torpedo boats. He could scarcely afford to lose one heavy ship.

In the event he appeared to compromise between necessary caution and necessary close range, with the emphasis on caution. While he steered to cross ahead of the Russian course, bringing down the range and inducing a manoeuvring contest, he kept well outside what was regarded as decisive range, generally passing and paralleling at about 7,000 yards. At this distance the Russian preponderance of heavy pieces should have given them an advantage, and probably did: a British naval attaché observing the action from the battleship, *Asahi*, wrote afterwards:

> Looking back upon the action the impression that Russian marksmanship at long range was superior to that of the Japanese remains vivid and unshaken. Time after time the Russian projectiles fell so close on either side of the opposite line that those falling to leeward might, many of them, have almost been dropped out of the lee boats. The only explanation of the disparity between results and appearances would seem to be that the Japanese were befriended by chance...[8]

After his preliminary manoeuvring against the Russian van, Togo concentrated on the weak Russian rear without success and then, as the Russians continued steaming hard south-easterly on their way out of the Gulf of Korea, he followed and, catching them, continued the action on a parallel course at ranges generally outside 7,000 yards. So the firing continued down a long afternoon, both sides concentrating on the leader of the opposite line, but neither Admiral willing to close in to decisive range. Slowly the hits mounted. By late afternoon both flagships had been struck by some dozen projectiles. Of the two the *Mikasa* was probably faring worse; her after turret was out of action from a direct hit and she was taking in water from holes and shaken plates in the hull. Togo himself had narrowly escaped death as he directed the battle from the exposed top of the pilot house.

Then at 5.40 chance took a decisive hand. A 12-inch shell from one of the Japanese guns struck the sea short of the *Tsarevitch* and ricochetted up inside the mushroom roof of the armoured conning tower, where it burst, killing the admiral and several of his staff inside, wounding the captain, gunnery officer and signal ratings. At about the same time there was a failure in one of the valves in the steering engine right aft in the tiller flat and the ship began to circle out of control, eventually making a complete circle towards the Japanese line.[9] The second Russian ship, *Retvisan*, meanwhile followed her towards the *Mikasa* but when the flagship continued turning and she found that she was on her own she made back. The ships behind each turned different ways, and in a moment the Russian formation was in disorder. Whereupon the admiral second-in-command apparently panicked and signalling, 'FOLLOW ME' led round north-westerly back towards Port Arthur. Togo, seeing his opportunity, pressed in towards decisive range, 5,000 to 4,000 yards, where his superiority in QF guns and the superior training of these guns' crews at last began to tell. But by then it was too late. The light began to fade, and he soon called off the pursuit. In the darkness the Russian squadron split up, some like the *Tsarevitch* under the command of her gunnery officer breaking south to try to escape into the Pacific as originally intended, the majority returning to Port Arthur after the new flagship—although it was very evident that this was a mousetrap.

So it proved. Early in December, after heavy fighting the Japanese soldiers captured a vital hill commanding the harbour, and within a very few days their guns had put paid to all the big ships save one, which the Russians took outside and anchored, a splendid target for repeated Japanese torpedo boat attacks, which eventually sank her.

This was a sad misuse of the Russian fleet reminiscent of the Black Sea fleet's suicide in the Crimean War. As on that occasion the Russian guns were taken ashore to help defend the port. Perhaps the small size of the Russian heavy ships had something to do with their complete subjection to Togo's will. The two oldest ones, designed on the lines of reduced 'Royal Sovereigns' with armoured gun towers instead of barbettes, were some 11,000 tons, the next class 12,700 tons but of the old French style with high, unprotected sides particularly vulnerable to QF fire; only the two latest ships, the *Retvisan*, similar to recent British classes, and the *Tsarevitch*, similar to the latest French 'Republiques', were individually a match for the large Japanese ships; even these were only 13,000 tons, 2,000 tons less than the *Mikasa*, *Asahi*, *Shikishima*, and similar to the older *Fuji*. However, it is striking that the Battle of 10 August actually turned on chance. Until the coincidental demolition of Admiral Vitgeft and the flagship's steering, the Russians were probably giving as good as they got and in view of the flooding in the *Mikasa* it is doubtful if Togo would have pressed in had they preserved their line. As for the *Tsarevitch* she was struck by some 15 12-inch shells and a number of lighter ones, but none penetrated her 16-inch belt or the 8-inch to 2-inch armour strake above, nor her gun turrets, one of which was struck full on and she was in full fighting condition at the end of the day. Most seriously damaged were her funnels; these were so riddled that the boiler draft was affected and coal consumption increased to such an extent that she had after all to make for the German port of Tsingtau to refuel; here she was interned until the end of the war.

The main lessons to be drawn from the battle were the indecisiveness of fire outside 5,000 yards and, once again, the value of armour protection. After the best part of a day's fighting and the expenditure of upwards of 10,000 shells, the total Russian casualties had been 79 killed, 404 wounded, the total Japanese 68 killed, 168 wounded;

of these 32 killed and 93 wounded were from the *Mikasa*, which had received 22 out of 32 hits on the whole Japanese line. And no ships on either side had been lost. By contrast three battleships had succumbed to mines since the start of the war.

After the action the Japanese stepped up their already thorough gunnery training; combined 'dotters and deflection teachers' began to appear aboard and came into continual use, as did telescopic sights, manufactured by J. Hicks of London for the 6-inch QF guns. A British observer with the fleet wrote, 'the improvement in training had not ended with an amelioration of the dexterity of the gun pointers. Among both officers and men shooting has formed the principle topic of thought and conversation for months...'[10]

Meanwhile Russia had started the main units of her Baltic fleet on a Homeric voyage around Europe, Africa and Asia in an attempt to retrieve her desperate fortunes in the East. This 'cumbersome mass' of warships, supply and hospital vessels was headed by four new first class battleships of the 'Borodino' class, of 13,600 tons designed displacement, but with modifications and extra bunkers and stores nearer 15,000 tons. Similar to the *Tsarevitch* in style, these had a complete waterline belt of a maximum 10-inch thickness, a 6-inch thick strake above tapering to 2½-inch at bow and stern, and above that a lightly-protected anti-torpedo boat battery of 12-pounders at mid-length. Two decks higher at either end of a long superstructure were two 11-inch armoured turrets housing a pair of 12-inch guns each, and there were six smaller turrets each housing a pair of 6-inch guns, an armament and armour arrangement which might have been produced by White for a French *directeur du matériel*; but the waterline belts were lower than anything White could have sanctioned—were in fact completely submerged by overloading when the ships eventually reached the East—the armoured strake above rose only 6 feet higher, and the 12-pounder gunports were only two feet above that; also the sides had a distinct French tumble-home culminating in a high superstructure, so dangerous to stability when combined with a low belt.

The Baltic fleet sailed from Kronstadt towards the end of September under the command of Admiral Rozhestvensky, an imposing disciplinarian with a towering temper who kept his own counsel about important matters, but had an interesting command of coarse nicknames for his Captains and subordinates. There were plenty of opportunities to air these at the start of the voyage, as the ill-practised fleet suffered a number of delays and accidents before it eventually steamed out of the Baltic and altered southerly for the Straits of Dover.

By this time the depressing news from the Far East and rumours of

Japanese torpedo-boats ready to beset them in their own waters had created a near-panic among officers and men, and when on the night of 22 October the lookouts saw flares from some British fishing trawlers off the Dogger Bank, they were immediately taken for enemy recognition signals and the flagship, *Suvoroff*, opened fire, which soon spread down the lines to port and starboard as bugles blared, drums rumbled. Men tumbled on deck in confusion and up to the flying bridges where the smaller quick-firers were mounted, peering out into the darkness rent by flashes from the great guns. Amid the thunder, the shouted orders and rattle of ammunition trucks the question burned on all lips, 'The destroyers? Where are they? How many?'[11]

After some twelve minutes of battle four Hull trawlers were on fire, another was listing and sinking and the chaplain of the first class cruiser, *Aurora*, was dying of wounds received from the guns of the *Oryol*.

The prestige of the Russian Navy, already low, touched bottom. In England there was expectation of war. The Channel Squadron under Lord Charles Beresford was ordered to raise steam and get the shell up and fused; British cruisers were despatched to shadow the Russians who, briefly fouling the nets of another fishing fleet, passed Dover and headed for the Atlantic. As they steamed southwards off Spain the British cruisers 'became more and more provocative in their behaviour. At night they steamed abreast of us, only two or three cables' length away, following by day a couple of miles in our wake...'[12]

Lord Charles Beresford drew up a battle plan:

Being quite satisfied with the gunnery of the Channel fleet I should only have engaged the Russians...with four of my battleships at a distance of from 5,000 to 6,000 yards. It appeared to me that this would only be chivalrous. If the Russian ships had commenced to knock my ships about I would have engaged them with the whole eight Channel Fleet battleships...[13]

It was evident that a war would have been popular in England, as in the fleet. But the threat passed. The Russians continued south, around the bulge of West Africa, stopping where they could at French or German ports to coal from a fleet of colliers chartered from the Hamburg-Amerika line. They rounded the Cape of Good Hope in December and steered up for the French island of Madagascar, arriving just before Christmas; here the men heard of the destruction of the Port Arthur fleet and the fall of Port Arthur itself. Their spirits fell further still. On Christmas day a midshipman in the *Oryol* who had been drinking freely voiced many thoughts: 'They are sending us to Golgotha. But if I don't want to be crucified, what then? Will they drag me to the cross?'

Rozhestvensky waited in Madagascar through January and February for reinforcing divisions which were making their way through the Mediterranean and Suez, meanwhile carrying out exercises and target practices whose lack of skill displeased him greatly. In early March he sailed on the penultimate lap across the Indian Ocean for the Sunda Islands. As this stretch took almost a month and as the only island coaling stations were British the ships had to coal at intervals at sea, a feat tried by various navies in exercises, but never from necessity. The colliers had been provided with special barges for the purpose; these and the warships' own boats were used to ferry the sacks across the water. And to make sure of a sufficiency while the weather permitted the operation, coal was stowed in every available space, even in the mess decks; the men slept on heaps of it, swallowed its dust with their food, felt their teeth gritty and the very pores of their skin blocked with coal. It became an obsession, as if the business of the squadron was 'not to fight but simply to get to Japan.'[14]

They passed Singapore at the end of March and the Russian consul came out in a launch with the news that the Japanese fleet under Togo was waiting for them on the north-west coast of Borneo — quite inaccurate as it turned out, but enough to set all hands stowing timber furniture below and at night turning uneasily as they tried to sleep. No hostile ships were sighted. Some days later they put into a bay in French Indo-China (the first land touched since Madagascar) where they coaled, heard about the latest disasters in Manchuria, then steamed on, finally meeting the reinforcements which Rozhestvensky had been ordered to attach to his flag. As they were headed by an obsolete 9,700-ton battleship, *Nicholas I*, and three 4,000-ton coast defence armourclads, it was more of an incubus than a source of strength. It raised their spirits all the same. The bands played, the sea sparkled, the heat shimmered over the black ships; Rozhestvensky issued an order of the day: 'The reinforcement which has just arrived has made our strength not merely equal to that of the enemy, but actually superior in respect of battleships. Even though the Japanese ships are swifter than ours, this is of no importance since we do not intend to run away.' The complete Second Pacific Squadron, now formed in three columns, steamed north-east up the Chinese coast towards their appointment with fate.

Officers and men speculated on Rozhestvensky's plans, wondering whether he would alter easterly and make a circuit around the Japanese islands to break into the Sea of Japan from the north where mist or fog might conceal them from Togo's fleet, or whether he would steer directly for the Straits of Tsushima which formed the southern entrance to the sea they must enter to reach Vladivostok. When they stopped in the ocean to take on the last of the coal from their colliers, again stowing it wherever they could find space and loading the ships well beyond their normal displacement, it began to seem as if they might take the long way around. But this was not Rozhestvensky's idea. The Japanese had the interior position and the faster fleet; their cruisers would be able to shadow him and there would be no escape however devious his route: he set course direct for Tsushima.

Togo was waiting for him. His cruisers sighted the Russians in the early hours of 27 May as they approached the Straits of Tsushima, and as Rozhestvensky was taking considerably more trouble celebrating the anniversary of the Tsar's coronation than spreading cruisers to find or repel the enemy's scouting forces, they were able to press in and wireless full details of the Russian composition, formation, course and speed to Togo, who put to sea to intercept. Rozhestvensky pressed on, perhaps inspired by supreme confidence in the strength of his ships or by the auspicious date, meanwhile forming his battleships into single line headed by the four largest, *Suvoroff*, *Alexander III*, *Borodino*, *Oryol*; behind them came four older battleships with the *Osliaba* in the lead, and behind them the thoroughly unbattleworthy reinforcing division of coast defence vessels.

Togo, steering towards them unseen on their starboard bow, led with his only four battleships joined by two armoured cruisers of 7,700 tons as his first division, followed by a second division of six other armoured cruisers of nearly 10,000 tons, each mounting four 8-inch guns and six or seven 6-inch on each broadside. All told Togo had 16 12-inch guns (on his four battleships) and 112 8-inch and 6-inch able to fire on any one broadside. Rozhestvensky had no less than 26 12-inch guns (only 16 of them modern weapons mounted in ships of modern construction), 17 10-inch guns and 121 8-inch to 6-inch on one broadside—an apparently overwhelming superiority of heavy guns but roughly equal secondary batteries. However, his rear four ships were so slow that the fleet speed was only 9 knots; Togo's was practically double. In addition of course the Japanese fleet was battle-tried, flushed with victory, intensively practised in gunnery and led by an admiral who had passed through the valley of extreme caution, digested the lessons, and prepared his mind to what appeared instinctive decisive action.

At about 1.30 in the afternoon of what had turned into a misty day, Togo steering south-south-westerly, sighted the leading ships of the Russian fleet ahead and on his starboard bow, steering up towards him on a reciprocal course. The wind was strong in the south-west, flecking the sea with streaks of foam, and as he had already decided to fight with it behind him, he altered north-west across the Russian course, coming round to west after a while and then south-west so that he was approaching the enemy on his port bow, meanwhile flying a signal reminiscent of Nelson's at Trafalgar: 'THE FATE OF OUR EMPIRE HANGS ON THIS ONE ACTION; YOU WILL ALL EXERT YOURSELVES AND DO YOUR UTMOST.'

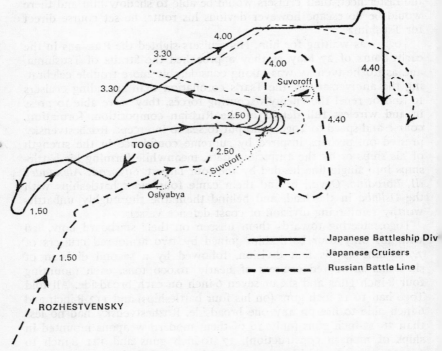

Figure 2. Battle of Tsushima. First phase of the battle – Diagram only; accuracy of courses and deviations has been sacrificed for clarity.

As the *Mikasa* came within 7,000 yards of the Russian leader, *Suvoroff*, Togo ordered a turn to port, ships in succession, and led around towards the enemy nearly 180 degrees, until he was steaming in the same direction as Rozhestvensky on a slightly converging course. As he came round the Russians opened an accurate fire at 6,500 yards—the first shot falling just 22 yards astern of the *Mikasa* —and continued to rain a volume of shells on the turning point as each Japanese ship in turn came up to it and put her helm over. Captain Packenham, one of the British observers, noted:

This commencement was made notable by the close shooting of the Russians. Shells were falling alongside the Japanese ships throwing heavy bodies of water on to their decks; some 6-inch shell fell on upper works and others splashed on armour belts, but no larger projectile seemed to get home.[15]

Meanwhile only those Japanese ships which had actually turned could open their own broadsides in reply; it was undoubtedly a bold if not a contemptuous manoeuvre very different from the distant promenadings at the start of the battle of 10 August, and while it was designed to bring a concentration to bear across the head of the Russian column it sacrificed the opening minutes to the chance of a few big hits from the most powerful Russian ships. However, it paid off; by 2-p.m. the two lines were steaming in the same direction and firing at 5,500–5,700 yards range, all the leading Japanese ships concentrating on the Russian flagship *Suvoroff*, which frequently disappeared behind columns of water and smoke. As the Japanese guns found the range Rozhestvensky altered two points towards them; this had the effect of allowing the Japanese ships, steaming at 15 knots, to forge ahead, so he soon turned away four points to bring them abeam again.

However it was not long before Togo's superior speed took him ahead again, and he turned in across the Russian course, closing the range rapidly. Rozhestvensky bore away once more, then made a sharp turn to port across the Japanese wake, at which Togo turned all his first division to port together and made to cross ahead from the other direction, again closing and punishing the *Suvoroff* in her upperworks and batteries, starting fires, scouring unprotected positions with a hail of splinters from shell fragments and the ship's own fittings, which even entered the observation slits of the conning tower, wounding Rozhestvensky and the officers crowded with him. The flagship swayed out of the line, lost in the smoke from her own fires.

Behind the Japanese first division, the cruisers had been concentrating on the leading ship of the Russian second division, *Osliaba*, to such good effect that she was already sinking. She was one of the earlier battleships in the French style with great tumble-home, and she had entered the battle so overloaded that her 9-inch belt was awash, thus leaving the protection of her waterline to a short mid-length belt of 5-inch steel. Early in the battle she had been struck by an 8-inch shell low in the bows and soon after by another which had penetrated her side low down, letting in the sea. She had begun to settle by the head and heel, until the water reached her perforated funnels and, flooding down, carried her quickly to the bottom.

By this time the Japanese cruisers which had done the damage had passed ahead of the Russian van. But the Russians soon doubled back under pressure from Togo's battleships and so came under the fire of the cruisers again. Once more they twisted to port, apparently trying to break through between the two Japanese divisions, now acting independently, and escape in the smoke and mist. Meanwhile the battered *Suvoroff* had become separated from the rest of the fleet and, passing alone close by the Japanese battleship division, received a concentrated fire at ranges which closed to little over 1,000 yards:

> It seemed impossible to count the shells which hit us. Not only had I never seen such a barrage, I could not have imagined anything like it. Shells seemed to rain down on us without pause. Steel plates and parts of our superstructure were blown to pieces, and flying splinters did a lot of damage... the high temperature of the explosions spread a kind of liquid fire which smothered everything, further enhancing the terrifying effects of the shells ...there were times when it was impossible to see anything through binoculars for the quivering of the overheated air confused everything...[16]

Packenham, watching the destruction, wrote:

> The forward funnel was gone and a raging fire had conquered the space between the other and the after barbette—in spite of which she continued in action...flames crept to the stern and the dense smoke emitted was being rolled horizontally away by the wind...a 12-inch shell made its way into her 'tween decks... the explosion was accompanied by a tremendous backrush of flame that must have been projected 50 feet from her side, and then through the enormous rent revealed, the glow of her newly-ignited interior could be seen...Projectiles continued to rain upon her. Her mainmast and foremast were shot away and a big explosion in her after part was thought to have finished her, but though only her bow and the upper part of her foc's'le could be seen she still maintained the unequal contest...the unexampled lengths to which human bravery and fortitude were carried in defence of this ship were such as reflect an undying glory, not only on her gallant crew, but on their navy, on their country, on humanity...this hero, not of a day, but of time.[17]

All the Russian ships were by now in confusion, circling away from the faster Japanese divisions as they bore down to decisive range. 'It appeared as if every ship in the Baltic fleet that was still able to move had got into a sort of pool, in which they were circling or standing to and fro aimlessly.'[18] Clouds of smoke and mist hid different ships or groups of ships at intervals so that it was impossible to tell how many were still together, while all the time the Japanese, keeping perfect station in line ahead in their two separate divisions, wheeling together in response to their admirals' signals, steamed around outside, keeping the range generally between 6,000 and 3,000 yards, pouring in fire whenever their gunners saw a target clearly. So it continued through the afternoon, the Russian ships outsteamed and outclassed in gunnery, yet keeping up a stout resistance, their fire-fighting parties constantly at work as the timber decks and bridges and all the boats, furniture and fittings that some ships had failed to clear away before the battle, rose in flames and smoke; the stretcher parties carried the burnt, asphyxiated, shocked, torn casualties below to the surgeons who operated without anaesthetics as the queues grew.

Later in the day the *Suvoroff*, still burning and steering aimlessly by herself, came under attack from a group of destroyers and received a torpedo in her port quarter which caused her to list but failed to sink her. Meanwhile the main body of Russian ships were following a new leader, *Borodino*, making northwesterly for Vladivostok as mist and smoke hid them briefly from the Japanese. Their respite was not long. Togo's battlefleet soon appeared again on their starboard quarter overhauling them on a parallel course closing to 5,700 yards distance, concentrating on the two leaders and as they forged past cutting in and forcing them round. The *Alexander III* staggered out of the line with her upperworks demolished and on fire, the choppy sea flooding in through holes in the unprotected parts of the side and numerous leaks between and behind the shaken armour plates; she heeled over, taking in more water through the low 12-pounder gun ports, then capsized and sank. The Japanese fire now concentrated on the *Borodino* and *Oryol*, which had so far suffered comparatively lightly.

Some minutes later the third Japanese battleship, *Fuji*, put a 12-inch shell into the *Borodino* close by her forward 6-inch turret, starting a fire which spread to her ammunition train and ignited it; a great column of smoke, ruddied by the explosion and other fires in her upperworks, rushed up to the height of the funnel tops.

From every opening in the upper parts of the stokeholds and engine rooms steam rushed, and in two or three minutes the ship from foremast to stern was wrapped in fiercely-whirling spirals of smoke and vapour, gaily-illuminated every now and then by the momentary breaking through of a tall shaft of flame... while all were watching, the unfortunate ship disappeared, her

G

departure only marked by a roar not greatly louder than that of the explosion of one of her own shells. At one moment the ship was there; the next moment she had gone, that was all...[19]

The flames had reached one of her magazines.

The time was 7.20; sunset. Togo steamed on ahead, opening the range beyond 8,000 yards and ceasing fire. Then the destroyers came in, tossing green seas from their foredecks, harrying the remnants of the fleet as they tried to reform behind the *Nicholas I*, flagship of the relatively little-damaged third division. Way astern another group of boats found the blackened, listing wreck of the *Suvoroff*. Admiral Rozhestvensky and his staff had been taken off by destroyer some time since, but her undamaged guns were still manned, and these opened up on the attackers as they approached, forcing them to manoeuvre around to the port side before they closed; then they struck her with three torpedoes from 300 yards range and she rolled over and sank.

Other torpedo attacks that night accounted for two of the older battleships and a coast defence armourclad, and as one other older battleship had succumbed to gunfire from the cruiser line earlier, the Russian battle line steaming for Vladivostok on the following morning was composed of only four ships; of these the *Oryol* was the one modern battleship of force, but she was listing badly and had been so punished about the upperworks and in the batteries, turrets and ammunition hoists, that she scarcely retained half her fighting strength. When Togo appeared with all his ships in fighting trim this pitiful Russian force, having no choice between surrender or annihilation, lowered their colours. Elsewhere Rozhestvensky's destroyer was captured and taken in tow by a Japanese destroyer.

So ended the Battle of Tsushima, one of the most decisive naval actions ever fought, in material terms perhaps the most decisive; the Second Pacific Squadron had ceased to exist. The Russian Navy had been swept from the list of major powers, Japan had indisputable command of the sea, and with her victorious armies in Manchuria indisputable command of the eastern war. In the subsequent peace she kept Port Arthur, Dairen, the South Manchurian railway and her dominant position in Korea. Russia broke out in revolution.

The main reason for the victory was undoubtedly superior gunnery at decisive range. This is clear in all British observers' reports. While the Russian ships had kept up a constant, rapid fire whether they could see the target or not, the Japanese had carefully husbanded their nervous energy, only firing when within range and sure of their aim. Captain Jackson reported from the cruiser, *Adzuma*: 'The discipline in this respect was marvellous. From time to time the firing died away, not in consequence of any order, but because the numbers one did not think they were justified in firing into the brown on the off-chance of hitting...'[20] The Japanese had three bugle calls for opening fire, either 'deliberate', 'ordinary' or 'rapid'; 'on board the *Adzuma* rapid fire never sounded and that for ordinary fire only twice, each when the range was less than 4,000 yards. The deliberate fire call was used several times, generally to check quickening fire at long ranges.' This careful aim was as a result of war experience, rigorous training and the expectation that the battle would last at least two days.

Together with better marksmanship the Japanese probably had more effective shells. Since the battle of 10 August, when their fuses had proved unduly sensitive, sometimes exploding in the guns and certainly on the slightest graze on target, thus taking effect outside even the unprotected parts of the Russian ships, they had introduced modifications which had made them rather more effective. While still too sensitive to pierce the Russian armour, they had brought their bursting charges through the unprotected parts with devastating incendiary effect. As a result there was a great swing towards 'common', that is thin-walled shells with a large bursting charge, as against armour-piercing shells, which because of their thick metal carried only small bursters. As Sir John Fisher put it at the time, 'many officers are so insistent on using common shell largely in action as they maintain the enemy would be so wrecked, demoralized and put out of trim by the effect of these large explosions, as not to necessitate any attack on his thick armour, which forms so small a target and is so small a proportion of the visible hull.'[21]

As for tactics, the superior Japanese speed, 15 against nine knots, had given them an advantage which Togo had seized to dictate the range at which the battle should be fought and to concentrate all his ships' fire against the leading one or two Russians in each division; he had repeated the manoeuvre again and again as the smoke and mist permitted, at first in fleet line ahead and then in two divisions in line ahead acting independently; the crushing early results on the two flagships and the successes at the end of the day seemed to justify this, although by later gunnery standards it was a mistake to leave any ships in the line unfired at; moreover this 'concentration fire' was thoroughly unscientific and wasteful in ammunition and nervous energy, for the splashes of the dozens of shells together made it impossible for the gunlayers or their officers to 'spot' their own shell and thus correct their aim. The effect was generally a wall of 'short' splashes obscuring both the target and any 'overs' and giving the gunlayers a constant tendency to raise their sights. Tsushima was a victory for the Nelsonic 'hail of fire', some of which was bound to find its mark, and as William Sims pointed out after careful analysis of the battle, most of the hitting had occurred when the rate of change of range had been low or negligible.

Nevertheless, Togo, in his courageous decision to start this battle where that of 10 August had left off, in his persistence in closing to his chosen range, refusal to hazard his ships to chance at really close range, and in his superb combination of gun and torpedo attack had shown undoubted *coup d'oeil*; as Packenham summed it up:

On this day the prevailing mists...severely tested the degree in which the Japanese admiral possessed this great quality. Ships disappeared and went, none could mark where, and then with equal suddenness they were again discovered on unexpected bearings and in groups of unknown strength. Admiral Togo has had before no such opportunity for showing that he has the eye of a master. It seems as though this day has completed him, and that something wanted earlier has now been supplied.[22]

Fire Control and the Dreadnought

Tsushima, dramatic and decisive as it was, and apparently pregnant with lessons, was another example of how action experience generally lagged behind theoretical and technical advance. The ships and gunnery methods with which it was fought were, if not obsolete, in a process of change which was about to render many of the 'lessons' meaningless; this change was 'fire control'. Tsushima was the last great naval battle fought in the time-honoured way with each gunlayer responsible for his own aim and fire, and subject to no—or more correctly ineffective—central control. In this respect it was closer in spirit to Trafalgar than to the actions of the 1914 war. It is true that both Russian and Japanese ships had two Barr & Stroud rangefinders apiece, and that their operators passed the range to the gun positions either by electric telegraph or, in the Japanese organization, by voicepipe to the conning tower where the range telegraph was situated, also that an officer was stationed aloft to 'spot' the fall of shot for each battery, but it is evident from all reports that this organization broke down during the decisive periods of the engagement; the Japanese Captain Murakami considered that the experience of the war indicated 'that an officer should be stationed aloft to spot, not with any certainty that he would be of any use, but because he occasionally might be.'[1]

The British service had advanced beyond this stage. Centralized control of all the guns from an aloft position had been accepted, at least in ordnance circles, and the apparatus needed, which included range and deflection telegraphs, 'rate of change of range' clocks, and instruments known after their inventor as Dumaresqs, which indicated the necessary deflection when set with enemy range, bearing, course and speed, were being manufactured and installed in carefully-planned 'control tops' on the masts of the latest battleships; older battleships were being taken in hand as the new instruments became available. A new annual long-range firing test called 'battle

practice' had been instituted, and an Inspector of Target Practice—
Percy Scott—appointed to co-ordinate and disseminate methods and
results. While all this organization was still in its infancy at the time
of Tsushima and the battle practice that year was carried out at only
5,000–6,000 yards, it was nevertheless developing with an enthusiasm
and momentum which had begun to transform long-range hitting
from a matter of chance into a science—or at least a craft. All this
was a development of the gunnery revolution that Scott had inspired,
fostered by the gap between the great gun's potential accuracy and
its poor results in the 'long range' practices instituted from the turn
of the century. It had nothing to do with the naval actions of the
Russo-Japanese war. As Percy Scott remarked after a notable 'historian' suggested that Tsushima provided proof of the futility of long
range fire, 'There are many people who did not require this battle
evidence to teach them that trying to conduct a fight at long range
without the necessary tools for doing it with, is a useless expenditure
of ammunition.'

Among the 'tools' under development in Britain were two highly
advanced systems, the forerunners of all later methods. The inspiration for the earliest of these dated from 1901, the year that Lieutenant Dumaresq invented his calculator. It was a continuous action plot
showing both own ship and enemy on a moving paper, and it was
designed to eliminate the great difficulty of long range practice, which
was that target range and bearing could alter substantially during the
time of flight of the shell. As the inventor, Arthur Pollen, pointed out,
it was no use ordering a 'spotting' correction 'Down 200 yards' if
the target was also going to move 200 yards closer while the shell was
in the air.[2] For spotting corrections at long range to be of any use they
had to be associated with the relative movement of the target; this
was what his plot aimed to find. While the mechanism was probably
20 years ahead of its practical application, several of the ideas and
the scientific attitude to long range fire which he pioneered gave the
British service several years' start in this field.

Of more immediately practical effect was a design for 'director
firing' maturing in collaboration between Percy Scott and the
ordnance manufacturers, Vickers Ltd.[3] Scott drew up the first rough
designs in 1904; they were for a modern version of the nineteenth-
century system whereby all guns of the broadside could be laid to a
required elevation and angle of training and then fired simultaneously
by one man at a 'director sight', as the target moved on to the point
of 'concentration'. This system had been discontinued since separate
turrets and casemates had made communications between all the
guns difficult. Scott aimed to revive it because he considered that
long range firing would be most effective if the guns were fired all

together and the whole broadside 'spotted' as one. The only way to fire them together and eliminate the different reaction times and personal errors of the gunlayers was to take both sighting and firing out of their hands and entrust them to one quite independent man, a director layer. To give this vital man a clear field of view above smoke, spray and splinters in action, he aimed to put him aloft in close association with the control party already there. This was the most vital single gunnery invention of the twentieth century, and although it was resisted stoutly by those who claimed that the Navy, and no doubt the British Empire, had achieved its triumphant position because of the steadiness of the (British) man behind the gun, resisted also by the 'historical' school of close-range enthusiasts, and even by those gunnery officers who achieved the best results at long range in independent fire—because they were good and practice conditions were always ideal—Scott eventually succeeded in having it adopted. That is jumping ahead. In 1904–5 all these and many other ideas were just catching fire, releasing a wealth of inventive enthusiasm from the gunnery officers of the fleet who felt themselves valued at last, and who had a practically clear field in which to experiment. Exactly the same thing was happening in the United States under their Inspector of Target Practice, William Sims. In both services the competitive instincts of the officers and men were engaged to effect the revolution—for it was nothing less. Where before paint and polish had brightened the narrowing path to high rank, it was now gunnery, gunnery, gunnery, holes in canvas and lattice-work battle practice targets. Perhaps this was helped by the new uniform dull grey imposed on all ships since 1902 following the lead of the German service. And yet that was a symptom too; grey didn't hide a fleet, there was too much smoke for that, but it did make the gunlayers' task more difficult in misty weather.

Out of the convulsion was born the new type of capital ship. Just as the 'Royal Sovereigns', 'Majestics', and all, had come from the acceptance of the Colomb/Mahan view of strategy, so the all-big-gun ship came from the gunnery renaissance. And as the British and US navies were the leaders in the renaissance so the new type appeared first in these two services. It is true that *ideas* for a vessel with a great battery of the heaviest guns only were floating about like spores on the wind of navalism which blew freely throughout the world, but these were vague concepts of devastation from 'knock-out blows' more reminiscent of the 1880s than of the new scientific gunnery, and they would never, in themselves, have persuaded the leading navies to throw over their existing battleships with compromise armament—not at least until a lesser power had shown the way. The vital point which persuaded the American and

British services to take the plunge was fire control, which meant centralized 'spotting' on target. This was simplest if only one calibre of gun was involved as each different calibre had to be given a different elevation to achieve the same range, hence passed through different atmospheres on different trajectories, and arrived at different times, generally confusing the picture. As the latest successors to the 'Majestics' had main, secondary *and* intermediate or semi-heavy batteries—thus the 'King Edward VII' class from 1903 had four 12-inch, four 9.2-inch, 10 6-inch, the American 'Connecticut' class from 1904, four 12-inch, eight 8-inch, 12 7-inch, not to mention 3-inch anti-torpedo-boat guns—the whole thing had become almost impossible and some simplification was inevitable.

Really the only point to be decided was the calibre of the uniform battery; in America the argument revolved around 12-inch or 11-inch, in Britain 12-inch or 10-inch, the 10-inch favoured by many officers including Fisher at one time, because it could be carried in greater numbers and had a firing rate of four rounds a minute as against only two rounds for the heavier piece; it seemed to offer not only scientific control and armour-piercing capacity at decisive range, but also a 'hail of fire'. However, the 12-inch won the day, as it did in America, because it had a flatter trajectory at any given range, therefore a greater likelihood of hitting the target—a consideration amply demonstrated in actual practice—and carried a far greater bursting charge. As 'controlled' fire was necessarily slow at that date, the greater single bursting effect outweighed the possibility of more rapid fire from the 10-inch.

While design discussions were taking place, attachés' reports from the battle of 10 August came in; these were scathing about the Japanese attempts at long range fire control which 'ascended through different degrees of diminishing harmfulness until it had attained to total uselessness'[4] but suggested that despite this the battle had been decided *before* the secondary batteries came within effective range.

It is believed that an inspection of the ships would show that the fate of the day had lain with and had been entirely decided by heavy guns, if not by the heaviest only...[5]

The same report also said 'the effect of the fire of every gun is so much less than that of the next larger size, that when 12-inch guns are firing, shots from 10-inch pass unnoticed...this must be understood to refer only to moral effect.[6] A later report from Packenham stated that the whole fate of the naval war had revolved around the 12-inch gun: 'medium artillery has had its day and the natural progress of evolution demands it should now give place to primary artillery.'⁷ This action experience reinforcing practice results and theoretical argument decided the issue. In 1905 both British and American navies began detailed design work on battleships having a single battery of 12-inch guns supported only by anti-torpedo-boat batteries.

In one respect the American design was the better; this was in the disposition of all the turrets on the centre-line with two forward turrets arranged one higher than the other so that both could fire right ahead as well as on either broadside and two after turrets arranged in the reverse order for direct astern or broadside fire. This 'superfiring' method appeared in British sketch designs but was rejected because of the blast effect of the upper turret guns on the occupants of the lower turrets; the Americans got around this, literally, by replacing the sighting hoods, which in the normal way stood up above the turret roofs, with sighting periscopes which stuck out from the sides of each turret—an idea after Leonardo da Vinci. In contrast to the two simple and economic pairs of turrets in the American design the final British design had five 12-inch turrets spaced at more or less equal distances down the length of the ship, three on the centre-line and one on either beam between the second and third centre line positions. This gave a similar broadside of eight guns and a similar ahead fire for most angles off the bow, but a theoretical direct ahead fire of six guns and a direct astern fire of only two guns; British ships were not expected to show their sterns to the enemy. In both designs broadside fire was of prime importance.

But there was one feature which placed the British ship in a higher class altogether than the American: this was her great speed of 21 knots, equal to a contemporary cruiser and two or three knots more than a contemporary battleship. The requirement for speed was a reflection of the maturer strategic and tactical conceptions of the British service. The US Navy did not, and from its very recent battleship build-up could not, have the experience in fleet exercises and tactical evolutions that the British had. Since at least 1895, when line of battle was clearly evident in the British annual manoeuvres, scouting, signalling and manoeuvring techniques had been developed into a body of tactical lore which was unequalled for precision and range. It was criticized for over-centralization and for its un-*real* or peace-time quality, but it is doubtful if there were many other tacticians in any other navies of the calibre of Sir Arthur Wilson, for instance. As for unreality, the battle Wilson fought with X fleet against B fleet in the 1901 manoeuvres might almost have been a dress rehearsal for Togo's tactics at Tsushima, although he didn't hazard the opening minutes to chance by turning 16 points in succession within range of the enemy. This 'battle' is interesting for the sophistication of the tactics on each side and as an illustration of the value of speed. Wilson's fleet had a two knot advantage over B fleet and he used this to bring a concentration to bear on the head of the B line, opening fire at 7,000 yards while his own line was on a steady course converging on B line of advance; 'the fire of X fleet became more and more concentrated on the leading ships of B fleet...the ships of B fleet also became exposed to torpedo attack at long range by the ships of X fleet without the possibility of returning it'.[8]

As for tactics, so for battlefleet strategy; Britain had experience from decades of manoeuvres, also a greater need than any other power for rapid concentrations. She also had a First Sea Lord, Sir John Fisher, who understood the limitations now placed upon battle-fleet movement in narrow seas and coastal areas by flotilla attack—especially at night—also by the developing submarine. Apart from French concentration on this arm, the infant British submarine service had already shown in exercises that it could torpedo big ships steaming off ports, and Fisher had decided to use submarines to provide an extended coastal defence system, rather as mobile mine-fields. He saw clearly that all these developments fundamentally altered the role of the battleship.

SECRET AND PROFOUNDLY PRIVATE

Formerly the battleship was the ultimate protection to anything or any operation. NOW ALL THIS HAS BEEN ABSOLUTELY ALTERED. A battlefleet is no protection to anything or any operation during dark hours and in certain waters is *no protection in daytime!*

Hence what is the use of battleships as we have hither-to known them? None!...No one would seriously consider build-ing battleships merely to fight other battleships since if battle-ships have no function that first-class armoured cruisers cannot fulfil, then they are useless to the enemy and need not be fought.

Hence the history and justification of the designs of the battle-ship now proposed; for what else is she but a glorified armoured cruiser?[9]

To obtain cruiser speed without increasing the length and dis-placement excessively, Fisher and the engineer-in-chief of the Navy showed great courage in adopting turbines; this form of marine engine which used high pressure steam acting on a series of angled blades round the perimeter of a central rotor, had been under development by Sir Charles Parsons since 1892 and had first been used in the destroyers *Viper* and *Cobra* in 1899. On their success a cruiser had been ordered, and her trial results gave the Admiralty the necessary confidence to adopt the engine in their new battleship. It was a remarkably short development period. In the event the decision was triumphantly justified; turbines offered the great advantage of lightness and compactness, with the added bonus that they were more efficient at high speeds than the reciprocating engines they replaced and had fewer moving parts and were consequently less liable to failure.

As the main features of the British design were experimental, Fisher determined that only one ship should be built and she should be rushed through in order to obtain trial results and experience at the earliest possible date; in fact Fisher believed in rush for its own sake, and the new battleship, his own conception, really a materialization of his own naval philosophy, became a giant exercise in administration against the stopwatch, conducted with his usual flair for publicity before an amazed world audience. The keel plates were laid in Portsmouth on 2 October 1905 after armour plates, guns and mountings had been diverted from the last two conventional battleships under construction; she was launched just over four months later on 10 February 1906, and steamed out on her trials on 3 October, one year and a day after the start—an awesome demonstration of industrial strength. Her name was *Dreadnought*.

She was immediately recognized as a new class of capital ship. Her looks affirmed this view: the long clean deckline overhung with the menace of the great turrets spaced out along it, the brief uncluttered superstructure surmounted by two well-proportioned rectangular funnels and a tripod mast for the control top, all fused into an aspect of efficiency and stark fighting power. There was no compromise, no extravagance, no uncertainty in line or curve or armoured plane. She was the embodiment of confident shipbuilding harnessed to gunnery; she was a great gun platform. By contrast existing battleships looked strangely stubby and ineffectual as if their designers had been unable to think of what to do with the space between the two end turrets and had filled it with whatever miscellaneous armoury, flying decks, tall funnels they had been able to collect together.

On trials the *Dreadnought* fulfilled all expectations; her gunnery was particularly impressive, each piece proving capable of two aimed rounds a minute with good drill, and the ship's structure proving adequate to absorb the terrific shock of full eight-gun broadsides. It became evident that no pre-'*Dreadnought*' battleship could live with her. One odd fault in her design was that the tripod mast, hence the vital control top, was placed abaft the foremost funnel, thus subject to smoke and fumes in certain wind conditions; another was that the anti-torpedo-boat guns were too small for the job, another that the main belt of 11-inch Krupp armour was too low. These details were ironed out in her successors; they and the wing turrets rather than a super-firing system were minor flaws in what became the prototype for all future capital ships, particularly as the great increase in strength which she represented had been achieved on a displacement of just under 18,000 tons—only 1,400 tons more than the latest class of pre-Dreadnoughts —and at a cost of only £1¾ millions against over £1½ millions for the pre-Dreadnoughts.

However, she was too radical a change to be accepted without opposition, and she became the centre of fierce controversy both inside and outside the service. The critics fell into three main categories. First there were those who admired the concept but deplored the fact that Britain had given it shape and thus pushed into the second rank all her existing battleships which were in such preponderance over all other powers; by doing so she had virtually wiped out 15 years of intense naval building, given all nations a chance to start from scratch in the new capital ship stakes, and thus encouraged challenge and a new 'naval race'. These critics insisted that British policy had always been to *follow*, never to initiate change, relying on industrial supremacy to go one better, faster. A second body of critics deplored the escalation in size and cost that the *Dreadnought* represented, especially in view of the submarine and torpedo menace; it was putting too many eggs in one 'majestic but vulnerable' basket. Of course this had been a recurring theme throughout the armourclad's evolution. Thirdly there was the naval historical school led by Mahan who thought that the design itself was wrong both in the total elimination of a secondary battery and in the sacrifice of strength for speed. It is plain that these arguments stemmed from the eighteenth century when the three-decker ship of the line had been the battle-winner although slower than the two-decker, and when British close tactics had prevailed over French long-range tactics.

Mahan stressed that the propensity to long-range fire 'destroyed the mental attitude which keeps offensive power in the foreground' and that the navy which habitually sought to keep its enemy at a distance 'in the long run finds itself brought to battle at an unexpected moment under conditions unfavourable to it both materially and morally'.[10] This must have referred to the French service in the last two decades of the eighteenth century. As for more recent times, the great preponderance of secondary over primary guns in the Japanese fleet at Tsushima and their enormous inferiority to the Russians in heavy pieces made it easy to argue that it was the sheer volume of rapid fire from the secondary pieces which had decided the action, not the 12-inch guns. One of the foremost British 'historians', Admiral Custance, drew from this the conclusion:

> There need be no hesitation in saying that in a seaway a Dreadnought would be worsted by a battleship having a battery of 6-inch guns of high command, with a few 12-inch guns to put the finishing touches at short range when the personnel is cowed and its nerve shaken by the hail of despised 6-inch shell.[11]

When Fisher showed this article to Percy Scott, the great gunner remarked, 'if you are firing at a range when the light guns do not hit, I see no reason why the volume of well-directed fire from them should prevent a successful reply from 12-inch guns.'[12] His view was that of a practical modern gunnery expert, yet it accorded with the lessons of history far better than the 'historians'; had they examined gunnery actions less dogmatically they would have found that the longer effective range gun had always given victory, from the time of Vasco da Gama, through the Dutch wars to the Anglo-American war of 1812. In that conflict, when the British sailors at last found themselves up against an *equal* enemy the decision had invariably gone to the greater gun or the longer-range gun. Sir Howard Douglas in his influential *Treatise on Naval Gunnery* after the Anglo-American War had dwelt on the 'vast advantages that may be reaped in distant cannonade with powerful guns, directed with every resource of refined, minute expedient to gain accuracy'.[13] Unfortunately the historical school which had started so brilliantly with their exposition of the strategy of maritime power would not look further than Nelson's period for gunnery or tactical lessons and, becoming victims of their own 'offensive' dogma, increasingly confused the issue. It is significant that the practical men took no notice—even when historians were right (as Mahan was about convoy)—unless it accorded with their own analysis, when they gladly supported their arguments with the historians' analogies.

In America Sims countered the historical arguments that naval battles were decided by demoralization of guns' crews, thus:

> On the proposed all-big-gun-ships the heavy armour belt will be about 8 feet above the waterline and extending from end to end. The conning tower, barbettes etc. will be of heavy armour; and there being no intermediate battery (which could not be protected by armour on account of its extent) it follows that in battle all gunnery personnel, except the small single fire control party aloft, will be behind heavy armour, and therefore neither the

ship nor her personnel can be materially injured by small-calibre guns.[14]

As for the other arguments that Britain was wrong to initiate change or increase the size of capital ships, this had really ceased to apply in the late 1880s when the historical doctrine of command had been accepted and been given material form in the 'Royal Sovereigns', the largest battleships of their time. They and their successors in command, the 'Majestics', had been designed, not simply to keep up with other nations' designs, but to do a specific job; that was the vital point of departure, not the *Dreadnought* policy. In any case it was impossible to draw the line between 'following' and 'initiating' change as the whole design process had been evolutionary; the earlier *Devastation* or *Dreadnought*, even the *Warrior* right at the beginning, had taken the initiative and all had led to the modern battleship; the latest *Dreadnought* was simply another stage, the final stage in this process. As America already had two all-big-gun ships under construction it was not a process which could be halted. The increase in size was also inevitable—with indisputable historic and theoretical precedent throughout the sailing era—and applied as much to pre-Dreadnoughts as to the *Dreadnought*.

But, of course the real reason why the *Dreadnought* had to be built was that a country which meant to command the seas with the guns of her battlefleet had to build battleships which could use their guns to maximum advantage. It would have been absurd to do anything else. As the British Director of Naval Ordnance, Captain Jellicoe, put it in May 1906: 'The recent development of the prospect of hitting frequently at long range is the all-important fact which has brought the value of the heaviest guns forward, and which culminates in the design of the *Dreadnought*.'[15]

At the same time as the Dreadnought decision was taken, three Dreadnought armoured cruisers, soon to become known as 'battle cruisers', were also specified, and the first of the class, HMS *Invincible*, was laid down in February 1906, just before the *Dreadnought* herself was launched. The ships were in most respects a development of existing heavy cruisers which were designed not simply for commerce protection, but as adjuncts to the battle fleet, to press home a reconnaisance in the face of enemy scouting forces, to support the head of the battlefleet in action, thus bringing a decisive concentration to bear on the leading enemy ships or in the event of a chase, to catch the enemy fleet and delay it while the battleships caught up. These cruisers were also given 12-inch guns. Fisher's naval assistant, Captain Bacon, wrote afterwards:

The day was carried by the argument that the gun should be of the same calibre as that of the battleship so that cruisers could be used in a fleet action as a fast auxiliary squadron instead of having to remain inactive owing to the fact that their guns could not range their enemy until they themselves had been compelled to close near enough to be under a murderous fire.[16]

Of course the new class of cruiser was also designed to be able to catch and crush enemy commerce-raiding squadrons, indeed that may well have been the prime consideration; nevertheless it seems clear that the term 'battle cruiser' was a true functional description.

Having decided on a speed of 25 knots to be able to catch any cruiser or armed merchantman afloat, and a single calibre armament of 12-inch guns for fire control there was not much tonnage left for protection; the cruisers' main belt was consequently 6-inch tapering to 4-inch in the bow and ending short of the stern, against 11-inch, 8-inch and 4-inch for the battleship, their barbettes and turret fronts were 7-inch against 11-inch in the battleship and their sides above the belt were left unprotected, as against an 8-inch strake at mid-length on the battleship. This comparatively weak protection was criticized at the time, and has received regular attack since then for being incompatible with a ship which would have to stand a pounding in a fleet action. However, given the gunpower and speed required, the only alternative to thin armour would have been a quite unacceptable increase in displacement. And while there remains a great deal of doubt about whether any first generation battle cruisers were lost because their armour was pierced, there is no doubt that their speed and gunpower proved decisive on several occasions. In any case they were by no means the first battle cruisers; most Italian heavy ships could have been described thus, and the Japanese heavy cruisers had already shown what such ships could do in a fleet action.

The extra speed of the battle cruisers was not gained simply by lighter protection; they had one less centre-line turret than the *Dreadnought* turbines which developed 80 per cent more horsepower—in fact the most powerful engines put aboard any ship up to that time—and they were longer by some 40 feet, and slimmer. Nevertheless they *looked* like capital ships, were naturally regarded as such and always featured in the Dreadnought counts that began to replace battleship counts as the chief concern of British admirals and politicians.

Meanwhile Germany had replaced France and Russia as the chief rival. The Russian battlefleet had, of course, been knocked out by Japan, the French had veered off on one of their periodic enthusiasms for small craft, in this case submarines, and had fallen behind in their battlefleet programmes, but the Germans, steadily proceeding on Tirpitz's chosen course, had launched 14 battleships since the supplementary Navy Law of 1900, and were potentially, if not actually, the second naval power in Europe. British naval dispositions, political attitudes and popular opinion had all swung round to meet this new threat. An *entente* concluded with France before the Russo-Japanese war had stiffened into something like an alliance based on mistrust of German aims. Wilhelm's diplomacy did nothing to allay mistrust. Nor of course did his battleships. In Britain it was noted that they had small cruising radius and cramped accommodation and it was concluded that they were designed to fight in the North Sea against Britain.[17] Such a powerful fleet would scarcely be needed against France and Russia; as a 1902 Cabinet paper put it, 'the issue of such a war can only be decided by armies and on land, and the great naval expenditure on which Germany has embarked involves a deliberate diminution of the military strength which Germany might otherwise have attained in relation to France and Russia.'[18]

Wilhelm declared that his navy was not directed *against* any power, but was being built to match Germany's growing maritime trade and the needs of her colonies throughout the world. 'It is absolutely *nonsensical* and *untrue* that the German Naval Bill is to provide a navy meant as a challenge to British naval supremacy...'[19]

In that case, went the British retort in countless articles and Admiralty memos, why short-haul battleships and destroyers instead of long-range cruisers which would be able to defend trade and colonies? This was verbal sparring. Both sides knew precisely what the battlefleet was for; it was being built as a tool for German diplomacy, specifically as a counter to the British battlefleet because that was the decisive factor in the balance of European, therefore world power. As in the Franco-Russian build-up of the 1880s and 90s it was the overwhelming strength of the British fleet, and the force that this gave to the smooth phrases of British statesmen protecting British interests, which drew naval expansion in its wake, and inevitably so. British navalists professed not to understand this. They pointed out that Britain needed an irresistible navy because she was an island and her very existence depended upon imports of food and raw materials, just as the existence of her empire depended upon command of the sea; her navy was therefore entirely 'defensive'. On the other hand Germany was a 'land power'; she did not depend upon imports by sea to live. Therefore if she built a powerful navy, it was 'offensive'. More, it was dangerous, as it was well known that a strong—by which they meant crushing—British Navy was the best guarantee of peace in the world. This was a useful rationalization; it rested on two assumptions which would not have stood up under scrutiny; first that it was possible to draw a line between 'defensive' and 'offensive' fighting forces, second that the British Navy *had* preserved the peace of Europe—no doubt it had on occasion usually by threat of highly 'offensive' action, but only *when* it suited the British interest to step in! Nevertheless it was the only practical line for the British Admiralty to take. It was also traditional, and in the nineteenth century had produced something like a stable world order; this was justification enough.

As for the Germans, they had an equally strong case; they were the fastest growing European power, second only to the United States in world terms; they had nearly doubled British steel production, had developed strong sea-borne trade and an efficient merchant marine which, while not yet a quarter the size of Britain's, was second in the world. They needed naval power corresponding to this strength and expansive momentum; without it they were, in Tirpitz's phrase, 'erecting a perfectly hollow structure...' And as Tirpitz believed in the battlefleet theory so they had to have a fleet of battleships. On another level, a battlefleet was the current symbol of technological exuberance—like the cathedrals of the Middle Ages.

In 1905, when Fisher's plans for an all-big-gun battleship became known, the Germans were working on some remarkably obsolescent ships with powerful secondary batteries which would have delighted the historical school; it is clear that they were some way behind the British and US services in fire control. They immediately stopped all construction work and spent two years planning their answers to the *Dreadnought*. As it was necessary to make them considerably larger than existing classes they also had to deepen the Kiel Canal, widen the locks and dredge deeper Channels from Wilhelmshaven, an added bonus for Fisher's policy which never ceased to delight him although it had formed no part of his plan. Finally, in July and August 1907, they laid down four Dreadnought battleships of just under 19,000 tons, the 'Nassau' class. These were technically inferior to the *Dreadnought*, mainly because there was only one firm in Germany which could build large turbines, and as Tirpitz wanted these engines for his cruisers, the battleships retained reciprocating engines. These took up a great deal of room at midlength to obtain a speed 1½ knots less than the British prototype, and required an arrangement of two wing turrets each side at midlength instead of the one centreline, one wing turret in the British design. There were of course two end turrets as well, making a total of no less than 12 heavy guns to obtain a broadside of eight guns. These were 11-inch pieces against the *Dreadnought*'s 12-inch. The *Nassau*'s main belt was however 11¾-inch thick against the *Dreadnought's* 11-inch. One undoubted German superiority was the anti-torpedo protection provided by a steel bulkhead inboard of side coal bunkers and cofferdams and carried the whole length of their vital magazine and engineroom spaces. All these features, smaller-calibre guns, thicker and generally more extensive armour protection and better underwater protection than contemporary British ships were continued in successive German classes down to 1914.

While the 'Nassaus' were building in 1908 Tirpitz again amended the Naval Law: the keels of four large armoured ships were to be laid down every year until 1911, and thereafter two. This accelerated construction of the Dreadnought type, and as it was also decided that large cruisers of the previous law should be built as battle cruisers, following the British lead, it increased the proposed establishment from 38 battleships and 20 large cruisers to 58 Dreadnoughts.

The British had meanwhile been building successors to the *Dreadnought* in comparatively leisurely style under a Liberal government anxious to increase the living standards of the people rather than spend money on 'bloated armaments'. In any case the British Navy was satisfyingly ahead of any possible rivals, and the idealists in the party who wanted Britain to give a lead in halting the international arms build-up were allowed a hearing. Thus, while six battleship successors to the *Dreadnought* and three battle cruisers had been laid down up to 1908, the estimates that year only allowed for one battleship, one battle cruiser. This was the year that Germany stepped up her building programme to four big keels a year: the situation had all the makings of a naval scare like those which had distinguished the 1890s, and true to form the navalists in the country started howling for Liberal blood. At first Fisher and the Board were not impressed: the British fleet stood to the German in the proportion 4:1, in Dreadnoughts built and building 10:4. No other European power had a single Dreadnought under construction; the French were still building ships similar to the British pre-Dreadnought 'Lord Nelsons' in point of armament.

Nevertheless the agitation continued, feeding on the wilder elements of German nationalism who looked forward very publicly to the day when Germany would be able to challenge Britain on the seas, break the ring of battleships and alliances that Britain had placed around her, and emerge as the supreme military and naval *world* power. For this it was not necessary to build a stronger fleet than Britain, only one which was strong enough to challenge at its own chosen moment when units of the British fleet were engaged elsewhere, perhaps in the Far East or in the Mediterranean against Russia. The alarm that this caused in British navalist circles and their reflex responses to call for more battleships in turn fed the violent outpourings; it was added proof of Anglo-Saxon determination to keep Germany and Germanism hemmed in in central Europe. So the fever on both sides spiralled upwards.

The Board of Admiralty, while keeping cool heads throughout this paper challenge, were nevertheless affected by the attaché's reports stressing Germany's increased shipbuilding capacity, the efficiency of her naval officers, the great efforts they were putting into training and the general feeling that they were working towards a showdown with the British Navy. Then in December, intelligence from various sources indicated that she was stockpiling nickel for guns and armour, and had stepped up her heavy ordnance capacity. As guns and mountings were the chief limiting factor in both the number and speed of construction of battleships, this removed the last vestiges of Admiralty complacency.

Here is one of the vital reports, dated 23 December 1908, from the military attaché at Constantinople; it dwelt on the importance of Krupp's works to Germany and their corresponding 'menace to England'.

During recent years (as can be proved) enormous quantities of heavy machinery have been purchased by Krupp, which can be required for no other purpose than that of manufacturing big guns and big naval mountings. This present machinery is far in excess of any requirements for the existing naval programme of Germany. German naval mountings are simpler in construction than English ones, and are designed particularly with the object of being manufactured quickly. The date of delivery of a battleship depends upon the date when the big guns and mountings can be delivered and erected. The ship can (with pressure) be built in about half the time necessary for the guns and mountings...From information received it seems safe to say that it is, or was, the intention of the Emperor to secretly prepare all the mountings, ships, plates, ammunition etc. at Krupps, and then to suddenly commence the creation of a number of battleships sufficient to at least equal the naval strength of England...[20]

Here was a situation such as no British Board had ever faced. It had always been an axiom that Britain could outbuild her chief rivals; now this seemed to be under challenge, and when it was learned that the first two financial instalments for Germany's 1908–9 ships came to almost as much as the first *three* instalments for previous programmes, and that 1909–10 contracts had been given out six months in advance of the usual time and before the Reichstag had approved the money, it seemed as if a most serious threat to British naval supremacy had already begun. The Board were convinced of it. They concluded that Germany would have 17 'Dreadnoughts' by May 1912 instead of the 13 that should result from her amended Naval Law, and that if they built up to their full capacity they could even have 21. Against this Britain would have 16 if she laid down four heavy ships during 1909, 18 if she laid down six. Even taking the lower German and the higher British figures and allowing for Britain's preponderance in pre-Dreadnought battleships this was an obviously unacceptable margin against Germany alone, without considering any other powers; the Board recommended a programme of eight big ships for the current year—the most that could be built with the ordnance capacity available in the country.

Wilhelm and his ministers vigorously denied that the Naval Law was being exceeded and insisted that Germany would only have 13 Dreadnoughts by the *end* of 1912. A powerful section of the Liberal government was prepared to believe them, but there could be no proof as the Germans repeatedly and angrily refused to agree to inspections or to pool building and completion dates with the Admiralty; they were naturally sensitive about having their numbers checked, it smacked of being kept in their place, just as previous British attempts at agreeing a ratio of capital ships had seemed like a design to maintain the *status quo*—with Germany the perpetual underdog at sea. In the uncertainty the British government compromised by approving estimates for four Dreadnoughts in 1909, and making four contingent upon German acceleration.

The Board of Admiralty had no doubt that the 'contingent' four were as good as in the bag, and there would have been resignations if the government had weakened. In the event, the situation was resolved by the disclosure of Austrian plans for building Dreadnoughts, plans which sparked off an immediate Italian reaction, and with the prospect of each of these Mediterranean rivals laying down four the government announced that the four British 'contingent' ships would be laid down in 1910 without prejudice to that year's programme. The Board had their 'eight'.

After this it was the turn of the German politicians, anxious to lower the temperature of Anglo-German relations, to propose various naval building agreements; they saw Britain's instinctive fear of losing her naval supremacy as the chief cause of the extraordinary enmity that now existed. Others in both countries saw trade rivalry as the main factor, thus Fisher to King Edward, 'that we have to fight

Germany is just as sure as anything can be, solely because she can't expand commercially without it.'[21] Whatever the complex of cause and emotion, the British now took their traditional attitude that they could not agree to limit their building against one country alone as this might prejudice their position against other navies, and would in any case give rise to difficulties of inspection and interpretation which might lead to even greater mutual mistrust. In short, they held that a natural balance of power was a surer safeguard against war than an artificial balance which did not represent the true interests of the powers concerned. This accorded with Fisher's philosophy that the best way to prevent war was to make sure that the enemy knew that you were prepared to fight with every unit of your strength in the first line and 'hit him in the belly and kick him when he's down'.[22]

So the great naval race took its course. Succeeding classes of Dreadnoughts, in accordance with all precedent, grew larger and more powerful and soon followed the American pattern of super-firing guns fore and aft with an additional centre-line turret to give full 10-gun broadsides. Other powers followed, first the United States and Japan, then the Mediterranean powers, Italy, Austria and France with initially four apiece, and Russia with four for the Baltic, three for the Black Sea; even the rival South American countries joined in. Everywhere the number of Dreadnought battleships was regarded as the chief measure of strength of a navy; by such reckoning Britain and Germany stood well at the head of the League with the United States a strong third. By the end of 1912 the table was: British Empire 21 built, 12 building; Germany 13 built, 10 building; USA eight built, four building; elsewhere only five had been completed.

This was the year that Tirpitz made the final amendment to his Naval Law, increasing the final establishment of the fleet from 58 to 61 Dreadnoughts, and even more significant, increasing the ships in full commission at any time from 17 battleships, four battle cruisers, 66 destroyers to 25 battleships, eight battle cruisers, 144 destroyers, a proportion of the fleet in instant readiness which Winston Churchill, the new First Lord of the Admiralty, considered 'remarkable...so far as I am aware [it] finds no example in the previous practice of modern naval powers'.[23] The Naval Intelligence Department of the British Admiralty, trying to penetrate the true cause of this inexorable and alarming expansion, produced a lengthy memorandum for the Cabinet:

The whole character of the German fleet shows that it is designed for aggression and offensive action on the largest possible scale in the North Sea or the North Atlantic. The structure of the German battleships shows clearly that they are intended for attack in a fleet action. The disposition of their guns, torpedo tubes, armour, the system of naval tactics which the Germans practice and the naval principles which they inculcate upon their officers leave no room to doubt that the idea of sudden and aggressive action is the primary cause for which they have been prepared...

The claim from Germany that she has no expectation of victory over the strongest naval power, but has simply created a 'risk fleet' is scarcely respectful of the sagacity of the German Government...Whatever purpose has animated the creators of the German Navy, and induced them to make so many exertions and sacrifices it is not the foolish purpose of certainly coming off second best on the day of trial...[24]

This estimate is absolutely confirmed by the German naval archives; they make it clear that Tirpitz's policy was directed against England from the beginning, as was his Imperial master's—despite extravagant protestations of friendship. A secret memorandum drawn up by Tirpitz when he assumed office in June 1897, which set the new course for the German Navy and which was followed thereafter with blind obstinacy, picked out England as Germany's 'most dangerous naval enemy' and the enemy 'against which we most urgently require a certain measure of naval force as a political power factor.' It went on:

> Commerce raiding and transatlantic war against England is so hopeless because of the shortage of bases on our side and the superfluity on England's side, that we must ignore this type of war against England in our plans for the constitution of our fleet. Our fleet must be so constructed that it can unfold its greatest military potential between Heligoland and the Thames.'[25]

To return to the British Intelligence Department memorandum: it admitted that the purpose of the German fleet might be unconnected with her desire to use it, and so long as Great Britain kept her superiority they would be unlikely to do so. *But* 'the German Empire has been built up by a series of sudden and successful wars...'

The Prime Minister, Asquith, jotted down the Admiralty projections forward to 1915:[26]

	GB		Germ
Dread.	25 + 2 in hand	}	17
Battle Cr.	10 4 in hand	} 6	6
Pre-D^t battleships	8 King Ed.		8
	8 Formidables		4
	5 Duncans		
	8 Majestics		
	8 Canopus & Swiftsure		
Arm^d Cruisers	22		7

It is difficult to make comparisons between the Dreadnoughts of the two principal powers in the naval race up to the First War; the officers on both sides criticized their own ships freely, and often found their opponents' vessels better, which was not surprising as each navy had a different emphasis in design, the Germans concentrating on thicker and more comprehensive armour, the British on heavier guns. Consequently each could point to their own inferiority in one vital department. Since the war the argument has acquired some elements of myth because of the dramatic destruction of no less than three British battle cruisers at Jutland, apparently proving all criticisms of weak protection on the British side. However, it is probable that the real cause of the losses was the sensitivity of the British cordite—in marked contrast to the German propellant which had a stabilizing ingredient and burned without exploding when German ships were destroyed. The vital point in any comparison, particularly between the battleships, is that although the German vessels had thicker armour, they needed it; they were facing heavier shells. In general it is probably true that the strategic initiative which Fisher grasped with the sudden and shocking design of the *Dreadnought* herself, was held throughout the period. The German service constantly followed, both in turret arrangement and gun-calibre, and while Jellicoe held their classes from 1910 to be superior fighting units, as they had between 1,300 and 3,000 tons more displacement than contemporary British classes, the British always followed with one better, eventually producing what is acknowledged by all—even the cautious Jellicoe—as incomparably the finest battleship class of the era, the 'Queen Elizabeths'.

These vessels, the first of which were laid down in 1912, can be considered as a new type of capital ship altogether. The features which distinguished them from previous Dreadnought battleships were their high speed of 25 knots—equal to the earlier battle cruisers —and 15-inch calibre guns, which were the heaviest naval guns of the period and thoroughly outclassed German ordnance, whose calibre had risen to 12-inch after the 'Nassaus' and stuck there. The 15-inch projectile was double the weight of the German 12-inch, 1,950 against 890 lbs, and although the muzzle velocity was somewhat lower the heavier projectile retained its velocity longer and had a flatter trajectory for any given range. It was therefore a more effective hitter, and while some of its enormously greater power was in the event lost by inferior shells and oversensitive bursting charges, it was still the most formidable weapon afloat at the time. The 'Queen Elizabeths' had eight of these pieces in two pairs of superfiring turrets, the whole system weighing approximately the same as the five 13.5-inch turrets of previous British classes. Their protection was also similar to previous classes although the main belt and turret armour was increased from 12-inch and 11-inch to a uniform 13-inch; above the belt 6-inch armour extended up to the anti-torpedo boat battery of six 6-inch guns each side.

The high speed of the 'Queen Elizabeths' resulted from a naval staff requirement for a squadron which would be able to turn the head of the (retreating) enemy fleet and bring a concentration to bear on the van. It was obtained by using oil-fired boilers driving 75,000 horse-power turbines—against 29,000 horse power for previous battleships. They were also rather longer than previous battleships and at 27,500 tons displacement, some 2,500 tons larger. However, the vital factor which allowed their great speed was the change from coal fuel to oil, which had a higher thermal efficiency, and by giving 40 per cent greater radius of action for the same weight released displacement for offence and defence.

Oil firing had been pioneered by the Italian Navy in the 1890s; it had been adopted for British high-speed destroyers soon after the turn of the century when it had also come in as an alternative system in the big ships, but there had been powerful arguments against its full adoption. First, Britain had unlimited supplies of the best steam coal in the world—but the only oil supplies within the British Empire lay far away from the home base in Assam and Burma; second, coal bunkers provided excellent protection against both underwater and shell damage. The arguments were generating considerable heat when Fisher went to the Admiralty as First Sea Lord; one of his first acts was to set up an oil committee. The committee, like Fisher, soon realized that the technical arguments in favour of oil were overwhelming, and hearing that an enterprising Englishman named D'Arcy had obtained oil rights in southern Persia, they introduced him to the Burmah Oil Company, which already had an agreement to supply oil to the Navy. This was in 1905. Burmah put up the capital for further exploration and four years later when a rich field of oil had been found at the head of the Persian Gulf they put in another million pounds and formed the Anglo-Persian Oil Company. As southern Persia and the Gulf had long been a sphere of British interest because of its strategic position as a buffer between Russia and India and as a vital flank to the Suez-Far East shipping route, and as the importance of a British presence had increased with the advance of German influence through Turkey and down the axis of the Berlin-Baghdad railway, the new oilfield which promised adequate supplies for the Navy could be regarded as a reasonably secure source within the British world system. Hence Churchill's decision in 1912 to change from coal to oil in future ships; hence the high speed *and* high offensive and defensive powers of the 'Queen Elizabeths'. Churchill records that the actual decisions occurred the other way round; the determination to produce a fast squadron led to the change to oil.

The Anglo-Persian refinery began drawing oil in 1913, and in November that year its first shipment of 6,000 tons passed through the Suez Canal in a Japanese tanker and was discharged at Sheerness for the Royal Navy. In May 1914 the British government bought a controlling interest in the Company for £2.2 millions, a purchase which has been compared to Disraeli's purchase of Suez Canal shares in the previous century. Indeed the whole story is a good example of the way in which British command of the sea, exercised through her world system, allowed her to exploit commercial opportunities which in their turn increased her command—and how the British presence seemed to block and encircle every German outward thrust. In this case Tirpitz could not turn over to oil for his own big ships because of the impossibility of ensuring supplies in a war.

As the material for the naval race built up, so did intensity of training. Gone were the carefree days of the 1890s when officers could devote their energies to sport or artistic battery decks; now it was preparation for WAR. The striving for efficiency was carried to such lengths that 'the strain and stress of peace resembles closely the actual conditions of war'.[27] While this process had begun in the Mediterranean and the Far East at the turn of the century with the advent of a new breed of scientific officer, epitomized by Fisher, it was the German naval challenge which sustained and deepened it as contention moved up into the grey mists of the North Sea and Baltic.

On both sides the historic theory of naval warfare was paramount; everything, it was believed, would turn on the opposing battlefleets arrayed in the traditional manner, the British in a close blockade, the Germans as the weaker fleet, blockaded until they could break out and reverse the decision of Trafalgar. All classes of ships and tactics were designed with this situation in mind. The Germans concentrated on short-range torpedo-boats, designed to attack battleships near her own coasts, and practised combined battleship and torpedo-boat tactics for a fleet action, a system rendered more effective than earlier French efforts by the development of the 'heater' torpedo in 1907; this employed a superheater for the compressed air before it entered the turbine, increasing the maximum speed to over 40 knots, or the effective range to over 7,000 yards. At about the same date Germany embarked on a programme of submarines designed to attack battleships; although she was the last major power to start development she began immediately on large 'overseas' boats, soon outstripped the pioneer, France, and by 1914 had placed herself first in the world in this arm. By the outbreak of war she had 29 'overseas' U-boats and 16 building; all were attached to the scouting forces around Heligoland to watch for the arrival of the expected blockading fleets and patrols, and attempt to whittle down their numbers. Had the war broken out in 1912 or before, it is possible that the British would have obliged, that at least was the aim in the War Plans, and that was the invariable practice of senior officers in the strategic exercises at the War College.

The invisible menace of the submarine and to a lesser extent mines and surface torpedo-boats which could dart out at sunset and return before dawn made this policy increasingly dangerous as German strength in these arms grew, and just before the outbreak of war 'observation blockade' was officially dropped in favour of 'distant blockade' which sought to control the northern exit to the North Sea with the main battlefleet based upon the 'Scottish coast and islands', and the English Channel exit with flotilla vessels supported by older battleships of the Channel fleet. The main fleet could also come south in time to intercept the German battlefleet before it could return to base after any foray into the Channel. This last-minute change of plan was a stroke of practical genius which upset all the premises on which Tirpitz had based his plans; on the outbreak of war the German scouting forces and torpedo craft lay waiting for a fleet that never came.

Undoubtedly the main concentration of effort during the lead up to the war was in great gunnery, and battlefleet tactics designed for great gunnery. Thus, the British fleet destroyers were armed with larger guns than the German torpedo boats and were given the prime function of knocking out the enemy flotillas before they could interfere with the gun action between the battlefleets. Tactical evolutions, mock battles and scaled down exercises on the tactical board at the War College were concerned mainly with forming one long line of battle from cruising formation in the shortest time, and either across the line of advance of the enemy—crossing his T —or so as to concentrate on his van, force him round and disorganize his line. There were critics, especially those officers with a historical bent, who thought the single line tactics too rigid and too highly centralized in the commander-in-chief, who pointed to the utter failure of fleet line in the eighteenth century and who advocated attack by divisions or divided tactics to achieve decisive concentrations on sections of the enemy line. Such tactics were tried in exercises, but they never beat the single line, and it was pointed out that with long-range fire and the possibility of concentrating *guns* it was unnecessary to concentrate *ships*. In any case the battle cruisers would be there to add the weight of their fire where it would cause most disruption on the van of the enemy.

Meanwhile fire control made immense progress. A gunnery lieutenant named Dreyer took over some of the elements of Pollen's original enemy-plotting apparatus and had by 1913 produced a fire control table,[28] which had separate continuous plots of enemy range and bearing derived from a Dumaresq (trigonometrical computer), both of which were under continual 'tuning' from actual observations from the rangefinders and from the control top; thus if the theoretical range worked from own ship's and enemy courses fell out of step with the actual range as observed by rangefinder it was 'tuned' to conform; this then fed back to the other theoretical components of the problem and so altered the bearing plot—and *vice versa*. In short it was a highly complex and ingenious mix of observation and computation continually cross-checking each other to arrive at a truer approximation of the relative movement of the enemy, and keeping the vital factors, gun range and deflection under constant scrutiny. This elaborate 'on-line' computer, which was housed in a transmitting station way down in the bowels of each ship, was well in advance of anything in either the American or German services, both of whom used a similar device to the Dumaresq allied with range rate clocks. But while the fire control table gave adequate results in the artificial and, as it turned out, short range peace-time practices, it was probably no better than the simpler systems when it came to the extremely long range, high speed encounters during the war.

Probably more important was the immense amount of time and effort devoted to training the control top personnel in 'spotting' and correcting the guns from the fall of shot. This art was tested annually in the battle practices, which had become the most keenly contested events in the calendar, not only in the service, but in the country at large. An enormous amount of newspaper space was given to the results—expressed on a points basis so as to give no information away to the enemy—winning ships and control officers were accorded enthusiastic write-ups, those at the bottom of the table were slated. In the service itself an officer's promotion had become linked to his ship's shooting performance; one of the great gunnery officers of the day wrote afterwards: 'It was not so much the anticipation of war but the competitive spirit and the quest for promotion which drove the Navy with a sharp spur to unexampled standards of endeavour...'[29]

From 1908 the battle practice target—stationary in the early days —was towed on unknown courses at unknown speeds, and the firing ship had to make previously unknown alterations while steaming at 14 knots at ranges between 9,000 and 10,000 yards; so much had accuracy improved since the start of the gunnery rennaisance that ships were making better results in these conditions than they had at the old prizefiring target at ranges of 1,400 yards at the turn of the century. The method evolved was to fire a single 'ranging' gun set with the mean of the rangefinder readings, wait for the splash of the shell, correct 'up' or 'down', 'left' or 'right' and fire another single gun or perhaps two, wait for their splashes and correct again, only firing a full salvo, that is one of each of the turret guns, when the correct range has been found. When a salvo 'straddled' the target—two or three 'short', the rest 'over'—rapid fire was commenced and salvoes were fired without waiting for spotting corrections—until the range was lost again. Gunlayers aimed their own guns, but all ranges and sight-setting corrections were passed from the control top on the foremast *via* the transmitting station, also all the orders to fire.

'Bong!' The ship shuddered and a belch of orange smoke came from B turret, then silence while the projectile mounted skywards on its lengthy journey. After a long pause a white pillar of water became dimly visible, streaking the distant grey. It was near the target but to the left and almost automatically I gave the correcting order, 'Right six!' Then, after a short pause, 'Fire!' The resulting splash was behind the target...'Down 400! Fire!' This time the splash was in front and still in line. Good! We now had the range. 'Up 200! All left guns fire!' Faintly one heard the fire gongs ringing in the nearer turrets, then came a rippling roar, Bong-bong-bong-bong! The mast kicked like a mule's hind leg, hot breath from the guns hit one's forehead like a gust of desert wind, and for several seconds the orange cordite smoke obliterated everything.

Looking down on the bridge I spied the solitary figure of Commander W. W. Fisher, who was umpiring. From the turrets came the hiss of air blasts, and a whiff of blue smoke trickled from each muzzle. Then followed the roar of the chain rammers as the next round was being rammed home. It was glorious music. Little lights in the control position told that the right guns were ready to fire, but the fall of the last salvo must be awaited. Now the smoke was clearing and the target became visible once more, when suddenly a forest of white pillars shot up all around it. Looking carefully through a high powered glass one could see three were behind and two in front of it. Perfect!...'Right guns, fire!'[30]

While this method was being developed to such hair-lines of precision that more intelligent officers began to regard shooting at 10,000 yards as far too easy, and to advocate longer-range practices lest the enemy get in the first hits, Percy Scott was fighting with all the fire of thwarted genius to have his director firing gear adopted in the fleet. Fortunately Jellicoe and other scientifically-minded officers were with him, and after exhaustive tests through 1912 and 1913 when a director-fitted battleship, HMS *Thunderer*, decisively beat the top-shooting ship in the navy, it was decided to fit all Dreadnoughts with the system. It was not a moment too soon. The German service already had a part director system: the turrets were trained by following a pointer actuated by the movements of a director telescope in the control position abaft the fore bridge, but the guns were still laid on target by individual gunlayers. Adopting a complete director system in which all the guns of the broadside were trained and laid by ratings who never saw the target, but simply followed pointers from a director sight situated on the foremast just below the control top, British gunnery potential moved decisively ahead of the chief rival—even further ahead of America, which had neither system. For when peace practice was replaced by war experience, it became evident that the director was essential; it ensured that all guns were laid on the *same* target, that the single aiming position was above smoke and spray, and of course that the guns were fired absolutely simultaneously and with a constant personal error—that of the director layer—which came out in the spotting corrections.

There was one respect, however, in which British gunnery lagged behind German—in the rangefinding apparatus. The original Barr & Stroud 4-feet 6-inch rangefinder first issued in 1892 had grown into a 9-foot baselength instrument as battle practice ranges had increased, but there it had stuck; it was not until just before the war that the latest battleships were fitted with 15-foot base-length instruments.

The Germans, on the other hand, had turret-mounted rangefinders manufactured by Carl Zeiss which were nearly 20 feet for 11-inch turrets and up to 27 feet for 12-inch turrets. As accuracy is directly proportional to base length, these were naturally far more effective instruments, and usually gave better opening ranges in the unexpectedly long-range encounters which occurred during the war. It is probable too that they were better adapted to give accurate readings when the ships were juddering at high speed; whereas the British instruments were operated on a 'coincidence' principle in which two horizontal sections of the target had to be exactly lined up so that vertical lines formed exact continuations, the German ones were 'stereoscopic', which meant that there was no lining up of images, but simply a subjective comparison of two complete images, one entering each eye. However, there were disadvantages to this method too, particularly when the observer was thrown off balance physically or mentally, and there is every indication that the excitement of hot action tended to do just this. In any case the decisive advantage the Germans enjoyed was in the opening ranges; after that 'spotting' played an increasingly important part. It is not certain why the Germans were allowed to gain this opening advantage; certainly they had no greater expectation of long-range battle than the British. Their tactical exercises had convinced them that visibility in the North Sea, where they expected to fight, would seldom allow ranges over about 10,000 yards, and in their war games on the tactical board no results were allowed from any firing above 11,000 yards. Now 10,000 yards was the precise range at which all British organization and instrumentation was aimed; at this distance the Barr & Stroud 9-foot instrument was adequate. Just before the war when a few British squadrons were allowed to practice at 'long range', from 12,000 to 16,000 yards, the inadequacy of the 9-foot rangefinder was shown up, but nothing was done to re-equip existing ships as it was generally considered that firing or practising at such a distance was simply throwing ammunition away. The service in general looked to action at 'decisive' range—probably not so much a historical as a scientific or materialist viewpoint:

> Fire may be considered *effective* if perforation at 30 degrees to the normal can be counted upon against the main armour of any given ship...[31]

In July 1914, as Continental Europe moved towards war with the elegance of a carefully laid row of collapsing card houses, the Dreadnought line-up was decidedly in Britain's favour—completed battleships 20:14, battle cruisers 9:4. In total weight of broadside, and in Dreadnoughts under construction the balance was even more favourable for Britain, particularly as the first of the new super-class of five 15-inch 'Queen Elizabeths' were nearing completion. And practically the whole of this force was available for concentration against Germany, strategic talks with the French having already established the principle that the French battlefleet would mark the Austrian and if necessary the Italian fleets in the Mediterranean, as it were holding the ring for the major contestants in the North Sea.

The main British force, to be aptly named the Grand Fleet, was to have its wartime base at Scapa Flow in the Orkney Islands off Scotland, where it was hoped that the ships would be out of reach of German submarines; it comprised one fleet flagship and four battle squadrons, the first and second having eight Dreadnought battleships each, the third eight of the most powerful pre-Dreadnoughts, and the fourth four of the earlier 12-inch-gunned Dreadnoughts. There was also a squadron of four of the latest 13.5-inch-gunned Dreadnought battle cruisers, three cruiser squadrons and 76 destroyers; other cruisers and destroyers worked from East and South coast bases. Against this the German High Seas Fleet consisted of one fleet flagship and three battle squadrons, the first of eight Dreadnoughts, the second of eight pre-Dreadnoughts (main battery four 11-inch guns), and the third of four of the latest 12-inch-gunned Dreadnoughts; there was also a battle cruiser squadron of three 11-inch ships with one 12-inch ship nearing completion, a light cruiser squadron and some 150 destroyers or large torpedo boats. So while the Germans had a strong torpedo arm, it was evident that, given anything like equality in material and training, their battlefleet was quite unequal to a stand-up gun battle with the British Grand Fleet. And while most of their older, indeed obsolescent pre-Dreadnought battleships were formed into a fleet to gain control of the Baltic from the Russian Baltic fleet, the far more powerful and numerous British pre-Dreadnoughts were formed into a second fleet to watch the English Channel. Like the geographical position, the maritime odds were overwhelmingly against Germany.

For this reason the chief fear in the British fleet was of a surprise torpedo attack in the Japanese mode before a formal declaration of war. So it was that towards the end of July as the final desperate efforts were being made to keep the Continental powers from rushing at each other, the Grand Fleet was ordered to take up its war station at Scapa Flow out of reach of such a *coup*; it made an early stage of the journey by night showing no lights.

As we threaded our way like dark, shapeless monsters of another world through the myriad lights of crowded Dover Straits, past the Thames Estuary and up through the North Sea with ships' companies at night action stations, all attention was focussed on the urgent problem of defending ourselves against a night attack... Nobody really knew how we stood in this matter, for we had never fired at night at real, live destroyers attacking at full speed. We had engaged hundreds of floating targets and with certain precautions a good many towed targets, but what would the situation be like when some 20 or 30 destroyers charged down upon us in a mass and loosed their torpedoes?[32]

A surprise attack was the last thing the Germans were contemplating; while there was any doubt about Britain entering a war on the side of France and Russia they intended to do nothing to provoke her. In any case the German service suffered from a grave sense of inferiority to the British fleet, its preponderant size, greater guns and long and triumphant history, and their plans were based on the British coming to them and being reduced to something like an equality in Dreadnoughts as they attempted a close blockade.

On 31 July the Grand Fleet reached the Orkneys without incident, passed between the towering island outposts of the Flow in a file stretching some fifteen miles down the Pentland Firth, and came to anchor by divisions under the northern shore, a quiet and supremely confident armada holding more power in its long guns than any naval force before—the one ultimate sanction of the British 'Empire of the Seas'. On 4 August the ageing commander-in-chief, who was due to retire in October, was replaced over the heads of several more senior candidates by Admiral Sir John Jellicoe, the man whom Fisher had groomed for the post in war.

Jellicoe was an appropriate choice. He had specialized in gunnery, and had an intellect which worked with the order and precision of the great machines he was to command. He joined to this a tremendous capacity for detailed work and a practical efficiency in everything he undertook which had marked him as the outstanding professional in the higher ranks of the service.

A suppressed excitement pervaded all ranks of the fleet he took over; it seemed that the years of arduous training were behind, and the weapon they had forged would be put to the test at any moment.

It was nearly dark on the 4 August when the bugle sounded the 'Still'. The colliers winches suddenly stopped and the Bosun's mate passed the word, 'Hostilities will commence against Germany at midnight.' The loud cheers which followed were soon silenced by the renewed clatter of the winches and the thud of the bags as they came in with increased speed and more clearly-defined purpose...[33, 34]

War

The pace of the pre-war naval race and the emotional charge it had acquired as a challenge to British supremacy led both sides to expect an almost immediate fleet action to decide once and for all who had command at sea. In the ships of the Grand Fleet all extraneous timber fittings and other combustible materials or shell-bursting structures were pulled out and sent ashore; even ships' boats were discarded. Similarly in the German ships waiting in the Jade, all hands expected the British fleet to appear to draw them out for the 'inevitable clash'. But of course the Grand Fleet was blockading the North Sea, not the German coast, and the German High Command had no intention of seeking it out. Nor had the Commander-in-Chief, High Seas Fleet, any intention of leaving the protection of the coastal batteries and minefields in the Heligoland Bight, lest Jellicoe by some fiendish stratagem should 'ambush' him. 'We must not do the enemy this favour. Although we are all anxious to prove our determination to fight, we must remain very patient. In the end they shall have to come to us. Then, with God's help we shall beat them.'¹ Jellicoe, meanwhile, felt much the same about the ingenious underwater ambushes the Germans must be devising for him, and as he was very conscious of the supreme importance of the Grand Fleet, the loss of which would lose Britain the war, he had no intention of being drawn anywhere near the minefields and submarine defences of the Heligoland Bight.

Both parties to this unexpected situation have received constant criticism since for their 'defensive mentality', particularly the Germans, whose shipping was swept off the face of the oceans, whose few cruiser squadrons were dogged and eventually crushed and who did practically nothing to dispute the passage of British troops to France—in short who lost control of the sea. This catalogue is the best answer to any criticisms of the British Grand Fleet under whose umbrella all these things happened. It was Jellicoe's overwhelming strength which prevented the High Seas Fleet acting up to its name, and allowed the British cruisers and flotilla craft to 'control sea communications' as in the classic doctrine of command by blockade. And with total effective command of the surface outside the Baltic and Black Seas Jellicoe had no need to risk any of the Dreadnoughts on which that command ultimately rested; on the contrary he had every reason *not* to risk them.

As for the Germans, there was no reason for them to risk the High Seas Fleet in an action with a force which they believed to be so much stronger than themselves, backed up by reserves of twice their own strength. The truth was that Tirpitz had impaled Germany on the English doctrine, and Tirpitz and the German statesmen combined had isolated the central powers, so that their 'alliance value' fleet had no ally to value it. As for its twin role of 'risk fleet' there was no naval power Britain had to fear however many ships she might lose in a struggle with Germany. Tirpitz blamed the ruin of his policy on the devilish subtlety of British diplomacy. This may be true, particularly perhaps in the Japanese alliance, which was shortly invoked to clear the Pacific of German bases and commerce raiders, but the real cause of the ring around Germany was her own growing strength endangering the other great powers and so operating an automatic balancing mechanism against her.

Other reasons for the inactivity of the High Seas Fleet were that Wilhelm wished to preserve it intact as a bargaining counter at the Peace Conference after the short, Bismarckian war he envisaged, and that Germany was, despite all Tirpitz's efforts, still predominantly a land power viewing strategy through a soldier's monocle. The Military High Command was certain that they could crush any British soldiers on the Continent of Europe—let them come! In this respect there is truth in the historical school's distinction between a true sea power and a land power.

To sum up the position in 1914, here is the official historian of the war at sea, Julian Corbett:

> ...it was but a repetition of what had occurred in the old French wars when France had the inferior fleet. By massing an overwhelming concentration at the vital point the Admiralty had made sure of the command of the Narrow Seas upon which their whole system was built up. They had also made sure of a crushing decision on 'the day', but incidentally they had made it inevitable that 'the day' would be indefinitely postponed. All experience shows that in conditions such as our home concentration had set up an enemy will never risk a battle except for some vital end which cannot be obtained in any other way...[2]

A similar situation had arisen in the Mediterranean where the French battlefleet composed of her only two Dreadnoughts and ten heavy pre-Dreadnoughts blockaded the Austrian fleet by patrolling the Straits of Otranto.

When it became clear to Germany that the British main fleet was not going to sweep into the Heligoland Bight and attack them in their own nest, they changed their strategy, released their submarine fleet from its defensive role and sent it out on a 'guerilla offensive' against the British fleet in its own waters. This had an immediate effect; it caused the Grand Fleet to adopt zig-zag courses wherever it went, ensured that battle squadrons never moved without an escort of destroyers, which decreased their sea-keeping ability, and caused a temporary evacuation of Scapa Flow while it was rendered U-boat proof. It accounted for one Dreadnought battleship, *Audacious*, sunk by mine off the west coast while the fleet was avoiding the submarine peril to the east, one pre-Dreadnought battleship in the Channel, and several cruisers. Much the same happened in the Mediterranean where the Dreadnought *Jean Bart* was torpedoed by a submarine, and although she managed to make port, the French blockade was removed to Malta and then to the island of Cephalonia. A contributory factor in both cases was the wear and tear on boilers and machinery which constant sea-keeping imposed on a fleet that had to keep moving for fear of submarine attack.

While this war of attrition strained British nerves and machinery and made it certain that the Grand Fleet would not be drawn into the south-eastern quarter of the North Sea, it neither altered the essential strategic position, which was that Britain could draw in food and strength from the shipping routes of the world, while German trade was severed, nor did it offer any prospect of reducing the Grand Fleet to equality with the High Seas Fleet. The submarine was as yet too slow underwater—maximum 8 knots—and too deaf to communication to do much more than keep blockading squadrons at a respectful distance; it could not alter the blockade doctrine itself because battleships had the strategic and tactical advantages of much greater speed.

However, it soon became clear that the German 'overseas' submarine was an ideal commerce raider and in November 1914 all the arguments which had distinguished the controversy between the *jeune école* and their opponents who declared that neutral opinion would be outraged by the breaches of international law and 'civilized values' inevitable in a submarine *guerre de course*, were thrashed out in Germany. The Navy wanted to use U-boats to retaliate for the British mercantile blockade which was already causing shortages in Germany. They believed that by scaring all neutral shipping away from British waters they could deal a heavy, if not decisive, blow against Britain's capacity to fight the war. The politicians were afraid of alienating neutral opinion, particularly American opinion. In the event the Navy won the first round; a war zone was declared around Britain in February 1915 and all neutrals were warned that any ships within it were liable to be sunk. But the outcry, particularly from the United States, was so great that before it could come into operation Germany was forced to declare that ships flying a neutral flag would not be attacked unless identified as enemy, a restriction which handicapped the U-boats and vitiated the policy; while British cruiser squadrons could stop and examine neutral ships in accordance with international law, U-boats risked losing their prey, and at worst being decoyed to destruction when they surfaced to examine a ship. So during this period German submarines were only half as successful as privateers had been in the great French Wars; at the height of their activity they only destroyed 1 per cent of British ships. While this comparative failure was partly due to the small number of submarines available—for the underwater *guerre de course* had been no part of the German pre-war policy—it seemed that the doctrine of battlefleet command still held good.

Besides the material effects of the British battlefleet grip, the old demoralizing effects were beginning to make themselves felt in the High Seas Fleet; Seaman Richard Stumpf of the Dreadnought *Heligoland* confided to his diary the 'deep disappointment mingled with boredom'³ which had affected his shipmates and how the best and most intelligent officers had been transferred to submarines and torpedo boats, leaving many who only thought in terms of making unnecessary work and harrassing the men; a division had arisen between officers and men.

Meanwhile the battle cruisers of both sides saw action. As early as August 1914 'offensive' British spirits planned a flotilla and cruiser sortie right into the Heligoland Bight. Jellicoe heard of the operation and sent his battle cruisers under Sir David Beatty in support, a fortunate stroke, as the light forces ran into trouble from a German cruiser squadron and Beatty had to go to their rescue. He arrived through mist at a critical juncture, chased the German cruisers off and, catching two of them at 8,000 coming down to 4,000 yards, practically blasted them out of the water. This bold stroke depressed the German service out of all proportion to their material losses; Wilhelm gave instructions that the Battle Fleet was not to fight an action outside the Bight and not even inside if faced with superior forces.

Big ships saw action again after the German Pacific cruiser squadron under Admiral von Spee had annihilated a weaker and less trained British squadron off Coronel in November 1914. The Admiralty had immediately despatched two battle cruisers, *Invincible* and *Inflexible*, to find and destroy Spee, and partly by virtue of their great speed and partly by good fortune they accomplished this in remarkably short time—strategically-speaking. Tactically it took rather a long time for despite the superiority of the battle cruisers' 12-inch over the German 8.2-inch main batteries, the British admiral, Sturdee, kept the range long, generally between 14,000 and 12,500 yards in the decisive phase of the battle. This was because the German 8.2-inch fire proved extremely accurate and at 12,500 yards Spee was able to open with his secondary batteries of 5.9-inch as well. The battle cruisers had no secondary battery. Added to this the wind was blowing directly down range from the British as they chased, and both their fire control and sighting were hampered by their own dense funnel smoke; this was exaggerated by the fact that neither ship had yet been fitted with director gear, although Vickers' engineers were aboard the *Invincible* for this purpose.

Spee's ships put up a heroic fight, constantly trying to close and bring their smaller guns into effective range, but Sturdee had the speed advantage, and held them at his own chosen distance where the flatter trajectory of the great 12-inch pieces eventually told. While these tactics did not accord with British close range tactics in the French wars, nor even with pre-1914 'decisive range' tactics, they were nevertheless the tactics that had always been employed between *equal enemies*, and in this case they were doubly important because the battle cruisers were needed back with the fleet in home waters. The action was an even more triumphant vindication of Fisher's big-gun battle cruiser policy than the action in the Heligoland Bight.

The next time British battle cruisers fought it was in the North Sea again, and against their own kind. The action came about after Wilhelm, in response to pressures for a more offensive use of the fleet, had given the commander-in-chief a freer hand to carry out sorties on his own initiative—still making the preservation of the ships a ruling principle. Vice Admiral Hipper, in command of the scouting force of battle cruisers, was accordingly sent to make a reconnaisance into the middle of the North Sea, and to hammer any light forces he might meet. Unbeknown to him, British Intelligence had intercepted and decoded his wirelessed instructions and although the Grand Fleet was, for some reason, not informed until too late, the British battle cruisers under Beatty were ordered out to meet him.

At 7.15 in the morning of 24 January 1915 the flanking cruisers of the two forces met just to the east of the Dogger Bank and Hipper, believing from wireless signals that he had run into a battle squadron, altered south-easterly for home, while Beatty increased speed in the same direction to cut him off. Visibility was splendid; 'the day was so clear', a cruiser commodore recalled, 'that only the shape of the earth prevented one from seeing everything on it', and it was not long before Beatty, leading in the *Lion*, sighted Hipper's big ships off his port bow some 14 miles distant; he called for maximum speed and chased.

Beatty's force consisted of three 13.5-inch-gun ships and two older 12-inch-gun vessels which formed the second Battle Cruiser Squadron and were under a rear admiral, his second in command. Only the most recent ship, the lovely and formidable *Tiger*, had director firing gear, but she lacked practice and as it turned out she failed to make a single hit in the action that ensued. The German force was far weaker in primary gunpower; Hipper flew his flag and led the line in the 11-inch gun *Seydlitz*, and he was followed by one other 11-inch gun ship, one 12-inch gun vessel and in the rear the much smaller and slower *Blücher*, which was little more than a heavy cruiser with a Dreadnought arrangement of her main battery of twelve 8.2-inch guns. It was on this weak and unfortunate rear ship that Beatty opened with deliberate single shots as his superior speed brought him within extreme range, around 20,000 yards—*twice* the pre-war expectation. The other ships joined in as they came up, punishing her severely as the distance dropped to 16,000 yards, the *Lion* meanwhile shifting her sights up the line to the *Seydlitz* which she engaged at 17,000 yards.

All Hipper's ships were meanwhile concentrating on the *Lion*, and were soon shooting with great accuracy, scoring hits and raising forests of splashes which drenched her conning position and rained down on decks and turrets, making sighting extremely difficult. Beatty zig-zagged to throw out the range and kept up a spirited reply, indeed the *Lion* had already knocked out two of the *Seydlitz's* after turrets with one shell which had penetrated D turret barbette and caused a catastrophic ammunition fire. However, the concentration proved too hot. The hits on the *Lion* mounted and two particularly damaging 12-inch shells which drove in the waterline armour abreast of a boiler room, allowed seawater to enter the feed tank, effectively crippling the port engine.

As the British flagship began to drop astern Beatty sent out a series of signals by flag urging the rest of his force to continue closing the German squadron as rapidly as possible; by the standards of eighteenth century 'chase' tactics this rash of hoists was quite unnecessary, and in the event it led to a fatal misinterpretation: all the British ships closed on the unfortunate *Blücher* which was circling out of control and finished her off while the rest of the German ships escaped.

This error of interpretation and the lack of initiative displayed was much debated afterwards. Equally serious, although unrecognized at the time, was the poor British gunnery. Apart from the early hits on the *Blücher*, Beatty's powerful squadron made only three other hits, two by the *Lion* on the *Seydlitz* and one on the second in the line, *Derfflinger*. Against this the *Lion* received 16, which crippled her, and the *Tiger* six. The main reason for this was the long range of the action and the consequent inaccuracy of the short-base British rangefinders. As these fed the fire control plots and the 'rate'-finding instruments they threw the whole elaborate gunnery organization out and control officers were driven back to simple 'spotting', but this again proved unexpectedly difficult as 'overs' could not be seen at all at that distance, and whenever the range was found the enemy ships started weaving off course. In addition to this the British ships were juddering forward at full tilt and were not equipped with director gear; the low turret sights were dulled with spray and cordite smoke, green water poured in through the sighting hoods, soaking and freezing the layers and trainers who only saw the enemy as smoke columns on the horizon. The Germans on the other hand had their longer-base rangefinders which gave good results, a part director system which only required the gunlayers, not the turret trainers, to keep the sights on target, and they were pointing their guns astern, away from the spray and wind.

However, it is also probable that there was a degree of over-confidence in the British battle cruisers' attitude which worked against such thorough gunnery training as the Germans—as the weaker force—practised. This did not apply to the battleships up in Scapa Flow; Jellicoe was the supreme gunnery training enthusiast, was constantly making the point that even the most modern ships were unfit to lie in the line unless their gunnery organization had been worked up to the high standards required in a modern action, and his battle squadrons were practising constantly off the Orkneys. While Beatty's ships had no such opportunities for practice, as they were based further south in the restricted waters of the Forth, the memoirs of the time suggest that the battle cruiser officers and men regarded themselves as an élite 'cavalry of the sea', certainly more than a match for the Germans. Carried too far this was bound to work against *making* opportunities for gunnery practice. The Dogger Bank did nothing to shake this confidence: how small the number of hits on the leading Germans was not realized and it was in any case easy to blame the comparative failure of the action on the lack of director gear, and particularly the fatal turn against the *Blücher*. Besides, it had been a victory; the Germans had run as fast as they could, leaving one of their number behind.

As for the Germans, shaken by the extraordinary range of the fight, they set about increasing the angles of maximum elevation of all their primary guns from 13 ½ degrees to 16 degrees;[4] this pushed the maximum range of their 12-inch pieces out 3,000 yards to 22,400 yards. They were also alerted by the loss of the *Seydlitz*'s after turrets to the danger of 'flash' from the ignition of charges on their way to the guns. The single shell from the *Lion* that had penetrated the 9-inch barbette of D turret had started a fire whose effects had jumped along a train of no less than 62 cartridges on their way to the guns on both D and C turrets, and had wiped out both turrets' crews in flames which had leaped funnel high. After this lesson 'anti-flash' doors were fitted at various stages of the loading cycle and rigid rules were imposed about the number of cartridges in each flash-tight stage.

Naturally the result of the battle did nothing to raise German morale; the *Blücher* had fought splendidly and with phenomenal discipline in the face of an overwhelming volume of heavy shell, but she should never have been with Hipper's faster ships in the first place, and the sortie, which had no clear purpose, should, it was felt, have been backed up by the battle fleet. The commander-in-chief was replaced; women and children openly jeered him in the streets of Wilhelmshaven.

> *Lieb Vaterland magst ruhig sein*
> *Die Flotte schlaft in Hafen ein.**

The new commander-in-chief, while leading the High Seas Fleet out of harbour on seven occasions during 1915, was scarcely less cautious about risking an action, and it was not until he was replaced by Vice Admiral Reinhard Scheer in February 1916 that the Germans had a commander with a positive offensive outlook. Scheer, of course, knew that he could not challenge the Grand Fleet as things stood, but he believed, like Tirpitz, that by taking the initiative and forcing the British to react he might be able to draw them over submarine traps or entice them into a position near his own minefields where the German strength in flotilla craft and training in combined battle-fleet and flotilla tactics could reduce their superiority in battleships. It was just such a sortie that, on 31 May, led to the Battle of Jutland, the nearest approach to a decisive test of strength which the great Dreadnought fleets ever managed.

Scheer's plan envisaged 20 U-boats placed along the east coast of Britain and the mining of the Grand Fleet's and battle cruisers'

---

* Dear Fatherland, rest in peace, the fleet is sleeping in port.

exits, to be followed by a battle cruiser attack on the east coast to draw the British ships out over the mines and submarines. However, to ensure the safety of his supporting battlefleet he needed to know where the Grand Fleet was at all times, and as continuous bad weather precluded airship reconnaisance he gave up the original idea and sent Hipper on a compromise sortie north from Heligoland towards the Skagerrak—following him with all the ships of the High Seas Fleet.

British Admiralty intelligence had known that something was afoot for days as the great number of U-boat departures and the lack of any subsequent sinkings had been noted. When on the morning of 30 May the Admiralty intercepted wirelessed instructions to the High Seas Fleet to prepare for sea and assemble in the Jade, the British fleet was immediately alerted, and Jellicoe made plans to rendezvous with Beatty's battle cruisers in the north-eastern part of the North Sea, ready to fall upon the Germans or upon their line of retreat wherever they might go. By chance the rendezvous Jellicoe chose was off the Skagerrak, whither Hipper's course was directed. So it was that both fleets steamed towards each other through a bright morning on 31 May, the Germans steering north in two groups, Hipper's battle cruiser force leading, Scheer following with the more ponderous battle fleet, the British converging upon them also in two groups, Beatty's battle cruisers steering east from Rosyth, the Grand Fleet under Jellicoe south-easterly from Scapa Flow.

The forces contained almost the entire Dreadnought strength of both sides giving the British a superiority of almost 2:1. Beatty, flying his flag in the *Lion*, led a force of six battle cruisers and four of the new super-class of fast 'Queen Elizabeth' battleships against Hipper's five battle cruisers; Jellicoe, flying his flag in the *Iron Duke*, led 24 Dreadnought battleships and three battle cruisers against Scheer's 16 Dreadnought battleships. Scheer also had a squadron of six pre-Dreadnoughts, but with their slower speed and weak armament these were actually a liability. In total gunpower the British mustered 324 heavy guns on each broadside against 196 German heavy pieces; the weight ratio of the broadsides was nearly 400,000 lbs: 200,000 lbs, against the Germans. In addition to this all British ships had by now been fitted and practised with director firing gear; the Germans still had their part director system. The only German advantages were the number of their torpedo tubes and their generally heavier secondary batteries, which were controlled with a director system similar to their main armament system—indeed they were intended for use with the main armament in a fleet action once the range had been found. The British secondary batteries, on the other hand, were in independent gunlayer control and were exclusively anti-torpedo boat batteries; they were not for use with the main armament for fear of hindering the primary fire control. On either side of the battle squadrons were screens of destroyers, ahead were light cruisers spread for scouting.

By 2.15 p.m. Hipper and Beatty had reached the same latitude and were only some 50 miles apart; the most easterly cruiser of Beatty's screen and the most westerly of Hipper's were a bare 16 miles from each other—just below the curve of the horizon. Splitting the distance between them was a neutral merchantman, and as both sides closed to investigate they sighted each other, wirelessed enemy contact and opened fire. Beatty and Hipper reacted immediately, wheeling their big ships towards the sound of the guns, although Beatty's move was marred by a signalling error which allowed the powerful Fifth Battle Squadron of four 'Queen Elizabeths' to diverge 10 miles north of the battle cruisers. Meanwhile the British light cruisers still closing on the enemy saw smoke as from a fleet on the eastern horizon and reported it by wireless; way to the north, Jellicoe, who had already ordered steam for full speed at the first contact report, abandoned the zig-zag he was on, and made straight for the conflict at 17 rising to 18 knots.

Meanwhile both battle cruiser commanders, drawn towards the light cruiser action, sighted each other at 14 miles hull down; Beatty swung east to cut across the German route home, and Hipper, seeing this, turned SE to fall back on Scheer, 50 miles behind, and spread his big ships on a line of bearing so that the smoke from his leading ships would not obscure the range. He knew the trap was sprung: Beatty would undoubtedly follow him as he had at the Dogger Bank. Of course Beatty had to; he pressed on to close the range.

For the British these were intensely exciting minutes; they had been waiting over a year to settle the issue begun at the Dogger Bank, and this time they meant to make no mistake. While Beatty has been criticised for his headlong charge at Hipper and his impetuosity in not waiting to concentrate with his Fifth Battle Squadron which was steaming hard to make up the original lost ground, he knew that time was the supreme factor in a chase, and even without the battleships he was six to Hipper's five. Besides he was Beatty and his only experience had been German retreat, this was the Royal Navy and its only traditions were offensive superiority and victory.

The Germans waited resolutely at their guns as the range closed. There had been a marked hush in the control positions at the first news of the British battle cruisers, but this had only lasted a minute or so, 'then humour broke out again, and everything went on in perfect order and calm'.[5] The gunnery officers in their armoured positions abaft the conning tower gazed at the British force through their periscopes, 'six tall, broad-beamed giants steaming in two columns...

showed up clearly on the horizon and even at this distance they looked powerful, massive...[5]

The British battlecruisers formed in one line of battle as they came on at 25 rising to 26 knots, the *Lion* leading; the rangefinder numbers intoned the shortening distance and Beatty's flag Captain, Chatfield, waited impatiently on the compass platform while Beatty on the bridge below composed a message for Jellicoe. Finally, as the rangefinders, which were actually overestimating the distance, indicated 16,000 yards, Chatfield could wait no longer, and gave the order to fire himself. Hipper opened at about the same time, 3.48. Beatty came up to the compass platform.

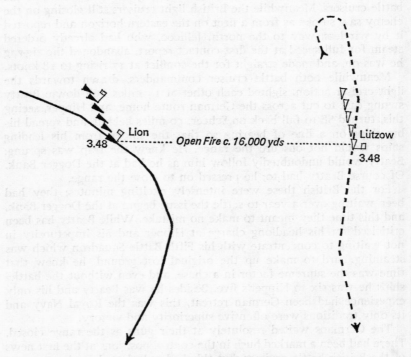

Figure 3. Battle of Jutland. The opening of battle cruiser action. Diagram only – not to scale.

As the first shells rose in the bright afternoon sunlight all the advantages save numbers were with Hipper. In the first place he was on a steady course right across Beatty's T, and Beatty had to spread on a line of bearing and alter south-easterly by degrees to parallel him during the vital opening minutes when a steady course for gunnery control should have been a prime object; his rear ships were not even in a position to open fire. The necessary turns also had the effect of creating a rash of flag hoists in which the distribution of fire signal, made at 3.46, was misinterpreted: while his two leading ships correctly concentrated on Hipper's flagship, Lützow, the third ship took the third ship in the German line, leaving the second ship, Derfflinger, to make unmolested target practice. Two other factors which Beatty could do nothing about were the westerly sun and the westerly breeze; the sun tended to silhouette the British ships and give the Germans a slight visibility advantage—although not a great one as the Lion's gunnery officer made clear, 'The Germans were showing up splendidly...'⁶—the breeze blew the funnel and gun smoke right down the range, and despite the line of bearing which Beatty adopted, seriously hampered the rear ships. This situation was aggravated by a part flotilla of destroyers which were straining up the engaged side of the British battle line to gain position ahead, further befouling the range with their dense funnel smoke.

Probably the severest British disadvantage was the short base length of their rangefinders; while their opening salvoes were falling as much as a mile over their targets many of the German salvoes were right on for range. The first salvo from the Moltke landed just 200 yards short of the Tiger and the next straddled her. Before the rear two ships in the British line had even opened fire, the Lion had been hit twice by the Lützow, and shortly afterwards the Tiger received two hits. Hipper's men were giving a superlative exhibition of shooting, their shells falling in tight bunches, while the British fire control was still overestimating the range and in some cases underestimating the rate of change of range, indeed it was closing so fast before Beatty's alterations gradually brought the two lines in parallel, that the Derfflinger, having straddled the Princess Royal, was able to go into rapid fire including secondary armament and a salvo was leaving her guns every seven seconds. Meanwhile the rear two British ships watched for the splashes of their opening salvoes, guns silent. Such was the advantage reaped by Hipper's steady tactics and his Zeiss rangefinders; such was the price paid for Beatty's overconfidence.

British officers, who had thought the German squadron looked a 'sitter' and had wondered only how long it would take to put them all on the bottom, settled down to a long struggle; up aloft gunnery control officers conducted their monosyllabic quick question and answer with spotters and the transmitting station way below.

'Did you see that?'

'No.'

'Down 400—close the rate 200!'

'Can't.'

'Make it one.'

'Down 400 on the plot.'

'Put it on and close 100!'

'Rate 250—closing.'

'Shoot!'

Their opposite numbers in the German ships were making the same quick judgements, and while waiting for the splashes of their own salvoes, found themselves watching the British shooting.

> I was able to see distinctly four or five shells coming through the air. They looked like elongated black specks. Gradually they grew bigger and then, Crash! they were here. They exploded on striking the water or the ship with a terrific roar. After a bit I could tell from watching the shells fairly accurately whether they were over or short or whether they would do us the honour of a visit.[7]

By 4 o'clock the British ships had received between 12 and 15 hits, the Germans probably four. The range had closed to under 14,000 yards and the noise and concussion were deafening. The grey paint on the gun barrels had blistered into several shades of yellow and brown, 'dense masses of smoke accumulated round the muzzles, growing into clouds as high as houses'. Tall columns of water with a poisonous yellow-green tinge from the base to about half the height stood up around the ships full five seconds before collapsing, overs', ricochets, and steel splinters hurtled through the air with whistling noises. Through it all the great ships worked up to full speed, their funnels belching volumes of black smoke, 'huge bow and stern waves being thrown up, straining to the uttermost'.

It was too hot to last. Both admirals turned two points away. Shortly afterwards the *Lützow* caught the *Lion* in a storm of accurate salvoes and Beatty turned away another three points so that the range began to open fast. Meanwhile at the rear of the line the *Von der Tann* found the *Indefatigable* with no less than three shells from a four-gun salvo at 16,000 yards—a startling feat. Smoke started billowing from the stern of the British ship, and she failed to follow round on the alteration of course. The torpedo officer of the next ahead laid his glasses on her in time to see the next salvo straddle as well, one shell hitting her foc's'le, another her forward turret. He continued watching for some 30 seconds until quite suddenly she erupted in front of his eyes. The explosion started from forward with sheets of flame followed immediately afterwards by thick, dark smoke, which obscured the ship from view. Debris were hurled high in the air and fell in all directions from the rising tower of smoke; a 50-foot picket boat hovered upside down but intact 200 feet above the water, and beneath it, almost entirely hidden from view, all that remained of the riven hull of the battle cruiser turned over and dived beneath the surface.

Evidently the flames had reached her magazines. Now it was five against five. But as Beatty's superior speed and opening course drew the leading battle cruisers out of range and the guns fell silent, the Fifth Battle Squadron, which had been cutting corners to catch up, at last made out Hipper's ships and opened fire at 19,000 yards. Although the director layers only had the high, white stern waves of the rear two German ships to aim on, they were soon making good practice—aided by more effective 15-foot rangefinders, the flatter trajectory of their 15-inch shells, and by intense gunnery training which they had undergone recently in Scapa Flow. Within six minutes of opening fire the flagship, *Barham*, had hit the *Von der Tann*, and the German ships were snaking out of line to confuse the control.

Beatty, no doubt heartened by this powerful reinforcement, altered back to close Hipper, who had meanwhile also altered to close Beatty and get within gun range of at least one of his opponents. So the two battle cruiser forces fired on each other once more. For Hipper and his men this stage of the action marks as heroic and successful a feat of arms as is to be found in modern naval history. While Beatty's battle cruisers and the Fifth Battle Squadron converged on him from positions just before and slightly abaft his beam, bringing an overwhelming volume of shell on to his five vessels, he held on resolutely, weaving due south to bring his shorter range pieces into effective action. His boldness brought early rewards. Almost as soon as the *Lion* came within range and hit his flagship, the *Lützow* replied with such devastating effect that the *Lion* herself disappeared temporarily beneath a cloud of smoke. The second German ship, *Derfflinger*, losing sight of her, shifted sights to what now appeared to be the second British ship, the *Queen Mary*, which was already engaged by the *Seydlitz*. The *Queen Mary* herself was already firing at the *Derfflinger* with beautiful precision and accuracy, and she got in the first two blows, starting fires and then almost immediately extinguishing them with near misses which deluged the decks. As the range closed rapidly the action grew to a crescendo, the *Queen Mary* firing full eight-gun broadsides, according to the gunnery officer on *Derfflinger*, with 'fabulous rapidity', and the *Derfflinger* attempting to beat her to the shoot, but severely handicapped by gun smoke blurring the low turret sights and even the control periscope lens.

Then the *Derfflinger* straddled her at 15,000 yards, and went into rapid fire. The ammunition numbers stepped up their drill to a peak of disciplined speed and for the next two minutes as the range closed to 14,400 yards a salvo left her guns every 20 seconds. Each one straddled the *Queen Mary*. Once again the close bunching of the German shells produced a fatal combination, three striking out of four from one salvo, two from the next. The *Derfflinger*'s gunnery officer watched through his periscope as internal explosions began:

First of all a vivid red flame shot up from her forepart. Then came an explosion forward which was followed by a much heavier explosion amidships, black debris of the ship flew into the air, and immediately afterwards the ship blew up with a terrific explosion. A gigantic cloud of smoke arose, the masts collapsed inwards, the smoke cloud hid everything and rose higher and higher...[8]

An officer in the conning tower of her next astern, *Tiger*, had a closer view; he saw a dull red glow amidships, 'and then the ship seemed to open out like a puffball or one of those toadstool things when one squeezes it...the whole ship seemed to collapse inwards. The funnels and masts fell into the middle and the hull was blown outwards. The roofs of the turrets were blown 100 feet high, then everything was smoke...'[9] The *Tiger* put her helm over sharply to avoid the wreck but was completely unsighted as she plunged into the smoke; debris rained down upon her decks. Astern of her the *New Zealand* put her helm the other way as they saw, fantastically to port, the stern of the stricken ship projecting seventy feet out of the water, her propellers still revolving, and clouds of white paper, torn by the wind, rising giddily above the smoke.

It is almost impossible to describe one's feelings on witnessing this disaster...but I think the principle sensation was one of astonishment that a ship should disappear in an instant without leaving a trace. One could not realize all that it meant...[9]

Meanwhile Beatty had ordered the British destroyers to attack, and having strained past the big ships, they had at last reached a position ahead of Hipper's line of advance and were turning to close. Hipper,

Top German Dreadnought battleship, *Friedrich der Grosse*, steaming to internment at Scapa Flow. (*Imperial War Museum*)

Bottom The battlecruiser, *Derfflinger*, sinking after scuttling at Scapa Flow. (*Imperial War Museum*)

Top The German 15-inch-gun 'Badens' bore a striking resemblance to the British 'Queen Elizabeths' (*Collection Unimare/E Groner*)

Middle The threat to the battleship: aircraft carriers with the British Mediterranean fleet of the 1930s. (*Cdr J. Hale, D.S.O.*)

Opposite 16-inch-gun battleship, U S S *New Jersey* firing a broadside. (*U S Navy*)

Opposite middle U S triple 16-inch-gun turret and loading complex. (*U S Navy*)

Bottom Final development of the 'super-Dreadnought': the Japanese 18-inch-gun *Yamato* on trials, 1941. (*Imperial War Museum*)

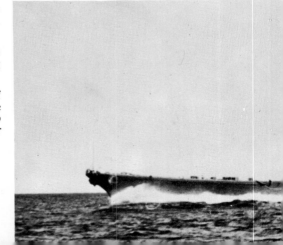

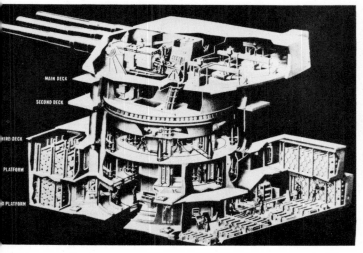

MAIN DECK

SECOND DECK

THIRD DECK

PLATFORM

D PLATFORM

Yamato under the U S Navy fleet air attack which finished her – and the battleship type. *Ichabod!* (*U S Navy*)

who had been undeterred by all the great guns opposed to him, immediately turned his battle cruisers 6 points away together, and then a further 2 points; it was the standard counter in all navies. And from his disengaged side the German destroyers raced out to repel the attack, forcing 'a glorious sort of disorganized mêlée in which the destroyers of both sides were dashing about at 30 knots in all directions'; the battle cruisers were momentarily forgotten as quick firing guns went into rapid independent, maximum rate of fire, maximum deflection.

At this point Beatty's Second Light Cruiser Squadron, some 9,000 yards ahead of the battle cruisers, saw on the rim of the southern horizon the masts and upperworks of heavy ships, and signalling 'BATTLESHIPS SOUTH EAST', pressed on to investigate: eight minutes later they were able to send a more detailed report: 'HAVE SIGHTED ENEMY BATTLEFLEET BEARING APPROXIMATELY SOUTH-EAST COURSE OF ENEMY NORTH.[10]

> ...on our port bow the German fleet coming to the rescue of the battle cruisers, and an imposing sight they looked, ship after ship in single line melting away into the haze, all showing up white, lit by the sun.[11]

By this time the head of Scheer's line could be seen from the *Lion* herself. It was a momentous and thrilling sight, the first glimpse for the British officers in two long years of war of the main strength of the German naval challenge. More important, the whole complexion of the battle had changed suddenly and dramatically. The protagonists had changed roles. Beatty, the hunter, who had been led by Hipper almost into Scheer's arms, had turned into Beatty, the hunted, whose task was to lead both Hipper and Scheer into Jellicoe's arms. He ordered an immediate alteration of 16 points and retraced his tracks; the Fifth Battle Squadron, thundering down on his heels, failed to distinguish the flags until they were passing on a reciprocal course, and so came within 21,000 yards of Scheer's leading ships and a holocaust of shell before they too turned back.

Way to the north, the Grand Fleet, formed in six columns of four ships, was sweeping towards the scene at 20 knots; Jellicoe signalled the Admiralty, 'FLEET ACTION IMMINENT'.

> Shortly afterwards I noticed that several ships were flying, instead of the customary one ensign, three or four ensigns from various parts of the rigging...in about 10 minutes the air seemed to be thick with white ensigns, large and small, silk and bunting, hoisted wherever halyards could be rove.[12]

It is interesting to compare the hitting rates of the two forces up to this point where the battle took a reverse turn; in the vital opening minutes Hipper had established an ascendancy with 12–15 hits against about four received, thus one hit per minute with five ships against Beatty's one every three minutes with six ships. During the rest of the southerly action Beatty's five ships scored probably nine hits against between 24 and 27 received, and allowing for time outside effective range this gives very similar relative hitting rates; the Fifth Battle Squadron, after coming into range, had scored eight hits against none received. It is evident that Hipper won the round decisively in hitting rate as well as ships lost.

At the turn the Fifth Battle Squadron received nine hits from the head of Scheer's battle line, but despite this they soon found Hipper's range as he too turned north to follow Beatty, and during the next 10 minutes, 5.05 to 5.15, they scored another 11 hits on the German battle cruisers against only two received at ranges starting at 20,000 yards coming down to 18,000 yards—a remarkable performance, and testimony to the British big gun policy. Here is the *Derfflinger*'s gunnery officer:

> This part of the action, fought against a numerically inferior, but more powerfully armed enemy who kept us under fire at ranges at which we were helpless was highly depressing, nerve-wracking and exasperating. Our only means of defence was to leave the line for a short time when we saw that the enemy had our range...[13]

Hipper was by now restricted to 22 knots speed as the British destroyers, having beaten off the German counter attack, had pressed in to 3,000 yards and caught his third ship, *Seydlitz*, with a torpedo as she turned north. She was in no danger of sinking and remained in the line, but the reduced speed she forced on the squadron allowed the British forces to draw ahead so that the gunfire became spasmodic, and at times ceased altogether.

A curious feature of this race to the north is that Beatty, heading directly for a junction with Jellicoe, could by no stretch of the imagination have been making for any British bases; all were westerly. It seems astonishing in retrospect that neither Hipper nor Scheer apparently realized this but in the heat of the chase followed him blindly into a trap.

By 5.35, with Jellicoe's fleet only some 16 miles to the northward and the forces closing each other at a combined speed of nearly 40 knots, Beatty altered from his north north-westerly course to north-easterly for the double purpose of regaining contact with Hipper, and heading him off from any sight of the Grand Fleet as it bore down. It was a well-conceived manoeuvre and brilliantly fulfilled its purpose. As Hipper had already altered two points towards the British forces, also in an effort to regain contact, the battle cruisers soon sighted each other again and re-opened fire. This time all the advantages were with Beatty; he was crossing Hipper's T, and the sun at last clear and low in the north-west both dazzled the German gunlayers and lit their ships for the British who found spotting conditions better than ever before. About the same time the Fifth Battle Squadron also re-opened fire and, caught between these two, Hipper turned north east, then east as Beatty closed. The Grand Fleet was now only 10 miles to the north, but Hipper caught no glimpse of it; instead he heard gunfire ahead of his course in a position which none of Beatty's forces could possibly have reached. This came from an advance detachment of cruisers and three battle cruisers led by Rear Admiral Hood in the *Invincible* which Jellicoe had sent on ahead to support Beatty. They had arrived some 20 miles east of Beatty, and one of the light cruisers had run into a German cruiser squadron. By this time the earlier good visibility was giving way to mist patches and the lone British cruiser actually approached within 7,000 yards of the Germans before being chased off. Both Hood and Hipper turned their big ships towards the sound of the action and Hood, arriving first, reduced one German cruiser, *Wiesbaden*, to a blazing wreck at something under 12,000 yards before he was forced to turn away by the threat of torpedoes. The destroyers with him pressed in to make a counter attack and shortly coming in sight of Hipper's big ships forced Hipper in his turn to alter away; he went south towards Scheer.

At this point none of the commanders on either side had any clear idea of what was happening, Scheer and Hipper least of all. The cruisers attacked by Hood had reported battleships in the north-east—they were of course battle cruisers—but their number was uncertain; the only certain point was that they could not be part of Beatty's force. However Scheer was not a man to be frightened by shapes in the mist, and believing from earlier and erroneous U-boat reports that the Grand Fleet was split in several directions, he altered north-easterly to probe this new force; Hipper, coming towards him, made an about turn and reformed at the head of the battle line.

As for Jellicoe, he was scarcely better informed. Cruisers ahead of Beatty's force had sighted the most westerly of the Grand Fleet advanced cruiser screen about the time of Beatty's easterly alteration to regain contact with Hipper but they had not signalled the position of the enemy relative to themselves or relative to Jellicoe's cruisers —as the Grand Fleet Battle Orders stipulated—nor had Beatty himself given any indication of where the enemy lay; meanwhile Jellicoe could make out nothing for himself; the light south-westerly breeze was blowing all the smoke and haze of the northing action across his front and the slow mists of the North Sea were gathering in pockets so that visibility varied from moment to moment and from sector to sector:

> The average visibility was never greater than 12,000 yards (at this time), and was in most cases far less. In exceptional cases in certain directions, objects could be seen up to 16,000 yards, but in other directions they could only be seen 2,000 to 3,000 yards.[14]

Jellicoe had already instructed his Flag Captain to take bearings all round the compass and find the best direction for gunnery; the report had been that it was clearer to the south, but the advantage to an easterly force would grow as the sun set and threw the western horizon into silhouette; in addition the westerly wind would blow the smoke clear of the easterly force. This was ideal from the point of view of cutting the Germans off from their base. But where were the Germans? Although gunfire could be heard to the southward it was vital for Jellicoe to know much more about their bearing and course before he deployed his own fleet from cruising formation into line of battle; so far the few reports had been baffling.

The first had been from the most westerly of his own cruiser screen, 'BATTLECRUISERS IN ACTION SOUTH SOUTH-WESTERLY.' But whose? A few minutes later another of his cruisers screen had reported 'SHIPS IN ACTION SOUTH SOUTH-WESTERLY STEERING NORTH-EASTERLY. Next one of Beatty's cruisers had signalled her own position followed by 'ENEMY ALTERED COURSE NORTH NORTH-WESTERLY.' As the estimated position of Beatty's forces was some seven miles east of true and of Jellicoe's four miles west of true, this signal was not helpful about the relative position—although by this time Jellicoe must have realised that there was a discrepancy between the navigators, and that the enemy whom he had expected to meet ahead was somewhere to the west, or starboard of his starboard column. A few minutes later the same cruiser from Beatty's force signalled 'ENEMY ALTERED COURSE TO NORTH. ENEMY BATTLECRUISERS BEAR SOUTH-WESTERLY FROM BATTLESHIPS.' This further confused the issue as the battle cruisers bore north-east not south-west from their battlefleet. Jellicoe remarked testily to his flag captain, 'I wish someone would tell me who is firing and what they are firing at.' And in desperation he signalled to the leading ship of his starboard division, 'WHAT CAN YOU SEE?'

He received a model answer: 'OUR BATTLECRUISERS BEARING SOUTH

SOUTH-WESTERLY THREE TO FOUR MILES STEERING EAST. LION LEADING SHIP.' At the same moment Jellicoe saw the battle cruisers himself two points before his starboard beam and heading easterly across his course; Beatty was obviously engaging an enemy somewhere to the south and Jellicoe altered his six columns due south together to face them, at the same time flashing Beatty: 'WHERE IS THE ENEMY'S BATTLEFLEET?' Beatty was not sure; he replied, 'ENEMY BATTLECRUISERS BEARING SOUTH-EAST.' This didn't help Jellicoe, but as the direction of the battle appeared to be drifting easterly, and he wished to cut the Germans from their base he altered his columns back to their original south-easterly direction. It may be that as he did so the idea of a deployment on the port column came into his mind, for at the same time he ordered two destroyer flotillas to port, only one to starboard.

The situation was now critical; it was essential for the Grand Fleet to be formed in line of battle by the time the enemy came in sight or it would be at a crippling disadvantage with nearly all guns masked; it is a measure of Jellicoe's stature that despite this he held on at 20 knots, determined to wait for precise information before committing himself.

> Many had been the critical situations which British Admirals in the past had been called upon suddenly to solve, but never had there been one which demanded higher qualities of leadership, ripe judgement and quick decision than that which confronted Admiral Jellicoe in this supreme moment of the naval war...[15]

Almost at the last moment, the veil was lifted. The Fifth Battle Squadron which had now come into sight some way astern of Beatty's battle cruisers signalled 'ENEMY IN SIGHT SOUTH-SOUTH-EAST,' and at the same time Beatty himself saw Scheer's ships and flashed 'SIGHTED ENEMY'S BATTLEFLEET SOUTH-SOUTH-WEST.' Jellicoe made a quick mental cross between the lines of bearing, and working on a visibility of five miles, placed the enemy almost due south of his starboard column of battleships. He stepped towards the central compass platform where his flag captain was watching the course being steered.

> I heard the sharp, distinctive step of the Commander-in-Chief approaching—he had steel strips on his heels. He stepped quickly on to the platform around the compass and looked in silence at the magnetic compass card for about 20 seconds. I watched his keen, weather-beaten face with tremendous interest, wondering what he would do...I realized as I watched that he was as

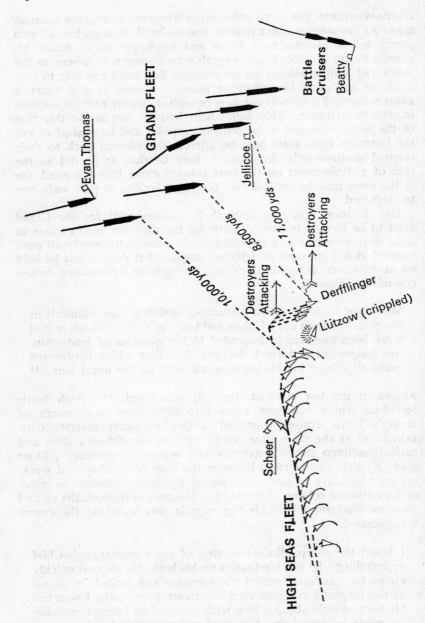

Figure 4. Jutland. 6.25 p.m. The grand deployment.

cool and unmoved as ever. Then he looked up and broke the silence...'Hoist equal speed pendant south-east!'[16]

The effect of the signal was that while the port wing column continued on its south-easterly course, the leaders of all other columns turned 90 degrees to port, followed by the ships behind as they reached the leader's turning points, thus forming one line heading towards the port column—then swinging round south-easterly in its wake. It was undoubtedly a masterstroke. It gave the Grand Fleet every advantage it could wish for, cutting the Germans from their base, crossing their T as they advanced north-easterly, ensuring the advantage of the light, of the wind and of the visibility for gunnery. It also ensured that the whole fleet would be in line in four minutes and at a sufficient distance from the German van to prevent its own van from becoming embroiled in a torpedo boat melée.

As the line was forming Beatty was steaming easterly across its front belching funnel and gun smoke, a squadron of Jellicoe's cruisers was bearing down to finish off the cruiser *Wiesbaden*, which Hood's battle cruisers had previously stopped and set ablaze, and at the rear the *Warspite* of the Fifth Battle Squadron was circling towards the Germans with a jammed rudder. So Hipper was denied any sight of the Grand Fleet as he steamed up at the head of Scheer's battle line. It was not until these distractions had dispersed and he had come within 12,000 yards of the British van that he gradually became aware that the battle cruisers he had been engaging had been reinforced by a much larger fleet. The ships of the fleet were invisible though; all he could make out were their gun flashes which stretched in a ring from the north-eastern to the north-western horizon, and as he closed to 9,000 yards the salvoes rained thickly about his ships. Still so little was visible that his gunnery officers could only reply by ranging on the enemy flashes, and he shortly turned south, reporting to Scheer 'TURNING AWAY BECAUSE OBSERVATION AGAINST THE SUN IMPOSSIBLE.'

Meanwhile Scheer's leading battleships were also coming under fire. Jellicoe's flagship, *Iron Duke* (gunnery officer Geoffrey Blake) had the *König* in her sights and scored six hits in as many minutes. And Jellicoe, eager to press his advantage, ordered a signal for the fleet to turn by divisions three points closer to the enemy. Before it was made executive he realized that half the fleet were not yet around the turning point to a south-easterly course, and it must lead to confusion, so he cancelled it.

At the head of the line Beatty had placed his squadron before the leading ships of the Grand Fleet and Hood, rejoining, had added

234

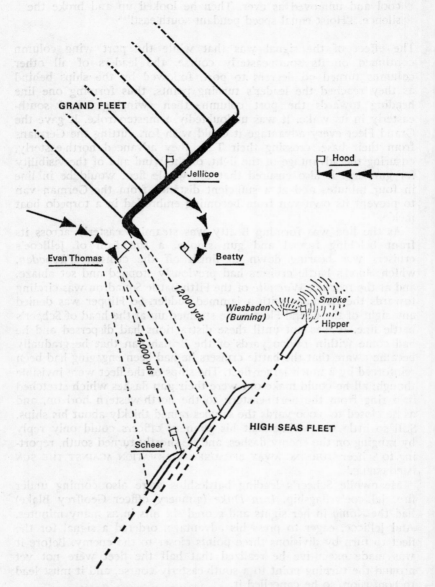

Figure 5. Jutland. Hypothetical position at 6.20 p.m. – if Jellicoe had deployed on his starboard wing column.

his three battle cruisers ahead of Beatty, so that the *Invincible* led the entire British force strung out across what had been the German line of advance. She was engaging Hipper's flagship, the *Lützow*, which had already taken tremendous punishment; the German ship shortly fell out of the line ablaze with most of her armament out of action and Hipper boarded a destroyer to transfer his flag. The *Invincible* switched her sights to the next astern, *Derfflinger*, which suddenly saw her too as the mist curtain parted momentarily. The range was 10,000 yards and a fierce duel developed for a space of four salvoes. Then the British battle cruiser blew up; 'as with the other ships there occurred a rapid succession of heavy explosions, masts collapsed debris was hurled into the air...'[17] The *Derfflinger* herself was heavily damaged, on fire in several places, taking in water through a gash in the bows and with her torpedo nets shot loose and in danger of fouling her propellers.

Scheer's leading battleships were faring almost as badly without being able to make any effective reply, and Scheer ordered a battle turn away, all ships together. This was a difficult evolution which had been practised many times in manoeuvres for just such an eventuality; it involved the rear ship turning first through 180 degrees, followed by her next ahead, and so on until the whole line had reversed its course. It was now carried out brilliantly under fire. To the British the Germans appeared to melt away into the haze and it was suddenly quiet. After a few minutes Jellicoe altered the fleet course by divisions to south to probe for the enemy and at the van Beatty set off to search south-westerly.

Scheer, meanwhile, performed another battle turn and again advanced north-easterly, battle cruisers in the lead. Why will never be known for certain. His subsequent explanation was that he had decided upon a bold initiative to surprise the British Commander-in-Chief while his massed torpedo attack threw the British fleet into confusion—a Nelson-like thrust. Perhaps the most widely-held theory is that, having been led to believe by Hipper's earlier report that the British van was ahead of where it actually was, he attempted to get around the tail of the British fleet in the gathering dusk, then strike for home. This leaves out of account the fact that he had *seen* the gunflashes to the north and could scarcely have believed that this entire line could have moved so far south as to give him a clear passage. The probable answer is that, like Jellicoe, he had no clear idea of what he was up against—he probed easterly for more certain knowledge. And once again his van, already severely punished, ran into the entire Grand Fleet, now heading south across his T. The firing started from the rear divisions of the Grand Fleet at 10,000 yards, gradually spreading forward until even the battle

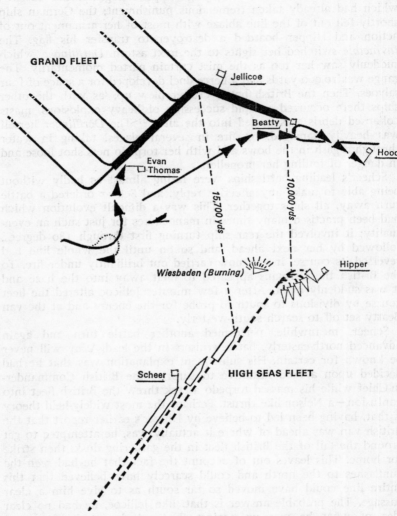

Figure 6. Jutland. 7.20 p.m. The second battle – turn away.

cruisers at the head were engaged, and once again the German range-takers and gunlayers found it impossible to see much more of the enemy than the bright flashes of the guns like batteries of red search-lights opening momentarily. As the hits mounted and the leading German ships were forced southwards Scheer realized that he was advancing towards certain annihilation, and ordering yet another battle turn away, he sent his destroyers in to attack and cover the big ships with smoke screens. But even this was not judged sufficient to save the battle fleet, and he added an order to the battle cruisers to charge the enemy regardless of consequences.

Captain Hertog of the *Derfflinger*, still leading as Hipper had not yet found a sufficiently undamaged ship in which to hoist his flag, ordered 'FULL SPEED, COURSE SOUTH-EAST!' and there began a suicidal charge towards the British guns—a splendid, headlong attempt to retrieve at least the battleships from a tactically hopeless position. An inferno of shell exploded about the already battered ships as they pressed forward; the *Derfflinger* lost two turrets to ammunition fires in rapid succession, then a shell struck the fore control, shaking it 'as though by the hands of some portentous giant', and although the armour kept the full effect outside, poisonous, greenish-yellow gases poured in; the control party donned gasmasks.

Without much hope of hurting the enemy I ordered the two forward turrets to fire salvo after salvo. I could feel that our fire soothed the nerves of the ship's company. If we had ceased fire at this time the whole ship's company would have been over-whelmed by despair...[18]

Then Scheer completed his turn away successfully and felt able to call off the charge; at the same time the German destroyers, approaching to some 8,000 yards through a barrage from the British secondary batteries, forced Jellicoe to turn two points away, then a further two points so that the range opened. As the British ships manoeuvred individually to evade 21 torpedo tracks bearing down upon them, the German battle cruisers turned back towards Scheer and escaped.

This virtually concluded the daylight actions. Beatty probing westerly did sight and engage the German battle cruisers briefly, but the rest of the Grand Fleet, despite altering south after the torpedoes had passed, then westerly at 7.59, never sighted the Germans again. Nevertheless they were extraordinarily close as darkness fell; Scheer was heading southerly with his main battle fleet in single line, Jellicoe barely 12,000 yards to the east of him was heading south-westerly and the fleets were set for a collision point some nine miles ahead.

But as in the earlier stages of the battle neither fleet commander had any idea of the real situation; both were ill-served by their scouts. While Scheer thought that Jellicoe had turned easterly for good, Jellicoe had a mental picture of the action as a revolving encounter with the Germans always occupying the interior position with an overlap, and he therefore imagined that they were well ahead of him. It was this idea that they were ahead and to the west that coloured his thinking when he decided on his course for the night.

He had already discarded night action as it was both theoretically chancy and had been proved so in manoeuvres, nor had he any intention of risking the Grand Fleet to massed torpedo attack in the darkness when the tracks would be invisible, so his problem was how to keep between the High Seas Fleet and its base during the six hours before first light—about 2 a.m.—the following morning. Scheer's shortest route home was by the Horn's Reef Channel (105 miles from 9 p.m.); other possibilities were the Ems Channel (180 miles) or a gap in the minefields (135 miles). The two last were longer but more westerly, and Jellicoe, with his picture of Scheer well to the west, selected them as the most likely, and shaped his night course south by east at 17 knots, to be 40 miles from the gap in the minefields at daylight; at the same time he gathered his battleships together in three compact columns and massed the destroyers five miles astern so that they would not be mistaken for enemy craft in the darkness. Beatty, who also had a mental picture of the Germans way to the west, was stationed 12 miles on the starboard, thus westerly, bow of the Grand Fleet.

Scheer, however, was concerned about the possibilities of the Grand Fleet being reinforced from the British southern bases the following morning, and was determined to make for home by the shortest, most easterly route. He therefore altered south-south-easterly for the Horns Reef, which Jellicoe's movement left uncovered, and pressed on at 16 knots. By these movements of the commanders within 10 minutes of each other shortly after 9 o'clock, the former collision courses of the fleets were transformed into near-miss courses with the British fleet passing the point of intersection some five miles ahead of the Germans. It was the British destroyers, five miles astern of the battlefleet, who were now on collision course with Scheer.

So the two fleets steamed almost side by side some nine miles apart on this most incredible night. Despite the loss of three battle cruisers —still unknown to Jellicoe—the Grand Fleet was relatively stronger than it had been at the beginning of the day, having 23 untouched Dreadnought battleships, and four more with main batteries unimpaired against Scheer's six; in battle cruisers the British had six which retained 90 per cent of their fighting capacity, the Germans only one. Hipper's flagship, *Lützow*, was miles astern and sinking, the *Seydlitz* was also sinking, the *Derfflinger* and *Von der Tann* were straggling behind with about one turret each in working order. However, there was one field in which the darkness was to prove the Germans immeasurably superior: this was in the training and control for night action. The German secondary batteries were in part director control, the searchlight batteries were in remote control, and they had star shell to illuminate the enemy; the British fleet had none of these devices and this led to a general lack of confidence in night fighting, consequently less intensive training.

This soon told as Scheer's van converged on the massed British flotilla and the cruiser screens. The British made out the shadowy forms in the darkness, trained their guns, searchlights and torpedo tubes and challenged; in answer the German shutters fell from their lights and the broadsides crashed out at point blank range with devastating effect. And while British destroyer attacks deflected the German battleships temporarily they soon probed back again, pressing through, leaving a trail of wrecked and burning vessels after a series of the closest, most rapid and deadly encounters that had yet been seen in naval warfare.

At the stern of the German fleet the battle cruiser officers watched the results of the struggle:

> One blazing, red hot vessel after another passed us. I could not help thinking of the living torches driven about by the Romans in their orgies of cruelty. All metal parts were aglow and the destroyers looked like fine filigree work in red and gold...[19]

While these desperate actions were taking place just astern, the Grand Fleet itself held a steady course southwards. Although the gunfire could be heard plainly, and the flashes, searchlights and bursts of flame could be seen during the night passing gradually from the starboard quarter to right astern, then over to the port quarter, Jellicoe and Beatty thought that they were caused by the British flotillas repulsing German destroyer attacks. No one told them otherwise. A cruiser and a few destroyers tried to get messages through but they were either jammed by the enemy or not passed quickly enough. Perhaps the most inexplicable event of this extraordinary night was when German battleships were plainly seen and recognized from the rear ships of the Fifth Battle Squadron at the tail of the Grand Fleet and no message was passed to Jellicoe. This was an inexcusable failure. So Scheer passed east with the loss of only one heavy ship, the pre-Dreadnought *Pommern* by torpedo attack in the early hours. Jellicoe continued south, leaving the way to Horns Reef clear.

As daylight broke, the Grand Fleet, whose officers fully expected to repeat the deeds of their forebears on the 'Glorious First of June', turned north and formed into line of battle; Beatty, whose first inclination had been to sweep south-westerly to find the enemy, followed. But the mist and the sea were empty as they peered through their glasses. To the east of them the officers of the High Seas Fleet were also gazing anxiously through the early haze with binoculars. 'As we could then discover no signs of the enemy, far and wide, I confess frankly, a load fell from my heart.'[20]

The only fleet action of the war, indeed the only fleet action between Dreadnought battleships, ended in anti-climax. For the British, Navy and public alike, it was a great disappointment. They had been brought up on the Nelson legend, and felt let down. In fact the consequences of the battle were quite as decisive as Trafalgar. The German fleet had been driven home, and no thinking German officer could ever contemplate another action with the Grand Fleet except in terms of a final suicide sortie to retrieve the honour they felt they had lost through inaction while the army took the brunt of the war. The High Seas Fleet made other occasional sorties, but never with the intention of fighting a fleet action, nor with the hope of altering the basic strategic position in which they were locked by the steel ring of Grand Fleet battleships.

The Germans made much of the spectacular British losses in battle cruisers, three against only one of their own (the *Lützow* failed to make Horn's Reef), and as they had started much the inferior fleet they claimed a victory—with such success that the myth has persisted. However, it must strike impartial observers as a curious victory that allowed the beaten side to hold the field of battle and forced the victors to escape by the shortest possible route regardless of consequences! Hipper certainly defeated Beatty in the battle cruiser skirmishes—although the margin of defeat was exaggerated by the fickleness of the British cordite. As for the main action, Beatty and Jellicoe combined outmanoeuvred the German fleet to such an extent that the Grand Fleet received only two hits, both from Hipper's battle cruisers in their final charge; altogether in the two brief fleet encounters the German battleships and bzattlecruisers received some 70 hits and made perhaps 20 themselves on three ships, *Warspite* (Fifth Battle Squadron), *Invincible* and *Colossus*—leaving out of account both sides, hits on lghter craft. And while the British shells appeared liable to break up on oblique impact to armour, and their lyddite bursting charges proved too sensitive so that they often blew up outside instead of inside the ship, they still succeeded in piercing

11 inches of Krupp steel at over 17,000 yards, 10-inch at greater distances—again causing complete destruction of battle cruisers' turrets by ammunition fires—while the thickest British armour pierced appears to have been a 9-inch tapered plate. That the British shells *were* capable of wrecking a ship is proved by the loss of the *Lützow*, and the severe damage to all other German battle cruisers. Men seeing the *Derfflinger* after she had limped home gazed with awe at her wounds. The deck aft looked as though a volcano had erupted; forward a whole armour plate had been torn from the side and driven into the battery deck, while the superstructure 'looked like a madhouse' with bent, rolled-up, torn, twisted, blackened plates and fittings, guns shorn or pointing unnaturally in all directions.[21]

The main reason that the German ships were able to take this kind of punishment and survive, whereas the British battle cruisers succumbed to far less, has nothing to do with their armour protection, everything to do with the composition of their cordite charges and the neglect of the various precautions built in to the turret complex to prevent fire being passed down the ammunition hoists to the magazines. While the ammunition hoists had been broken deliberately at a working chamber fitted with flash-tight covers to guard against this danger, and the magazines had been provided with vents to the open air to dissipate the effects of an explosion, these devices had been nullified in action by the enthusiasm of the magazine parties to feed the guns as rapidly as possible; thus the lids of the ammunition cases in the magazine were taken off before the charges were needed, the magazine doors were left open, a stack of charges were piled outside the doors, with igniters uncovered, ready for loading, and access ladders to the gunhouse which by-passed the anti-flash devices in the hoists were left open. All this would have been viewed with amazement, indeed terror by an eighteenth century sailor, but since the introduction of the supposedly safer smokeless ammunition in place of gunpowder the old fear of internal explosion had been lost. Added to this, the cordite itself proved unstable; whereas the German charges burnt and wiped out whole turrets, the British charges exploded and destroyed whole ships. While it is true that the Germans adopted various anti-flash precautions after the disaster to the *Seydlitz*'s turrets at the Dogger Bank, these were extemporized devices which did *not* eliminate the flash danger according to the British officers who inspected the High Seas Fleet after the war. Thus it was not so much the anti-flash precautions of the German ships at Jutland which saved their ships from the fate of their British counterparts as the stabilizing ingredient in their charges.

After Jutland all British ships were fitted with anti-flash devices, safety routines were instituted in the loading cycles and in deference to the strong opinion in the fleet that the magazines were insufficiently protected from dropping shells, extra horizontal armour was fitted. To increase offensive power new shells were designed to withstand oblique impact, and fire control received a radical overhaul, the leisurely, peace-begotten method of ranging salvoes—which the Germans also practised—was speeded up so that two salvoes were in the air at the same time, spread first for deflection, then for range; 'concentration' fire of two or more ships against one of the enemy was perfected, and in the *matériel* field director firing was fitted to secondary as well as main armament, while the director gear itself was improved with gyro-stabilization so that the guns were fired automatically when the ship reached an even keel; in addition all the aids to night firing perfected by the Germans were faithfully copied. By the end of the war, the Grand Fleet was perhaps twice as effective a hitting unit as it had been in 1916. This is not to decry Grand Fleet gunnery at Jutland; it had been fully equal to German gunnery, and the chances are that it would have proved a great deal better in heavy weather because of full director control and the higher and better sighting position aloft.

So much for *matériel* and training. As for the fleet commanders, both have received regular and frequently hysterical criticism since the battle. Yet the fact which stands out above all is the poor intelligence with which they had to work. While Scheer and Jellicoe both confirmed the adage that in the stress of action a man will do as he has been trained (or in this case trained himself to do beforehand) their scouting forces did not. Pre-war exercises reveal model reports from cruisers and battle cruisers of the position, course, speed, composition and formation of 'enemy' forces, yet in the 'real thing' scarcely any scout commanders obeyed the rules, and few appeared to think themselves into the position of their commander-in-chief some distance away and quite blind to what they were seeing themselves. Beatty, a man of towering courage, presence of mind and fighting inspiration who was no stranger to hot action, was so immersed in the stunning concussion of events that he completely failed to put himself in Jellicoe's position. And while Jellicoe's Grand Fleet Battle Orders spelled out that navigational discrepancies were inevitable between two separated forces and it was therefore essential that once visual contact was made between the advanced cruisers all reports should give *relative* not geographical positions, this was not done. In all these respects pre-war training had failed, and most lamentably during the night action. The Dreadnoughts' powerful armaments had exceeded their sensory apparatus; they had groped about the field like half-blind monsters, lashing out whenever they

saw an opponent briefly through the mist, drawing blood and occasionally killing, but seldom knowing the true position—consequently
unable to take advantage of it.

For this reason the main criticism levelled against Jellicoe, that he
turned away from torpedo attack and failed to pursue the German
fleet as it fled for the second time, is invalid. Jellicoe turned away
like every other commander faced with torpedo attack because it was
the safest and had been proved in countless exercises the safest way
to avoid massed torpedoes. He did not know that the German battle
cruisers were almost finished—no one had told him—nor that their
battleships were on the run, and when the German fleet disappeared
in the mist and destroyer smoke screens he didn't know where they
had gone.

Jutland was indecisive because the main action was joined late in
mist, and because Scheer naturally declined to stand and be pummel-
led by greatly superior force; Trafalgar would have been quite as
indecisive if Villeneuve had run, indeed it would never have been
fought. Against this, Jellicoe's masterly deployment across the
German T and the tactical pre-thinking which allowed him to hold his
great force perfectly poised for the next blow will undoubtedly out-
live the historical and largely redundant criticisms of his 'cautious'
attitude, and he will surely be numbered among the greatest of
British fighting admirals.*

British battle tactics after Jutland remained unchanged in essentials; the main differences were that destroyers were given a more
offensive function against the enemy battle fleet, and in the later
stages of the war great steam-powered submarines which could keep
up with the fleet were exercised with the battleships; their function
in a fleet action was to dive on contact with the enemy and work
around the flanks to cut off his route home. But the main weapon
of command remained the great gun, and the ruling tactical principle remained that 'the Dreadnought fleet as a whole keeps together,
attacks by division or squadron on a portion of the enemy line being
avoided as liable to lead to isolation of the ships which attempt the
movement...'[22] It is interesting that this passage, particularly abhor-
rent to the tactical school that drew inspiration from the Nelson
tradition, might have been a paraphrase of the great English fleet

---

* It is true that a more 'offensive' attitude and more individual
initiative paid dividends in the Second World War, but then conditions
were entirely different; the weapons had changed, as had the relative
strengths, and there were no great Dreadnought fleets to control as
one massed body. But chiefly, the great gun was no longer the supreme
tactical weapon.

I

commanders in the Dutch wars of the seventeenth century. Jellicoe continued, 'so long as the fleets are engaged on approximately equal courses, the squadrons should form one line of battle'. And he stated his unaltered intention to make 'full use of the fire of our heavier guns in the early stages at long range' for 'close action is to the German advantage'.[23] When Jellicoe went to the Admiralty as First Sea Lord and Beatty succeeded him as Commander-in-Chief, Grand Fleet, the ruling principles remained unchanged. All the diagrams in the confidential book *Tactics* brought out at this time had a dotted line drawn parallel to the enemy formation and 15,000 yards from it; this marked the danger area for enemy torpedo fire. The gun battle was to be fought outside it.[24]

In the event no gun battle was fought. The German service was forced by overwhelming battlefleet odds and the apparent impossibility of reducing them to turn seriously to the *guerre de course* — as the French had after Trafalgar. It was evident that the comparatively gentlemanly campaign the U-boats were carrying on under the restrictions imposed by international law and neutral opinion had no hope of achieving decisive results, so once again they urged an unrestricted campaign. They believed that this could frighten all neutral shipping away from the British Isles and sink 600,000 tons of British shipping per month, a rate which would destroy Britain's capacity to fight within six months. German statesmen doubted these figures and were anxious not to provoke the neutrals, but when the Army High Command supported the naval view as the only way to bring the war to a successful conclusion, Wilhelm overruled the statesmen and sanctioned an 'unrestricted' campaign. It began in February 1917. As one of the main planks in the soldiers' argument had been the effects of the British maritime blockade which made them doubt whether Germany could stand another winter, it is apparent that it was the double success of the British battlefleet supporting both naval and commercial blockades which forced Germany into her desperate gambit.

That same month Seaman Richard Stumpf of the *Heligoland* noted in his diary that the 'usual' crowd of dockers were begging for food scraps on the dock below; a shipmate gave one of them, a crippled soldier with a stiff leg, half his portion of turnips.[25]

By this time Germany had a fleet of 111 operational U-boats, almost 50 of which were at sea; in the first month of the unrestricted campaign they sank 250 ships, in the next month 430, mostly by torpedo and without warning. As had been expected neutral shipping to the British Isles fell away to a quarter of its normal volume. The British Admiralty had no efficient means either of finding or destroying submarines unless they were caught on the surface, and in April,

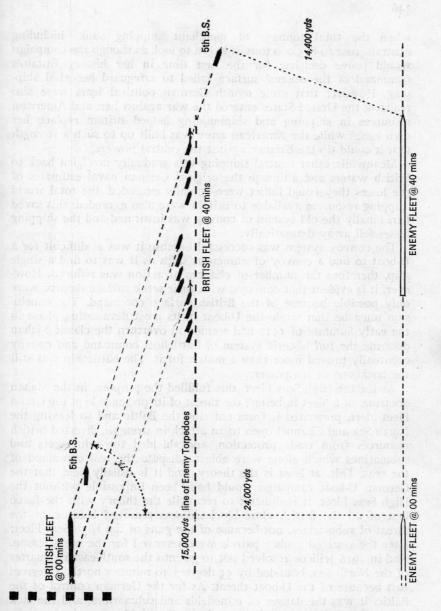

Figure 7. Re-drawn from British Admiralty Secret Book *Tactics* evolved during 1916–17. 'High visibility situation I – Battle fleets abeam of each other, range 24,000 yards, it is desired to close the range.'

Labels within figure:
5th B.S. — 14,400 yds
ENEMY FLEET @ 40 mins
BRITISH FLEET @ 40 mins
5th B.S.
BRITISH FLEET @ 00 mins
24,000 yds
15,000 yds : line of Enemy Torpedoes
ENEMY FLEET @ 00 mins

when the total tonnage of merchant shipping sunk, including neutrals, rose to 875,000 tons, it began to look as though the campaign would prove decisive; for the first time in her history Britain's command of the oceans' surface failed to safeguard her vital shipping. However that same month German political fears were also realized; the United States entered the war against her, and American resources in shipping and shipbuilding helped Britain replace her own losses while the American army was built up to such a strength that it could tip the balance against the central powers.

Meanwhile other neutral shipping was gradually inveigled back to British waters and although the original German naval estimates of the losses they could inflict were actually exceeded, the total world shipping resources available to Britain were also exceeded; this saved her. Finally the old system of convoy was instituted and the shipping losses fell away dramatically.

The convoy system was successful because it was as difficult for a U-boat to find a convoy of numerous ships as it was to find a single ship, therefore the number of chances of action was reduced. However, it is evident that convoys, with their weak surface escorts, were only possible because of the British surface command. The conclusion must be that while the U-boat in its most devastating phase in the early Summer of 1917 had seemed to overturn the classic Mahan doctrine the *full* historic system of battlefleet command *and convoy* eventually proved more than a match for it. The battleship was still the backbone of sea power.

As for the High Seas Fleet, this fulfilled the purpose, in the Mahan doctrine, of a 'fleet in being'; the threat of its presence kept the Grand Fleet alert, prevented it from entering the Baltic and so leaving the North Sea and Channel open to an attack in strength, diverted British resources from trade protection, and shielded the minelayers and submarines which alone were able to dispute the real command of the seas. This, at least is the theory, and it is usually held that the German U-boat campaign would have been impossible without the High Seas Fleet. It is difficult to reconcile the theory with the facts: first of all the British close blockade was removed because of the threat of submarines, not because of the guns of the High Seas Fleet; later the vestigial cruiser patrols were removed for the same reason. And in 1916 Jellicoe resolved not to go into the south-eastern quarter of the North Sea, bounded by 55 degrees 30 minutes north, 4 degrees east because of the U-boat threat. As for the German control of the Baltic, it was the danger of minefields and submarines, and the lack of suitable bases which hampered the Grand Fleet as much as the threat of a German counter sortie into the North Sea. It is arguable therefore that the High Seas Fleet diverted a greater proportion of resources from the attack on trade than the Grand Fleet diverted from trade protection, and was therefore counter-productive. The argument itself is not important; what is significant is that there can be argument, for it suggests that the Mahan doctrine was being undermined by the submarine, that naval warfare was in yet another stage of transition in which the old certainties no longer applied.

Whether or not the High Seas Fleet served any useful purpose it suffered a tragic end. In October 1918 it was ordered to sea to fight one great engagement before the Armistice, but the ratings, suspecting their officers of a desire to retrieve their honour and the honour of their fleet by a glorious death in battle, refused to weigh anchor. This was not so much a bloodless victory for the Grand Fleet as a symptom of the complete collapse of German morale consequent on food shortage, a hopeless position, and a feeling that the whole world was antagonistic to 'Germanism'. After the Armistice the great ships with their guns laid fore and aft followed meekly between the lines of the Grand Fleet to anchor in Scapa Flow; some months later the skeleton crews opened their tightly compartmented hulls to the sea as a final act of defiance.

As a postscript to the naval war, here is Admiral Beatty, Commander-in-Chief, Grand Fleet, describing his negotiations with Admiral Meurer for the internment of the High Seas Fleet:

> I read him my prepared instructions and refused to discuss them, but said they must be thought over and answered on the morrow. They were greatly depressed, overwhelmingly so...Meurer, in a voice like lead with an ashen face, said 'I must think the Commander-in-Chief is aware of the conditions in Germany, and then, in dull, low weary tones began to retail the effect of the Blockade. It had brought revolution in the north, which had spread to the south, then the east and finally to the west, that Anarchy was rampant, the seed was sown...Men, women and children were dying of starvation and dropping down in the streets and died where they lay. Children under six were non-existent, that Germany was destroyed utterly... It had no effect. I only said to myself, Thank God for the British Navy. This is your work. Without it no victory on land would have availed or ever been possible.[26]

Challenge from the New World

As the ships of the former High Seas Fleet gathered weed at the bottom of Scapa Flow, a new naval race was starting up between three of the victorious powers. The Royal Navy was well in the lead with existing ships, with no less than 42 first line Dreadnoughts against only 15 for the new runner-up, the US Navy, but the United States was feeling the compulsion of power and industrial supremacy, and was no longer willing to take second place. Vocal sections of service and popular opinion were calling for a 'navy second to none', adducing anti-British arguments reminiscent of those from Germany during the pre-war naval race. Indeed the results of that race seemed to lend them strength; for centuries, it appeared, Britain had used naval supremacy to dominate world markets and carrying, and impose her will on Europe; she had countered every naval challenge, and had crushed the latest one ruthlessly in war. Now the United States was Britain's main commercial rival, and with a merchant marine inflated by war from two million to 12½ million tons, against Britain's 18 million, she was the chief maritime rival as well. The portents seemed alarming; a naval staff memorandum declared: 'Every great commercial rival of the British Empire has eventually found itself at war with Britain—and has been defeated.'[1]

On top of this there was the unfortunate political fact of the Anglo-Japanese naval alliance. This had stood Japan in good stead during the war; in return for her help in dealing with German bases and commerce raiders in the Pacific, she had been able to expand into the former German-held island groups, the Marshalls, Marianas and Carolines, which commanded the US strategic route Hawaii-Guam-Philippines. She had subsequently taken advantage of the Russian revolution to move into the Russian sphere of southern Manchuria. Meanwhile her merchant marine had moved into the British routes in the Pacific as British ships were withdrawn for more vital war services, an expansion which was helped by the US La Follette Act banning Asiatic crews from US ships, thereby pricing

American tonnage out of the Pacific. The Japanese merchant marine had almost doubled as a result to three million tons by 1920, and was third in the world; her shipowners had grown fat on wartime profits, her exports had more than doubled and the Pacific was beginning to look like a Japanese lake. Taken together, the remarkable maritime/commercial expansion, the ruthless imperialist spirit Japan had shown during the war, and her new strategic position flanking US western Pacific bases, were so ominous that prophets of an imminent Pacific war were not lacking arguments.

Yet another reason canvassed for American naval expansion was President Wilson's aim to set up a League of Nations (ironically America never joined it) which would sort out the problems of the world without wars. The League would need an armed force to restrain aggression and impose sanctions. As such a force must rely heavily on naval power to be world-wide it was essential that no *one* navy be supreme, otherwise the League could become a vehicle for that nation's policies. Hence, it was argued, the US Navy should be built up to parity with the British. The pre-war Pax Britannica was to be replaced by a Pax Anglo-Americana working through the League of Nations. A similar attitude had been prevalent in British and American naval circles before the World War, but it formed no part of British post-war naval policy; with her own war-expanded navy more powerful in relation to any European nation's than it had ever been, Britain was in no mood to reverse her traditional policy for what was regarded as a hopelessly idealistic approach to international affairs. She maintained, as of old, that her scattered empire and unique dependence on sea communications demanded naval supremacy. And while it could hardly be maintained after the recent blood-bath that a supreme British Navy was the best guarantee for peace in the world, it was not difficult to twist the old saw into an equally splendid ideal: a supreme British Navy was the best guarantee against successful aggression. The position of Germany demonstrated it.

Naturally there were opposite views in both countries; some Americans like Theodore Roosevelt sympathized with British naval necessities, many British—and of course Americans—deplored all arms, believing that it was the pre-war arms build-up, particularly perhaps the naval race, which had caused the World War. Such views were not reflected by the British delegation to the Peace Conference in 1919; they came determined, in the Prime Minister's words, 'to keep a navy superior to that of the United States or any other power'.[2]

Meanwhile the momentum of the US Navy's wartime expansion had carried through authorizations for construction programmes

designed to bring its strength up to no less than 51 first-class Dreadnoughts, most of them post-Jutland 16-inch gun ships of some 43,000
tons, twice the size of the original *Dreadnought* and far more powerful than Britain's existing battleships. The Navy Department justified
this with the best Mahan phrases — 'find and defeat the hostile fleet
...protect our seaborne commerce...drive that of the enemy from
the sea...Sea Power...vast importance in international relations...'
It seasoned these with high moral ideas like 'the protection of small
nations, the preservation of the freedom of the seas' and even (a
new contribution to navalist jargon) 'the fulfilment of the United
States' destiny[3] as a leader of democratic impulse'. However, there
is little doubt that so far as Wilson's administration was concerned
the authorization was intended as a means of bringing Great Britain
to heel. The programmes had an escape clause which provided that
if a competent international tribunal were established to settle
disputes peacefully then construction might be suspended. The idea
was to force Great Britain to support a League of Nations, and following this a general reduction of armaments during which she would
accept naval parity with the United States. This was over-optimistic
and in the event a compromise formula was worked out by which
Britain agreed to support the American proposals for a League of
Nations but not to surrender naval supremacy, and the Americans
agreed to consider postponing work on ships authorized but not yet
laid down. The day of reckoning was postponed; that was all. Inside
America strong navalist and expansionist forces supported demands
for 'the greatest navy in the world'. Was not America the richest and
greatest country in the world?

Meanwhile American building programmes and navalist propaganda against Japan forced a corresponding increase in Japanese
programmes — or, by the very nature of such races, *vice versa*. Japan
already had the first 16-inch gun battleships *Nagato* and *Mutsu* nearing completion, and in 1920 a programme was authorized which
would bring the strength in 16-inch gun super-Dreadnoughts up to
16 by 1927. Intelligence sources reported Japanese plans for 18-inch
gun battleships. This all provided fuel for American naval expansion.
And of course it threatened British supremacy: none of the British
pre-'Queen Elizabeth' class ships would be any match for these
monsters. She had to respond. In 1921 Parliament sanctioned a
programme of four 48,000-ton battle cruisers mounting nine 16-inch
guns each; these would be followed by four rather larger battleships
each mounting nine 18-inch guns.

The naval race was on. To many in Britain and America the situation was scarcely credible; the Allies had defeated German militarism
only to start on a similar path themselves, which must lead if not to

war, certainly to friction, rapidly escalating cost, and probably financial ruin. For while America had by far the greater industrial capacity there could be no doubt that the British Admiralty would extend itself to the limit and beyond rather than give up its historic supremacy. In this situation those sections of opinion favouring an international agreement on arms limitation gained more public support than they had been able to muster during the Anglo-French or Anglo-German naval races. They were helped by the recent illustration of the horrors of modern war and the tide of pacifism which had resulted. When on top of this, Europe and America began to slide into a financial and industrial depression, a revolt against navalism and its growing cost swept through both countries, carrying the governments before it. The American navy estimates for 1921 were cut in half by the House of Representatives, and as passed were quite insufficient to complete the construction programmes authorized; the British government put out feelers towards the incoming President, Harding, for an Arms Limitation Conference, and made it clear that they would accept naval parity with America—a truly historic change of attitude. With both major powers now agreed in principle, the United States government shortly issued invitations to Great Britain, Japan, France and Italy to attend a Conference at Washington to discuss arms limitation and to reach 'a common understanding' on the problems of the Pacific; the 'Washington Conference' opened on 21 November 1921.

From the start it was clear that the United States meant business. In his opening speech President Harding referred to the pious but futile recommendations that had resulted from previous peace conferences in 1899 and 1907 and went on, 'The time has come and this Conference has been called, not for general resolutions or mutual advice, but for action.'⁴ Then, instead of delegating the discussion of ways and means to technical committees, he outlined a concrete plan which his government had prepared; it was based on four main premises: that capital ship tonnage should be used as the measure of naval strength, that the comparative strengths of the various navies should remain approximately the same after 'limitation' as before, that all capital ship building programmes should be abandoned and that there should be a 'naval holiday'—that is a stop to the construction of all capital ships for a period of not less than 10 years. He followed this up by announcing a breath-taking programme for scrapping 845,000 tons of American, 583,000 tons of British and 449,000 tons of Japanese capital ships built or building. These proposals startled the delegates, but captured the imagination of the world, as they were intended to do. More—they gave the United States the initiative. She had by far the largest building programme authorized, one which would give her incomparably the most powerful battlefleet in the world when complete (if the current mood of the American people did not make that impossible), and by offering to scrap it all, and her older battleships, she placed the ball squarely in her rivals' court—where she kept it with great skill throughout the Conference.

The tactics succeeded; there was hard bargaining over the actual ratios, but none of the countries concerned was prepared to take responsibility for wrecking the vision held out by the President of relieving 'humanity of the crushing burden created by competition in armament.' And after all the manoeuvring agreement was reached in February 1922: Great Britain was to retain 22 capital ships of 580,000 tons in total, the United States 18 of 500,000 tons, Japan 10 of 301,000 tons, France 10 of 221,000 tons and Italy 10 of 182,000 tons,[5] thus roughly in the proportions 10:10:6:4:4; these ships could be replaced 20 years after the date of their completion with ships not exceeding 35,000 tons displacement, nor mounting guns larger than 16-inch calibre. However, as the latest American and Japanese battleships already mounted 16-inch guns and Britain had nothing larger than a 15-inch gun battleship, she was allowed to build two new ships of this size immediately. There were various other points, the most important of which were an agreement by America and Japan not to construct new bases in the Pacific, and the replacement of the Anglo-Japanese naval alliance with a nine-power treaty designed to maintain the integrity of China and prevent national spheres of interest there.

This was a considerable achievement. It failed to limit competition in submarines or military aircraft, both of which were potentially more important weapons than battleships, but this is more apparent with hindsight than it was in 1922; at the time battlefleets were generally regarded as the backbone of any navy, and it was reasonable to assume that the vicious, rising spiral of suspicion, response and counter response had been cut. So the majority in the English-speaking world saw it. Others were not so happy; for the French, the agreement meant relegation to the second rank, and in Japan there was considerable bitterness both at the ratio allotted and because her British alliance had been severed. It seemed to nationalists that the Japanese had suffered a crushing diplomatic defeat.

British naval, as opposed to popular, opinion was equally unenthusiastic; it would have been unreasonable to expect anything else. Admirals who had been brought up on 'two-power' superiority, and the balancing and peace-keeping role of a commanding Royal Navy, would have been more (or perhaps less) than human if they had been able to accept this voluntary sharing of the trident without alarm, particularly as the British Empire had far greater need of a navy than the virtually self-sufficient United States. Naval opinion in the United States, which had slipped so effortlessly into equal first place, was also violently critical; this was mainly because of the agreement to build no bases in the Western Pacific and the impossible strategic position *vis-à-vis* Japan in which this left them. There was also pique at not being allowed a 'two-power' navy 'second to none'.

While the hurt suffered by naval and nationalist opinion might be a measure of the Treaty's success, it is clear in retrospect that the admirals and their publicists were wasting powder on a measure of naval strength which was losing its validity. The battleship was on the way out! This was already recognized by the most perceptive thinkers on both sides of the Atlantic; the three who had done most to bring about its final development, Fisher, Scott and Sims, had all turned away from the gunned capital ship and were more interested in naval aviation and submarines. They were supported by the enthusiastic specialists in these branches, and a battle royal was being waged in the popular press and in service journals. In *The Times*, the regular correspondence on the subject was headed 'Great Ships or—?' One of the earliest contributors was Scott:

> 9 December 1920
> Sir...We are on the eve of declaring a new naval programme. Let us not forget that the submarine and aeroplane have revolutionized naval warfare; that battleships on the Ocean are in great danger; that when not on the Ocean they must be in a hermetically sealed harbour; that you cannot hide a fleet from the eye of an aeroplane; that enemy submarines will come to our coasts and destroy everything...During the war the submarine dominated everything and very nearly lost us the war...We want forethought now, and we must not too lightly scrap Jackie Fisher's idea that air fighting dominates future warfare...[6]

He was supported strongly by Rear Admiral S. S. Hall, who had been in charge of the British submarine service from 1915 to 1918:

> The present so-called capital ship is a fraud. She is certainly the most powerful surface ship, and in the last war our Grand Fleet was the dominating factor, if you like, but it was certainly not the arbiter of the sea conflict. The vital sea conflict that went on without ceasing for two years was a submarine war on our trade...The true role of our navy is to devise a means of defeating the enemy's capital ships, not the bolstering up of the so-called capital ship. The accomplishment of this purpose, the

final defeat of the mammoth surface vessel, will leave us with a more mobile and economical navy, available for attack or defence, and not equipped purely for a battle which may never take place, and which will be indecisive if it does.[7]

Similar views were being promoted in America by Admiral W. H. Fullam, among many others who saw air power as the vital factor in future naval warfare—a particularly important factor in the Pacific: 'A strong air force, allied with submarines, torpedo planes, mines and torpedoes, may suffice, unaided by a [battle] fleet, to at least hold off an attack, if not completely defeat a hostile fleet.'

Sims tested the theory on the gameboard at the War College; he gave each side an equal amount of money, one to build 16 battleships, six airplane carriers, the other to build 22 airplane carriers. Three weeks later he gave his opinion that the days of the battleship were over. He wrote to his brilliant colleague, Rear Admiral Bradley Fiske, who had invented a torpedo-carrying plane as early as 1912.

I assume that you are sufficiently acquainted with the history of the introduction of new weapons of warfare to know that the first decision in the case, as in practically all previous cases will be wrong, because the great majority of opinion will be of the unreasoned and therefore conservative kind...If I had my way, I would arrest the building of great battleships and put money into the development of the new devices and not wait to see what other nations are doing...[8]

Sims's strictures on conservative opinion were justified; in Britain Admiral Beatty, now First Sea Lord, was worried because the constant propaganda about aeroplanes and submarines was affecting the judgement of his political masters and he called in one of his advisors, Rear Admiral Richmond: 'It will be impossible to obtain money for battleships if this campaign continues. I want arguments to show that battleships are necessary.'[9] Richmond confided to his diary that this was the wrong way to tackle the problem.

The conservatives, however, did have good arguments; in practical terms the gun was still the weapon of greatest range and accuracy —its shells could not be dodged. Both torpedo and bomb were inaccurate by comparison and so slow in flight that, if delivered from the range to which it seemed the gun must drive their carriers, they might be evaded. Besides, by building larger ships and providing underwater bulges which could take the explosion of torpedoes outside the hull proper, and by increasing the horizontal armour to withstand bombs, it seemed that the great surface ship could be made invulnerable to aerial and submarine attack. There was good historical precedent: time and again the large gunned ship had been pronounced dead by enthusiasts for torpedoes and small, swift craft, and each time it had simply grown larger, mounted longer range and more rapid-firing guns and drawing a host of lesser craft to its protection had continued to wield supreme power at sea. If history were anything to go by this process would simply be repeated in the air age; the lesser craft would be fighter aeroplanes from a few aircraft carriers deployed with the far more numerous battle fleet.

As in the transition period of the 1850s before the armourclad herself took over as capital ship, various experiments to test the question could not be staged in sufficiently realistic war conditions to provide definite conclusions and both sides usually gained ammunition for their own cause. The first full-scale tests were conducted off the east coast of America in the Spring and Summer of 1921 against several old American and German ships, including the Dreadnought battleship, *Ostfriesland*, completed in 1911. The lighter ships were soon put on the bottom by aircraft bombs, but the *Ostfriesland* survived 16 hits before she was eventually sunk by two one-ton bombs which exploded in the water under her quarter and stove in her side. The air power enthusiasts were jubilant; more cautious observers pointed out that the visibility had been perfect, there had been no anti-aircraft fire to distract or drive off the pilots and no manoeuvring to throw out their aim; besides it had taken more than 16 hits to put paid to an elderly Dreadnought. The following year tests in Britain on the modern German battleship, *Baden*, showed the comparative insignificance of bomb damage above the armoured decks, and pointed to the need for specially designed armour-piercing bombs (with resulting smaller bursting charges) or bombs designed to explode in the water close by ships for a mining effect. Then in 1924 the new US battleship, *Washington*, scrapped under the Washington Treaty, resisted all efforts to sink her with bombs. These and other tests, together with the development of anti-aircraft guns, suggested to the responsible departments in all navies that the claims made for air power were greatly exaggerated.

This is not to say that any major navy neglected air power; all followed the lead set by Britain during the First War, converted battle cruisers into aircraft carriers and used them in fleet exercises building up a volume of data which was supplemented by ingenious 'damage assessment' and 'chances of success' tables. In 1925, for instance, the Admiralty estimated that no bombs below 500 lbs weight could seriously damage a heavy ship, and that it would take 12 500-pounders to put a modern battleship out of action: these would have to be dropped from at least 5,000 feet to penetrate armour decks, and at this height the chances of a direct hit were only seven in a hundred.[10] The Director of Naval Construction minuted:

> ...such figures must be almost entirely speculative and therefore of little value...500 lb bombs would not effect damage to the battleships *Nelson* and *Rodney* (the new 16-inch gun ships allowed Britain under the Treaty) which are provided with considerable deck and underwater protection.[11]

Torpedo-carrying planes promised better results. During British exercises in 1926 five hits were made from 18 torpedoes fired, thus 30 per cent, and when ships' avoiding action was restricted by divisional formation five out of eight were achieved, 62 per cent. Even these results were treated with extreme caution: 'Estimates of probability of hitting are most difficult to make since peace conditions limit the defence far more than the attack.'[12] It was deduced that in action the results would be only 11 per cent hits.

The cautious way in which the statistics and probabilities were analyzed by *matériel* departments in these years stand in marked contrast to the optimistic manner in which similar gunnery tests had been analyzed during the lead up to the First War, when the chances of hitting and the effect of each hit had been vastly overestimated, the range of action vastly under-estimated and the 'x' factor for enemy hits in action had scarcely been considered. Percy Scott knew the reason:

> Naval men do not commit suicide, and battleships are vital to their profession and vital to their comfort. To be captain of a battleship is the ambition of every naval officer. Who else in the world travels about in the same comfort as the captain of a battleship? He has a large drawing room, a dining room in which he can seat 25 or 30 guests, a commodious bedroom with bathroom attached and spare bedrooms...[13]

Scott was apt to overstate his case; so was Sims, who put the same answer in another way:

> ...it is an astonishing thing, the conservatism of the military mind. It is absolutely historical that they never give in. You have got to shed their blood before they do it...[14]

The truth was that it required a great deal of imagination to see the prime creations of the naval constructor's art succumbing to such insignificant and frail silk and string machines as contemporary aeroplanes—not only imagination, but faith in the development of better aeroplanes, bombs and torpedoes and ways of using them. The fire control revolution at the beginning of the century had needed just the same optimism and imagination, so it is not surprising that the prime movers in the earlier struggle, Scott, Fiske, Sims, Fisher, were some of the most confident voices heralding the end of the battleship. While the naval staffs and naval historians generally looked backwards to extract 'lessons', they looked forwards and arrived at their conclusions not so much by statistical speculation or analogy as by applied common sense. The history of naval development in the nineteenth century suggests that this was in reality the only 'historically' correct way to go about things as most so-called 'lessons' had been out of date almost before they could be analyzed. In any case, here is Sims giving evidence before a House of Representatives Committee investigating the whole subject in 1925:

> No surface vessels can long escape disablement or destruction if they remain within reach of aeroplanes that are in control of the air. This is not disputed even by those who claim that the battleship is still 'the backbone of the fleet'...this means that a fleet, however powerful in surface vessels, cannot successfully operate against any country or any position that is defended by more planes than can be brought to bear against it...It follows from the above that an airplane carrier of 35 knots and carrying 100 planes...is in reality a capital ship of much greater offensive power than any battleship.[15]

Rear Admiral Hall put the same case from the British point of view and in the context of British battlefleet strategy:

> The reasons why these two capital ships (allowed Britain by the Washington Treaty) will be a waste of money are that close blockade is dead and there is no one we can distantly blockade as in the last war, by reason of the submarine, which has also cut down the capabilities of capital ships in other directions too much to leave them the power to accomplish anything. By the time they are completed the inevitable development of air warfare will have left them entirely out of the picture...The attack of the future will be by clouds of planes at dusk, early dawn or moonlight on the ships before they go to sea...[16]

Conventional opinion, however, continued to insist that there was no proof that aeroplanes could master battleships in action, continued to cite Mahan battlefleet theory, and held it an article of faith that the Grand Fleet had been the dominating factor in the war against Germany. Aeroplanes and carriers were seen, not as the main striking force of the future, but as indispensible accessories to the battlefleet, increasing its range of vision, 'spotting' its fall of shot, helping to bring a fleeing fleet up short by slowing one or two units with torpedoes.

As the battlefleet was held to remain the arbiter of sea power tactical exercises continued to revolve around the massed fleet action; Jutland was re-fought countless times on tactical boards and in staff college lectures throughout the world, the 'lessons' of the encounter were extracted and debated, the mistakes analyzed and the *matériel* deficiencies corrected. The next time the enemy would not escape. Destroyers were trained in 'every conceivable method of search and attack by night. New methods were constantly being evolved and tried out.' By daylight 'the massed and simultaneous attack upon an enemy's battlefleet by three, four or more flotillas during a fleet action...still held pride of place.'[17] As for the great ships themselves their guns were given higher maximum elevation for longer range daylight action, long-base rangefinders were fitted to turrets, the fire control table and organization were refined to cope with ranges out to 30,000 yards—still on the same basic lines as before—and night training was carried to such lengths that it became an axiom that a well-handled fleet had nothing to lose and much to gain by fighting at night. Up aloft the fixed position for the gunnery control team and the separate revolving position for the director layer's team were amalgamated into a single revolving gunnery control tower so that all members of the vital hitting personnel were in close touch and kept the same relative position one to another wherever the enemy appeared. Year by year countless battle practice targets shivered under salvoes from over the horizon.

Majestically the squadron forms into line astern of the flag-ship...the staccato notes of 'Action stations' are sounded on the bugle. Away we run...Follow me to the forecastle, up a vertical ladder to B turret, and up through the armoured base into the gunhouse. I scramble over steel platforms until I am in my action station...the scene in the gunhouse is dominated by the rear ends of the enormous twin gun barrels and their breeches...Hydraulic pipes and mechanisms fill every unoccupied space and voice pipes snake their way around and about. Indicator dials for range, deflection, elevation, training and fire control orders are the pictures in this futuristic compartment. Electric lights gleam on white paintwork, burnished steel, polished brass, gunmetal and copper. The only sounds are the distant pounding of the hydraulic pumps, the hiss and whine of fan motors, and the clicking of instruments. There is a smell of gun oil, metal polish and stale, confined air. It is cold and dank...

'Load, load, load!' and far below there is a clash and clang of machinery followed by a further series of clangs in crescendo as the shell hoist rises on its slide through a succession of flash-tight doors finally emerging to rest with a last great clatter at the rear of the breech. This ponderous door of brass and steel has been opened by number two using hydraulic power...a further ear-splitting din succeeds as the projectile and cordite charges are moved to the loading tray, power-rammed into the gun and the breech closed. The disciplined uproar is duplicated as the left gun is loaded at the same time. When both are loaded the loading cages descend to the magazine and shell room for re-loading with a last hiss! clang! clang! clash!

'Salvoes!' I hear, and 'Salvoes!' I roar and feel a tightening of the stomach as I wait for hell to break loose. 'Right gun ready! Left gun ready!' from the numbers two, followed by a tense moment of silence, broken only by the hiss and whine of hydraulics as gunlayers and trainers move guns and turrets to follow the movements of the director pointers. Then 'Ding! Ding!', a puny noise on the fire bell, followed a fraction of a second later by another 'Ding!' scarcely heard in the shattering roar that fills the turret. The next thing I can appreciate is the great barrels sliding back through the cradles to their firing positions after their recoil...Bedlam breaks loose as the breech is opened, jets of water play on the chamber and the fiendish clatter, clang and rattle of the loading operation begins again...

Again and again the bedlam repeats itself as salvo after salvo is fired...The awe-inspiring movements of the guns and cataclysmic noise continue for some 25 minutes and then, suddenly, 'Ammunition expended!' comes up from the shell room and B turret is quiet. Then for the first time we hear and feel the discharges of the other turrets. Some or all have missed more salvoes than we and are still firing. The bellow of other turrets is quite a different noise from the all-pervading, ear-compressing blast of our own turret's guns. Now also we can appreciate, though we must have experienced it during the whole firing, the heel-over of the 35,000 ton ship as each broadside is fired.

I feel weak and dazed, as if the tremendous energy just unloosed had in some part come from me. My palms are wet, my knees trembling slightly. My head aches and there is a singing in my ears. Cordite fumes tickle my nose and throat...[18]

The power so evident from within the turrets of the great ships was quite as apparent to observers. Here is an American reporter cabling a despatch after witnessing a show put on by the British Mediterranean fleet of 1935:

> ...Britain's mightiest men of war five large battleships in line ahead led by flagship *Queen Elizabeth*...all England's heaviest and toughest looking bulldogs of the sea. Salvo after salvo of shells one ton each and landing in groups of twenty at a time salvo after salvo continued to keep sea in constant tormented upheaval...There's 50 thousand men and 400 thousand tons of steel-clad dynamite waiting here with guns loaded and steam up and decks cleared for action. It's certainly going to be hell if it's ever turned loose.[19]

This was the year when Italy invaded Abyssinia, and it seemed briefly as though it might be turned loose for the League of Nations against the Italian fleet. But the French refused to co-operate, the United States was not a member of the League, and the British government was unwilling to act unilaterally. The Royal Navy had no fear of Italy's ships, and the Admiralty policy in the event of war was to destroy her fleet as the surest way of bringing her to terms; however, they did not expect to accomplish it without loss which, in the current phase of naval 'limitation', would leave the Empire dangerously exposed should any third power come in against her. The Italian Navy backed by the Italian Air Force was thus a 'risk fleet' such as Tirpitz had wanted before the First War. This was due to Italy's position across the narrow Mediterranean-Suez shipping route to the Far East, and particularly because of Japan's militant hostility. The British Navy could not fight a war in Europe and the Far East at the same time; what it needed was the backing of the US Navy, which had demanded parity stridently and had achieved it effortlessly by virtue of industrial supremacy. However the United States had passed from Wilsonian idealism into isolation and declined the responsibility; Britain was left with the responsibility but little power. Perhaps what she really lacked was confidence. Caught between the popular ideal of 'collective security' under the Covenant of the League of Nations, but without the collective backing, and the old political realities of the 'balance' of European and world power, but without the power—or perhaps just without the confidence—she saved face with economic sanctions. The great guns of the Mediterranean fleet remained silent.

The Italians, in defiance of the League, transported troops through the Suez Canal and quickly over-ran Abyssinia.

Admiralty instructions to the Commander-in-Chief, Mediterranean Fleet during this period of tension make interesting reading in the light of the aeroplane *versus* battleship controversy. The danger at Malta of Italian air attack was considered so great that the Commander-in-Chief was ordered to set up a new fleet base at Navarino in southern Greece, to be known as Port X for secrecy, and to keep his ships dispersed as much as possible. His own plans were also much concerned with the air; he proposed to take two aircraft carriers, three destroyer flotillas and two oilers, covered by three battleships, into the central Mediterranean and make carrier strikes on the Sicilian air bases at Port Augusta and Catania. Following this, the light and air forces of the fleet would 'take the offensive' against the Italian North African coast, cut the Italian communications with these African territories and thus—hopefully—provoke the Italian battlefleet out for a deciding action with the British fleet.[20]

Evidently the supreme purpose of the fleet was still great gun action, but the dangers and possibilities of air power were well understood in the British service. What was not fully understood was that the strategic and tactical potential of naval air strike forces had overtaken that of gunned battlefleets. The British service was by no means unique in this. Every other navy was still controlled by men who worshipped great guns and the majestic super-Dreadnoughts which mounted them; even in the American service, which had taken the lead in the development of naval air power, there was a clique centred around the Bureau of Ordnance and known as the 'Gun Club' which virtually monopolized the higher posts in the Navy Department and at sea, to the exclusion of airmen and other specialists. In Japan a similar group of great gunnery enthusiasts planned to take the battleship into hitherto unparalleled dimensions.

Japan now bore much the same relation to Britain and America as Germany had to the British Empire before the First War; she was set on expansion in the Pacific, but faced by British territories and bases, and the naval presence and hostility of the USA, the richest nation in the world. Out of this conflict had come two main schools of militarist thought, one that Britain and America would eventually fight one another—as Britain had always fought commercial rivals— the other that Britain and America would combine to attack Japan. Both thought war with Britain, America or both inevitable sooner or later. In October 1934 the Japanese naval staff in violation of the spirit of the naval treaties still in force—still bitterly resented—

requested their Bureau of Naval Construction to prepare studies for a class of new battleships which would be a double jump up the evolutionary scale of size.[21] They reasoned that Japan could not compete industrially or economically with the United States so their only hope was to make each battleship so powerful that although numerically inferior they would be more than a match for any battle-fleet of the United States, which would not be able to equal their great size for many years. This reasoning was buttressed by the practical certainty that America would not build ships too large for the Panama Canal. As their own estimate of the largest ship which could negotiate the locks in the Canal was 63,000 tons, ten 16-inch guns and 23 knots, they asked their constructors for something incomparably superior, a battleship of 30 knots mounting 18-inch guns and with armour to match. This followed the natural line of evolution by which battleship and battle cruiser merged into the fast battleship.

The first blueprints were completed in March 1935; they showed an immensely broad, flat and shallow hull 964 feet long displacing almost 70,000 tons and theoretically capable of 31 knots from 200,000 HP turbines. With these mammoth figures set out the Japanese strategists reduced the speed requirement to 27 knots; meanwhile hull resistance and ordnance experiments were carried out in great secrecy and Japanese armour plants were expanded so they could produce 16.1 thick plates each of which weighed 68 tons. Two years, 50 ship models and 23 blueprints later the final design was ready and the keel of the first giant was laid in the utmost secrecy behind great fences and sisal curtains. She was intended to be the first of four. Her name was to be *Yamato*. This was the ultimate development of the battleship, the largest, most powerfully-armed leviathan ever conceived.

She was to displace between 68,000 and 72,000 tons and mount nine 18-inch guns in three triple turrets, whose barbettes were protected by no less than 22-inch armour. Her vitals were to be protected by 16.1-inch armour, sloped outwards to increase angle of impact of falling shells, and capable of withstanding 18-inch projec-tiles—which no other navy possessed—fired at any range greater than 22,000 yards. The line of this armour was continued down to the bottom plates as a torpedo bulkhead inside a light bulge to take the force of torpedo explosion. From the upper edge of the 16-inch plates a horizontal armoured deck 7.8-inch thick was to extend over all the vitals. This was impervious to 18-inch shells fired from *inside* 32,800 yards and to bombs less than 2,200 lbs armour piercing, which in any case had to be dropped from 10,000 feet to stand any chance of getting through. This remarkable concentration of heavy steel, reminiscent of the great skins of compound armour over the ironclads of the eighties of the previous century, was made possible by squeezing the vital parts into a length which was only 53½ per cent of the waterline length—hence the immensely broad hull. To decrease water resistance at her designed full speed of 27 knots she was to be given a bulbous forefoot. Below the level of the armour deck no less than 1,065 watertight compartments were planned, together with a complex system of damage control, and above this level a further 82 watertight compartments.

So much for her prodigious defensive powers; for offence, her 18-inch guns throwing a shell weighing 3,200 lbs—1,000 lbs more than a 16-inch shell—were to be ranged on target by a complex of three 49 feet rangefinders, one of which was stereoscopic, mounted with the fire director atop a tall tower superstructure. There were in addition, numerous batteries of anti-torpedo boat and anti-aircraft guns, and it was planned to equip her with several aircraft.

British naval intelligence got a small hint of the extraordinary power of the class towards the end of December that year, 1937. 'Information from Secret Sources indicates that there remains a definite possibility of Japanese ships having 18-inch guns.'[22]

By this time the naval treaty position was in some chaos. 'Washington' had been followed by two other naval conferences in 1930 and 1935, at the last of which capital ships had been limited to 35,000 tons and their guns to 14-inch calibre; not unnaturally Japan had refused to co-operate and had not ratified the Treaty. Consequently an escalation clause had been agreed whereby the signatories were allowed to mount 16-inch pieces if they received information that any country was exceeding treaty limits or if the treaty was not ratified by the end of 1936. This had placed Britain in a particularly difficult position, for by that time there were plain signs that Germany was re-arming to challenge the verdict of the First War, equally plain signs that League of Nations 'collective security' was breaking down. Germany was completing three so-called 'pocket' battleships armed with 11-inch guns, building two larger battle cruisers of 32 knots, and laying down two 15-inch gun battleships, all designed for commerce raiding. France and Italy were also building fast, modern battleships and Britain urgently needed to rejuvenate her ageing battle line. Unfortunately for her she had been sticking strictly to the spirit of the various treaties and had made no preparations for guns larger than 14-inch; mainly for this reason she was forced to commence her re-building with a class of ships mounting 14-inch guns, the 'King George Vs' of 35,000–37,000 tons displacement. The first was laid down in January 1936.

As America was preparing a 16-inch gun class, Japan the 18-inch gun 'Yamatos' and Germany, Italy and France 15-inch gun classes, it is plain that Britain's traditional qualitative superiority in gunned battleships was about to be lost; she had already lost her absolute numerical superiority outside Europe. While British naval men were apt to blame the Washington and subsequent naval treaties for this loss of 'command' it is plain that Britain could not have maintained her nineteenth century dominance even with an unrestricted building race. The prime fact was that she had been overtaken industrially by the USA.

Besides Britain's relative industrial decline, the naval build-up in the Pacific rendered world superiority impossible for her. This had, of course, been recognized from the earliest days of the century, hence the Anglo-Japanese alliance. Now it was more so. Again, while America's ambition to become the supreme naval power and her extreme suspicion of the imperial and commercial aims behind the British habit of naval superiority were regarded by the British as brash and unnecessary, they were a very real factor and if they had been brushed aside in another building race—which Britain could not have won—the consequences would have been incalculable. Overshadowing all else was the loss of life in the First War, and the popular feeling that this must not happen again. British politicians, reflecting this mood in 1923, introduced a rule whereby the services were not to expect a major war for ten years; this 'ten year rule' commenced afresh each year till 1932, and gave Chancellors of the Exchequer an unrivalled weapon for cutting down service estimates.[23] So, while the limitation treaties were the immediate cause of Britain's battle fleet decline, there were many other factors which rendered it inevitable.

Meanwhile, Britain, the United States and France together sent a note to Japan asking for information on her capital ship building, but Japan refused to divulge her plans. The British Ambassador in Tokyo pressed hard for details which might avert a new building race in size, but for his pains he was thoroughly misled: the Japanese were *not* building ships of 'such extravagant size' as 40,000 tons! American intelligence was also wide of the mark, but both countries recognized that Japan's reluctance to give details meant that she was exceeding Treaty limits—of course she was not a signatory to the Treaties any longer. There now began a diplomatic tussle between the three 'Western' powers who *were* signatories; the United States Navy wished to have all size restrictions lifted, Britain and France wished simply to raise the limit from 35,000 tons to 40,000 tons. On France's part this seems to have been caused by economic distress, on Britain's by a desire that her new 14-inch gun 'King George Vs' would not be outclassed before they were built. The British felt that a satisfactory and balanced ship could be designed on 40,000 tons with nine 16-inch guns, and that this would not provoke Germany and Italy, building classes with eight 15-inch guns, to go one better.[24] The only point of doubt seemed to be Russia, for she was affected by Japanese as well as European building and if, as seemed likely, there was about to be a resumption of the Pacific naval race, Russia would be obliged to follow Japan. Germany would then build up to Russia's standard, and France would have to follow—and so Italy—the Pacific escalation would be imported to Europe east-about.

Another consideration for the British Admiralty was that any increase over about 43,000 tons would mean enlarging their docks, which would add to the already excessive cost of such great ships, estimated at £11 millions. For all these reasons, but mainly because she wished to avoid downgrading her 'King George V's', she limited her 1938 capital ships to 40,000 tons; these were the 'Lions' with nine 16-inch guns and 30 knots speed, the first two of which were laid down in the Summer of 1939. They were, however, overtaken by events and never completed.

The United States, meanwhile, would accept a 45,000 ton limit or none at all, and in 1939 two 'Iowa' class battleships of this size were authorized; each had nine 16-inch guns, a 19-inch main belt—the heaviest steel armour given to any battleship—and a speed of 33 knots. The following year another four 'Iowas' were authorized, together with five 58,000 tonners mounting twelve 16-inch guns—although, like the British 'Lions', these were never completed.

So the brief period of limitations after the First War was succeeded by a rush of new building. The arbitrary ceiling on size was swept away, this time by the Pacific rivalry, and the natural tendency towards increased power and displacement continued—although with various inhibitions and complications arising from the treaty period. As the Second World War approached there were over 30 great ships taking shape in the arsenals of the world. In European waters Britain still held naval supremacy, at least in numbers, but elsewhere she was being overhauled: Japan was building the most powerfully armed battleships in the world and America was about to begin the most heavily armoured and fastest battleships; Britain's 'King George Vs' could not match either.

Far more serious was the way in which Great Britain had been overtaken in fleet *air* power by both Japan and the United States.[25] But the full realization of this lay in the future. The British Admiralty, like the naval departments of all other powers, still believed in the gunned battleship as the backbone of the fleet, the unit on which command rested. When they were driven to explain their position during a full-scale national row provoked by 'air' enthusiasts, they rested their case finally on lack of action experience. The airmen had no battle proof for their confident assertions.

If we rebuild the battlefleet and spend many millions on doing so, and then war comes and the airmen are right, and all our battleships are rapidly destroyed by air attack, our money will have been largely thrown away. But if we do not rebuild it and war comes, and the airman is wrong and *our* airmen cannot destroy the enemy's capital ships, and they are left to range with impunity on the world's oceans and destroy our convoys, then we shall lose the British Empire.[26]

This argument carried the day. It was a historic British argument, a paraphrase of that used by the Surveyor of the Navy in 1859, when experiments had seemed to indicate that iron-sided frigates would supersede timber ships-of-the-line as the capital ships of the future: 'No prudent man would at present consider it safe to risk, upon the performance of ships of this novel character, the naval superiority of Great Britain.' It may be clear with hindsight that the resources allocated to the 'King George Vs' would have been better spent on carriers and modern strike aircraft to operate from them, but the Board of Admiralty acted as responsible Boards always had: they built gunned ships against the threat of enemy gunned ships.

Naval historians were no more prescient: 'It is necessary not to make the same over-estimation of the flying torpedo craft as has been made in earlier times of the surface types'. The value of history in prediction is certainly questionable![27]

The End of the Battleship

The German military challenge began in September 1939, fortunately for Great Britain, some five years before the date Hitler had forecast for his naval staff. Consequently a great fleet of some 13 super-Dreadnoughts, four aircraft carriers and over 200 U-boats, which the German service had planned to deploy against British merchant shipping, was nowhere near completion. All they had ready were three 'pocket battleships', really light battle cruisers each mounting six 11-inch guns and powerful secondary armament, two 32,000 ton battle cruisers, *Scharnhorst* and *Gneisenau*, more properly fast battleships, mounting nine 11-inch guns and also strong secondary armament, various other cruisers and armed merchantmen and some 50 U-boats, less than half of them long-range ocean-going types.

To meet the surface threat Great Britain had 13 battleships, three battle cruisers, six aircraft carriers and 58 cruisers, on the face of it overwhelming superiority, especially with French support. However, the Admiralty had to be prepared for Italy to join Hitler, and possibly Spain and Japan as well. More important immediately, while all the German ships were fast and modern, Britain's heavy ships were all veterans of her First War Grand Fleet, bar the two 16-inch gun 'Washington Treaty' battleships, *Nelson* and *Rodney*, and nearly all, except the three battle cruisers, *Hood*, *Renown* and *Repulse*, were too slow by modern standards. Britain had the five 'King George Vs' under construction, but even these were only designed for 28½ knots, insufficient to catch the German battle cruisers or even the 15-inch gun, 28-knot battleships, *Bismarck* and *Tirpitz*, then nearing completion. These, built ostensibly to conform to the Treaty limit of 35,000 tons, were in fact 42,000 tonners and thus out-classed the 'King George Vs'. It is plain that lack of money, and British good faith in sticking to the letter of the various limitation treaties while others cheated, had reduced the former mistress of the seas to such a low *matériel* state that survival against only one power seemed at hazard. Fortunately for her, aeroplanes were about to revolutionize naval warfare, and German Navy-Air Force co-operation was running through more turbulent waters even than her own.

The opening moves followed the pattern of 1914–18, indeed they might almost have been a continuation of that struggle with better air scouting. The British Home Fleet, consisting of five battleships, two battle cruisers, and two aircraft carriers together with cruisers and destroyers, worked from Scapa Flow in support of northern cruiser patrols for the twin purpose of commercial blockade and distant blockade of the enemy surface raiders. Other patrols supplemented by heavy ships were established to block the Straits of Dover, and those German surface raiders already at sea at the beginning of the war were chased by distant squadrons. Meanwhile a British Expeditionary Force was landed safely in France, and British merchant ships and troop transports from all over the Empire were organized to sail in convoy.

At first the results were quite as successful as at the beginning of the First War; the two powerful German battle cruisers, *Gneisenau* and *Scharnhorst*, made a sortie into the area of the northern patrols to dislocate the merchant ships there, but when their position was reported by an armed merchant cruiser, which they shortly sank, they made back to base. And in the South Atlantic three British cruisers drove one of the two 'pocket battleships' at large at the beginning of the war to scuttle herself. This was the *Admiral Graf Spee*, and the action occurred off the River Plate on 13 December 1939, a welcome boost to British morale, although in retrospect it is plain that the action should have gone the other way.

The *Graf Spee*'s sister ship, *Deutschland*, had meanwhile returned to base via the Denmark Strait between Iceland and Greenland after sinking only two merchantmen; as the *Graf Spee*'s bag had been nine ships, the 'exchange rate' like the general maritime surface control and the commercial blockade was decidedly in Britain's favour.

The following year the old pattern changed drastically; the German army burst through all restraints, overran Norway, France, Holland, and Belgium. Italy came in on her side, completely upsetting the naval and geographical balance.

Up to this point the results of air attacks on ships either at sea or in harbour had quite failed to come up to the expectations of the pre-war air enthusiasts. There were many reasons for this: bad visibility in the North Sea, lack of *enough* aircraft for this purpose, perhaps above all the pre-war failure on both sides to train pilots adequately in anti-ship work or develop efficient anti-ship bombs. However, during the Norwegian campaigns it became clear that the Royal

Navy, despite surface command, could not carry out its traditional function of preventing the passage of enemy sea-borne troops and supply transports, nor even cover landings of its own troops effectively if the enemy held command of the air—like the Germans over Norway. This was precisely what the US Admirals Fullam and Sims, the British Admirals Fisher, Scott and Hall, among many others in all countries had been saying from 1920.

The British First Sea Lord wrote to his Commander-in-Chief, Mediterranean, Admiral A. B. Cunningham:

> I am afraid that you are terribly short of 'air', but there again I do not see what can be done because as you will realize every available aircraft carrier is wanted in home waters. The one lesson we have learnt here is that it is essential to have fighter protection over the fleet whenever they are within range of enemy bombers...[1]

With Italy in the war, France knocked out, and a question mark hanging over the French fleet, whose main units had steamed to French North Africa, the British position in the Mediterranean was critical, particularly so because its central base, Malta, was inadequately defended against air attack from Sicilian air bases only a hundred miles to the north, and its eastern base, Alexandria, was threatened by Italian forces in Libya. However the decision was taken to hold the Mediterranean, the French heavy ships were destroyed or neutralized by gunfire, air attack and (in one case) negotiation, and during the following months the British Mediterranean Fleet gave a remarkable demonstration of one of the favourite recurring themes of the historical school, the supreme importance of moral factors and training over purely material factors; its commander-in-chief, A. B. Cunningham, was an 'offensive' admiral in the most triumphant British tradition, the ships had been superbly trained between the wars.

The first engagement occurred off the toe of Italy in July 1940 soon after the actions against the French heavy ships. Cunningham was flying his flag in the modernized 'Queen Elizabeth' class battleship, *Warspite*, with one other unmodernized ship of the same class, another unmodernized and even slower veteran of the First War, *Royal Sovereign*, and the small aircraft carrier, *Eagle*. He was covering two convoys. An Italian squadron headed by two battleships was meanwhile covering an Italian convoy to North Africa. As Cunningham recalled afterwards, the action which resulted 'followed almost exactly the lines of the battles we used to fight out on the table at the Tactical School at Portsmouth'.[2] The Italian heavy ships were first sighted by long range reconnaissance aircraft from the *Eagle*, their position, course and speed were reported back, a strike force of torpedo bombers went in to attack—in the event unsuccessfully—and the British cruisers, spreading on a line of bearing ahead of the battle fleet, pressed in and were engaged by the enemy cruisers as they made visual contact. Shortly afterwards the *Warspite* came into action at 26,000 yards range against the Italian flagship, *Guilio Cesare*, a First War ship which had been modernized in the thirties with ten 12.6-inch guns on high-angle mountings which permitted long range fire. Her fire and that of her similar consort was excellent and the *Warspite* was soon straddled; however, the *Warspite*'s salvoes, flashing out in rapid ranging ladders, were also straddling in short time and seven minutes after the main action opened she scored first: Cunningham saw 'the great orange-coloured flash of a heavy explosion at the base of the enemy flagship's funnels. It was followed by an upheaval of smoke and I knew that she had been heavily hit at the prodigious range of 13 miles.'[3] The Italian Admiral then broke off the engagement under cover of smoke. Cunningham followed, but his squadron speed was too slow and as he approached the Italian coast and came under heavy bombing attack from the Italian Air Force, he gave up the chase.

> Here let me settle once and for all the question of the efficiency of the Italian bombing and general air work over the sea...To us at the time it appeared that they had some squadrons specially trained for anti-ship work. Their reconnaissance was highly efficient and seldom failed to find and report our ships at sea. The bombers invariably arrived within an hour or two. They carried out high level attacks from about 12,000 feet pressed home in formation in the face of the heavy AA fire of the fleet, and for this type of attack their accuracy was very great. We were fortunate to escape being hit...[4]

This first action in the Italian war had important consequences; the single hit by the *Warspite* reinforced the moral ascendancy that the British fleet already had over the Italian fleet, who never thereafter stood to receive the fire of British battleships. From Cunningham's point of view, it demonstrated the need for at least one other modernized ship which could fire at the range at which the *Warspite* had been straddled, and the need for a larger carrier than the *Eagle* to provide fighter cover over the fleet. He asked for both, and the following month received the modernized 'Queen Elizabeth' class battleship, *Valiant*, the new fleet carrier, *Illustrious*, which had an armoured flight deck and capacity for 70 aircraft, also two anti-aircraft cruisers fitted with radio direction finding (radar) apparatus. These essential tools for detecting and meeting any air threat over the fleet shifted the balance against the Italians, and Cunningham established a remarkable surface command over the Mediterranean; however, this did not make it possible to push merchant convoys through the narrow sea without loss from air or submarine attack, and the shipping route through the Mediterranean was closed to British merchant ships apart from those needed to supply the fleet base at Malta. Practically all British supplies for the land campaign against Italian North Africa had to go the long way round the Cape—as did shipping serving India, Australasia and the East. As for Italian shipping supplies for their North African army, these naturally had to come through the Mediterranean; the quantity that arrived safely was, throughout the campaign, inversely proportional to the British ability to operate naval and air forces from Malta, itself largely dependant on British control of the air over Malta.[5] It is clear from this that air power had completely upset the literal interpretation of Mahan battlefleet theory; surface command based on battleships was no longer adequate for real command at sea.

Towards the end of the year there was a more dramatic demonstration of this: the main strength of the Italian fleet, including four modernized First War battleships and two new 15-inch gun, 30-knot battleships of the 'Littorio' class which should have tipped the balance of surface power decisively against the British fleet, was lying in the fortified harbour of Taranto when Cunningham launched an aircraft torpedo strike against them from the carrier, *Illustrious*. Although a number of other aircraft were involved in the operation, first in reconnaissance, then in flare-dropping and diversionary bombing attacks, the number of torpedo planes was only 20; these took off from the carrier in the evening of 11 November 1940 in two waves, flew 170 miles to Taranto and pressing in under balloon defence in the face of heavy anti-aircraft fire scored a total of six hits, four on the new *Littorio* (later re-named *Italia*) and one on each of the modernized older battleships *Duilio* and *Cavour*, sinking all three at their moorings for the loss of only two planes. It was, as Cunningham remarked, an unprecedented example of economy of force; he wrote afterwards:

November 11th–12th, 1940 should be remembered for ever as having shown once and for all that in the Fleet Air Arm the Navy had its most devastating weapon. In a total flying time of about six and a half hours—carrier to carrier—twenty aircraft had inflicted more damage upon the Italian fleet than was inflicted upon the German High Seas Fleet in the daylight action at the Battle of Jutland.[6]

The lesson was not lost on the Japanese, nor for that matter on the Germans. Since their earlier comparative failures at bombing ship targets they had trained several dive bombing squadrons up to extraordinary standards of precision against ships and at the end of 1940 these were sent to the Mediterranean to relieve their Italian allies by attacking Cunningham's fleet. It is significant that in their first major assault against the fleet at sea they concentrated on the carrier, *Illustrious*, almost to the exclusion of the battleships.

At times she was completely hidden in a forest of great bomb splashes. One was too interested in this new form of dive-bombing attack really to be frightened, and there was no doubt that we were watching complete experts. Formed roughly in a large circle over the fleet they peeled off one by one when reaching the attacking position...The attacks were pressed home to point blank range and as they pulled out of their dives some of them were seen to fly along the flight deck of the *Illustrious* below the level of her funnel.[7]

The carrier suffered six hits and several near misses in short time, and was put out of action, only her armoured deck saving her from complete destruction; however, she managed to limp into Malta after dark, and later she escaped to Alexandria from where she was sent to America to be repaired fully. Her sister ship, *Formidable*, was ordered to the Mediterranean, but in the meantime Cunningham had lost command over the central basin, and Malta came under attack and siege from the air which virtually neutralized it as a fleet base.

The major surface action in the Mediterranean occurred three months later at the end of March 1941. Aircraft reconnaissance revealed that an Italian fleet headed by their new 'Littorio' class battleship, *Vittorio Veneto*, and several powerful 8-inch gun cruisers was steaming into the eastern part of the Mediterranean to attack British convoys, and Cunningham set out to intercept with a powerful force of three 'Queen Elizabeths', the *Warspite* (flag), *Barham* and *Valiant*, followed in the line by the *Formidable*. As in the earlier action off the toe of Italy the engagement followed the pattern anticipated in pre-war tactical instruction, at least in the early stages: first the *Formidable*'s reconnaissance aircraft reported the enemy forces, then the British cruiser squadron ahead of the battle fleet made contact with the enemy cruiser and battleship divisions, and then Cunningham sent in a carrier strike force to relieve the cruisers, also to slow the *Vittorio Veneto* so that his battleships could bring her to action. In the event the torpedo planes failed to obtain any hits, but the Italian forces made off westward for home. It is interesting that before the British cruisers were relieved, the *Vittorio Veneto* had been straddling them at the remarkable distance of 16 miles, and they had to retreat under cover of smoke and snake the line to avoid very close shooting; this was approximately twice the range at which Beatty's advanced cruiser division had twisted from the fire of the High Seas Fleet at Jutland.

The action then settled into a chase, with the Italians some 60 miles ahead and Cunningham sending off air strike forces to try and slow them; five torpedo planes attacked the Italian battleship scoring one hit—20 per cent success—and six attacked a cruiser division in the evening also scoring one hit—16 per cent. These hits slowed the battleship and stopped the heavy cruiser, *Pola*, whereupon the Italian commander-in-chief, believing the British fleet to be further behind than it actually was, ordered two other heavy cruisers, together with a division of destroyers, to stand by the crippled cruiser. Cunningham was unaware of this. His information was that the battleship he was chasing was 45 miles ahead, making 15 knots, and that the latest air strike had scored four torpedo hits, although whether any of those were on the battleship was not clear. As darkness fell he had to decide whether to continue the chase and put his valuable ships within reach of enemy dive bombers the following morning, besides exposing them to torpedo attacks from the retreating destroyers during the night, or whether discretion was the better part, as some of his staff advised. He mulled the problem over with his dinner.

My morale was reasonably high when I returned to the bridge, and I ordered the destroyer striking force off to find and attack the enemy. We settled down to a steady pursuit...[8]

Soon afterwards his advanced cruisers' radar picked up an unknown ship—actually the cruiser *Pola*—stopped to port of their course and about five miles ahead; Cunningham altered to close her and an hour later the radar-fitted *Valiant* picked up the echo of the ship under eight miles, still to port. Cunningham swung all his heavy ships towards her together, still at full speed, and all his main armament guns turned on to the reported bearing. Then before the stopped ship could be made out visually the Chief-of-Staff, sweeping the starboard bow with his binoculars, reported two large cruisers and a smaller ship crossing ahead of the new course from starboard to port; Cunningham, using short-wave wireless, turned the battleships together to starboard, thus back into line ahead again.

I shall never forget the next few minutes. In the dead silence, a silence that could almost be felt, one heard only the voices of the control personnel putting the guns on to the new target. One heard the orders repeated in the director tower behind and above the bridge. Looking forward one saw the turrets swing and steady when the 15-inch guns pointed at the enemy cruisers. Never in the whole of my life have I experienced a more thrilling moment than when I heard a calm voice from the director tower—'Director layer sees the target'; sure sign that the guns were ready and that his finger was on the trigger. The enemy was at a range of no more than 3,800 yards—point blank...[9]

Then came the 'ting-ting-ting' of the fire gongs, great orange flashes, shudder and heel of the ship and at the same time the searchlights opened to illumine the cruiser target as a 'silvery blue shape in the darkness'. Six 15-inch shells could be seen flying towards her through the beams of light and the next instant five of them struck with devastating effect. The other two battleships astern meanwhile opened on the other heavy cruiser, and in a short time the unfortunate Italian vessels, caught entirely unprepared, 'were nothing but glowing torches and on fire from stem to stern'. After the battleships had wheeled away at speed the destroyers were ordered in to finish off the wrecks, and did so, adding the third cruiser and two destroyers in company to the bag. So ended the Battle off Cape Matapan, for the *Vittorio Veneto* succeeded in making her way home the following day while Cunningham was forced to break off the chase as he came within range of enemy land-based bombers. Although the battleship had eluded him the result of the action was a tonic for the British; the enemy had lost three powerful cruisers and two destroyers, against one aircraft.

The whole engagement is also an interesting demonstration of how the new technology, aircraft, radar and effective wireless, had given to the battlefleet all the sensory attributes it lacked at the time of Jutland—just at the point when the same technology used *against* the battlefleet was about to destroy the concept altogether. Thus the fleeing enemy had been spotted, reported and slowed by aircraft, then in darkness found by radar and held until within visual range. The action also revealed the effectiveness of British night-fighting training between the wars; the Italians had scarcely advanced beyond the British position at the time of Jutland, and they lacked radar.

It is appropriate here, to add a word about radar—'radio detection and ranging'. This was an electronic device which detected objects by sending out radio pulses of very short wave-length and picking up those echoes which were bounced back from anything in the way. The time the pulses took to make the journey out and back was translated into distance—in fact the radar observer saw a heightening of an electronic trace as it moved along a distance scale—and the bearing was given by the direction the transmitting aerial pointed at the time. The German Navy was the first service to start serious work on the idea; this was in 1933, and their efforts were directed specifically towards producing ranges for fire control. The US Navy started similar experiments the following year and in 1935 Britain began development for the quite different but more compelling reason of aircraft warning. By 1939 all three countries had developed primitive sets and had installed a few afloat. However, while German radar scientists were subsequently diverted into what was considered more serious war work, the British team was spurred to greater efforts by the need for early detection of German bombing attacks on the country and in 1940 they achieved a major break-through by producing a shorter wavelength than had been possible hitherto; this gave greater accuracy and allowed a far smaller aerial—an important factor for shipboard use. As these 'centimetric' wavelength sets showed the potential eventually to replace optical rangefinders for feeding ranges to the fire control computer they were fitted to the director control towers of British ships from 1941—thus fulfilling the original requirement set by the German service. Subsequent development of shorter and shorter wavelengths and more refined sets fulfilled all expectations and by the end of the conflict Britain and the United States—the two collaborated—had shipborne gunnery radar sets accurate out beyond 30,000 yards, other sets which could 'spot' the fall of shot up to 50,000 yards, and numerous types for air and surface warning, navigation and close-range detail work.

Perhaps the first time that radar played a really crucial part in the maritime war between surface ships was two months after Matapan when the new German battleship, *Bismarck*, made a sortie into the North Atlantic. This superb example of the modern capital ship combined the best qualities of battleship and battle cruiser in one large hull. She was undoubtedly the most formidable gunned ship in the fleet of any belligerent power, and as Britain had nothing that could catch and destroy her, she represented the most serious threat to British shipping since the unrestricted U-boat campaign of the First War.

The Admiralty had warning of her approaching sortie from air reconnaissance before she sailed with the heavy cruiser, *Prince Eugen*, in company from a Norwegian fiord on 21 May; consequently

K

the Commander-in-Chief, Home Fleet had made his dispositions, alerted his cruiser patrol lines between Scotland and Iceland and between Iceland and Greenland (the Denmark Strait) and sent his battle cruiser Squadron, consisting of the *Hood* (flag) and the brand new 'King George V' class battleship, *Prince of Wales*, northwards to be in a position to intercept. Although these two ships outgunned the German squadron they were really no match; the *Hood* was in essence a First War battle cruiser which had received no full-scale modernization since commission in 1920; the horizontal armour over her magazines was 7-inch in total, but was made up of three separate decks, and was in theory penetrable by plunging shells of the calibre of the *Bismarck*'s. And although her main belt was 12 inches thick at mid-length it was far shallower and less extensive than that of the German battleship. Her main armament was eight 15-inch guns in four turrets. As for the *Prince of Wales*, she was at the other end of the scale, only recently commissioned, not fully worked up, and with dockyard fitters still aboard. She was slower than the *Hood* so that her maximum speed of 28½ knots dictated the squadron speed, and her main armament was of a different calibre—ten 14-inch guns in two quadruple turrets at either end and one superfiring double turret forward. Both British ships were fitted with the new gunnery radar which was capable of accurate ranging out to 20,000 yards, but this was a considerable novelty in the service and although the ships had exercised with it, both radar and fire control personnel were naturally inexperienced, and it is doubtful if it played any part in the subsequent gun action. Both German ships also had radar, but it is doubtful if this was as good as the new British types, nor as accurate as their magnificent optical rangefinders.

Radar's main contribution was in shadowing; on 23 May, the cruiser *Suffolk* on patrol in squally weather in the Denmark Strait sighted the German squadron and held on with her search radar while she followed, passing positions and courses by wireless. Admiral Holland in the *Hood* then set course westerly for an interception position which he planned to reach in the very early hours of 24 May, another significant pointer to the changed British attitude to night action. But shortly before reaching this position the *Suffolk*, which had been joined by the cruiser *Norfolk*, lost the quarry and Admiral Holland, no doubt thinking that the German ships had made a large alteration to shake off their shadows, reduced speed and altered course, meanwhile detaching his destroyers on a separate search. In fact the German Admiral Lütjens, had made no such change; this became clear when the *Suffolk* regained contact at 2.47 a.m. But by then the British battle cruiser Squadron was roughly abreast of the German squadron instead of on an interception course cutting across ahead, an important point in the engagement which followed, for Holland's battle plan (it is supposed) was to close the *Bismarck* quickly to get inside the range at which the German ship's fire would plunge and threaten the *Hood's* vulnerable horizontal armour. The new relative positions of the two squadrons made this impossible unless the British ships turned in towards the German broadsides and deliberately offered the German Admiral the initial advantage of crossing their T.

In the event, this is what Admiral Holland did shortly after sighting the German squadron at 5.35 a.m. While the Germans had the two British ships on a favourable bearing for gunnery just forward of their beam, the British pressed in in line ahead, *Hood* leading, with the Germans on their starboard bow, rear turrets masked and heavy seas sweeping over the foc's'les making it impossible for ranges to be taken from the long-base turret rangefinders. In addition the flagship, *Hood*, made an initial mistake in identification which caused her to fire at the leading German, in fact the cruiser *Prince Eugen*, while the *Prince of Wales* opened correctly on the *Bismarck*. Both German ships meanwhile opened up on the British flagship. There are remarkable similarities here with Beatty's charge at Hipper in the opening phase of the battle cruiser action at Jutland; as on that occasion when fire was opened at 26,000 yards the British ranging salvoes went winging way over the target while the German salvoes were immediately correct. The *Hood* received the first hit from the *Prince Eugen* barely a minute after fire commenced, a superlative feat of arms by the 8-inch gun cruiser, then five minutes later, just as Admiral Holland ordered a port turn to bring his full broadside to bear, she received another hit or possibly two, this time from the *Bismarck*, and there occurred the final, shocking similarity with the earlier encounter as the battle cruiser's after magazines blew up; there was a blinding sheet of flame which appeared to encircle the ship, a violent lurch which threw men to the deck and within four minutes the riven hull had listed over and sunk beneath a huge pall of smoke.

The *Prince of Wales*, following in close order, had to put her helm over to avoid the wreck and immediately came under the German concentration which already had the range, some 18,000 yards. She was in difficulties immediately; while one of her forward guns and her entire after turret developed mechanical defects, she was struck by four 15-inch and three 8-inch shells and was forced to turn away under smoke and then break off the action. However, in the brief time during which her forward turrets had been firing she had made two hits on the German flagship, and one of these up in the bows had caused fuel leakage and contamination which persuaded Admiral Lütjens to break off his Atlantic cruise and make for St Nazaire—a demonstration of the effect of even comparatively minor damage on a commerce raider.

The loss of the *Hood* was a shattering blow to the British service; between the wars she had been the proudest symbol of British naval power, with her long, graceful lines and nicely proportioned turret and superstructure arrangement—the epitome of the balanced capital ship. That she should be annihilated within seven minutes was far more shocking than the defeat of the new *Prince of Wales*. Admiral Holland, who went down with his ship, has been criticized since on several counts, mainly for his close 'line' tactics controlled from the flagship; these were appropriate for the great battle squadrons of the First War and the tactical games during the interwar years, indeed they were necessary to prevent confusion and the masking of friendly fire, but they were quite unnecessary for a squadron of only two vessels. In this case they were actually harmful for they forced both British ships to enter the action with rear turrets out of bearing, thus reducing an initial superiority in heavy guns to equality with the *Bismarck*; when the *Hood* mistook her target this equality became an actual inferiority so far as that ship was concerned. It has been suggested that if the British ships had acted independently the *Prince of Wales* could have covered the *Hood*'s advance to close range with her full broadside, and then closed herself.

Admiral Holland's reasoning will never be known for certain as none of his staff survived, but in retrospect it seems that the errors he made were forced by the inadequacy of the *Hood*'s protection against plunging fire, and by interwar tactical doctrine based on the great battlefleet action and thus the 'line of battle' controlled by the commander-in-chief. And, of course, he was allowed no time to retrieve them; this was the decisive factor. The German salvoes in the opening minutes which the British hazarded to fortune were devastatingly accurate.

However the British squadron had done just enough to stop what could have been a disastrous foray into the convoy routes, and the *Prince of Wales* together with the two cruisers, *Norfolk* and *Suffolk* was still shadowing Lütjens and reporting his position and course for the benefit of a vast concentration of heavy ships which the Admiralty was bringing into the area. The drama of the resulting chase as the *Bismarck* made south-easterly for western France has been described many times; it is sufficient here to note that the main hope for the British forces lay in their two carriers, the *Victorious* with the Home Fleet and the *Ark Royal* some way to the southwards. If strike planes could slow or halt the *Bismarck* British battleships would be able to intercept and put paid to her with an overwhelming weight of fire, if not the chances were that the German ship's great speed would enable her to escape.

In the event 15 torpedo bombers from the *Ark Royal* succeeded almost at the last moment in obtaining two hits; one was right aft, damaging the propellers and jamming the rudder to port. Attempts to free the rudder were unsuccessful and with the ship making a slow and erratic progress the crew resigned themselves to their inevitable fate. They knew that British heavy ships were closing in; it only remained for them to give a good account of themselves before they were destroyed. Seldom can any body of men have been so certain of death.

As dawn broke the following day the Commander-in-Chief of the British Home Fleet, Admiral Sir J. Tovey, flying his flag in the new battleship, *King George V*, with the 16-inch gun battleship *Rodney* in company, approached from the westward. The strong wind and rough sea was on his port quarter and the sun was low in the east, tending to favour the westerly force. Even so the visibility was poor, and as the British ships opened fire at 8.47 a.m. with the *Bismarck* making directly towards them about 25,000 yards distant, they did so on an estimated range.[10] The German gunnery control, despite being in a position of disadvantage down wind and sea, opened as usual with an almost correct range for the *Rodney*, and nearly hit her. However, as the distance closed rapidly to 16,000 yards, both British ships turned south independently and opening their full broadsides soon began to hit hard and frequently. By 9.20 the *Bismarck* was consumed with flames and her fire was losing all accuracy. The British ships turned and closed, pouring in broadsides from ranges which soon shortened to 4,000 yards. The destruction was incessant and appalling, and at 10.20, by which time the German guns had been reduced to silence, Tovey ceased fire and made off northwards, leaving it to accompanying cruisers to finish off the tortured wreck with torpedoes.

So ended the most vital series of gun actions British ships had fought since Jutland, perhaps the most vital actions since the Armada campaign. As for the *Bismarck*, she had been defended with great heroism and had gone down either scuttled or torpedoed, with her flag flying. In material terms she provided one more proof of the immense defensive powers built into German ships, and she went some way towards vindicating those big ship men in all navies who had put their faith in the battleship's ability to resist torpedoes and bombs from aeroplanes. Nevertheless it had been the air strike from the *Ark Royal*, a mere 15 obsolescent Swordfish, which had sealed her fate.

Up to mid-1941 it could have been held that the battleship had maintained her ancient position as 'backbone of the fleet'. The Norwegian campaign, the air siege of Malta, and then a brief and abortive British campaign in Greece at the beginning of that year had shown that a surface fleet, with or without battleships, could not perform its traditional functions when the enemy held command of the air above the sea, but as none of Britain's continental enemies had developed carrier air forces, this only applied within range of shore-based aircraft. On the wide oceans the battleship retained command; the *Bismarck* action was proof enough, as were the times when battleship convoy escorts caused surface raiders to sheer off. Moreover Britain's Home Fleet still formed a strong barrier against the breakout of these raiders, while supporting an effective commercial blockade of Germany by cruiser patrols. Against the main threat to merchant shipping, cruiser U-boats, battleships were little use, but of course they protected the ships that could and did fight the U-boats.

By the end of 1941 it would have been more difficult to maintain this position. The blockade of enemy surface units was increasingly maintained by aircraft, and although their attacks frequently failed to destroy heavy ships they inflicted sufficient damage to neutralize them in port. Aircraft were also recognized as the most effective counter to the U-boat threat to convoys, and both specially-designed escort carriers and converted merchant ships were being ordered to provide convoys with their own 'air'. But perhaps the main factor in the changed position was a series of sudden demonstrations of the vulnerability of battleships. The first to go was the *Barham*, a 'Queen Elizabeth' class ship of the Mediterranean fleet; she was torpedoed by U331 on 25 November and the explosion triggered off her magazines so that she blew up and sank with heavy loss of life. She was not the first battleship to be sunk by submarine, but she was the first Dreadnought to be so sunk while steaming at sea. Next, on the fatal Sunday 7 December 1941, Japan declared war on the USA in her traditional manner with an attack on the American fleet base at Pearl Harbor, catching the defences even more lamentably unprepared than those at Port Arthur at the beginning of the century, and wrecking, sinking or damaging every battleship there with waves of carrier-based bomb and torpedo planes. Fortunately for the Americans their fleet carrier force was absent from Pearl Harbor at the time and escaped damage.

That same night Japanese forces started landing troops halfway down the Malay peninsula, at the tip of which lay the great British naval base of Singapore. In Singapore were two British capital ships, the battleship *Prince of Wales*, formerly of Admiral Holland's squadron, and the battle cruiser *Repulse*; these had been sent east originally as a political gesture in the hope of deterring Japan from her increasingly belligerent posture, probably the last example of this traditional use of a British battleship squadron. It is significant that the ships were to have been accompanied by the carrier, *Formidable*, but she was under repair at the time and could not go. As the Japanese pre-emptive strikes against both her Pacific rivals were carried out the position of the two British heavy ships became critical, indeed impossible. With American naval power temporarily eliminated from the western Pacific by the success at Pearl Harbor they stood practically alone against the full potential of the entire Japanese Navy whose heavy units comprised six modernized battleships, two of which mounted eight 16-inch guns apiece, four modernized 14-inch gun battle cruisers capable of over 30 knots, and nine aircraft carriers; nearing completion were two of the giant, 18-inch gun 'Yamatos', either of which outmatched the British squadron. In London it was felt that the only course for the ships to adopt was to 'go to sea and vanish among the innumerable islands'. However, in Singapore the intelligence was that no Japanese battleships were in the vicinity of the Malayan landings and the British Commander-in-Chief, Admiral Phillips, believing that he could surprise the assault forces, called for shore-based fighter cover over the area of the landings, and on the evening of 8 December took his two capital ships and four destroyers out of Singapore and set course northwards.

The following morning he received a message that fighter cover could not be provided, also a warning that the Japanese were believed to have strong bomber forces in southern Indo-China, thus within range of their landings. Still believing that he might achieve surprise and wreak some havoc on the supply line, Admiral Phillips continued northwards until that evening when a Japanese aircraft was sighted. Then, with all chance of surprise lost, the probability of air attacks on the following day and his ships naked of any protection save their own quite inadequate anti-aircraft batteries, he abandoned the sortie and reversed course. That night he received another, as it turned out false report of new Japanese landings further south on the Malay peninsula, and as these were between his own position and Singapore, he altered towards the land to investigate. It was while he was searching inshore off Kuantan early the following morning, 10 December, that he was sighted by Japanese reconnaissance aircraft who were out looking for him, and then attacked by flight after flight of high level bombing and torpedo planes which had been despatched at first light from three fields in French Indo-China (Vietnam) over 400 miles away. The first wave succeeded in hitting the *Repulse* with a 250 kilogramme bomb aft, and then the torpedo planes came, attacking from all angles, pressing in below mast height and so close that the British AA gunners could almost have seen the dark eyes of the pilots before they released their torpedoes and banked sharply away. The *Prince of Wales* was hit twice; one right aft damaged her propellers and steering gear. Then a third wave of torpedo planes hit the *Repulse* once despite evasive manoeuvring and the *Prince of Wales*, which could not manoeuvre, four times. Following this another wave came in and crippled the *Repulse*'s steering so that she, too, lay a helpless target to succeeding waves. Within a short time it was all over; the battlecruiser took 14 torpedo hits in all down both sides, heeled right over and at the end hung for a few minutes at about 60 degrees, then capsized and sank.[11] Destroyers rescued over half her complement while the *Prince of Wales*, also listing heavily and sinking lower and lower, steamed slowly northwards. Altogether she had taken seven torpedo hits and a 500 kilogramme bomb; she took another bomb and a near miss before she, too, turned turtle, and went under at 1.20 p.m., less than two and a half hours since the attacks had begun.

The aircraft which accomplished this historic success – the first time capital ships had been destroyed while steaming at sea – were from the Japanese Navy's First Air Group, and comprised 99 bombers and torpedo planes, 39 fighters and six reconnaissance aircraft. According to their estimates their torpedo planes scored 14 times out of 34 against the *Repulse*—41 per cent—and seven times out of 15 against the *Prince of Wales*—46 per cent—in both cases a higher proportion than had been achieved in practice. While many had been achieved after fortunate hits had crippled both ships' steering, and all in the face of thin anti-aircraft batteries and no fighter protection whatsoever, it was the most significant pointer to the decline of the battleship. For while the *Repulse* had been an old battle cruiser, insufficiently protected against air and underwater attack, the *Prince of Wales* was of the very latest construction with sandwich compartmentation below her armour belt designed and tested to withstand the effects of torpedoes; yet seven had done for her.

So ended the brief period of transition to a new style of sea power, in which the prime unit was the aircraft carrier and the former capital unit, the great gunned battleship, was relegated largely to the carrier's defence. This new style, foreseen by the prophets in the early twenties and made possible by the development in the naval air techniques of the Pacific powers by the thirties was demonstrated beyond doubt in 1942. The first occasion was May, when two American task forces formed around the carriers *Lexington* and *Yorktown* disputed a Japanese expedition to seize Port Moresby in

New Guinea. A series of carrier air battles was fought over the Coral Sea to the east of Australia during which, for the first time in history, the ships of the two opposing fleets never sighted each other. Both side's carriers were severely mauled and both lost one, but the Americans prevented a landing in New Guinea, giving the Japanese the first real setback they had suffered since the opening of their spectacularly triumphant campaign of territorial conquest.

Next came the Battle of Midway on 4–5 June 1942: a strong Japanese fleet spearheaded by four fleet carriers with some 270 planes, and no less than seven battleships, moved eastwards to support an assault on the US island of Midway for the double purpose of pushing out the perimeter of their own Pacific empire and forcing a fleet action when the Americans came to retrieve the island. However, the incredible run of success that they had achieved over the first six months, during which their naval air forces in particular had roamed at will over the eastern possessions of the British Empire, bombing bases, supporting troop landings, sinking merchant ships and warships alike and receiving only one brief set-back at the Coral Sea, had inspired a feeling of arrogant superiority which contributed to their undoing. First of all they relaxed wireless security, and US intelligence, having broken the codes, came to learn almost as much of the Midway operation plans as the Japanese fleet commanders themselves. Hence three carriers under the command of Admiral Nimitz were on hand to dispute the assault early in the morning of 4 June. The Japanese failed to take sufficient account of the possibility of US carriers in the vicinity; Nimitz was thus able to surprise them with their aircraft refuelling after a first strike; his dive bombers put paid to three of the four carriers in a brilliantly executed series of attacks. The one remaining struck back, but was lost in turn next morning. With all his carriers gone, the Japanese commander-in-chief withdrew.

Midway is always regarded as one of the decisive battles of the world. In one forenoon the tide of Japanese success was halted and the main instrument of that success, the superbly trained and experienced aircrews of Admiral Naguno's four fleet carriers, was smashed. This was accomplished by three US carriers of ancient design, deploying some 230 aircraft. From the point of view of the battleship, Midway marked the end of the line; the Japanese Midway fleet included seven with an overwhelming gun superiority over the American force but once the carriers were lost they withdrew. It was the final lesson: in Japan the third of the 'Yamato' class giants, *Shinano*, was altered on the stocks to be completed as an aircraft carrier, and the battleships *Ise* and *Hyuga* were converted. In Britain that year no less than 52 carriers were included in the estimates, an impossible total, much of which had to be farmed out to America, along with the provision of suitable aircraft.

Naturally battleships were not immediately relegated to the breaker's yard; much capital and ingenuity had gone into their design, radar and air reconnaissance had increased their effectiveness, and against those European powers which had not developed carrier arms their usefulness was as great as ever. Even in the Pacific campaign battleships played a part as the gun component of carrier task forces and by night when air strike forces were blind. Thus it was that on the night of 14 November 1942 a battleship action took place in the fiercely contested campaign for Guadalcanal: on the American side were the *Washington*, flying the flag of Admiral Augustus Lee, and the *South Dakota*, both 35,000 ton ships started after the expiry of the Washington Treaties and armed with nine 16-inch guns, on the Japanese side the *Kirishima*, built originally as a battle cruiser to pre-1914 designs but re-built in the thirties with extra protection; she mounted eight 14-inch guns in her main armament. However, the decisive factor in the engagement was not so much the heavier American broadsides as their radar; the *Washington* carried an air/surface search set, a surface fire control set with the after 16-inch fire control position, and several sets for secondary armament and surface search. The Japanese lacked radar altogether, relying on keen eyes and superb night-fighting training. While the *Kirishima* was engaging the *South Dakota*, illuminated by searchlights at the commencement, the *Washington*, keeping dark, picked the Japanese heavy ship up by radar, fed the ranges into her fire control and opened at 18,500 yards with her main batteries and some of her secondary 5-inch guns, achieving complete surprise and devastating accuracy as she was able to spot the fall of shot with her surface fire control sets; within seven minutes she had put nine out of 75 16-inch shells into the Japanese ship together with 40 5-inch, wrecking her steering gear, setting her ablaze and deciding the action there and then. The following morning the Japanese abandoned the wreck under threat of daylight air attack.

A year later, far away in the northern darkness beyond the North Cape of Norway, radar superiority played an equally important part in the end of the last German Dreadnought to be sunk in surface action. The 'King George V' class battleship *Duke of York*, flying the flag of Admiral Fraser, accompanied by cruisers and destroyers in defence of a convoy to Russia, picked up the *Scharnhorst* at 22 miles by radar, and steered through heavy seas to intercept. The British flagship was slower than the German battle cruiser and Fraser's intention was to get in to decisive range to try and make certain of the business before she could escape; he accordingly closed to 12,000 yards before illuminating with starshell and opening fire. The *Scharnhorst*, despite having radar, was caught completely by surprise with her guns fore and aft, and it took her some moments to reply as she turned away. During the ensuing chase both vessels shot well but the *Duke of York* had the advantage of a flatter trajectory to her heavier shells and accurate radar spotting and she made the most effective practice, straddling 31 times out of 52 broadsides, putting one German turret out of action and damaging the battle cruiser under water. This slowed her down and enabled Fraser's destroyers to reduce her speed still further with torpedoes, after which the *Duke of York* and a cruiser closed and completed her destruction. Once again the crew fought long after all hope had vanished, and the vitals of the ship withstood tremendous punishment. Eventually she had to be finished off with torpedoes from the cruisers.

This action, a good example of the final development of gun and torpedo tactics in combination, was the last time a British battleship fought her own kind. It was still necessary to retain a powerful Home Battle fleet reinforced by US battleships to contain the 'Bismarck' class *Tirpitz* and the remaining German pocket battleships and battle cruiser based in Norway, but these were either destroyed or neutralized from the air and the great guns of the big ships found their chief employment in shore bombardments to support troop landings.

The final battleship action took place in the Pacific war. Here the Japanese Navy, to borrow a phrase from Masanori Ito, had been 'overwhelmed from the sky'. The destruction of her aircraft and trained aircrews, begun at Midway, had been continued during the vicious struggle for Guadalcanal, and by the end of 1943 she had lost over 7,000 planes which could not be replaced. Meanwhile American production lines had gathered momentum and given her practically complete command of the air, enhanced by radar. The Japanese Combined Fleet, headed by the *Yamato* and *Musashi* with their fiercely-towering control structures and enormous guns, still gave an appearance of immense strength, and the crews still trained as rigorously as ever, heartened by the recent addition of a primitive radar which they believed would restore the edge they had lost to the Americans. But nothing could restore their lost command of the air. Their four fleet carriers and two converted battleship carriers had scarcely 100 planes between them, even fewer fully-trained pilots.

Thus, when in October 1944 the Combined Fleet made its final sortie against American landings at Leyte in the Philippines, the carrier force was used, not as the spearhead of the attack, as in any conventional campaign of that date, but as a decoy to draw the US carrier force away from Leyte Gulf and permit two battleship squadrons to move in from different directions and destroy the landings and their supply craft. In the event the ruse worked brilliantly; the Japanese carrier admiral sent his few and ill-practised pilots against the carriers of Admiral Halsey's Third Fleet from a position some 200 miles to the north, and although they did scarcely any damage and suffered great losses this was beside the point. Halsey turned and pursued him with the whole of his immensely powerful carrier force, no less than 15 fleet carriers and eight battleships, leaving the defence of the American landings to a bombardment and support group of six older battleships and various cruiser and destroyer divisions under Rear Admiral Oldendorf, and three groups of escort carriers and destroyers under Rear Admiral Sprague. Halsey felt safe to do this as his carrier strike forces had been making repeated attacks on the main Japanese battleship division as it approached the Philippines that day, and his latest intelligence was that it was in retreat. In fact the US aircrews had concentrated on *Yamato* and *Musashi*, mainly the latter, damaging her mortally but leaving most of the other heavy ships with powers intact, and what was taken as a retreat was only a brief diversionary alteration by the Japanese Admiral, Kurita, who hoped to escape further attacks. Thus while the main weight of the American forces went haring off after six impotent carriers with barely 30 planes between them, Kurita, flying his flag in the *Yamato* and with the battleships *Nagato*, *Kongo* and *Haruna*, 11 cruisers and several destroyers, reversed course again and made towards the San Bernardino Strait, the northern approach to Leyte Gulf. This strait had been left undefended because of a signal misinterpretation after Halsey's precipitate chase, a stroke of fortune which the bold, indeed suicidal, Japanese operation perhaps deserved, but which could never have been anticipated. The main strength of the remaining US forces, the battleships and cruisers under Oldendorf, was concentrated across the entrance to the Suriago Strait, the southern approach to Leyte Gulf, to which a smaller Japanese force was heading.

The super-battleship *Musashi*, incidentally, had taken more punishment from the US Third Fleet carrier forces that day, 24 October, than any ship had ever taken before, for no fighters had come to her aid, and her attackers had approached in wave after wave from 10.15 a.m. until after 3.0 p.m. At first the bombs had simply bounced off her thick skin doing superficial damage only, and one torpedo hit had failed to slow her; it was only when a third wave of 29 planes, concentrating on her scored three more torpedo hits, ripping her starboard bow open so that she had to force the torn plates through the sea like a plough, that her speed was checked. Counter-flooding to keep her on an even keel sank her bows and further reduced her speed to something like 22 knots. Then a fourth wave of more than 30 planes reduced her to 12. At 3.0 p.m. Kurita ordered her to retire; he also ordered a fleet reversal of course to confuse the attackers, but the ships had scarcely turned before another wave of more than 100 planes fell upon them and the *Musashi* received another 10 torpedo hits which reduced her to 6 knots. She was now a wallowing wreck, her upperworks twisted and blackened, her bows sinking lower and lower and a starboard list increasing to such an extent that her Captain felt unable to use the rudder lest a change of direction capsize her; he continued the efforts at counterflooding until the foredeck was completely awash with only the forward turrets poking out of the sea like islands, and had all movable weights shifted to the port side. Still she continued to settle and heel and soon after 5.0 the order was given to abandon ship. It was none too soon; by 5.35 her effective waterplane had been reduced so much by the flooding that she lost all stability, rolled suddenly to port and plunged to the bottom, taking with her some thousand of her 2,200 crew, including her captain—and any lingering doubts about the ability of the huge armoured ship to survive air attack. In all she had received 20 torpedoes, 17 bombs and at least 15 near misses.[12]

Meanwhile the two Japanese forces steamed towards Leyte Gulf to carry out their pincer movement from the north and south entrances. There was no effective co-ordination between them, nor had they any air reconnaissance. Their movements were consequently blind and individualistic, and the southern group of two battleships, *Yamashiro* and *Fuso*, a heavy cruiser, *Mogami* and destroyers under the command of Vice Admiral Nishimura reached the approaches to the Straits of Suriago that evening rather before the main force under Kurita reached the northern entrance. Guarding the straits as Nishimura approached were all the heavy ships of Oldendorf's landing support group, together with destroyers and radar-equipped patrol (PT) boats which acted as the eyes of the fleet during the dark hours. The main gun strength of this force resided in the six elderly battleships, the *Maryland* and *West Virginia*, each mounting eight 16-inch guns, and the *Mississippi*, *Tennessee*, *California* and *Pennsylvania* from earlier programmes mounting twelve 14-inch apiece. Once again, as important as the weight of guns was the radar equipment aboard; here the *West Virginia*, *Tennessee* and *California* had a decisive advantage as they were fitted with the latest Mark 8 fire control sets, capable of scanning to 60,000 yards and precision ranging to 44,000 yards.

Oldendorf had arranged his forces so that the battleships steamed back and forth across the 12-miles wide strait in a roughly east-west direction, while two cruiser divisions two and a half miles south of them also steamed east-west in line ahead to cover the gap at each end of the battleship line. Further south still were the destroyer flotillas, and even further south the PT boats. These first picked up the Japanese ships soon after 10.30 that night as Nishimura steamed, unsuspecting, into the jaws of the trap. They reported to Oldendorf and then made unsuccessful torpedo attacks. Nishimura held on, four destroyers in the van, followed by the *Yamashiro*, then at intervals of one kilometer, the *Fuso* and *Mogami*. As he neared the Straits at 3 o'clock the US destroyers were advancing from both sides, and the first group attacked shortly afterwards from between 8,000 and 9,000 yards range, hitting the *Fuso*; then the second group came in and hit the *Yamashiro* and three of the Japanese destroyers, blowing up one and forcing the others to sheer out of formation. Still Nishimura pressed on, unaware that this was only a preliminary and his approach was, to quote the US naval historian, Samuel Morison, like 'an answer to the prayers of a War College strategist or a gunnery tactician'[18], right up to the T of a powerful battleship force waiting in line with all broadsides open. Then a second wave of US destroyers came in, again in two groups fron opposite sides, sinking another destroyer, scoring again on the *Yamashiro* and the *Fuso*, which blew up a quarter of an hour later. Afterwards as Nishimura steamed doggedly on, a third wave completed the destruction of the Japanese formation, so that only Nishimura's flagship, *Yamashiro* and the *Mogami*, both badly damaged underwater and escorted by only one destroyer, were left as the gun attack began.

The American battleships, which had reached the western end of their traverse, were steaming easterly as the last destroyer attacks began. The three ships with Mark 8 radar had been scanning the Japanese force from long before it came within range, and all were keeping the fire control solution up to date as Nishimura advanced inside gun range. Oldendorf was concerned about his comparative lack of armour-piercing shell however—his was a shore bombardment group—and he had decided to wait for decisive range before opening fire. So it was not until 3.51, when the nearest cruiser division was under 16,000 yards from the Japanese force, that he gave the order to fire. The battle line was then some 22,000 yards distant from the enemy, and at first only the three ships with Mark 8 radar opened between 3.53 and 3.55; they were followed a few minutes later by the *West Virginia* ranging on the splashes, and by the fleet flagship, *Mississippi*. The battle line meanwhile altered together towards the enemy bringing the range inside 20,000 yards, then altered due west together, opening the other side. By this time the Japanese flagship, on which most of the fire was concentrated, was a wreck, blazing fiercely throughout her entire length, and Nishimura had turned south to try and escape the sudden holocaust. It was too late; his flagship shortly capsized and sank taking nearly all her crew with her. The *Mogami*, which was also burning brightly, fired torpedoes then made smoke and retired southwards.

The *Yamashiro* has the distinction of being the last battleship to be sunk in a surface action with her own kind; after suffering an unknown number of torpedo hits from the destroyer attacks, she had been the target for an astonishing total of 3,100 shells from the cruisers and 285 heavy armour-piercing shells from the battleship line at what was decisive range by the standards of the day; how many hit her will never be known but the shooting was described by observers as 'devastatingly accurate'. To the US flagship, *Mississippi*, which fired the last broadside, full 12 guns at 19,790 yards range at eight minutes past four that morning, 25 October 1944, goes the distinction of being the last battleship to fire her guns in anger at another: as Samuel Morison put it so well, she was not only giving the *coup de grâce* to the *Yamashiro* 'but firing a funeral salute to a finished era of naval warfare'.[14]

Hardly had the echoes of this one-sided encounter died away than Kurita's battleship division, which had made an unopposed passage through the San Bernardino Strait, fell upon the northernmost of the US escort carrier groups to the east of the island of Samar just north of Leyte Gulf. The carriers immediately fled but the *Yamato* opened fire at the portentous range of 17 miles, the first time the Japanese 18-inch guns had been discharged in earnest, and was soon straddling the unfortunate carriers. Had Kurita pressed straight in to close the range he must have destroyed the American force, for the carriers were small and slower than the battleships, while their aircraft, intended for shore support, were only armed with light bombs as they flew off hastily to attack. Moreover Kurita's other battleships, all armed with 16-inch guns, soon proved that their intensive training off Singapore during the Summer and early Autumn had toned their gunnery up to high standards. However, Kurita, in the absence of air reconnaissance, had mistaken the escort carriers for fleet carriers and when he was attacked by a wave of aircraft from another escort group, abandoned the chase. After some manoeuvring towards the landing areas in Leyte he abandoned the mission altogether and retired. The brilliant opportunity created by the Japanese decoy force —which Halsey destroyed—was wasted.

After this disastrous episode, there remained one final sortie for the Japanese battleships; it was ordered on 5 April the following year, ostensibly to damage US naval forces, but apparently in the desperate hope of drawing off American bombers from the Japanese army on Okinawa, whose loss would mean disaster. The sortie, like Ozawa's, was a suicide mission from the first:

> Second Fleet is to charge the enemy anchorage of Kadeno, off Okinawa Island at daybreak of 8 April. Fuel for only a one-way passage will be supplied.[15]

The ships, headed by the great *Yamato*, sailed on 6 April under Vice-Admiral Ito. Early the following morning they were detected by the US Third Fleet's reconnaissance aircraft and 380 dive and torpedo bombers took off to intercept, reaching Ito soon after 12.30 and starting a series of attacks which did not end until his squadron had been utterly destroyed. The *Yamato* herself lasted three hours before she succumbed to the rain of bombs and torpedoes, and then she capsized after an internal explosion.

The active career of the Japanese Combined Fleet ended in useless sacrifice. Her other battleships and carriers had all been sunk or immobilized from the air or by submarine, including the *Yamato*'s one-time sister, the giant carrier, *Shinano*, which had gone down less than a day out on her maiden voyage, struck by four torpedoes from the US submarine *Archerfish*. Retribution had been exacted in full for Pearl Harbor and the giant battleships laid down in bad faith. The US production machine had overwhelmed the island empire.

And so ends the story of the battleship. She was no longer in command. The conflict in both European and Pacific theatres had been won and lost by all arms, submarines and torpedoes, mines, aircraft and bombs. Surface ships had played their part, but the great gunned ships, though more powerful than ever, had lost their major role at sea, and the Anglo-Mahan doctrines of command, which shone through all the complex actions of the war, needed redefinition in terms of carrier task forces.

Appendix

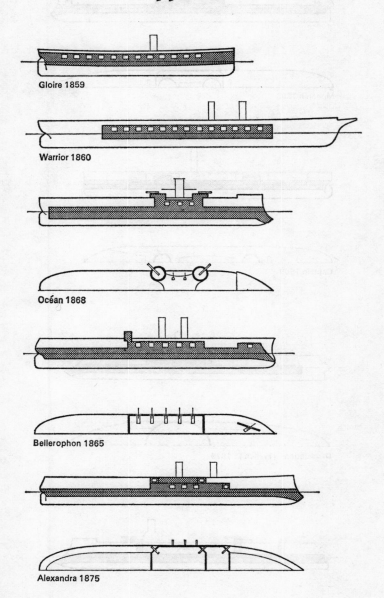

Gloire 1859

Warrior 1860

Océan 1868

Bellerophon 1865

Alexandra 1875

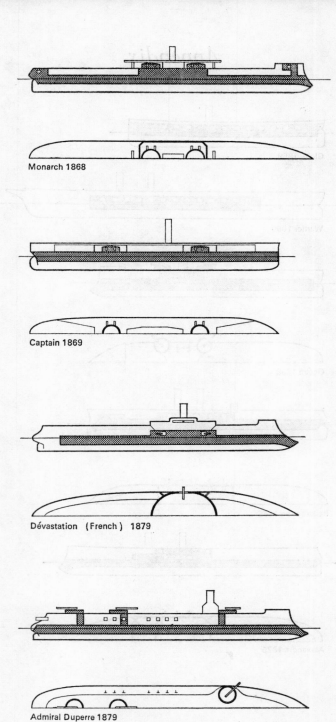

Monarch 1868

Captain 1869

Dévastation (French) 1879

Admiral Duperre 1879

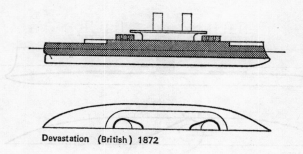

Devastation (British) 1872

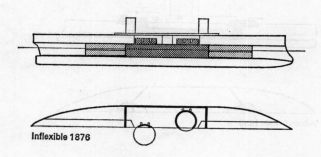

Inflexible 1876

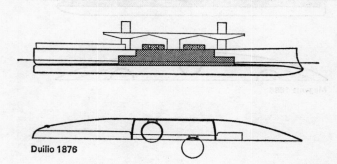

Duilio 1876

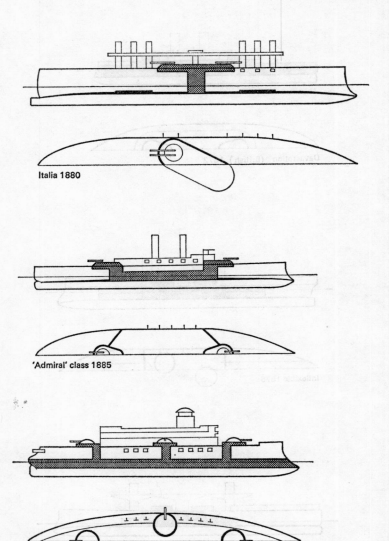

Italia 1880

'Admiral' class 1885

Magenta 1886

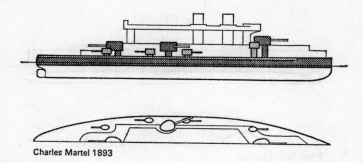

Charles Martel 1893

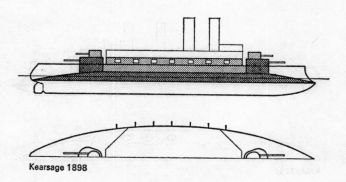

Kearsage 1898

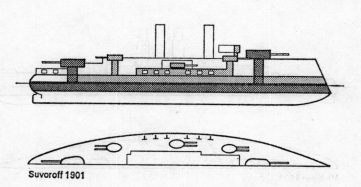

Suvoroff 1901

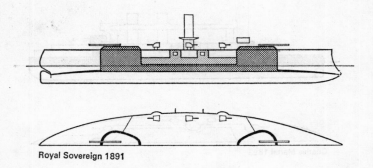

Royal Sovereign 1891

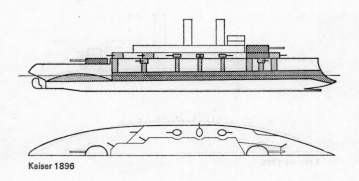

Kaiser 1896

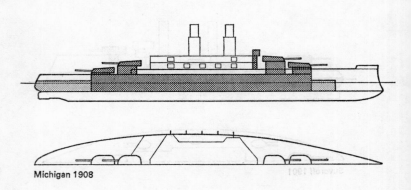

Michigan 1908

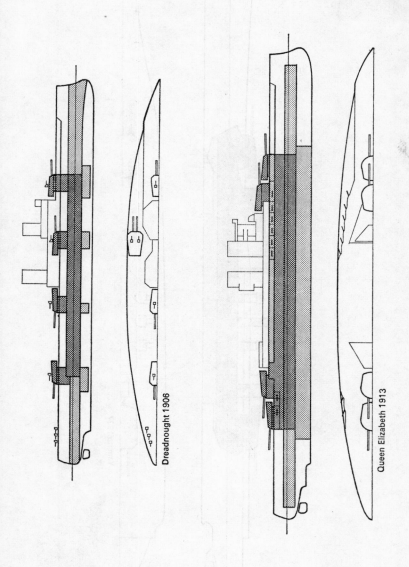

Dreadnought 1906

Queen Elizabeth 1913

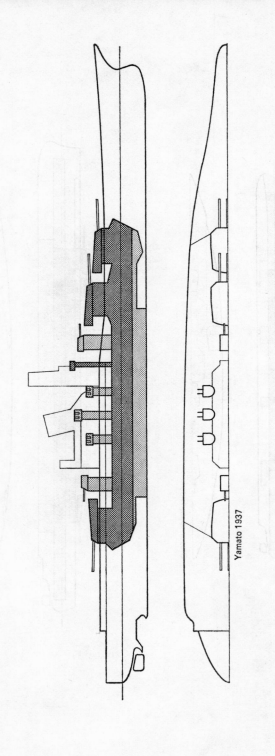

Yamato 1937

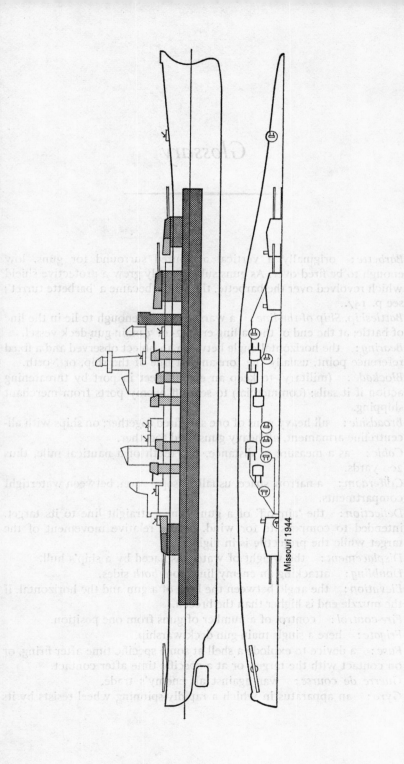

Missouri 1944

Glossary

Barbette: originally a vertical armoured surround for guns, low enough to be fired over. As guns subsequently grew a protective shield which revolved over the barbette, the whole became a 'barbette turret'; see p. 147.

Battleship, Ship-of-the-line: a warship strong enough to lie in the line of battle; at the end of the sailing era a 2- or 3-main-gun-deck vessel.

Bearing: the horizontal angle between an object observed and a fixed reference point, usually the fore-and-aft line of the ship, or North.

Blockade: (military) to keep an enemy fleet in port by threatening action if it sails; (commercial) to seal off enemy ports from merchant shipping.

Broadside: all heavy guns of one side fired together; on ships with all-centreline armament, *all* heavy guns fired together.

Cable: as a measure of distance, one tenth of a nautical mile, thus 200 yards.

Cofferdam: a narrow space, usually a separation, between watertight compartments.

Deflection: the 'aim-off' of a gun from a straight line to its target, intended to compensate for wind, or the relative movement of the target while the projectile is in flight.

Displacement: the weight of water displaced by a ship's hull.

Doubling: attacking an enemy line from *both* sides.

Elevation: the angle between the bore of a gun and the horizontal, if the muzzle end is higher than the breech.

Fire-control: control of a number of guns from one position.

Frigate: here a single-main-gun-deck warship.

Fuse: a device to explode a shell at some specific time after firing, or on contact with the target, or at a specific time after contact.

Guerre de course: war against an enemy's trade.

Gyro: an apparatus in which a rapidly-spinning wheel resists by its motion any change of direction; thus a gyro compass can be set to point north through any movements of the platform on which it rests.

Laying: giving a gun its correct angle of elevation.

Leeward: the opposite side to windward.

Plot: the graphical indication of the position and movement of another vessel and/or one's own vessel; a *true plot* shows a vessel's true geographical movement, a *relative plot* shows another vessel's movement relative to one's own.

Raking: firing up the *length* of another vessel from a position off her bow or stern.

Salvo: one gun from each turret fired simultaneously.

Shell: a hollow projectile containing a bursting charge.

Shot: a solid projectile.

Sponson: extension outwards from a ship's side above water—e.g. to house paddle wheels.

Spotting: correcting fire by observing the fall of the previous salvo.

Stability: the ability of a ship to return to an even keel after being heeled.

Strake: a line (horizontally disposed) of hull side plating.

Tack: to turn a sailing vessel so that the wind falls on the other side of the sails.

Trajectory: flight path of a projectile.

Tumble-home: inward-slope of a ship's side from waterline to upper deck.

Weather gage: a position on the windward side of the enemy.

Windward: the side from which the wind is blowing.

References, Notes and Bibliography

The chief sources for the technical development of battleships are Hovgaards' *Modern History of Battleships*, Brassey's *The British Navy*, 1882 (both in Chapter 5 references below) and subsequent Brassey's *Naval Annuals*, and in the twentieth century *Jane's Fighting Ships*. Most of the British Directors of Naval Construction wrote books (see References below), and gave addresses about their craft recorded in *Transactions of the Institution of Naval Architects*. The Naval Intelligence Department at the Admiralty kept detailed records of foreign warships, which are now in the Naval Library, London (N.I.D. Reports). Other valuable sources are, of course, Dr Oscar Parkes' classic *British Battleships* (Chapter 3 below) and Admiral Ballard's series on early battleships in *The Mariner's Mirror* through the mid-thirties. For strategical development the sources start with Philip Colomb, some of whose works are cited below, Mahan (Section 1), Custance for an interesting diversion — e.g. *The Ship of the Line in Battle*, Blackwood, 1912 — through Julian Corbett — e.g. the important *Some Principles of Maritime Strategy*, Longmans, 1911 — and H. Richmond (Chapter 18) to S. W. Roskill, *The Strategy of Sea Power*, Collins, 1962. It would be impossible to leave out of this list Arthur Marder's *British Naval Policy* (Chapter 12) and the five volumes of *From the Dreadnought to Scapa Flow*, Oxford, 1961–70. The development of guns, fire control and armour is based on my own *Guns at Sea* (Chapter 1), where the sources are quoted; they are chiefly Admiralty gunnery manuals and collections of papers at H.M.S. *Excellent*, the British naval gunnery establishment. The development of tactics is traced from the reports of the British Annual Manoeuvres in the Naval Library (Chapter 13), Signal and Manoeuvring Manuals, British and foreign, and N.I.D. Reports, all in the same place. The merchant naval background is chiefly from S. G. Sturmey's *British Shipping and World Competition*, Athlone Press, 1962.

In the references which follow the author's name or key words in the document are in capitals on their first appearance; thereafter only the author's name is given (and shortened title if necessary) together with the number of the chapter (in brackets) where the full reference can be found, but if the first reference is in the same section op. cit. is used.

Chapter 1. The Sailing Navy

1 For detailed discussion and references for early stand-off gun tactics and period of transition, galley to gunned sailer, see P. PADFIELD, *Guns at Sea*, Evelyn, 1972

2 GREENLEE (ed.), *Cabral's Voyage to Brazil and India*, Hakluyt Society, 1938, p. 183

3 Evolution of sailing ship tactics, see J. S. CORBETT, *Fighting Instructions 1530–1816*, Navy Records Society, 1904

4 S. R. GARDINER (ed.), *The First Dutch War*, Navy Records Society, 1899, p. 100

5 DE GUICHE, *Memoirs*, London, 1743, pp. 234–64, quoted A. T. MAHAN, *The Influence of Sea Power upon History 1660–1783*, Little Brown, 1890, p. 126

6 DE MOROGUES, *Tactique Navale*, Paris, 1763, trans., London, 1767, p. xx

7 P. Broke to H. Douglas, Broke Papers HA 93 877/16, Ipswich Record Office

8 J. GRAVIÈRE, *Guerres Martimes*, Vol. 2. pp. 175–6, quoted H. DOUGLAS, *Naval Gunnery*, London, 1855 edition, p. 314

Chapter 2. French Challenge

1 Parliamentary Papers 1861 v No. 438, p. 231, quoted J. P. BAXTER, *The Introduction of the Ironclad Warship*, Harvard, 1933

2 H. DOUGLAS, *Naval Warfare with Steam*, London, 1858, p. x

3 See H. Douglas (1), p. 309

4 ibid., p. 608

5 ibid., p. 302 quoting Paixhans, *Moniteur*, February 1854

6 Quoted J. P. Baxter, op. cit., p. 301

7 See also Report of Committee . . . into Navy Estimates, 1852–8, and J. Ross, *A Treatise on Navigation by Steam*, London, 1828

Chapter 3. Riposte

1 C. BERESFORD, *Memoirs*, Methuen, 1914, p. 1

2 Controller's Submission Book 20, quoted J. P. Baxter (2), p. 120

3 ibid., p. 123

4 Quoted O. Parkes, *British Battleships*, Seeley Service, 1966, p. 16

5 C. Beresford, op. cit., p. 42

6 J. FISHER, *Memories*, Hodder, 1919, pp. 148–9

Chapter 4. Battle Proof

1 H. W. WILSON, *Ironclads in Action*, Sampson Low, 1896, i, p. 3
2 Ericsson to Welles, 23 December 1861, quoted J. P. Baxter (2), p. 358
3 *Revue des Deux Mondes*, lxvi, p. 203, quoted H. W. Wilson, op. cit., i, p. 217

Chapter 5. The Iron Thickens

1 N. BARNABY, *Transactions of the Institute of Naval Architects*, March 1860, p. 154
2 Armour-piercing experiments, see J. P. Baxter (2), p. 204 ff., and O. Parkes (3), p. 21 ff.
3 Ordnance methods and statistics, see T. BRASSEY, *The British Navy*, 1882, Vol. ii
4 Evolution of types of ironclad, ibid., Vol. i, and HOVGAARD, *Modern History of Warships*, Spon, 1920
5 Report of Committee on Designs . . ., H.M.S.O., London, 1871, Q. 2640
6 ibid., Q. 2552

Chapter 6. Turrets

1 K. C. BARNABY, *Some Ship Disasters and their causes*, Hutchinson, 1968, p. 22
2 ibid.
3 Quoted idem.
4 *Revue Maritime*, 1872, Vol. ii, quoted T. Brassey (5), i, p. 113
5 Quoted K. C. Barnaby, op. cit., p. 29
6 Reed quoted A. HAWKEY, *H.M.S. Captain*, Bell, 1963
7 K. C. Barnaby, op. cit., p. 40
8 Quoted F. T. Jane, *The British Battlefleet*, Library Press, 1915, pp. 282–3

Chapter 7. Torpedoes

1 C. C. P. FITZGERALD, *Memories of the Sea*, E. Arnold, 1913, p. 295
2 R. D. EVANS, *A Sailor's Log*, Appleton, 1938, p. 172
3 C.-in-C. Mediterranean to Admiralty, 25 August 1868, Public Record Office ADM 116 135
4 Committee Designs (5), Q. 3321
5 Report of the TORPEDO Committee, 1873–6, pp. xxix, xxii, Public Record Office ADM 116 163

Chapter 8. Naval Supremacy in the 1870s

1 C. C. P. FITZGERALD, *Memories of the Sea* (7), p. 118
2 C. Beresford (3), p. 41
3 R. D. Evans (7), p. 61

4 Committee Designs (5), Q. 868
5 Quoted B. MCL. RANFT, *The Naval Defence of Seaborne Trade*, unpublished dissertation, D.Phil. Oxford 1967
6 S. E. MORISON, *Men, Machines and Modern Times*, M.I.T., Cambridge, Mass, 1966, p. 108
7 Quoted P. COLOMB, *Royal United Service Institution Journal*, 1887, p. 768
8 See also for this section evidence in First Report Royal (CARNARVON) Commission ... Defence of British Possessions; Milne Papers, National Maritime Museum

Chapter 9. Tactics and Design: the 1870s
1 Quoted P. Colomb (8), p. 770
2 Quoted E. J. REED, *Our Ironclad Ships*, Murray, 1869, p. 259
3 Committee Designs (5), p. xix
4 G. H. NOEL, *The Gun, Ram and Torpedo*, London, 1874, p. 59
5 Vocabulary Signal Book 1968, Naval Library, Ec 167
6 Gunnery details from Committee Designs (5), Q. 1920 ff.
7 P. SCOTT, *Fifty Years in the Royal Navy*, Murray, 1919, p. 31
8 Admiral BALLARD, *Battleships of 1870*, Mariner's Mirror, 1934
9 Signal Book 1853, p. 29, Instruction XV, Signal Books 1879, 1889, etc. Instruction 3, Naval Library
10 Quoted H. DOUGLAS, *Naval Gunnery* (1)
11 See G. H. Noel, op. cit., p. 62
12 Committee Designs (5), p. 17
13 See N.I.D. Report No. 260, 1891, Naval Library
14 G. H. Noel, op. cit., p. 13
15 Signal Books 1853, 1868, 1879, 1889, 1898, Naval Library
16 Committee Designs (5), p. 67
17 ibid., p. xx
18 ibid., p. xiv
19 ibid., p. xvii
20 ibid., Qs. 3198, 3205, 4325, 632, 1491

Chapter 10. Ships of the 1870s
1 N. BARNABY, *Naval Development in the Century*, London, 1904, p. 75
2 C. C. P. Fitzgerald (7), p. 28
3 T. Brassey (5), Vol. i, Part 1, p. 351
4 ibid., p. 281
5 N. BARNABY, *Transactions of the Institution of Naval Architects* March 1874
6 E. Reed to *The Times*, 18 June 1876
7 N. Barnaby to *The Times*, quoted T. Brassey, op. cit., p. 411

8 ibid., p. 411 ff.
9 Report *Inflexible* Committee, quoted idem.
10 R. BACON, *From 1900 Onwards*, Hutchinson, 1940, pp. 96–7
11 Quoted G. PENN, *Up Funnel, Down Screw*, Hollis & Carter, 1955, p. 109
12 N. BARNABY, *Naval Development*, op. cit., p. 77
13 *The Times*, 10 June 1879, quoted T. Brassey (5), p. 422
14 *Broad Arrow*, 1876, quoted ibid., p. 251
15 N. Barnaby, quoted idem.
16 O. Parkes (3), p. 232
17 T. Brassey (5), p. 363

Chapter 11. Actions, Accidents and Other Alarms
1 P. Scott (9), p. 14
2 A. LEDIEU and E. CADIAT, *Le Nouveau Matériel Naval*, Paris, 1889, ii, p. 495
3 Quoted D. A. FARNIE, *East and West of Suez*, Clarendon Press, 1969, p. 239
4 *The Times*, 27 May 1878, quoted ibid., p. 267
5 Reports from C.-in-C. and Captains, Egyptian Campaign, Naval Library Ca 872, 430, 435

Chapter 12. The Development of the Battleship
1 P. Colomb, *Royal United Services Institute Journal*, 1871, p. 765
2 Carnarvon Commission (8), Q. 3982
3 R. BACON, *A Naval Scrapbook*, Hutchinson, p. 174
4 C. C. P. FITZGERALD, *From Sail to Steam*, M. Arnold, 1916, p. 180
5 Quoted Hovgaard (5)
6 Gen. von Stosch, memo. quoted A. HURD, *The German Fleet*, Hodder, 1915
7 Quoted O. Parkes (3)
8 Quoted A. MARDER, *British Naval Policy, 1880–1905*, Putnam, 1941
9 Quoted F.O. Intelligence Committee Report No. 58, 10 December 1884
10 P. COLOMB, *Royal United Services Institute Journal*, 1887, p. 783
11 Report British Naval Manoeuvres, 1885, Naval Library Eb 06
12 ibid.
13 N.I.D. Report 1887, No. 149, Naval Library
14 Reports of British Naval Manoeuvres, Naval Library
15 Report Committee on Naval Estimates, quoted Ranft (8)
16 P. FONTIN, 'Submarines and the Naval policy of England', *Revue Maritime*, October 1902, N.I.D. Report No. 676, Naval Library
17 Quoted F. T. Jane, (6)

18 *Alternative Designs for First Class Battleships*, H.M.S.O. C–5635, February 1889
19 ibid.
20 W. WHITE, *Manual of Naval Architecture*, quoted E. ATTWOOD, *Warships*, Longmans, 1908, pp. 275–6
21 O. Parkes (3)
22 R. BACON, *Scrapbook*, op. cit., p. 264
23 A. T. Mahan (1), p. 526
24 ibid., p. 132

Chapter 13. Usage and Abusage: 1880s and 1890s
1 British Manual of Naval Manoeuvres, 1889, p. 109, Naval Library
2 Report of 1889 Manoeuvres, Naval Library Eb 06
3 N.I.D. Report No. 267 on formations adopted in French manoeuvres, Naval Library
4 Report of 1895 Tactical Exercises, Naval Library Eb 06
5 E. CHATFIELD, *The Navy and Defence*, Heinemann, 1942, p. 16
6 K. G. B. DEWAR, *The Navy from Within*, Gollancz, 1939, p. 21
7 ibid.
8 L. YEXLEY, *The Inner Life of the Navy*, Pitman, 1908, pp. 173–4, 176
9 C. C. P. FITZGERALD, 'On Mastless Ships of War', *Royal United Services Institute Journal*, 1887, p. 115
10 L. Yexley, op. cit., pp. 177–8
11 K. G. B. Dewar, op. cit., p. 25
12 *Victoria* Court Martial, Markham's evidence, Naval Library
13 MARK KERR, *The Navy in My Time*, Rich & Cowan, p. 31
14 E. E. MORISON, *Admiral Sims and the Modern American Navy*, Houghton Mifflin, 1942, p. 114
15 Sims to President Roosevelt, 16 November 1901, quoted ibid.
16 R. D. Evans (7), p. 391
17 ibid., p. 445

Chapter 14. The Age of Battleships
1 M. Bardoux's Report, quoted Brassey's *Naval Annual*, 1890
2 *Le Yacht*, quoted ibid.
3 Aube, quoted ibid., p. iv
4 P. COLOMB, 'Coaling Stations . . . our trade routes', pamphlet November 1893, Naval Library
5 N.I.D. Report, 1893, Naval Library
6 F. Richards minutes 'Requirements in cruisers', Public Record Office ADM 116 878
7 P. MAGNUS, *Gladstone*, John Murray, 1954, p. 416
8 F. Richards memo., 1893, Public Record Office ADM 116 878
9 Commandant Z, quoted Brassey's *Naval Annual*, 1890, p. 197

10 F. Richards memo., 'Dimensions of Capital Ships', November 1895, Public Record Office ADM 116 878
11 ibid.
12 W. White minute 'Characteristics and dimensions of battleships', ibid.
13 E. Chatfield (13), p. 37
14 P. Fontin (12)
15 ibid.
16 Quoted A. Hurd (12), p. 158
17 A. TIRPITZ, *My Memoirs*, Hurst & Blackett, 1919, i, pp. 59–60
18 ibid., p. 117
19 ibid., p. 122
20 Quoted from A. Hurd (12), pp. 183–8
21 Fisher to Lord Lansdowne, 22 April 1905, A. MARDER, *Fear God and Dread Nought*, Cape, 1959, ii, p. 55
22 P. Fontin (12)

Chapter 15. Gunnery Renaissance, in Practice and Anger

1 L. Yexley (13), p. 197
2 Plans for Battle, Mediterranean Fleet, 1898, Public Record Office ADM 116 434
3 P. Scott (9), p. 60
4 See E. E. MORISON, *Sims* (13), and P. PADFIELD, *Aim Straight*, Hodder, 1966
5 Captain DARAGAN, Russian Imperial Navy, to author, 18 October 1968
6 Marder (12), p. 436, quoting T. ROPP, *The Development of a Modern Navy*, unpublished dissertation Harvard 1937
7 Daragan, op. cit.
8 NAVAL ATTACHES' Reports, Russo-Japanese War, Vol. 1, p. 166, Naval Library Ca 1263
9 Daragan, op. cit.
10 Naval Attaches', op. cit., Vol. 3, p. 47
11 See A. NOVIKOFF-PRIBOY, *Tsushima*, Allen & Unwin, 1936, p. 48
12 See ibid., p. 61
13 Quoted Marder (12), p. 440
14 See Novikoff-Priboy, op. cit., p. 103
15 Naval Attaches', op. cit., Vol. 3, p. 64
16 Semenov, *Rasplata*, quoted G. BLOND, *Admiral Togo*, Jarrolds
17 Naval Attaches', op. cit., Vol. 3, p. 69
18 idem.
19 idem.
20 ibid., p. 115

21 J. FISHER, *Naval Necessities*, private circulation, Public Record Office ADM 116 942
22 Naval Attaches', op. cit., Vol. 3, p. 81
23 See also for this section I. A. NISH, *The Anglo-Japanese Alliance*, Athlone Press, 1966, and G. MONGER, *The End of Isolation*, Nelson, 1963

Chapter 16. Fire Control and the Dreadnought
1 Naval Attaches' (15), Vol. 3, Captain Jackson's Report
2 See the 'Jupiter Letters' by ARTHUR POLLEN, private circulation, 1905, H.M.S. *Excellent* Library, Whale Island
3 See P. Padfield (15)
4 Naval Attaches' (15), p. 162
5 ibid., p. 167
6 ibid., p. 165
7 Quoted Marder (12), p. 531
8 N.I.D. Report, No. 641, 1901, Naval Library Eb 06
9 J. Fisher memo., 'The Fighting Characteristics of vessels of war', May 1904, Public Record Office ADM 116 942
10 Mahan's views on Battle of Japan Sea, *Proceedings of the U.S. Navy Institute* June 1906
11 Barfleur (Admiral Custance), 'Strategy, Tactics and Speed', *Royal United Services Institute Journal*, April 1907
12 Annotations to above by Percy Scott, *Fisher Papers*, ed. P. KEMP, Navy Records Society, 1960
13 H. Douglas, *Naval Gunnery* (1), p. 481
14 Sims in U.S. *Naval Institute Proceedings*, quoted A. Hurd (12)
15 Marder (12), p. 538, quoting FISHER'S *Naval Necessities*, 111, p. 249
16 R. Bacon, *From 1900* (10), p. 101
17 For details of the growth of Wilhelm II's Navy see: V. R. BERGHAHN, *Der Tirpitz Plan*, Dusseldorf, 1971; J. STEINBERG, *Yesterday's Deterrent*, MacDonald, 1965; J. C. G. ROHL, 'Admiral von Muller and the Approach of War', *Hist. Journal*, December 1969
18 Marder (12), p. 107 quoting Lord Selborne memo., 1902
19 Wilhelm II to Lord Tweedmouth, 14 November 1908, Asquith Papers, Bodleian Library, Box 19
20 In Asquith Papers, Bodleian Library, Box 21
21 Letter, March 1908, quoted J. FISHER, *Memories* (3), p. 4
22 R. BACON, *Lord Fisher*, Vol. i, Hodder, 1929, p. 122
23 W. Churchill in House of Commons, quoted A. Hurd (12)
24 Admiralty memo on naval situation, 26 August 1912, Asquith Papers, Bodleian Library, Box 24
25 Steinberg, op. cit., Appendix
26 Admiralty memo, 26 August 1912, op. cit.

27 A. Hurd (12), p. 141
28 See P. Padfield, *Guns* (1)
29 C. V. USBORNE, *Blast and Counterblast*, Murray, 1935, p. 6
30 ibid., pp. 7–11
31 Results of trials of 12 in. and 9.2 in. projectiles against KC armour, G 9407/09, Nav. Library, JA 010
32 C. V. Usborne, op. cit., pp. 25–7
33 K. G. B. Dewar (13), p. 161
34 See also for this chapter W. CHURCHILL, *The World Crisis, 1911–15*, Butterworth, 1923; R. HOUGH, *Dreadnought*, Michael Joseph, 1965; Admiralty paper: 'British and German Dreadnoughts compared', 1914 and 1917, Public Record Office ADM 116 0025

Chapter 17. War

1 von Ingenohl's message to Fleet, quoted in diary of Seaman R. STUMPF, (ed. D. Horn), Frewin, 1969, p. 33
2 J. CORBETT, *Naval Operations*, Longmans (revised edition), 1940, Vol. i, p. 157
3 See R. Stumpf, op. cit., pp. 74–5
4 See P. SCHMALENBACH, *Die Geschichte der deutsche Marineartillerie*, Koehlers, 1970, p. 79
5 G. VON HASE, *Kiel and Jutland*, Skeffington, 1921, p. 80
6 Gunnery Officer, H.M.S. *Lion*, writing in *The Fighting at Jutland* (ed. Fawcett and Hooper), Maclure, MacDonald, c.1918
7 von Hase, op. cit., p. 91
8 ibid.
9 Fighting at Jutland, op. cit.
10 All signals, courses etc. during battle of Jutland from three main sources: (i) J. Corbett, *Naval Operations*, op. cit., Vol. 3 and maps; (ii) *Narrative of the Battle of Jutland*, H.M.S.O., 1924; (iii) J. HARPER, *The Truth about Jutland*, Murray, 1927
11 Fighting at Jutland, op. cit.
12 ibid.
13 von Hase, op. cit., pp. 97–8
14 J. Harper, op. cit., p. 22
15 J. Corbett, op. cit., Vol. 3, p. 361
16 F. DREYER, *The Sea Heritage*, Museum Press
17 von Hase, op. cit., p. 103
18 ibid., p. 113
19 ibid., p. 121
20 ibid., p. 125
21 See R. Stumpf, op. cit., p. 214
22 The JELLICOE PAPERS, ed. A. Temple-Patterson, Navy Records Society, 1966, Vol. ii, p. 48

23 idem.
24 Admiralty. pub., *Tactics*, Confidential circulation, Naval Library Eb 011
25 See R. Stumpf, op. cit., p. 294
26 W. S. CHALMERS, *Life and Letters of David Beatty*, Hodder, 1951, pp. 344–5

Chapter 18. Challenge from the New World

1 U.S. Navy Staff memo prepared for Peace Conference 1919, quoted H. and M. SPROUT, *Towards a New Order of Seapower*, Princeton, 1946
2 Lloyd George, quoted ibid., p. 62
3 See ibid., pp. 59–66
4 See ibid., pp. 126–35, 153
5 Details from ibid., pp. 305–6
6 These are two of a fascinating series of letters in *The Times*, headed 'Great Ships or ... ?', extending through winter 1920–21 and re-vived at intervals later
7 Sprout, op. cit., p. 219
8 Morison, *Sims* (13)
9 A. MARDER, *Portrait of an Admiral*, Cape, 1952, quoting Admiral Richmond's diary, 10 November 1920: 'Beatty said the political people are very difficult to deal with. They said "but if battleships can only run away from each other when they meet, and if destroy-ing the enemy fleet would not have affected the submarine cam-paign ... why build battleships?" '
10 See 'Assessment of damage due to aircraft action in staff exercises and war games 1925–8', Public Record Office ADM 116 2464, and later: 'Vulnerability of capital ships to air attack, 1937', Public Record Office, ADM 116 3733, and 'Bomb and Torpedo Damage to battleships, 1937', Public Record Office ADM 116 5741
11 ADM 116 2464, op. cit.
12 ibid.
13 P. Scott to *The Times*, 7 April 1922
14 Sims' testimony before House of Representatives Committee into Operations of the U.S. Air Services, 1925 (Part 4 pp. 2959–3015), quoted Morison, *Sims* (13), p. 506
15 idem.
16 S. S. Hall to *The Times* 7 April 1922
17 A. B. CUNNINGHAM, *A Sailor's Odyssey*, Hutchinson, 1951, p. 161
18 Lt. Cdr. W. B. HARVEY, 'Broadside Mess' (4), *Navy*, October 1966, pp. 333, 341
19 Quoted in W. JAMES, *Admiral Sir William Fisher*, Macmillan, 1943, pp. 136–7

20 Admiralty papers 'Abyssinian Dispute', Public Record Office ADM 116 3476 for C-in-C's narrative; see also ADM 116 3297 for harbour defences etc., ADM 116 3487 for political aspect, and ADM 116 3476 for ship movements

21 See KITARO MATSUMOTO, Design and Construction of the Yamato and Musashi, U.S. Navy Institute Proceedings, October 1953

22 Admiralty papers, 'Capital ships—limit of 1936 Treaty exceeded by Japan', Public Record Office ADM 116 3735

23 See E. CHATFIELD, It Might Happen Again, Heinemann, 1947

24 ADM 116 3735, op. cit.

25 See S. ROSKILL, Naval Policy between the Wars, Collins, 1969, and for personal accounts of the scandalous situation in the British forces interwar : M. SEUTER, Airmen or Noahs, Pitman; and I. CAMERON, Wings of the Morning, Hodder

26 E. Chatfield to Lord Halifax, E. Chatfield, op. cit., p. 99

27 H. RICHMOND, Sea Power in the Modern World, Bell, 1934, p. 96

Chapter 19. The End of the Battleship

1 A. B. Cunningham (18), p. 227

2 ibid., p. 260

3 ibid., p. 262

4 ibid., p. 258

5 See ibid., Appendix 2

6 ibid., p. 286

7 ibid., p. 302

8 ibid., p. 330

9 ibid., p. 332

10 Gunnery Officer H.M.S. Rodney (now Admiral Sir. W. Crawford) to author, letter 25 March 1969

11 See MASANORI ITO, The End of the Imperial Japanese Navy, Wiedenfeld

12 See ibid., and Kitaro Matsumoto (18)

13 S. E. MORISON, U.S. Naval Operations in World War II, Little Brown, 1947, Vol. vi, p. 223

14 ibid., Vol. vi, p. 241

15 Admiral Kusaka's operation order, 5 April 1945, quoted Masanori Ito, op. cit.

Index

Ship names are listed in a separate index, following; battles are listed in chronological order under 'Battles', not in alphabetical order in the main body of the index; similarly aspects of 'Tactics', 'Strategy', 'Guns' and 'Gunnery'.

Index of Ships' Names